THE PLAINS CREE

Dr. S. Fritz Forkel
د. سليمان فريتس فوركل
ד״ר שלמה פריץ פורקל
Skén:nen Rón:nis

THE PLAINS CREE

AN ETHNOGRAPHIC, HISTORICAL, AND COMPARATIVE STUDY

DAVID G. MANDELBAUM

CANADIAN PLAINS STUDIES ■ 9

J. ARCHER, GENERAL EDITOR of OCCASIONAL PUBLICATIONS

CANADIAN PLAINS RESEARCH CENTER
UNIVERSITY OF REGINA
1979

Copyright 1979 by the Canadian Plains Research Center
First reprint 1985
Second reprint 1987
Third reprint 1990
Fourth reprint 1994
Fifth reprint 1996
Sixth reprint 2001

ISSN 0317-6290
ISBN 88977-013-1

Canadian Cataloguing in Publication Data

Mandelbaum, David G., 1911–1987
The Plains Cree
(Canadian plains studies; 9 ISSN 0317-6290)

Based on the author's thesis.
Part I was previously published in 1940 by the American
Museum of Natural History under title: The Plains Cree.
Bibliography: p.
ISBN 0-88977-013-1

1. Cree Indians. 2. Indians of North America—Great
Plains. I. University of Regina. Canadian Plains Research
Center. II. Title. III. Series.
E99.C88M36   970'.004'97   C78-002170-3

Canadian Plains Research Center
University of Regina
Regina, Saskatchewan
S4S 0A2

Printed and bound in Canada by Hignell Printing Limited
of Winnipeg

Contents

PREFACE xiii

EDITOR'S NOTE xvii

PART ONE—THE PLAINS CREE: A HISTORICAL AND ETHNOGRAPHIC STUDY
INTRODUCTION 3
TRIBAL DISTRIBUTION 7
    Terrain 7
    Band Divisions. 9
THE WESTWARD MOVEMENT 15
    First Contacts, 1640-1690 15
    The Establishment of Fur Trade, 1690-1740. 20
    Conquest of the Western Forests, 1740-1820 31
    Occupation of the Plains, 1820-1880 40
    Summary. 45
THE MAINSTAYS OF PLAINS CREE ECONOMY . 51
    The Buffalo. 51
        HUNTING METHODS 52
        BUTCHERING AND FOOD PREPARATION 58
        STORAGE 59
        TANNING 59
        BY-PRODUCTS. 60
    The Horse 60
        HISTORY. 60
        CONSEQUENCES OF ACQUISITION 62
        CARE 63
        RIDING AND TRANSPORT GEAR. 65
    The Dog. 66
        FUNCTION 66
        CARE AND TRAINING 66
    Other Elements of Economic Life 68
        LARGE GAME 68
        SMALL ANIMALS. 68
        FISH 71
        VEGETAL FOODS. 74
        ANNUAL CYCLE 77
        PROPERTY 78

MANUFACTURES AND ARTIFACTS............ 81
  Clothing 81
      MEN'S CLOTHING 81
      WOMEN'S DRESSES 83
      MOCCASINS 83
      MITTENS.................................. 83
      HEADGEAR............................... 84
  Personal Adornment 85
  Housing................................. 87
  Ceremonial Structures 90
  Household Furnishings and Utensils 91
  Weapons 94
  Smoking Utensils.......................... 96
  Musical Instruments 97
  Transport Devices 99
  Techniques of Ornamentation 100
SOCIAL LIFE 105
  The Basis of Band Divisions.................. 105
  Chieftainship............................. 106
  Rank and Societies......................... 110
  Camp Life 121
  Crime and Justice 122
  Kinship 124
  Games 127
      MEN'S GAMES........................... 127
        Striking the Bow 127
        Shooting Arrows 128
        Rolling Game......................... 128
        Hoop Game.......................... 128
        Hand Game.......................... 129
        Bone Game 130
        Shaking Game 131
        Stake Game 132
        Sliding Game 132
        Moccasin Game....................... 132
      GAMES PLAYED BY MEN AND WOMEN 132
        Stick Dropping Game 132
        Stick Striking Game 132
        Playing with a Ball.................... 133
        Tossing the Ball...................... 133
        Stringing the Bone Cups 133
      BOYS' GAMES 134
        Bouncing Stick Game 134
        Sliding Stick......................... 134
        Tops............................... 134
        Slings 134
        Gliding Stick 134
      WOMEN'S GAMES 134
        Testicle Game........................ 134
        Shooting Women's Arrows 136
      CONTESTS.............................. 136
      RIDDLES................................ 136
      STRING FIGURES........................ 137

THE INDIVIDUAL LIFE CYCLE 139
   Birth 139
   Names 140
   Childhood 142
   Puberty and Women's Observances 145
   Marriage 146
   Wife Exchange 149
   Death, Burial, and Mourning 150

RELIGION AND CEREMONIALISM 157
   Supernaturals 157
   Soul and Afterworld 158
   The Vision Quest 159
   Shamanism 162
   Bundles 170
   Vision Prerogatives 175
   Beliefs 178

CEREMONIALISM 183
   Vowed Ceremonies 183
      THE SUN DANCE 183
      THE SMOKING TIPI 199
      MASKED DANCE 204
      GIVE AWAY DANCE 206
      PRAIRIE-CHICKEN DANCE 207
      HORSE DANCE 208
      ELK DANCE 209
      BEAR DANCE 210
      PIPESTEM BUNDLE DANCE 210
      ROUND DANCE 211
      THE MITE•WIWIN 212
   Secular Dances 214
      POW-WOW DANCE 214
      DAKOTA DANCE 218
      TAIL WAGGING DANCE 218
      TEA DANCE 219
   Bear Ceremonialism 219
   Eagle Ceremonialism 222
   First Event Ceremonialism 222
   Dog Feast 224
   Tipi Painting 224
   Offering Pole 226
   The Elements of Ritualism 227
      USE OF THE PIPE 227
      OFFERINGS 228
      SONGS 229
      PRAYER 231
      THE VOW 233
      FOOD 233
      SERVERS 234
      SMUDGE 234
      MISCELLANEOUS RITUALISTIC ELEMENTS 235

SWEATBATH 236
BUNDLES 236
WARFARE. 239
Motives 239
Procedure of the Raid 239
The Return 244
Scalping. 245
War Exploits 246
Vengeance Party 247
Insignia 247
Metaphor of Battle 248
A War Record 249

**PART TWO—A COMPARATIVE STUDY OF
THE PLAINS CREE CULTURE** 261
I   THE PROBLEM 261
II   THE EASTERN AFFILIATIONS OF
     PLAINS CREE CULTURE 266
MATERIAL CULTURE AND ECONOMIC LIFE. . . 267
Housing. 267
Ceremonial Structures 269
Household Furnishings and Utensils 270
Dress   271
Personal Adornment 273
The Food Quest 274
Food Preparation 278
Transport 278
Weapons 280
Manufactures 281
Musical Instruments 283
SOCIAL ORGANIZATION 289
Chieftainship. 290
Societies. 291
Rank and Prestige 291
THE INDIVIDUAL LIFE CYCLE 292
Birth 292
Puberty 293
Marriage   294
Death, Burial, Mourning 295
RELIGION AND CEREMONIALISM. 301
Supernatural 301
The Vision Quest 304
Shamanism 305
Hunting Observances. 308
Elements of Ritualism 309

  Ceremonialism.............................312
  Secular Dances, Minor Ceremonialism, Beliefs 313
  WARFARE.................................319
  SUMMARY 323
III THE PLAINS AFFILIATIONS OF
     PLAINS CREE CULTURE 326
  *MATERIAL CULTURE AND ECONOMIC
  LIFE*......................................327
  Housing...................................327
  Household Furnishings 328
  Dress.....................................328
  Personal Adornment 329
  The Food Quest 330
  Food Preparation 330
  Transport 331
  Weapons 331
  Manufactures 332
  Musical Instruments 333
  SOCIAL ORGANIZATION....................337
  The Individual Life Cycle...................338
  RELIGION AND CEREMONIALISM..........341
  WARFARE................................347
  SUMMARY 349

PART THREE—CONCLUSIONS................353

APPENDIX
  A. *MONTH NAMES AND OTHER
      TERMINOLOGIES* 359
  B. *A VISION EXPERIENCE AND ITS
      CONSEQUENCES* 363
  C. *FIELD SKETCHES*.....................371

BIBLIOGRAPHY 377

List of Illustrations

1. A Group of Cree Surround the Author 5
2. Map Showing the Range of the Plains Cree,
   1860-1870 13
3. A Cree Elder by Sanford Fisher. 19
4. A Cree Indian by Paul Kane 27
5. Buffalo Pound 53
6. Detail of Entrance to Buffalo Pound. 53
7. Watching over his Horses by Michael Lonechild 64
8. Fish Weir 72
9. Painted Buffalo Robe 82
10. Tattoo Marks 86
11. Detail of Rabbit Robe Weaving. 94
12. Types of Snowshoes 100
13. Bow Loom 101
14. Woman's Shinny Game. 135
15. Fine-day near Center Pole. 168
16. Sun Dance Encampment 184
17. Preparing Drums for Sun Dance by Allen Sapp. 185
18. Sun Dance. Raising the Center Pole 189
19. Center Pole at Crooked Lake Sun Dance. 190
20. Inside the Sun Dance Lodge. Women Dancers. 192
21. Inside the Sun Dance Lodge. Men Dancers 192
22. Face Paintings. 194
23. Thunderbird Nest of Sun Dance Lodge 196
24. Structure of Old Sun Dance Lodge 198
25. Smoking Tipi Ceremony. Diagram of Lodge. 201
26. Tipi of Long-horned-sitting-bull 226
27. Consecrating the Sun Dance
    Pole by Henry Beaudry. 264
28. Pow-wow at the Battlefords by Allen Sapp 264
29. Kee-a-Kee-Ka-sa-coo-way by Paul Kane 265
30. Old Woman Getting Water in Early Spring
    by Michael Lonechild 268
31. Camp Circle 371
32. Braid Bundle Dance 372
33. Give Away Dance 373
34. Funeral Feast 373
35. Drum 374

Preface to New Edition

This edition of *The Plains Cree* includes that work as it was originally published in 1940 and also contains the final sections of my doctoral dissertation. In those sections, Plains Cree culture of the mid-Nineteenth Century is compared with the cultures of the forest peoples to the east and of the plains dwellers to the west and south of them.

I completed the dissertation at Yale University in the Spring of 1936; it bears the ponderous, if accurate, title *Changes in an Aboriginal Culture Following a Change in Environment, as Exemplified by the Plains Cree.* Later in 1936, before I left to do field work in India, I prepared the historical and ethnographic sections of the dissertation for publication. The comparative sections appear in print here for the first time, as they were written in 1935-36, with some slight revisions made about 1940.

On looking over this study across more than forty years, I find it heartening that a number of research workers and students still find it useful, and that they have suggested that it be made available again in this edition. It is also good to recognize how well anthropology and anthropologists have developed over those years. The data and concepts with which we were then concerned have been considerably enhanced. Many of our former ideas have been refined, revised, reoriented, or replaced. Yet a principal theoretical focus of the dissertation is on a subject that is receiving much current attention. As the title indicates, it attempts to assess why and how Cree culture was changed when some of the Cree changed their habitat, economy, and general environment. It deals, in part, with an ecological subject.

The ethnographic focus is on the buffalo-hunting way of life and not on the experiences of the Plains Cree on reservations as I witnessed them in the summers of 1934 and 1935. My field notes include observations on that situation; I was in it, temporarily part of it, and could scarcely avoid noticing its nature. But, following the example and suggestions of my mentors, I concentrated on the older culture. In the 1930s there were still men and women alive who could tell me, often in vivid and clear detail, about their free-ranging early life as buffalo hunters, gatherers, warriors, and providers. Despite the physical deprivations and personal tribulations that had overwhelmed them after the buffalo were killed off, many of them remained strong in their personalities, devoted to the aboriginal values and rituals, determined that they and their children were to remain Plains Cree in personal identity and group loyalty despite direct efforts by government officials and constant pressures by others to diminish that identity.

So a principal reason for concentrating on the older ways was because these survivors and their vivid memories would all too soon be gone and much of their knowledge lost unless we made special efforts to record it. Another reason why American anthropologists at that period devoted so much of their efforts to the aboriginal cultures of North America was that anthropology then had yet to assimilate and learn what could be made of those data before we travelled on (as I did immediately, both literally and figuratively) to other areas of research.

I have not tried to correct or bring up to date any of the following materials, except to delete three brief and now unneeded footnotes and to clarify several sentences. The work as it stands is a reasonably thorough outline of the culture and is not atypical of the ethnology of its time. I would now bring in much more comparative data because more is now available; I would be more careful about presenting the comparative data in a generalized "ethnographic present"; I would change some terms, as "Warrior Society." I certainly would deal with a wide range of concepts based not only on the books and articles about Plains Cree that have since appeared and on the vast newer literature on North American Indians but also on the newer development of social-cultural anthropology in general. But to do so adequately would involve a large enterprise that is better entrusted to other hands and minds.

Since leaving the Plains Cree in 1935, I have talked with some of them on three occasions. In March 1965 I met several younger members of the tribe when I came to the University of Saskatchewan, Saskatoon, to give a lecture that was published as Number 12 of the University Lectures (1967) under the title *Anthropology and People: the World of the Plains Cree*. That led to my attending a Sun Dance ("Thirsting Dance" in Cree) at Sweet Grass Reserve through the courtesy of the chief giver, Philip Favel, and with the help of my former student, now Professor Zenon Pohorecky. My son, Michael Mandelbaum, and I made a recording of parts of the ceremony for broadcast on educational radio. I was impressed by how faithfully the ceremony was performed, how respectfully it was attended by many Plains Cree. Then, as before, I was grateful for the courteous help given me by the many Plains Cree men and women with whom I talked.

Then, in October 1975, I attended a Plains Cree Conference sponsored by the Canadian Plains Research Center, University of Regina. There I found some old friends, a few of whom had also interpreted for me. I met young people who are of the fifth generation of Plains Cree whom I have known. I learned of the resurgence of interest in the aboriginal ways and of the rising assertiveness about one's identity as a Plains Cree. These trends are not unique to the Plains Cree—they are going on among other American Indian groups as well—but some of the Plains Cree are strongly involved in these efforts. After one of my talks to the conference there was a discussion session. One man whom I had known as a youngster and who is now a much-travelled participant in American Indian movements, rose to ask me a pointed question. He encased the question in the oratorical style of the old tradition, and when he spoke in English for my benefit, two other of my former helpers, Adam and Stan Cuthand (who at the time of the conference were both on the staff of the University of Manitoba), translated into Cree.

"What good," he asked me, "have all your efforts among us and your writings about us done for my children and my people?" I remembered enough about Plains Cree discourse to recognize that the question was partly a request for information and partly a statement about relations between Indians and Whites. I did not feel inclined to muster a fervent justification of my own efforts (I had, after all, collected material for my doctoral dissertation and received the degree), but I did think it reasonable to respond for my profession. What I tried to express was that the work I had done with the Plains Cree had given them, and might well continue to provide for their descendants, some record of their forefathers and of a way of life that many of them would increasingly want to know about. Together with their own oral traditions it could provide that sense of personal and social roots that most people want to have. These writings may also give the people living in the region, both Indians and non-Indians, some idea of what their predecessors on the land had been like, how they coped with the problems of that environment. Such knowledge, too, is something that the people of a place often want to know.

For students of the northern prairie country and of Plains Indians, the anthropological sources delineate the aboriginal cultures of the Plains Indians, try to explain their adaptations to the environment and to their neighbors, and analyze the processes by which they made their adaptations. And for an understanding of mankind generally, the studies of the Plains Cree and of other Plains Indians tell us about one general set of answers that these people developed to meet the life questions that all men and women must confront.

I am not sure whether the Plains Cree or the anthropologists and others who heard me were satisfied with that response. I do know that I am satisfied to have known and worked with Plains Cree. I am grateful to the late Professor Clark Wissler who originally made it possible, and to the Canadian Plains Research Center, especially to Deanna Christensen of that Center, who brought me back among the Plains Cree and found that there was interest enough in my writings about the Plains Cree to justify this new edition. I thank John Archer, George Arthur, Deanna Christensen, Les Crossman and Barbara ElDeiry for the fine work done in editing and preparing all of the material for publication.

David G. Mandelbaum
University of California, Berkeley
February 1978

Editor's Note

The Canadian Plains Research Center published the new edition of Dr. David G. Mandelbaum's *The Plains Cree: An Ethnographic, Historical, and Comparative Study* in 1979. That this basic work of scholarship remains useful to research workers and students alike is proven by the fact that the book has now been reprinted twice.

Dr. Mandelbaum pointed out in his "Preface to New Edition" that the book included work from his dissertation, originally published in 1940 as *The Plains Cree* in Anthropological Papers of the American Museum of Natural History (Part I), together with the historical and ethnographic section of the dissertation written in 1935–36, and slightly revised about 1940 (Parts II and III). The Canadian Plains Research Center, University of Regina, expresses its gratitude to the Trustees of the American Museum of Natural History for so generously granting permission to reprint Part I.

While the reconstitution of the original dissertation necessitated some editorial attention in order to standardize minor variations in spelling and footnoting, the work stands as Dr. Mandelbaum would have it stand—on its own strengths and as a basic contribution to scholarship in the field.

Dr. Mandelbaum was born in 1911 and he died in 1987. During the course of his life—more than three-quarters of a century—he took in many and varied activities, but he became best known, and will be long remembered, for his research and writing on the Plains Cree. In Western Canadian parameters he was born at a time when Saskatchewan was enjoying a period of rapid pioneer settlement. He died when the Canadian Plains Research Center was focussing efforts on understanding the maturing process of prairie settlement.

Dr. Mandelbaum left behind him an impressive heritage. His account of the Plains Cree has remained the definitive work on this subject for nearly half a century. Dr. Mandelbaum donated his research notes to the Saskatchewan Archives where they are available for scholars and researchers. The Canadian Plains Reserach Center and the Saskatchewan Indian Federated College more than most have profited from Dr. Mandelbaum's industry and generosity.

It is gratifying that the continuing demand for *The Plains Cree: An Ethnographic, Historical, and Comparative Study* has necessitated this second reprinting. This provides an opportunity to acknowledge once more the great contribution made by Dr. Mandelbaum to the world of scholarship and, in particular, to the Saskatchewan Indian community and to Western Canadian research. As I pointed out in the Editor's Note to the new edition in 1979, "This is a basic work of scholarship which will be sought out, and referred to, by scholars for many years." True words of prophesy and a tribute to a warm-hearted scholar, Dr. David G. Mandelbaum.

John H. Archer
President Emeritus
University of Regina
1987

PART ONE

**THE PLAINS CREE: AN ETHNOGRAPHIC AND
HISTORICAL STUDY OF THE PLAINS CREE**

Introduction

The last of the buffalo in the Plains Cree country were killed off about the year 1880. During the three decades prior to that date, the tribal culture was a full-fledged Plains way of life, sharing almost all of the traits and complexes commonly regarded as appertaining to the buffalo hunters of the northern plains. Yet, the historic literature and tribal traditions make it clear that the Cree were recent arrivals in the prairie country, coming in as invaders from the north and east.

The peopling of the plains has long excited the interest of ethnologists and is still a live problem which merits further study. The Plains Cree offer a strategic case example for the purposes of such study. Their migratory movements are relatively well documented; their pre-Plains culture may be surmised from the accounts of early observers and from the work of modern ethnographers among the parent stock, the Eastern Cree; the final phase of aboriginal Plains Cree life is described in the following pages. Thus the factors involved in the tribal movements and the cultural effects of a shift from a woodland to a plains environment may be more comprehensively envisaged for the Plains Cree than for most other Plains tribes.

The historic and descriptive materials presented in this paper are designed to be instrumental to a comparative and analytic study of the tribal culture. Anecdotal incidents have been given in some detail so that a certain insight into the leitmotifs of Plains Cree life might be obtained. The descriptive account refers to the period 1860-1870, before the buffalo had disappeared and within the memory of the oldest informants.

The material in Part One of this volume was originally published in Anthropological Papers of the American Museum of Natural History, Volume XXXVII, Part II, New York, 1940.

My principal informant was *Kamıokısıhkwew*, Fine-day, who was over eighty years old in 1934. He had earned a great reputation as a warrior in the days of inter-tribal warfare and during the native-uprising of 1885 was the military leader of his tribesmen.[1] He had been a skilled hunter and trapper. As he grew older his reputation as a powerful shaman increased. When *Maskwa* demurred at imparting some of his supernatural experiences (for to speak of one's own shamanistic powers overmuch is to court disaster), he seriously said, "I am sure that old Fine-day is not afraid when he speaks of the spirit powers. He is brave in all things." And Fine-day did give the desired information. Cooperative, intelligent, well-versed in many phases of the culture, he was an unexcelled informant.

Maskwa, Bear, also had been a famous warrior and was well acquainted with the old life. More taciturn than Fine-day, his shamanistic capabilities were renowned. *Kakıcikawpıhtokew*, Coming-day, had been Bloomfield's principal informant for the collecting of mythology.[2] He had been blind for many years and was particularly good for religious and mythological information.

These three were all of the River People band. Other informants from this band were *Pones, ıwe·sikan* (Fringe), *Sapostahıkan* (Shooting-through), *Kananıpatcipiskew* (Night-traveler). Women informants were: *Kopıecicimit* (Many-birds), *Askıhkowikit* (Lives-in-a-bear-den), and Mrs. John Fine-day.

Among the Calling River People band, some of Skinner's informants[3] were used. They were Four-clouds, Assiniboine, Neil Yellow-horse. At the File Hills Agency, where both Rabbit Skin and Calling River People now live, the principal informants were Red-dog, Otterskin, *Pıkats*, Feather, Day-walker, and Star-blanket. At the Qu'Appelle Agency, home of the Cree-Assiniboin band, Dragging-him and Little-Sioux were used. The Touchwood Hills People band are now at the Touchwood Hills Agency. In this band information was obtained from Thunder-mist, Standing-day, Going-about. Among the Parklands People at the Duck Lake Agency, Upturned-nose, Rattlesnake, Joe and Sam Wolf were informants. At the Carlton Agency, Peter Dreever, Tom Muchahaw, *Wa·pacuc*, all of the House People, supplied data. The conversations were conducted through interpreters. Solomon Blue-horn and Joe Poplar were the most satisfactory of several so employed.

4

On all reserves Cree is the common language; much of the old ceremonialism, and especially the Sun dance, flourishes; shamans are feared and respected; quillwork, tanning, moccasin-making, and many other aboriginal techniques are practised.[4]

The phonetic symbols are the same as those used by Bloomfield[5] except that long vowels are marked with a dot:—

a, as in English *father*
e, as in English *rate*
i, as in English *pin*
ı, as in French *rive*
c, as in English *she;* usually written by Bloomfield as *s.*

The kind hospitality of Mr. and Mrs. Walter Taylor and of Mr. and Mrs. Allan Waters facilitated my efforts. The many officials of the Canadian Department of Indian Affairs with whom I came in contact, all courteously gave their assistance.

The data upon which this study is based were secured during two field trips in 1934 and 1935 under the auspices of The American Museum of Natural History. The entire financial support for this work came from the Frederick G. Voss Fund of the Museum.

Fig. 1. A group of Cree surround the author. Sweet Grass Reserve, 1934.

My thanks are due to Professor Clark Wissler for acquainting me with, and generously aiding in, the Plains Cree study. I am under obligations to Professors Edward Sapir and Leslie Spier who helped me in many ways. It is a pleasure to acknowledge the kind aid of Miss Bella Weitzner.

David G. Mandelbaum
December 1, 1936.

FOOTNOTES

[1]FINE DAY, Incidents of the Rebellion (Canadian North-West Historical Society Publications, vol. 1, no. 1, Battleford, Saskatchewan, 1926), pp. 11-18. *See also* JEFFERSON, ROBERT, Fifty Years on the Saskatchewan (Canadian North-West Historical Society Publications, vol. 1, no. 5, Battleford, Saskatchewan, 1929), p. 114.
[2]BLOOMFIELD, LEONARD, Sacred Stories of the Sweet Grass Cree (Bulletin 60, Anthropological Series, no. 11, National Museum of Canada, Ottawa, 1930), p. 1.
[3]SKINNER, ALANSON, Political Organization, Cults and Ceremonies of the Plains Cree (Anthropological Papers, American Museum of Natural History, vol. 11, part 6, New York, 1914), pp. 515-541.
[4]The Parklands People, at the Duck Lake Agency, are much more deculturated than are the other bands. This may be due to their peculiar origin.
[5]BLOOMFIELD, Sacred Stories of the Sweet Grass Cree, pp. 2-7.

EDITOR'S NOTE: The format used in the footnotes is based on that followed in the Bibliography of the original monograph.

Tribal Distribution

TERRAIN

The Plains Cree live on the northern edge of the Great Plains, chiefly in the Park Belt, the transitional area between the forests and plains. They have occupied this territory only since the beginning of the nineteenth century, for it was formerly inhabited by the Assiniboin and Gros Ventre in the eastern part and by the Blackfoot in the western section.[1] That the Plains Cree invaded this area from the east is amply verified both by documentary evidence and by the testimony of living informants who assert that their parents or grandparents once lived farther to the east.

Just before the disappearance of the buffalo, the tribal lands extended across the present provinces of Saskatchewan and Alberta from the region where the Qu'Appelle River crosses the Manitoba line to the vicinity of Edmonton. The various bands of Plains Cree centered in the river basins included in this area and the tribal range may be defined in terms of the valleys of the Qu'Appelle, the lower North Saskatchewan, the lower South Saskatchewan, and the lower Battle rivers.

At present [1936] the Plains Cree are settled on some twenty-four small reserves in Saskatchewan and Alberta, and on one reserve, Rocky Boy, in Montana. The Montana reserve was largely composed of those Plains Cree who fled to the United States after the Riel Rebellion of 1885. The tribe now numbers approximately seven thousand, which was roughly the population estimated for them by Hayden in 1853 and given by the Canadian Government Reports in 1899.[2] This large, homogeneous population has made for a preservation of the native life despite the efforts of Government officials to discourage the aboriginal social and religious practices.

The Canadian Park Belt, within which the Plains Cree lived, is a black soil terrain characterized by luxuriant grass vegetation and dotted with patches of hilly woodland. Buffalo abounded in this region. Elk, deer, and other game were plentiful in the hills. This area now supports a denser population than the rest of the Canadian prairie country and also has a greater density of livestock, in proportion to the land occupied, than the Canadian Plains in general.[3] It is probable that in aboriginal times, also, the parklands were more favorable to the maintenance of men and animals than were the other sections of the Northern Plains.

The northern limits of the Park Belt also marked the boundary between the Plains Cree and their congeners, the Western Wood Cree. The Plains tribe called their northern neighbors *saka·wıyiniwak*, Forest People, and had relatively little contact with them, for the Forest Cree remained in the woodlands and infrequently came south of the North Saskatchewan. The Plains Cree mocked them for their lack of martial fervor but also feared them for their magical prowess.

On the east were the Plains Ojibwa, *nahka·wıyiniwak,* who are called Saulteaux in Canada. They were even later arrivals on the Plains than the Cree and were culturally more strongly attached to the Woodlands. They were friends and allies of the Plains Cree and exchanged their medicines, beadwork, and even their women for the horses of the Plains Cree.

To the south, were the Assiniboin, called *asını·pwat*, Stoney Sioux, or *opwa·sı·mu*, who were cultural godfathers to the Plains Cree in introducing them to many of the manners of Plains life. They often camped together and were their allies in warfare. The Plains Cree freely intermarried with them. The Cree now living on the *pıpıkisis* Reserve of the File Hills Agency stated that they descend from an Assiniboin band which came to have so great an admixture of Cree blood that they permanently attached themselves to a Plains Cree group, the Calling River People.

Visitors from the Eastern Cree, *omaskekowak*, and from the Ojibway, *otcipwewak*, were often entertained by the Plains Cree and treated as relatives.

The great enemies of the tribe were the bands of the Blackfoot confederacy which alternately retreated and advanced on the western front according to the fortunes of battle. The Cree names for the Blackfoot tribes were *pıkano·wıyiniwak,* Piegan, *kaskitewıyasitak,* literally, Black Feet, *mıhkowıyiniwak*, Blood People. The Sarsi, *sas·ıwak*, also made many forays against them.

To the south and southwest were several hostile peoples. The Dakota, *pwatak*, were always dangerous. The Crow, *kahkakıwaıtcanak*, Crow Foot, were noted as a tribe from whom it was particularly difficult to steal horses. The *pawistikowıyiniwak* Rapids People, Gros Ventre, were occasionally encountered. The village tribes of the Missouri were called *kotasiskıkamikowak*, Mud House People, and were sometimes raided. Tribes rarely met, but none the less known as enemies, were the Cheyenne, *kanehıaw estcik*, Cree Speakers (from the fact that the Cree could recognize some of the Cheyenne words), *kınepiko·wıyiniwak*, Snake, *paıpe·komak,* Nez Percé, and *napakstokwewak,* Flathead. All hostile peoples were included in the generic term, *ayahtcıyiniwak*. Since the Blackfoot in particular were the enemy tribe, this term came to be especially applied to them.

BAND DIVISIONS

The Plains Cree were divided into several loosely organized bands whose numbers and range varied a good deal over relatively short periods of time; hence, a precise statement of their locale is not possible. But it is clear that there were at least eight major divisions in the nineteenth century.

The easternmost groups were the Calling River People, *katepwewcıpı·wıyiniwak*, and the Rabbit Skin People, *wapucwayanak*. The latter hunted in the wooded country between the Assiniboine and Qu'Appelle rivers and were closely attached to their eastern neighbors, the Plains Ojibwa. The Calling River People roamed up and down the valley of the Qu'Appelle. In later years they expanded their territory to the south and southwest of that river. Both these bands were restrained in their westward movement by dependence on the trading posts, to which they returned annually. It was only when the Hudson's Bay Company established Forts Pelly and Ellice and other posts to the west, that they completely abandoned the Lake Winnipeg region. Most of the Cree were tethered in this wise to the trading posts from which they dared not stray too far lest their supplies be cut off. The two bands were settled on the Crooked Lake and File Hills reserves.

A band known as the *nehıopwat*, ''Cree-Assiniboin,'' was so called because of its close relations and frequent intermarriage with the Assiniboin. They occupied the area southwest of the Qu'Appelle River, in the vicinity of Wood Mountain. Of all the Cree groups, this band was deepest into the true plains. Its close kinship connections with the River People make it probable that it was an offshoot of that band. As did all of the Plains Cree, the Cree-Assiniboin, moved far to the south when the buffalo supply diminished. Their descendants are now on the Piapot Reserve, Qu'Appelle Agency.

A small group called the Touchwood Hills People, *pusakawatciwɪyiniwak*, occupied the territory between Long Lake and the Touchwood Hills. They are now on the Touchwood Reserves.

The House People, *waskahɪkanwɪyiniwak*, were so designated because they had long clustered about the houses of the Hudson Bay posts. They often met at Fort Carlton and hunted to the north and southwest of that post. In the middle of the last century there were two important chiefs of this band, each with his own following. *Mistawasis* lived exclusively on the prairie, hunted along the South Saskatchewan and supplied Fort Carlton with buffalo pelts and meat. *Atahkako·p*, Star Blanket, trapped in the bush to the north of Carlton and came to the plains in the summer for buffalo. One part of the band had divorced itself completely from the forest life; the other had effected a compromise between the two environments. This band was allotted to the Carlton Agency.

To the east of the House People was a group sometimes mentioned in the literature as Willow Indians.[4] Their Cree appellation is *paskuhkupawɪyiniwak*, Parklands People. They are now living on the reserves of the Duck Lake Agency. This group is distinctive in that practically all of the individuals in the band were descendants of a Scotch trader, one George Sutherland, who came from Scotland in 1790. He took a Cree wife and left the employ of the Hudson's Bay Company to live on the prairie as a native. He subsequently took two more wives and begot twenty-seven children who grew to adulthood and raised families. His offspring married with the surrounding people but always returned to live with the familial group. In this way Sutherland became the first chief of a band he had himself engendered.[5] The Parklands People associated but little with the other bands but they spoke Cree and regarded themselves as more closely related to the Cree than to any other tribe.

The River People, *cɪpɪwɪyiniwak*, lived between the North

Saskatchewan and Battle rivers, as far west as the present Alberta line. This was their usual locale, but they also hunted westward to the vicinity of Edmonton and went south to the forks of the South Saskatchewan. When the buffalo vanished from their country, they penetrated far into Montana in quest of the herds. This band was allocated to the Sweet Grass and Little Pine reserves of the Battleford Agency.

The most numerous of the bands was that known as *natimɪwɪyiniwak*, Upstream People, or *amiskwatcɪwɪyiniwak*, Beaver Hills People. They were the westernmost of the Plains Cree, roaming along the North Saskatchewan to the neighborhood of Edmonton and south to the Battle River. They bore the brunt of the Blackfoot raids, but were also richest in horses. Their present reserves, at Edmonton and Saddle Lake, are the only major Plains Cree groups not visited by the writer.

The eastern bands were given the collective name, *mamihkɪyiniwak*, Downstream People. In this division were the Calling River People, Rabbit Skins, and Touchwood Hills People. The western group were known collectively by the name applied to the westernmost band *natimɪwɪyiniwak*, Upstream People. Besides the Upstream People proper, this division included the House, Parklands, and River People. The Cree-Assiniboin were sometimes included in the latter term, sometimes called *paskwa wɪyiniwak*, Prairie People.

The cultural and dialectal differences between the two sections of the Plains Cree, were not of a major order. For example, the eastern bands erected grave-houses while the western bands did not. Other details of burial were similar.

All of the bands, except the Cree-Assiniboin, were geographically contiguous to the forests and, at the close of the buffalo period, were uniformly moving away from the woodlands into the true plains. The Rabbit Skin and Calling River People were erupting out of the Qu'Appelle Valley southward and westward. The House and Parklands People were extending their travels along the valley of the South Saskatchewan. The River and Upstream People, repulsed in their westward advance by the Blackfoot, were also drifting southward. These movements were suddenly accelerated by the passing of the buffalo before they were finally arrested by the institution of the reserve system.

The dialectal differences among the Plains Cree bands are minor, being chiefly matters of vowel length and degree of nasalization. Plains Cree differs from Woodland Cree in having "y" in certain words in place of n, l, or δ.[6] Michelson[7] classes Cree (both Plains and Woodland) with the Central subtype of the Algonkian stock. Montagnais is very closely related to it, as are Menomini, Sauk, Fox, Kickapoo, and Shawnee.

FOOTNOTES

[1]COUES, ELLIOTT, ed., New Light on the Early History of the Greater Northwest. The Manuscript Journals of Alexander Henry and of David Thompson, 3 vols., New York, 1897, vol. 2, pp. 516, 530.
[2]WISSLER, CLARK, Population Changes among the Northern Plains Indians (Yale University Publications in Anthropology, no. 1, New Haven, 1936), pp. 8-13. Note that Western Wood Cree numbers must be subtracted from total Western Cree figures to give Plains Cree population.
[3]MACKINTOSH, W.A., Prairie Settlement: The Geographic Setting, Toronto, 1934, pp. 89-104.
[4]*As in* SKINNER, Political Organization, p. 517.
[5]I am indebted to Father Chevalier of the Duck Lake Mission for the verification of this story. He has traced the genealogy of most of the members of the Duck Lake reserves and has reconstructed the Sutherland family tree.
[6]BLOOMFIELD, LEONARD, The Plains Cree Language (Atti del XXII Congresso Internazionale degli Americanisti, Roma, Settembre, 1926, Roma, 1928), p. 429.
[7]MICHELSON, TRUMAN, Preliminary Report on the Linguistic Classification of Algonquian Tribes (Twenty-Eighth Annual Report, Bureau of American Ethnology, Washington, 1912), pp. 238-247.

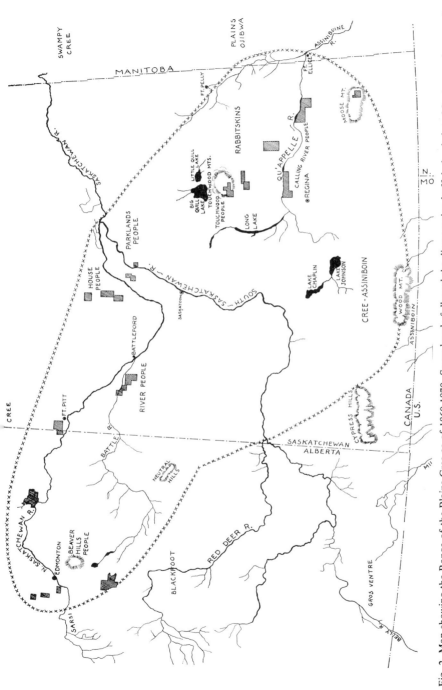

Fig. 2. Map showing the Range of the Plains Cree as of 1860-1870. Some bands followed the disappearing buffalo herds into Montana and scattered groups fled to the United States following the Riel rebellion. Some of the Plains Cree territory, enclosed in the line of crosses, was shared with bands of Assiniboin, especially in the south. Shaded areas are present-day [1936] reserves of Plains Cree.

13

The Westward Movement

The tribal locale, as described above, had been occupied by Plains Cree for less than a hundred years when the nomadic life came to an end. Although their culture in the latter part of the nineteenth century was overwhelmingly that of the Plains area, the historic evidence indicates that the forebears of the Plains Cree, at a not too remote date, lived in the Eastern Woodlands and shared the characteristic traits of that region. In order to envisage the factors which propelled the Cree westward and sent some of them into the plains, we may review the relatively abundant documentary material dealing with the historic career of the Woodland Cree, and later, with that of the Plains Cree.

FIRST CONTACTS, 1640-1690

The earliest glimpses of the Cree in the historical literature occur in the *Jesuit Relations*. The intrepid Jesuits were the first whites to see them and their reports begin the story of almost three centuries of contact and intercourse between the Cree and the carriers of European culture.

In the early records, they are designated by several variants of the Ojibwa name for them. Kristineaux, Kiristinous, Kilistinous, are a few of the variants from which the present term, Cree, was contracted. The Plains Cree called themselves *nehiawak,* a term which cannot be etymologized to my knowledge. The name, Kiristinon (Kilistinon), is first mentioned in the *Relations* of 1640, and is repeated at frequent intervals in the reports for the next twenty years although the priests themselves had not yet met any of the tribesmen at that time.[1] From other Indians the Jesuits learned that the Cree were a very powerful people who lived toward Hudson Bay. They fought the Nadouessis, Dakota, and were nomadic hunters. In the *Relations* of 1656-1658, four geographical subdivisions of the Cree were named. Thwaites, the editor of the *Jesuit Relations*, locates the four divisions, in so far as the evidence permits, as being in the region of Lake Nipigon, in the country west of James Bay, between Lake Nipigon and Moose River, and along the East Main River.[2] This would make the tribal boundaries in 1656 roughly coterminous with the range of the Eastern Cree as defined by Skinner[3] who visited them some two hundred and fifty years later.

In the reports for 1666-1667 we finally get some first-hand information on the Cree.[4] Father Allouez conducted a mission to the tribe and in a brief passage records some of his observations. He says that the Kilistinouc have their usual abode on the shores of the North Sea and their canoes ply along a river emptying into a great bay which he believes to be the Hudson. Allouez characterizes the Cree as being of a kind, docile disposition, but much more nomadic than the other tribes. They have no fixed abode, no fields, no villages, living upon hunting and a little "oats" (wild rice), which they gather in swampy places. They affix sacrifices of dogs on poles as an offering to the sun. Their language, Father Allouez affirms, is almost the same as that of the Poissons-Blancs, an Algonkin people who live on the headwaters of the St. Maurice.

In 1669 Father Dablon also tried to spread the gospel among the Cree. He laments the fact that they are nomadic, assembling only rarely for some market or festival and, therefore, most difficult to convert.[5] Dablon first saw the Cree when they came to the fishing places about Sault Ste. Marie from their lands near the North Sea, having been driven out of their country by famine.

A letter from Father Marquette in the *Relations* of 1669-1670 bears out Dablon's plaint.[6] Two hundred canoes of Cree called at the mission of St. Esprit, near the Sault, where Marquette was stationed. He describes them as a nomadic people always wandering in the woods and having only the bow to live by. Marquette says that their rendezvous is not yet well known, but they are toward the northwest of the mission. They all go into the woods during the winter but are seen on the shores of Lake Superior in the summer. They come down to the Sault to buy merchandise and corn. This last commodity was ever of importance to the fur trappers, since it furnished a highly nourishing, yet compact and easily transportable food. It appears that by 1670 certain of the Cree had become dependent upon the traders for part of their food supply.

16

Father Dablon reaffirms his previous statements concerning the Kilistinou in the *Relations* of 1670-1671.[7] Again he notes that they possess neither fields nor any fixed abode, but are forever wandering through the forests seeking their living by hunting. They are dispersed through the whole region to the north of Lake Superior, but other nations inhabit the same districts. From this passage, it seems that the territory between Lake Superior and Hudson Bay was then occupied by Cree bands intermingled with bands of various other tribes, lumped by Dablon under the title "the peoples of the interior" or of "the North Sea."

Some clues to the residents on the shores of the North Sea are proffered by Father Albanel in the 1671-1672 volume.[8] Albanel arrived at James Bay via Lake Mistassini and Rupert River. Kilistinous, he writes, are settled to the southward and upon the bay are the Mataoûakirinouek and the Monsounic. The former were a band of the Algonkin tribe, the latter are known as the Monsoni, a group closely allied with, if not part of, the Cree proper.[9] Unlike Dablon, who suggested that the tribes occupy the whole country in common, Albanel states that each nation is separated from its neighbors by large rivers.

While these missionaries were advancing farther and farther westward and northward, sending reports of their achievements and adventures back home, two French fur traders sought out the little known tribes about Lake Superior. The two, Radisson and Groseilliers, also beseeched the natives to live at peace with one another; but their motive was not to extend the blessings of Christian brotherhood to the heathen, but to divert their energies from bloody warfare to profitable fur trapping. The devastating effect of the Iroquois raids upon the French trade impelled the two explorers to recoup their declining commerce by tapping fresh resources to the west. Radisson, who later helped organize the Hudson's Bay Company, kept a journal of their experiences. He afterward wrote up the account, in what English was at his command, as a sort of investment prospectus for the newly established Hudson's Bay Company. In all, four voyages were recorded, but it was not until the third, in 1659, that we hear of the Cree.[10] In that year Radisson reached the Mascoutin, who lived on the Fox River in present day Wisconsin, and who were probably related to the Illinois.[11] The Mascoutin told him of

. . . another wandering nation, living onely uppon what they could come by. Their dwelling was on the side of the salt watter in summer time, & in the land in the winter time, for it's cold in their country. They calle themselves Christinos, and their confederats [of the Mascoutin] from all times, by reason of their speech, wch is ye same, & often have joyned together & have had companys of souldiers to warre against that great nation.[12]

The great nation referred to is the Dakota, who evidently bore the brunt of a united Algonkin attack.

The two *voyageurs* pushed their way into the regions described by the Mascoutin in 1661. Somewhere on the south shore of Lake Superior they chanced upon a band of Cree. Continuing along the shores of the lake, they met "the nation of the Boeuf" which Thwaites identifies as a band of Sioux. These Indians begged the Frenchmen to protect them from the attacks of the Cree. Radisson answered in a tone consistent with his desire to promote the fur trade, saying the French had extended their protection to all the tribes and that they would effect a peace between them.[13]

To carry out this promise to seal a "general peace," Radisson and Groseilliers set forth to hold council with the Cree and arrived at one of their encampments. The site of the camp is located by Thwaites as being seven days' journey north of the Mille Lacs region and perhaps was somewhere in the valley of the Albany River. The Cree assented to the plans of the traders and staged a grand feast to celebrate the event. Over a thousand people came. There was much dancing accompanied by the beating of drums made of earthen pots filled with water and covered with "stagg's" skin. The young men competed for a prize by climbing a greased pole. Radisson cuts short the description of the feast thus:—

> I ffor feare of being inuied I will obmitt onely that there weare playes, mirths, and bataills for sport, goeing and coming with cryes; each plaid his part.[14]

Before taking leave of the Cree, Radisson promised that he would meet them on their side of Lake Superior the following spring and would go with them into their country. However, this trip never materialized.

Efforts to stop native warfare were not very successful. The *Jesuit Relations* of 1672-1674 record the massacre of ten Dakota by the Kilistinons at Sault Ste. Marie.[15] Nicolas Perrot declares that the Sioux

> give all their attention to waging war against the Kiristinons (Cree), the Assiniboules, and all the nations of the North.[16]

At the time of Perrot's Memoire, 1658-1661, the Dakota had to contend with the raids of the Assiniboin, as well as with those of the Algonkin-speaking confederates. This seems to be the earliest indication of the firm alliance between the Cree and the Assiniboin that we shall have much occasion to notice at a later time.

The prowess of the Cree in warfare is documented by Lahontan, although his evidence is not very trustworthy. His journeys were in the Great Lakes area between 1685 and 1690. Lahontan tells that the number of Eskimo warriors is

> thirty thousand; but they are such cowardly fellows, that five hundred Clistino's from Hudson Bay, used to defeat five or six thousand of them.[17]

If we disregard the numerical exaggeration, it appears that the Cree fought the peoples to the north as well as those to the south.

Although the Cree raided the Dakota in this period, they probably traded with them also. H.A. Innis, in a chapter dealing with the fur trade in the years 1654 to 1666, remarks that the Cree, Assiniboin, and other Indians in the neighborhood of Hudson Bay, being most distant from the

Courtesy of John A. Warner

Fig. 3. A Cree Elder by Sanford Fisher.

French, valued European commodities most highly. The goods they did get came through the Sioux,[18] who traded in turn with the Ottawa and Saulteaux who had direct contact with the French. Following the establishment of the Hudson's Bay Company at the mouth of the Nelson River in 1670, the Cree themselves became middlemen to the fur trade.

The first fifty years of documented history reveal the Cree as a nomadic people occupying much the same territory between Lake Superior and Hudson Bay as do the Eastern Cree today and subdivided, as at present, into several geographically defined bands. They were a powerful tribe, feared by their enemies, the Dakota, against whom they waged a fierce warfare in company with their Assiniboin and Algonkin-speaking allies.

They are adjusted to a coastal habitat in summer and to an inland range in winter, manifesting a similarity to the Northeastern Algonkin and Northern Athapascans[19] in this trait. The Cree of this period use canoes, collect wild rice, gather in large encampments during the annual rendezvous, have pottery water drums, have not yet acquired firearms to any extent, are eager to obtain trade goods, and are friendly to the whites.

Although it is hardly to be expected that the early priests and traders could have known of the lands beyond Hudson Bay or even about Lake Winnipeg, yet there is not the slightest evidence that the Cree had a westward extension. Their travels were strictly in a north and south direction.

THE ESTABLISHMENT OF FUR TRADE, 1690-1740

The advent of the Hudson's Bay Company marked the opening of a new phase in tribal fortunes. No longer dependent upon intermediaries, the Cree thenceforward had easy and direct access to trading posts. The first English supply ship came into Hudson Bay in 1668. Two years later posts were established at the mouth of the Nelson, Moose, and Albany rivers, and the Cree flocked in to trade.

Both the tribal culture and locale changed greatly under the infuence of the English. The culture naturally altered with the influx of European goods and with the shift of occupational emphasis from food gathering to fur trapping during certain seasons of the year. The locale was enlarged because the traders sent the natives deeper and deeper into the back country to collect furs from the different tribes and to trap in virgin territory.

Like the French traders, the English implored the savages to stop fighting, and they too travelled among the tribes to attain this purpose. Henry Kelsey was the first of a long line of able agents sent out by the Hudson's Bay Company.[20] In 1690 he ran away from his position as servant at York Factory but returned in 1691 with some Assiniboin. He related his adventures among the inland tribes and persuaded the governor of York Factory to allow him to return and bring the "Naywattamee Poets" in to trade. It is not possible to ascertain just what tribe this was, but they were prevented from reaching the posts by the hostility of the Cree.

Kelsey kept a diary in which the Cree are mentioned several times. The introduction tells of a peace parley he held with the distant Indians. But no sooner was his back turned than the Home Indians killed six tents of those with whom he had concluded a pact and so his efforts were foiled. This incident is retold in the body of the journal and the name Nayhathaways is given instead of Home Indians. Kelsey knew the Cree both as Nayhathaways and as Home Indians.

An entry in the journal records that some Assiniboin brought the news that the Naywattamee Poets had killed three Nayhathaway women. They also said that the Naywattamee subsequently had fled so far that Kelsey would probably never meet them. This indication, together with some other hints as to their nature, leads me to believe that Kelsey meant the Cree when he wrote:—

But now of late they hunt their Enemies
And with our English guns do make ym flie[21]

The diary itself does not dwell on the relationship between the Assiniboin and the Cree, but it seems that it was generally a friendly one, although in one passage the Assiniboin fear lest the Cree "murder ym."

It is apparent that the Cree took immediate advantage of the turn of events and in the twenty years that the Hudson's Bay posts had been established, were already firmly entrenched as middlemen and allies of the English. They readily adapted themselves to the new weapons and artifacts. The annual trip to the trading post came to be a vital part of their yearly round.

The French keenly felt the effects of the English competition and took steps to check it. One measure was to attempt another truce between the Cree-Assiniboin alliance and the Sioux, who traded almost exclusively with the French. Duluth in 1679 arranged a pact at the head of Lake Superior, but nothing much came of it.[22] Somewhat more effective were the military means adopted by the French in establishing a line of forts and in capturing some of the English posts. York Factory and Fort Nelson at the mouths of the Hayes and Nelson rivers were twice taken by the French and twice regained by the English. First seized and burned by Radisson in 1682, Fort Nelson was rebuilt by an English expedition the following year. Meanwhile, two ships set out from New France to carry supplies to Fort Bourbon, the French name for Fort Nelson. But they arrived to find the fort in English hands again and spent a hard winter at anchor on a small tributary of the Hayes River. Father Antoine Silvy, chaplain to the party, tried his hand at Christianizing the natives, but like his predecessors, met with little success. Silvy writes that the Cree and Assiniboin come to the Fort, but are here today and gone tomorrow, and since they come to trade only, are incapable of absorbing religion.[23] Silvy qualifies his statement by adding that if a missionary could go to their country, fifteen or twenty days inland and live in their village for some time, the savages would listen to the words of salvation. The village was supposed to be situated beyond the great lake of the Assiniboin, which is probably Lake Winnipeg.

Father Gabriel Marest was chaplain to yet another military expedition against the English. In 1695 Fort Nelson was again captured and renamed Fort Bourbon. In a letter to one of his Jesuit superiors, Marest describes the tribes that came in to trade.[24] The most distant, numerous, and powerful are the Cree and Assiniboin. The language of the Cree is the same as that of the natives surrounding the Fort, with some slight shift in accent and vocabulary. Some Cree go to trade on the shores of Lake Superior, Marest himself having seen them at the Sault and at Michilimakinac. Several had even been as far as Montreal. Marest's name for Winnipeg is the "Lake of the Cree." The tribe has no village or fixed dwelling, roaming the forests in search of game. They assemble on the various lakes in the summer to harvest a store of wild rice, and so are relatively sedentary for two or three months. Father Marest remarks that despite their linguistic disparity the Cree and Assiniboin are the closest of allies. He says that many Cree speak Assiniboin and many Assiniboin can speak Cree.

H.A. Innis, citing Margery, dates this confederacy from the time of the establishment of the Hudson's Bay Company.[25] When the Assiniboin found themselves between the Cree who were armed with English guns, and the Sioux, armed with French muskets, they were forced to ally themselves with one or the other faction and, to the detriment of the French trade, chose the Cree. The account of a voyage up the Mississippi in 1669-1670 by the explorer, Le Sueur, is one of the early sources of this supposition.[26] Le Sueur makes the point, however, that the Cree obtained arms from the English before the Sioux received them from the French. The Assiniboin, neighboring the Cree, joined them to obtain supplies of guns and ammunition. Although the Cree proximity to a base of European supplies undoubtedly was a factor in cementing the alliance, the *Mémoire* of Perrot, which we have cited above, shows that as early as 1661 the Assiniboin were hostile to the Sioux.

In 1697 the French took York Factory again and this time kept possession until 1713. Bacqueville de la Potherie was an important member of this expedition and sent back a number of letters which included a description of the savages about Fort Nelson. The tribe nearest the Fort he calls "Ouenebigonhelinis." Michelson states that this term must apply to a Cree band inhabiting the shores of James and Hudson bays. La Potherie further names the "Monsaunis," the "Savannahs," and the "Christinaux." Tyrrell identifies the two former as the Monsoni and Swampy Cree, present divisions of the tribe. La Potherie says of the Cree proper that:—

> they are numerous people with an immense territory. They extend as far as Lake Superior.[27]

The tribal name "Savannahs" appears also in the letters of the noted explorer, Charlevoix, who includes all the peoples living on Hudson Bay, at least as far up as Fort Nelson, under the general term "Savanois."[28] L. P. Kellogg's editorial footnote to this letter of 1721 says that the term was applied to the people now known as Swampy Cree. Émile Petitot also refers to Charlevoix and identifies the Savanois as Maskegons or Swampies. The Cree themselves are located by Petitot between the Savanois on the east and the "Grandes-Pagnes" on the west.[29]

These sources make it clear that there were several bands or subtribes, of which the Cree proper were the largest and farthest to the southwest. Petitot takes the Grandes-Pagnes to be the forerunners of the contemporary Prairie Cree, but submits no reason for believing that Cree were living on the prairies at the time. No other source gives any definite indications of such a Cree band as early as the date of Charlevoix's voyages. Significant in Petitot's article is the reference to the warfare between the Algonkin tribes and the Athapascans to the north of them. According to Petitot, the Cree pushed back the timid inhabitants of the Lake Athabasca area to Great Slave Lake. The Cree advance was apparently going on before the advent of the English. When the conquerors obtained European goods, they carried on trade with the ousted "Slaves" and also with the Eskimo.

While this northern extension of the Cree in the first part of the eighteenth century is not clearly marked, their southerly bounds are more definite. The *Jesuit Relations* of 1720-1736 contain a communication from a missionary stationed at Fort Charles on the south shore of the Lake of the Woods, one of the fortifications erected by the French to stave off the encroachments of the English.[30] The letter, dated 1736, notes that the Assiniboin live to the south of Lake Winnipeg and that the other shores of the lake are inhabited by Cree, who occupy not only the northern part as far as the sea, but also all the immense stretch of territory beginning at the Lake of the Woods and extending far beyond Lake Winnipeg. Father Aulneau, unfortunately, did not specify in what direction the immense stretch extended, probably because he himself did not know. It may have been northwest to Lake Athabasca or westward into the plains. The Jesuit also tells of Cree travels to the southwest. He records his plans to accompany the Assiniboin on one of their annual winter journeys to the country of an agricultural people from whom they procure corn. Although the Cree are not specifically mentioned it is evident that they too followed the same trail. On his way to the land of the agriculturists, one of the village tribes of the Missouri, the missionary was killed, and we have no further description of the Cree corn trading expeditions. The native participation in the fur trade may have given an impetus to this intertribal commerce, since corn was in demand for the trappers.

As had many before him, Aulneau despairs of ever persuading the Cree to embrace the faith. The old complaint concerning the nomadism and superstition of the Cree is forwarded, with yet another fault which we find echoed and re-echoed in many other sources, that of drunkenness. By cleverly manipulating the native craving for liquor, the French were able to cling to a greater portion of the trade than was their economically justified share. But the English soon learned also to extract full advantage from the native love of liquor. Aulneau tried to make a systematic study of the Cree language during the winter of 1739, but relates that his purpose was retarded because all the Indians had been out on a raid upon the "Maskoutepoels or Prairie Sioux."

The French were continually attempting to call a halt to this hostility which was so detrimental to their commercial enterprises. St. Pierre held a peace conference for the Sioux and the Cree in 1729, but by 1742 we find a war party of Cree and their allies starting out to despoil the Sioux.[31] The expedition was composed chiefly of Cree and Assiniboin but the peoples of Nipigon, Kamanistiquia, Tekamamcouene, the Monsoni, as well as the tribe of the narrator, the Saulteaux, are also enumerated. The peoples about Lake Nipigon and Kamanistiquia were not then considered Cree. The Monsoni appear as a distinct group in earlier accounts, but are always so closely allied to the Cree in language and culture that they are in reality a Cree band. The Saulteaux were not always on friendly terms with the Cree, as is witnessed by a record of the year 1729 (which seems to have been a banner year for truces), noting that the Cree have carried gifts to the "Sauteux" of Pointe de Chagouamigon, on the south shore of Lake Superior and were going to conclude a peace.[32] This attempt, too, was unsuccessful. Beauharnois, who wrote of the peace efforts, sadly remarks in 1731 that the Cree have had an affray with the Saulteaux of Point de Chagouamigon and have killed some of their men. Six years later another Cree-Saulteaux peace was concluded, which lasted at least until 1742, when the two tribes set out as allies upon the Sioux expedition mentioned above.

The Chevalier de la Vérendrye was one of the last and most capable of the Frenchmen who labored to secure the western lands and trade for France. For nearly twenty years, from 1727, when first he was sent to Lake Nipigon, he and his sons worked for the gain and glory of New France. La Vérendrye's quest was a double one. He wanted to reach the "Western Sea" and he sought to divert the commerce of the natives from the Hudson's Bay Company to the French. The search for the sea led him to drive deeper into the Saskatchewan Basin than any Frenchman had before. His desire to monopolize the fur trade led him to reinforce and build a chain of forts from Nipigon almost to the Rockies. For a time he succeeded in restoring the commerce, but eventually factors beyond his control militated against him. The distance of the outposts from a base of supplies and the weakness of the home government worked to negate his purpose in the end. His journals are peppered with casual references to the Cree, with whom he travelled and among whom he lived.

Noteworthy is La Vérendrye's reference to the "Cree of the Prairies," the first authentic and plausible notice in the literature that Cree were living in the plains country south of the Saskatchewan. A map accompanying the journal cites the annual meeting place in the spring of the

> . . . Cree of the Mountains, Prairies and Rivers, to deliberate as to what they shall do—go and trade with the French or with the English.[33]

If this is not merely a rhetorical way of saying that Cree came from near and far, and it does not seem to be, then it appears that in 1730, a good part of the tribe was already out on the prairies. From other evidences in La Vérendrye's journal, the Cree of the Prairies seem to be just west of Lake Winnipegosis and those of the Mountains to the north of that lake. No sharp segregation had as yet been effected among the divisions, since they met annually to decide upon a mutual course of action.

From the incidental notes of La Vérendrye we may gather a good deal of information concerning the locations of the Cree groups. He remarks that living about Fort St. Charles on the western shores of the Lake of the Woods were Cree and Monsoni who had long been allies. Fort Maurepas was located on the southeast shore of Lake Winnipeg, near the mouth of the Winnipeg River. The tribe in its environs is called the Cree of Strong Woods or Thick Woods, "Cristinos de Bois Fort," a name that crops up later for the Cree north of the Saskatchewan. A post was established on the western shore of Lake Winnipegosis at the request of the Cree of the Prairies and the Canoe Assiniboin. A strange combination this is, since the Cree were predominantly Canoe people at that time and the Assiniboin more usually the plains dwellers. Farther north was Fort Bourbon situated on the northwest shore of Lake Winnipeg. Here were the "Cree of the Lakes and Little Rivers." At the request of the "Mountain Cree," Fort Dauphin was built at the head of Lake Winnipegosis.

The tribe extended south of Lake Winnipeg, for at the juncture of the Red and Assiniboine rivers, La Vérendrye met a band of Cree. A "Chief of the Cree" drew a map for La Vérendrye at Kamanistiquia in 1730, before the Frenchman had himself traversed the western territory. The chart

Fig. 4. A Cree Indian by Paul Kane.

indicates the Saskatchewan, the Red, and the Missouri rivers. This native had evidently traveled far beyond the eastern forests.

According to the journal, the country to the north of the Winnipeg River is held by the Cree. The peoples to the south of that river are not named, but were probably Assiniboin, since both the Cree and Assiniboin frequented Fort St. Charles in that vicinity. Fort Pointe du Bois was a rendezvous for the Assiniboin, Cree, and Monsoni, whence they started against the Sioux. The map of 1750 shows this point to be on the Red River, a little above its juncture with the Assiniboine.

The extension of the French posts into the heart of the Cree country brought a quickening of the demand for European goods. La Vérendrye tells of a council which reveals the eagerness for trade goods that constitutes the recurrent motif in all native councils of this period.

> The nephew of a chief spoke in the Cree language in the name of his whole tribe, which consists of seven villages, the smallest of which numbers a hundred cabins and the largest eight or nine hundred. He begged me to receive them all into the number of the children of our Father, to have pity on them and their families that they were in a general condition of destitution, lacking axes, knives, kettles, guns, etc., that they hoped to get all these things from me if I would let them come to my fort . . .[34]

The traders had little trouble in disposing of their wares.

The death of Chevalier de la Vérendrye was soon followed by the final defeat of the French and New France passed under the sovereignty of the British. This marked approximately one hundred years of European contact with the Cree. During that period many extraneous economic forces were influencing the historic career of the tribe and many far-reaching changes in their mode of life must have occurred. For some of these changes there is adequate documentation, but we may only surmise the nature of others from the indirect evidence of the literature.

Certain it is that the Cree flocked to the trading posts soon after their establishment. From the very first mention of the people in the Jesuit reports, throughout the two centuries following, the fur trade is by far the most important single factor to be reckoned with in an outline of the life of the tribe. In 1640 the Cree were already trading with the Nipissings, who probably were then the middlemen for the whites. In 1659 they earnestly beg the French to visit their country because the Iroquois have cut off their source of European supplies. In 1661 they are most eager to welcome the trader, Radisson, and extract a promise from him to tour their lands when next he voyages in the west. By 1659 they were coming down to Sault Ste. Marie in considerable numbers to trade for manufactures and corn.

The advent of the English nearer to their accustomed domain soon drew them to Hudson Bay. By 1682 they travel to York Factory and Fort Nelson in large numbers from their lands which are fifteen to twenty days' journey inland. In

1690 they have become allies and aides to the English and serve as guides to Kelsey. The trade sent them as far east as Montreal in 1695.

At the end of the first century of contact, we see them patronizing both the English posts to the north and the French forts to the south, and find them greatly dependent upon the aliens not only for arms, clothing, and utensils, but even for provisions. From the self-sufficing plane of aboriginal existence, by 1740 they have passed into a state of economic subservience. They were specialists in fur trapping. The vagaries of the London and Paris fur markets directly touched the Indian, in so far as they affected the returns he received for his labor. In addition to their dependence on the trader for articles which had become basic necessities, the Cree were perhaps more closely bound to the production of furs by their insatiable desires for liquor and tobacco.

The ready spread of the fur trade and its powerful hold may be attributed to several factors. It is well to note that the compelling grip exerted by the trade upon the Cree did not hold true for other peoples. The several men that the Hudson's Bay Company sent into the plains to induce tribes there to come to the posts, were not entirely successful. The plains dwellers proffered a variety of excuses to Kelsey and Henday, the upshot of them all being simply that they did not want to trap beaver for the English. What was there in the situation of the Cree that lent such a powerful impetus to the trade?

In the first place, the lively demand for beaver skins in Europe sent traders to Canada and caused them to exert all their influence toward increasing the fur harvest. The beaver hat came into vogue in the seventeenth century and the value placed on pelts rose as the gentlemen of Western Europe took a great fancy to this headgear. Once the lands nearer the settlements were drained of beaver this acceleration of the demand and the consequent profitability of the fur trade actuated the incursions into Cree territory. Had not this fad so excited European men, the British and French would hardly have been so eager to spread their authority through the wilds of Canada and over its native inhabitants. The fashion-plates of the time were certainly prime factors in starting the historic process which led to the transformation of Cree life. Eventually, the tribe would undoubtedly have come under the dominion of the invaders, but the rate of culture change and its accompanying vicissitudes might have differed. The pressure of European demand for beaver furs, the richness of the Cree range in this commodity, and the ready accessibility of the country to transportation by way of the Hudson Bay or the Great Lake-St. Lawrence route, all paved the way for a large scale fur trade.[35]

The natives themselves were well adapted to the demands of a trapper's existence. Being aboriginally a hunting people, dispersed in small groups over a wide territory, they fulfilled the prerequisite of the fur harvest imposed by the scattered nature of the source of supply and the disadvantages of too intensive trapping in any one area. Secondly, they were a canoe-using people and so were readily able to utilize the network of waterways in their terrain to transport the raw materials to the posts. This trait influenced their later status as middlemen. Their early introduction to the ways of the whites and ability to travel by canoe, gave them a great advantage over the more distant people who lacked both the early start and the technique of water transport. For the Cree could reach out into far lands and, armed with guns, repel the previous inhabitants.

The motives that made this fur gathering mechanism function at a rapid rate were strong. A host of new needs was stimulated by the introduction of manufactured commodities into the primitive economy. Knives, forks, pots, and axes soon became indispensable to the native life. The Cree at once grasped the potentialities of the gun in defeating their enemies and in easing the rigors of the hunt. Although in 1670 they are noted as having only the bow, in 1690 Kelsey remarks that the Cree and Assiniboin, armed with guns, have turned the tables on their enemies and have put them to rout. They soon had little use for the bow. Before long they became strongly addicted to whiskey and Brazil tobacco. These inelastic demands furnished plentiful motives to keep the system going. The price paid for the advantages derived was a twofold dependence upon the traders. Both the supply of pelts and of trade goods were subject to fluctuations. The richest streams were soon trapped bare of animals and the hunter had to range farther afield and work harder to bring an adequate load of furs to the post. Then the European demand was not constant, and while several beaver skins would buy a gun one year, it would take twice the amount to purchase one the next year.[36] Moreover, an Indian would often squander the fruits of a season's labor in one grand spree and thus be forced to penetrate still deeper into the untrapped territory and redouble his efforts in order to earn his supplies.

The consequences of the trade also affected Cree relations with other tribes. For one thing, the alliance with the Assiniboin was cemented, presumably because of the prior acquisition of guns by the Cree. Their old enemies, the Dakota, were repulsed, and later, the wave of Cree conquest swept over the Gros Ventre and Blackfoot in the west, and the Athapascans to the north.

Within one hundred years after the arrival of the whites, the Cree moved westward. The fur trade impelled the movement, the gun enabling them to push other people before them. They were brought to the fringes of the prairie country in their quest for fresh fur-trapping areas. Because of their function as middlemen in the trade, they traveled into the plains to carry trade goods to distant tribes. Their superior armament enabled them to gain a foothold in the plains.

CONQUEST OF THE WESTERN FORESTS,
1740-1820

As far as the Cree were concerned, the competition between the French and the English only brought them better trading facilities. When the English finally ousted the French, trade from York Factory to the interior developed rapidly. From then on the Cree and Assiniboin became important middlemen, trading between the people of the hinterland and the English. These middlemen probably trapped during the winter. In the spring they met at a rendezvous, built canoes, and journeyed to Hudson Bay with their furs.[37]

Such were the "Cree of the Prairies" mentioned by La Vérendrye, who were probably the progenitors of the Plains Cree. This group certainly lived on the plains only a part of the year, but later found the plains life so congenial that they severed all connections with the woodlands. The transition from forest to plains was not accomplished at once.

An interesting bit of evidence on the westernmost Cree of that time occurs in the narrative of David Thompson. He tells of coming upon an old man of Cree origin[38] among the Piegan, in the foothills of the Rockies. When the Indian was a very young man (Thompson estimates the date as about 1730), messengers came to the Cree asking them to join with the Piegan against the "Snake." About twenty warriors, including the youth and his father, responded to the call. The Cree left the few guns they had with those who stayed behind to provide food for and to protect the women and children. The encounter with the enemy was not particularly successful. Thompson's informant remained in the Piegan country and took a Piegan wife. Later he joined a party of Cree, Assiniboin, and Piegan against the Snake. By this time they had more guns. Although they had heard that the Snake had taken to riding strange animals, they were not discouraged. They managed to take some scalps and then wandered about the frontiers of the enemy country hoping to catch a glimpse of the wonderful new creatures the Snake possessed. Finally they came upon the carcass of a dead horse and were able to satisfy their curiosity.

The old man related that after this experience, he returned to his own people, the Cree. In four days' journey from the place where he saw the dead horse, he reached a camp of Assiniboin who directed him to a band of his own folk within a day's travel. From these he discovered that his parents had gone off to "the low countries of the lake" (probably Lake Winnipeg); whereupon he turned about and rejoined the Piegan.

Since the Piegan could call upon them for aid, the group to which the narrator originally belonged must have been well out in the lands west of Lake Winnipeg. The evidence is that a camp of Cree was only five days' journey from the boundaries of the Shoshonean territory. Yet, the Cree knew the lowlands about Lake Winnipeg well enough to travel there on occasion, as had the man's parents. It is reasonable to infer that the westernmost Cree were out on the plains about 1730, and yet were still familiar with the lakes and woodlands, probably shuttling in and out of the prairies, seasonally.

An account of the country surrounding Hudson Bay by Arthur Dobbs appeared in 1744. Lake Winnipeg is given as the boundary between the Cree and Assiniboin in this narrative.[39] Since Dobbs knew something of the prairies and their inhabitants, it is significant that he does not mention Plains Cree. Indeed, he talks of the "true nation of the Cris, or Christineaux" who live about a great lake, called Michinipi. In another place he mentions the Cree as the savages who dwell along the lakes, being a very numerous nation extending over a vast country, even as far as Lake Superior.

Carver traveled along the Great Lakes in 1766-1768. On the northwest shore of Lake Superior, at the Grand Portage, he chanced upon a large party of Cree and Assiniboin.[40] They had come down from the interior to meet the French traders from Michilimackinac. Carver camped with the Indians and made some inquiries as to their provenience. They told him of the French Fort La Reine and were evidently from the region of Portage La Prairie to the south of Lake Winnipeg. They were well acquainted with a great stretch of territory, for they were able to describe to him, not only Lake Winnipeg and the Lake of the Woods area, but indicated that they often roamed along the Red River and the upper Mississippi. Some of them had been to Hudson Bay. Despite the southerly range of this band, Carver remarks that the Cree dwell mainly about Lake Winnipeg and along the Nelson River, and generally trade at the English posts on Hudson Bay.

Matthew Cocking, a Hudson's Bay Company man, was dispatched to the Saskatchewan country to bring the Indians in to trade. His written observations of the Cree are meager, but on one matter in particular his evidence is significant. Under the date of September 24, 1772, he notes seeing some Cree and Assiniboin traveling eastward to trap wolves and impound buffalo. He was then probably somewhere along the North Saskatchewan. Several months later he makes another entry concerning the buffalo pounds. In 1772 the Cree were sufficiently acculturated to Plains life to build buffalo pounds.

Cocking several times talks about the "pound" as though the Cree, Assiniboin, and Blackfoot all congregated at the same place and partook in the common activity. He usually makes no distinction between the Cree and Assiniboin, with one exception: in referring to some Assiniboin who are unacquainted with canoes, he adds that others of the same tribe, however, accompany the Cree to the place where they annually build them. From this comment it seems that even though some of the Cree had become buffalo hunters in Cocking's time, they had not yet given up the use of the canoe as they did later.

The elder Alexander Henry first saw Cree in 1775 when he visited some of their villages on Lake Winnipeg.[41] This statement is somewhat surprising, for he had been at Michilimackinac since 1761. Apparently, by that time the Cree had completely ceased their former visits to this trading center. Yet another unusual reference in Henry's narrative is that the Assiniboin at Fort des Prairies, south of Lake Winnipeg,

> lived in fear of the Cristinaux, by whom they were not only frequently imposed upon, but pillaged, when the latter met their bands in smaller numbers than their own.[42]

The staunch alliance of the two tribes that many commentators implicitly and explicitly noted did not everywhere nor always prevail.

The banishment of the French did not enable the Hudson's Bay Company to monopolize the fur trade, for a rival organization soon came into existence largely as the result of the combination of British capital with French experience. The new North West Company also sent its men into the back country to develop the trade. In 1790 Edward Umfreville, a North West Company man, published a book which was in large part devoted to castigating the policies of the Hudson's Bay Company, but it does nevertheless contain some valuable information for our present purpose.

Umfreville says that his knowledge of the Nehethawa is more perfect than that concerning any other tribe and the description of native life contained in the volume is particularly applicable to them. Since they are scattered over a vast country, Umfreville continues, they do not seem to be as numerous as they really are. But were the different tribes of the Cree to be collected, they would wield a much greater influence among the others than they do now.

The Ojibwa Indians seem to Umfreville to be descended from the Cree, because the languages of the two people were similar and the two maintained a strict alliance. Indeed, many Ojibwa lived among the Cree. The last observation and many others like it, reveal the fact that the Cree became an amalgam of many different tribal stocks. Not only do we find that the Assiniboin, Monsoni, Ojibwa, and the Algonkin to the east and south lived among the Cree, but even their enemies, the Dakota, the Athapascans, and the Blackfoot, occasionally camped with and married into the bands of the Cree. One reason why the Cree attracted people from far places was that they had become, thanks to the fur trade, the wealthiest and most powerful tribe.

Umfreville makes several references to the Cree use of horses. The young men of the tribe are said to employ the greater part of their time in dress, play, and in the care of their horses. Little of their time was required for the hunt, since the country was superabundantly supplied with animals. In the summer they either went to make war on their enemies or stayed at home in a state of ease and satisfaction.

This passage hardly squares with Umfreville's other hints that the Cree were a woodland-dwelling, canoe-using people. Other passages, too, smack more of the plains than of the rivers and forests.

> . . . both parties [the Cree and their opponents] fight with great bravery, each side being provided with coats of mail, made of many folds of drest leather, which are impenetrable to the

force of arrows: they have also shields made of undrest Buffalo hides, which they shift about in the time of action with admirable dexterity and skill. If but one man is killed, the engagement is at an end and the losing party betake themselves to flight to lament their loss at leisure. . . .

Their horses are of great service to the Indians in these expeditions, and are much esteemed by them. Many of the men shew more affection for their horses than for their wives.[43]

The evidence of Umfreville is puzzling. He states that the Cree inhabit the vast woodland-lake-river area between Lake Winnipeg and Hudson Bay. He says that the Ojibwa, living on the upper Great Lakes, are their neighbors and allies. On the other hand, the Cree use of buffalo hide, their fondness for horses, their methods of warfare and hunting, point to a plains culture. We can only conclude that the Cree known to Umfreville were characterized by an ambivalence between two environments.

Among those bands in which the Forest culture was more powerful, the people clung mostly to the hilly, wooded country even though the buffalo herds and the plains were very near. Among those Cree to whom the prairie life was more attractive, the demands of the new environment overrode, in the most fundamental things, the necessities of the woodland culture. An incident in the journals of the younger Henry illustrates this potency:[44] in describing the Cree near Fort Vermilion on the North Saskatchewan, he states that though desperately poor in arms and ammunition, they nevertheless immediately exchanged any guns they were able to get for the horses of the Assiniboin.

The years, 1784 to 1812, included in the *Narrative* of David Thompson cover the period of the most rapid expansion of the fur trade. Administrators and traders plunged deeper and deeper into the unexplored lands to the west and to the north. The competing trade companies poured many men and much money into the Canadian North-West and reaped great profits as their employees opened enormous areas to direct trade contact. Thompson's record gives us an excellent picture of the tribe during that period, but it has more to say about the customs and ceremonies of the Cree than of their locale and peregrinations. Thompson does comment that of all the tribes east of the Rocky Mountains, the Nayhathaway deserve the most consideration. Under different group names, they occupied a great extent of country and though separated and unknown to each other, the main subdivisions differed but little in custom and belief.[45] The Cree

35

had already occupied the plains about the rapids of the Saskatchewan, having driven out the former occupants who were the Fall Indians, the Gros Ventre. Not all the Cree invaders took to the prairies, however. The *Narrative* reports a small group of Nayhathaway and Swampy Ground Assiniboin living somewhere above the North Saskatchewan River, who still preferred their ancient mode of life to living in the plains. The Cree of the west were now becoming socially disconnected from their eastern tribesmen, but still shared much of the eastern culture with them.

Alexander Mackenzie, who traveled widely in Canada and knew the land and its people well, is quite definite as to the limits of Cree expansion. His work of 1789 contains a chapter devoted entirely to an account of the Knisteneaux Indians.[46] In it the terrain of the Cree is specifically bounded. It stretches from the Ottawa River in the east, evidently including some of what is now Labrador, following the divide of the Hudson Bay and Great Lakes basins across to Lake Winnipeg whence it extends along the Saskatchewan and then along the North Saskatchewan River almost to where Edmonton now stands. Thence the boundary line swings northward to Lake Athabasca, including the territory to the south and east. The northern line is formed by the Churchill River and Hudson Bay. Of the great area encompassed by these bounds, Mackenzie declares:—

> The whole of the tract between this line and Hudson's Bay and the straits (except that of the Esquimaux in the latter), may be said to be exclusively the country of the Knisteneaux.[47]

Mackenzie adds that this does not include the ultimate expansion of the Cree, for they have penetrated south of Lake Winnipeg to the Red River Valley and southwest along the southern branch of the Saskatchewan. Furthermore, their forays to the north carried them far beyond Lake Athabasca. They raided the Slaves living on the shores of Great Slave Lake and even carried on war with the natives on the Mackenzie River below the mouth of the Liard. In 1789 the Cree were shouldering many Athapascan peoples out of their accustomed territory.

The immense territory inhabited by the Cree at this period is greater than that dominated by any other North American tribe. Since Mackenzie himself explored and even mapped much of the area, there can be little doubt that the outlines given in his record are substantially accurate.

Of course the term Cree defines no cohesive political or

social entity. There is no evidence that the Cree of Lake Athabasca, say, felt themselves at one with or even knew of the people also called Cree, living on the headwaters of the Ottawa River. But there was enough linguistic and cultural homogeneity to warrant the common appellation. From Mackenzie's statements it is clear that the Cree had not yet, in his time, consolidated for themselves the country south of the North Saskatchewan River, territory later inhabited by the Plains Cree. They had penetrated into this prairie country, but did not lay claim to it. Mackenzie says plainly that the Knisteneaux are, and have been, invaders into the Saskatchewan valley from the east. By virtue of their prior possession of firearms which, at first, overawed their opponents, they were able to conquer the original owners of the region. But as the other tribes themselves acquired guns, the tide turned, and the invincibility of the Cree faded. Mackenzie's comments on the situation disclose how quickly the conquerors lost their prestige. He says of the Cree:—

> Formerly, they struck terror into all the other tribes whom they met; but now they have lost the respect that was paid them; as those whom they formerly considered as barbarians are now their allies, and consequently become better acquainted with them and have acquired the use of fire-arms. The former are still proud without power and affect to consider the other as their inferiors: those consequently are extremely jealous of them, and, depending on their own superiority in numbers, will not submit tamely to their insults; so that the consequences often prove fatal, and the Kristeneaux are thereby decreasing both in power and in number; spirituous liquors also tend to their diminution.[48]

At the end of the eighteenth century, they were already on the down grade.

The decline is strongly emphasized by Doctor Richardson, a member of Sir John Franklin's expedition of 1819-1822. He says, as did Mackenzie, that the Cree reversals are due to the acquisition of arms by their enemies.[49] He adds that the debasement of Cree character is also to blame. Because of their complete dependence on the trader and their passion for liquor, they no longer are the warriors who swept before them the inhabitants of the Saskatchewan and the Mississippi.

It must be remembered that both Mackenzie and Richardson were opposed to the practices of the Hudson's Bay Company, especially to giving plentiful amounts of liquor to the Indians. Hence their decrial of the Cree must not be taken too literally, for there is considerable evidence to show the ascendancy of the Cree continued for over fifty years after these accounts were written.

The journal of the younger Henry, who spent the years 1808-1810 on the North Saskatchewan near the present site of Edmonton, portrays the Cree as a powerful, aggressive people, harassing the Blackfoot, Sarsi, "Snare", and Flathead, reaching the Rocky Mountains on war expeditions.[50] One of his chief concerns was to keep the Cree out of the plains and in the forests where they could trap for furs. He was not usually successful, for the buffalo pounds exerted too great an attraction for the tribesmen. He says:—

> when once they (the Cree) take the route for the pounds below (on the plains), we expect no more fur from them during the season. . . .[51]

In another instance he came upon a group of Cree along the North Saskatchewan and states that:—

> I remained . . . to . . . prevail on some of them to return above, this fall, to make their hunt as usual in the strong wood country.[52]

In this document we have clear evidence that the Cree were still partaking of both forest and plains habitat, were pushing southward into the prairie country. The territory they were to occupy in 1860, was held in 1810 by their allies, the Assiniboin, from whom they received horses and many Plains customs.[53] The Assiniboin were closely associated with the Cree in almost all their ventures, but differed in that they were more aptly adjusted to the Plains life; the Cree, for instance, do not seem to have taken over the use of the horse very readily. Mackenzie mentioned the horses of the Assiniboin several times, but little is said of the Cree animals. It is quite apparent that the Cree lagged behind their allies in adopting the new ways suited to the open country.

Lewis and Clark attempted to stop the traffic between the Cree and the Mandan, first observed by the Jesuit, Aulneau, in 1736. Although the Americans recount a ceremony of adoption and an exchange of property between the Assiniboin and the Cree and Mandan, they wrote as though the allies had a sinister hold upon the village dwellers. They argued that the Mandan should trade with the Americans and not with the native middlemen, because they were no longer obliged to accept the insults of the Cree and the Assiniboin. This source gives the range of the Cree as the valleys of the

Assiniboine and Qu'Appelle rivers southward to the Missouri. The Assiniboine and its tributaries apparently formed one route for the Cree invasion of the plains, the Saskatchewan the other. Lewis and Clark wrote that the Cree generally rove in the open plains, but that they also resort to marshy or wooded lands.

Daniel Harmon's journal of the years 1800 to 1819 graphically records the fur trade of the day. He was intimately acquainted with the Cree and married a Cree woman. Like the foregoing writers, he also pairs the Cree and Assiniboin, remarking in one place that they are similar in most things except language and horsemanship.[54] The Cree possessed horses, but were not very adept with them. The Assiniboin hunted the buffalo with bow and arrow, unlike the Cree who employed guns whenever possible. Harmon declares that the Cree have almost entirely abandoned the use of the bow and other aboriginal implements, and could obtain a livelihood only with great difficulty if deprived of European goods. In his journal we see again that not all the Cree living on the margins of the plains became buffalo hunters. In the vicinity of Swan River Fort, west of Lake Winnipegosis, a group of Cree remained in the forests to hunt moose, elk, and beaver, rarely venturing out into the nearby prairie lands.

Since the long account of native life in this work purports to cover all the aborigines east of the Rocky Mountains, it is usually difficult to tell which tribes Harmon had in mind. He repeatedly mentions raids on the Rapids Indians, the Gros Ventre, by war parties of Cree and Assiniboin.[55] The Gros Ventre, at one time, lived about the forks of the Saskatchewan. The Cree ousted them and then dislodged the Blackfoot farther to the west. Finally, the Cree moved into territory formerly occupied by their Assiniboin allies and were pushing southward in the last years of their independent existence.

At the end of Harmon's period, the Plains Cree were no longer vacillating between forest and woodlands, as they had in the middle of the eighteenth century. Although not yet firmly entrenched in the prairie lands, their woodland excursions were becoming less habitual.

The period from 1760 to 1820 includes the years when the forces indicated in the previous section propelled the Cree to their farthest extension. In the Mackenzie basin they overrode the timid Athapascans. The degree to which the Cree marauders were feared may be judged from a collection of Beaver tales. In eighteen out of seventy-two stories, twenty-five per cent, the Cree figure prominently as rapacious enemies.[56]

The Qu'Appelle and South Saskatchewan basins had been entered by the Cree intruders. But the Cree were not yet totally sundered from the forest. The same bands which roamed the open plains returned occasionally, or perhaps seasonally, to the marshes and forests.

At the close of this period, there was a general southward movement of people in the Saskatchewan area. The Assiniboin, who in Henry's day (circa 1809) occupied the valleys of the lower North Saskatchewan, lower South Saskatchewan, and Qu'Appelle rivers, moved down to the Missouri. The vast mortality caused by smallpox was probably an important factor in bringing about a shrinkage of Assiniboin territory. The Cree, whose numbers were being constantly augmented by recruits from the east,[57] expanded into the former Assiniboin lands. The withdrawal of the Cree from their northern range permitted the Chipewyan to press further southward than they formerly had done.[58]

OCCUPATION OF THE PLAINS, 1820-1880

By 1845, when Father de Smet visited the Plains Cree, they were a bona fide Plains tribe. Although they had gained the prairies they had not ceased their warfare for territory and booty. De Smet observed that they were the most formidable enemies of the Blackfoot and continually encroached upon the territory of their opponents. He accounted for the onslaught by saying that the Cree have been forced to migrate from the Hudson Bay territory because of the scarcity of game there. Of the Hudson Bay territory he says:—

> When the reindeer, buffalo and moose abounded, the Crees were then the peaceful possessors; the animals have disappeared and with them the ancient lords of the country. Scarcely do we meet with a solitary hut. . . . The Crees have gained the buffalo plains and they contend for them with the Black-feet, whose mortal foes they have become.[59]

Duncan Cameron, a trader who wrote in 1804, similarly argued that an increase in Cree population forced the tribe into territories they had not previously inhabited. His opinion was derived from his own experience in the region and from the following native evidence.

> Every old man with whom I conversed, and from whom I made some inquiry on this subject, told me that his father or grand father was from either of these two places (Hudson Bay or

Lake Superior), and that the reason they came so far back inland could be accounted for in no other way than the following: Population was on the increase, both in Hudson's Bay and on the shores of Lake Superior, and as Indians, who are obliged to rove from place to place for a good hunting ground, are equally at home in any place where they can find their living, they took to the interior of the country where they found innumerable rivers and lakes, swarming with a vast quantity of fish, beaver and otter.[60]

The prompting of the traders and the invincibility of the gun were not the only factors responsible for Cree expansion. The introduction of European techniques and artifacts effected an increase in the population. Exhausting the resources of their former habitat, the Cree were forced to extend their boundaries.

Bishop Taché visited the Plains Cree in 1850 and deplored their bloodthirsty nature as contrasted with the pacific disposition of their woods brethren who regaled themselves much more wisely by giving grand feasts rather than by massacring their neighbors.[61]

Hind, who led an expedition into the western plains, cites an attempt to arrange a truce between the Cree and Blackfoot.[62] All went smoothly until the Cree young men could no longer resist the temptation offered by the fine Blackfoot horses. They stole several, were pursued, caught, and some fatalities ensued. The Blackfoot were better supplied with horses than were the Cree who often attempted to replenish their stock from the plentiful Blackfoot herds.

The warfare, however, was not an unceasing affair. Captain John Palliser, whose report is one of the best sources of information on the Plains Cree, relates a tale told to him by a native[63] concerning a bloody massacre of the Cree by the Blackfoot, but begins with the statement that the Cree and Blackfoot had been at peace and were tenting together near the elbow of the South Saskatchewan. Again, the Cree could not keep away from the Blackfoot horses, were caught, and killed.

One of Palliser's subordinates, Lieutenant Blakiston, spent the year 1857 on the South Saskatchewan, often in the company of Cree. He submitted a report containing a history of the migrations of the Cree which summarizes other evidence we have examined and so is worth quoting. Blakiston says:—

In fact the Crees generally may thank the traders for the greater part of the interior they now have in their hands, for it is not a great many years since the Blackfeet held the whole Saskatchewan plains at which time the Stone Indians or Assiniboines inhabited the country lying along the river of that name, and the Crees were confined mostly to the thickly-wooded-country to the north of Lake Winnipeg, and between that lake and Hudson's Bay. On the fur trade, however, being pushed up the Saskatchewan and the Crees obtaining fire-arms of the traders, they drove the Blackfoot and Fall Indians, or Gros Ventres, west, at the same time taking to horses, they gradually became Prairie Indians and forming a league with the Stone Indians, who, as late as 1819 could not obtain guns in trade at the Forts, succeeded in confining Blackfeet to the limits they now rarely overstep, namely, from the upper waters of the Saskatchewan in a line towards Fort Union on the Missouri, as shown on the map. Crees also inhabit the country to the north of the Saskatchewan, where they are mostly what are called thick or strong-wood Indians, there being only a few horses among them.[64]

The dichotomy between those Cree who hunted buffalo and their eastern relatives became more and more sharply marked. So great was the separation that Hind warned against sending any of the Christianized Swampy Cree to preach among the Plains Cree, for the haughty and independent children of the prairies would never acknowledge or respect their docile tribesmen as teachers.[65]

Lacombe recorded the story of an old Plains Cree who said that not very long ago his people had lived to the east, among the Maskegon and Saulteaux.[66] They were separated because some of the bands went farther and farther afield in quest of the herds until the distance between them and those who remained in the river regions was considerable. The expansion of the Cree, writes Lacombe, has made it possible for one equipped with a knowledge of the Cree language to communicate with any Canadian tribe, even with the hostile Blackfoot and Sarsi, who have on occasion camped with them.

The Cree were not always the aggressors on the western frontier at this period. In 1858 Hind mentions some Cree who were fleeing from Blackfoot attacks.[67] By 1865 they were apparently in full retreat, for John McDougall observes that the region about old Fort Edmonton, once the scene of many battles, was now peaceful because the Cree had moved eastward.[68]

The Palliser report of 1857-1859 mentions the terrific ravages of disease, especially smallpox, as one of the contributing factors in the decline of the tribe. In one locality, over half the population had been carried off by the epidemic. Then also the buffalo herds were on the wane. Both Palliser and Hind remark that the scarcity of the buffalo often brought the Cree to the brink of starvation. But even in Palliser's day they were the most widespread and probably the most numerous tribe in Canada.

The Prairie Cree, according to the official report of the expedition, though similar in language and appearance to the Woodland Cree, differed very much in their disposition and manner of living. They habitually formed great encampments and followed the buffalo herds. During the summer they generally camped along the Qu'Appelle River and the Missouri Couteau, where they bordered on the Sioux and Assiniboin. At other seasons they were mostly in the valley of the Saskatchewan, from the Neutral Hills south of the Battle River to the Beaver Hills and Fort Edmonton where they impinged upon the Blackfoot.[69]

The first of a series of treaties made by the Dominion Government with the Cree was signed in 1871.[70] It confined them to a specific range and imposed obligations upon the Indians to keep peace. In return the government granted them certain gifts and annuities to relieve the starvation that was facing them. In 1874 another pact was drawn up with some bands of Cree and Saulteaux at the Qu'Appelle lakes. In 1875 all of the Swampy Cree came under the terms of a treaty drawn up at Lake Winnipeg. Finally, in 1876, the Plains Cree submitted to government authority at Forts Carlton and Pitt.

Throughout their long dealings with the white man, the Cree had been uniformly friendly to him. But after their confinement to reserves and their loss of power, some of them rebelled.[71] Under the leadership of Louis Riel an uprising against the whites occurred in 1885, centering in the Metis settlements in the Saskatchewan River area. The Cree near Carlton Agency, once a prized buffalo hunting ground, were subsisting largely upon muskrats, but even these became scarce. Several bands raided the traders and killed some white people. Other bands of Plains Cree, hearing of this, also took up arms against the whites. The uprising was soon quelled and some of the leaders were hanged. From then until the present, the tribe has gone through the trials and adjustments that most North American Indians have had to endure. Penned into smaller and smaller areas, cut down by disease, economically pauperized, they now subsist on small-scale farming and Government grants.

One important factor in the decline of the Plains Cree was the effect of the epidemics that struck the tribe periodically and diminished their numbers. By far the most virulent of the diseases that afflicted them was smallpox, wiping out whole bands. In later days the tuberculosis mortality reached epidemic proportions.

The first notice of smallpox occurs in the journals of La Vérendrye under the date of March 26, 1736.[72] The entry records that a group of Winnipeg Cree (i.e., a band living on the Winnipeg River) whom the author had left at Fort Maurepas, had all died of smallpox. The extent of this particular epidemic cannot be ascertained from the single reference. However, the extinction of an entire band must surely have been accompanied by similar fatalities among other groups of the people.

Another epidemic, that of 1781-1782, is better documented. The years are fairly certain, although F. V. Hayden in writing of the great mass of burials puts the date at 1776-1777, and F. E. Peeso says that one half the Cree died of the malady in 1786.[73] However, John McDonnell, Edward Umfreville, and David Thompson, all agree on "the years of the great plague," from 1780 to 1782.[74] This epidemic was not confined to the Cree alone, but struck all of the tribes of the Hudson Bay country. Umfreville vividly describes the baleful effects of the disease, saying:—

> That epidemical and raging disorder has spread an almost universal mortality throughout the country in the interior parts of Hudson's Bay, extending its destructive effect through every tribe and nation, sparing neither age nor sex. It is supposed that it was introduced among them by some of their war parties during the summer of 1781; and by the fall of the year 1782, it had diffused to every known part of the country.[75]

An old Cree whom Thompson encountered among the Piegan related that a Cree-Piegan war party had caught smallpox from the Snake Indians about 1730. More than half their number were swept away. This outbreak may coincide with the epidemic noted by La Vérendrye.

Thompson came on the scene soon after the 1780-1782 epidemic had burned through the native population. He states that according to best information the disease was caught by the

> Chipaways (the forest Indians) and the Sieux (of the Plains) at about the same time, in the year 1780.[76]

From them it spread to all the Indians so that more than one half died. The Cree slowly recovered from this blow. According to Thompson a peculiar circumstance accompanied the epidemic; the enormous fatalities were coincident with a corresponding decline in the numbers of the game animals; bison, deer, moose, and even wild fowl became scarce. Within a few years, however, the supply returned to normal, for Thompson records that when he again traveled in the country where the bison formerly had almost disappeared, the herds were far more numerous than they had been.

The interval between the first epidemic and that of 1780-1782 was about thirty-five or forty years. About the same span of time separates the second from the third epidemic. According to Hind, "a great mortality took place" in the Hudson Bay area because of smallpox and measles from 1816 to 1818. R. M. Martin gives the years 1810 to 1820 and adds that the Cree are increasing in numbers (about 1830). Some forty years later Palliser wrote that one half of a certain band had been carried off by smallpox. The pestilence then was almost a yearly occurrence among the Indians. The severe epidemics came thirty-five to forty years apart, perhaps flaring up with renewed intensity when a non-immunized generation grew up.[77]

Great as were the ravages of smallpox among the Plains Cree, they may have been even greater among the Assiniboin,[78] for during the epidemic of the 1780's, the Assiniboin were closer to true Plains life than were the Cree. They were living in larger groups for longer periods of the year; hence, they would furnish a ready field and a quick spread for the foci of infection. The Cree were scattered in small groups during a good part of the year and the malady was probably less catastrophic among them. This may explain why the Assiniboin withdrew from the Saskatchewan and Qu'Appelle basins to be supplanted by the Cree.

SUMMARY

A résumé of the historical narrative recounted in this section reveals the forest antecedents of the Plains Cree. In the period of earliest contact with Europeans, the Cree are depicted as a nomadic, powerful, war-like tribe. They lived in the forests between Hudson Bay and Lake Superior, appearing on the shores of these bodies of water in summer and spending the winter inland. Their culture is wholly Woodlands. There is no hint that they were reaching westward in the seventeenth century.

The period from 1690 to 1740 witnessed the establishment of trading posts in the Cree country. The tribesmen soon devoted much of their energy to fur trapping and became dependent upon trade goods. When intensive trapping exhausted the faunal resources of their lands, they were forced westward to exploit fresh territory. Armed with guns, they were able to force out the former inhabitants who, as yet, possessed no firearms. These forces brought the Cree close to the prairies; their function as middlemen to the fur trade sent them deep into lands beyond the scope of their conquests.

From 1740 to 1820 the Cree were expanding to their widest limits. Although some bands were out on the plains, they had not completely severed themselves from the forest. Toward the end of the period, the Cree on the prairies had largely ceased to waver between the two environments and were abandoning excursions into the woodlands.

The final era found the invaders firmly established in the plains as a true Plains tribe. They waged an unremitting warfare with the Blackfoot, were probably taking on new cultural forms, and were periodically decimated by smallpox. The influx of the white hunters and settlers put an end to their aboriginal existence.

A factor far removed from the North American forests and plains set in motion the historic forces to which the Plains Cree owed their existence as a tribal group. The European fad for the beaver hat created a great demand for beaver pelts. The quest for furs brought the Cree to the prairies; the congenial mode of Plains life induced some of them to stay there.

FOOTNOTES

[1]THWAITES, REUBEN GOLD, ed., The Jesuit Relations and Allied Documents. Travels and Explorations of the Jesuit Missionaries in New France, 1610-1791. The original French, Latin and Italian Texts, with English Translations and Notes. Illustrated by Portraits, Maps, and Facsimiles, 58 vols., Cleveland, 1896-1901, vol. 18, p. 229; vol. 21, p. 125; vol. 23, p. 225; vol. 42, p. 221; vol. 44, pp. 241, 243, 249, 325; vol. 45, p. 227; vol. 46, pp. 69, 249.
[2]THWAITES, Jesuit Relations, vol. 44, p. 325.
[3]SKINNER, ALANSON, Notes on the Eastern Cree and Northern Saulteaux (Anthropological Papers, American Museum of Natural History, vol. 9, part 1, New York, 1911), pp. 8-10.
[4]THWAITES, Jesuit Relations, vol. 51, p. 57; KELLOGG, LOUISE PHELPS, ed., Early Narratives of the Northwest, New York, 1917, p. 134; also VERWYST, CHRYSOSTOM, Missionary Labors of Fathers Marquette, Menard, and Allouez in the Lake Superior Region, Chicago, 1886, p. 69.
[5]THWAITES, Jesuit Relations, vol. 54, p. 135.
[6]Ibid., vol. 54, p. 193.

[7]*Ibid.*, vol. 55, p. 99.

[8]*Ibid.*, vol. 56, p. 203.

[9]HODGE, FREDERICK WEBB, ed., Handbook of American Indians North of Mexico (Bulletin 30, Bureau of American Ethnology, part 1, Washington, 1907, part 2, Washington, 1910), part 1, pp. 819, 932.

[10]SCULL, G. D., Voyages of Peter Esprit Radisson (Prince Society, Boston, 1885); THWAITES, REUBEN GOLD, ed., Radisson and Groseilliers in Wisconsin (Report and Collections of the State Historical Society of Wisconsin, vol. 11, Madison, 1888), pp. 66ff; CAMPBELL, HENRY COLIN, Radisson's Journal: Its Value in History (Proceedings, State Historical Society of Wisconsin at its Forty-Third Annual Meeting, Madison, 1896), pp. 96ff; KELLOGG, Early Narratives, pp. 46ff.

[11]MICHELSON, TRUMAN, The Identification of the Mascoutens (American Anthropologist, n.s., vol. 36, Menasha, 1934).

[12]THWAITES, Radisson and Groseilliers, pp. 68-69.

[13]*Ibid.*, p. 90.

[14]*Ibid.*, pp. 91, 92.

[15]THWAITES, Jesuit Relations. vol. 58. p. 257.

[16]PERROT, NICOLAS, Abstract from Memoire sur les Moeurs, Coutumes et Religion des Sauvages de l'Amerique Septentrionale: written about 1715-18 (Paris, 1864) in The French Regime in Wisconsin—I (Collections, State Historical Society of Wisconsin, vol. 16, Madison, 1902), p. 20.

[17]LAHONTAN, BARON, New Voyages to America, 2 vols., London, 1703, vol. 1, p. 210.

[18]INNIS, H. A., The Fur Trade in Canada, New Haven, 1930, p. 44.

[19]SPECK, FRANK G., Culture Problems in Northeastern North America (Proceedings, American Philosophical Society, vol. 65, Philadelphia, 1926), p. 304.

[20]KELSEY, HENRY, The Kelsey Papers. A Journal of a Voyage and Journey undertaken by Henry Kelsey—in anno 1691. With an Introduction by Arthur G. Doughty and Chester Martin (Ottawa, 1929); BELL, C. N., Journal of Henry Kelsey (Transactions, The Historical and Scientific Society of Manitoba, n.s., no. 4, Winnipeg 1928).

[21]*Ibid.*, pp. 3-4.

[22]KELLOGG, Early Narratives, p. 330.

[23]TYRRELL, J. B., ed., Documents Relating to the Early History of Hudson Bay. Edited with Introduction and Notes by J. B. Tyrrell (The Publications of the Champlain Society, XVIII, Toronto, 1931), p. 68.

[24]THWAITES, Jesuit Relations, vol. 66, pp. 107ff.

[25]INNIS, The Fur Trade in Canada, p. 47.

[26]SHEA, JOHN GILMARY, Early Voyages Up and Down the Mississippi by Cavelier, St. Cosme, Le Sueur, Gravier, and Guignas. With an Introduction, Notes and an Index by John Gilmary Shea, Albany, 1861, pp. 106ff.

[27]TYRRELL, Documents . . . of Hudson Bay, p. 263; MICHELSON, TRUMAN, Oüenebigonchelinis confounded with Winnebago (American Anthropologist, n.s., vol. 36, Menasha, 1934), p. 486.

[28]CHARLEVOIX, PIERRE FRANCOIS XAVIER DE, Journal of a Voyage to North America. Translated from the French of Pierre Francois de Charlevoix. Edited, with Historical Introduction, Notes and Index, by Louise Phelps Kellogg, Ph.D., 2 vols. (The Caxton Club, Chicago, 1923), vol. 1, p. 259.

[29]PETITOT, ÉMILE, On the Athabasca District of the Canadian North-West Territory (Proceedings, Royal Geographical Society, and Monthly Record of Geography, vol. 5, London, 1883), pp. 649ff.

[30]THWAITES, Jesuit Relations, vol. 68, pp. 287ff.

[31]THWAITES, REUBEN GOLD, ed., The French Regime in Wisconsin—II, 1727-1748 (Collections, State Historical Society of Wisconsin, vol. 17, Madison, 1906), p. 166, footnote, p. 418.

[32]*Ibid.*, pp. 262-263.

[33]BURPEE, LAWRENCE J., ed., Journals and Letters of Pierre Gaultier de Varennes de la Vérendrye and his Sons. With Correspondence between the Governors of Canada and the French Court, touching the Search for the Western Sea. With Introduction and Notes by Lawrence J. Burpee (The Champlain Society, Toronto, 1927), p. 25.

[34]*Ibid.*, p. 146.

[35]INNIS, The Fur Trade in Canada, pp. 84ff, 390ff.

[36]*Ibid.*, pp. 106ff.

[37]*See* UMFREVILLE, EDWARD, The Present State of Hudson's Bay, Containing a Full Description of that Settlement, and the Adjacent Country; and Likewise of the Fur Trade, London, 1790, pp. 56ff; *also* DOBBS, ARTHUR, An Account of the Countries Adjoining to Hudson's Bay in the Northwest Part of America, London, 1744, pp. 37ff.

[38]TYRRELL, J. B., ed., David Thompson's Narrative of his Explorations in Western America, 1784-1812 (The Champlain Society, XII, Toronto, 1916), pp. 328ff.

[39]DOBBS, An Account of Countries Adjoining to Hudson's Bay, pp. 24ff.

[40]CARVER, JOSEPH, Travels Through the Interior Parts of North America, in the Years 1766, 1767, and 1768, London, 1778, pp. 106ff.

[41]HENRY, ALEXANDER, Travels and Adventures in Canada and the Indian Territories between the Years 1760 and 1776, 2 parts, New York, 1809, p. 246.

[42]*Ibid.*, p. 313.

[43]UMFREVILLE, The Present State of Hudson's Bay, pp. 188-189.

[44]COUES, Early History of the Greater Northwest, vol. 2, p. 513.

[45]TYRRELL, David Thompson's Narrative, pp. 82, 235.

[46]MACKENZIE, ALEXANDER, Voyages from Montreal through the Continent of North America to the Frozen and Pacific Oceans in 1789 and 1793 with an Account of the Rise and State of the Fur Trade, 2 vols., New York, 1902, vol. 1, pp. cxl ff.

[47]*Ibid.*, vol. 1, p. cxli.

[48]*Ibid.*, vol. 1, p. cxii.

[49]FRANKLIN, JOHN, Narrative of a Journey to the Shores of the Poplar Sea in the Years 1819, 20, 21, & 22, Philadelphia, 1824, pp. 50-51, 62. Most of the quotations from this source that I have used are from the pen of Doctor Richardson.

[50]COUES, Early History of the Greater Northwest, vol. 2, pp. 495, 540, 596, 614, 644.

[51]*Ibid.*, vol. 2, p. 580.

[52]*Ibid.*, vol. 2, p. 501.

[53]*Ibid.*, vol. 1, p. 185.

[54]HARMON, D.W., A Journal of Voyages and Travels in the Interior of North America, D. Haskell, ed., Toronto, 1911, pp. 40, 73, 34.

[55]*Ibid.*, p. 25

[56]GODDARD, PLINY EARLE, Beaver Texts; Beaver Dialect (Anthropological Papers, American Museum of Natural History, vol. 10, parts 5 and 6, New York, 1917).

[57]COUES, Early History of the Greater Northwest, 1897, vol. 2, p. 576.

[58]TYRRELL, David Thompson's Narrative, pp. 131, 559.

[59]THWAITES, REUBEN GOLD, ed., Early Western Travels, 32 vols., Cleveland, 1904-07, vol. 29, p. 235; CHITTENDEN, HIRAM MARTIN, and RICHARDSON, ALFRED TALBOT, Life, Letters, and Travels of Father Pierre-Jean De Smet, S.J., 1801-1873, 4 vols., New York, 1905, vol. 2, p. 519.

[60]CAMERON, DUNCAN, The Nipigon Country, 1804. With Extracts from his Journal (In Les Bourgeois de la Compagnie du Nord-Ouest Récits de Voyages, Lettres et Rapports inédits Relatifs, au Nord-Ouest Canadien, Publié avec une Esquisse Historique et des Annotations, par L. R. Masson, Deuxième Série, Quebec, 1890), p. 242.

[61]TACHÉ, ALEXANDRE, Esquisse sur le Nord-Ouest de l'Amerique, Montreal, 1869, p. 82.

[62]HIND, HENRY YULE, Of Some of the Superstitions and Customs Common Among the Indians in the Valleys of the Assiniboine and Saskatchewan (The Canadian Journal, n.s., vol. 4, July, 1859), pp. 253-262.

[63]PALLISER, JOHN, Papers Relative to and Further Papers Relative to the Explorations by Captain Palliser of that Portion of British North America which lies between the North Branch of the River Saskatchewan and the Frontier of the United States; and between the Red River and Rocky Mountains, London, 1859, p. 53.

[64]*Ibid.*, p. 46.

[65]HIND, HENRY YULE, Narrative of the Canadian Red River Exploring Expedition of 1857 and of the Assiniboine and Saskatchewan Exploring Expedition of 1858, 2 vols., London, 1860, vol. 1, p. 324.

[66]LACOMBE, ALBERT, Dictionnaire et Grammaire de la Langue des Cris, Montreal, 1874, pp. x-xi.

[67]HIND, Narrative of the Canadian Red River, vol. 1, p. 318.

[68]McDOUGALL, JOHN, Pathfinding on Plain and Prairie, Toronto, 1898, p. 129.

[69]From an examination of the record of Cree camps encountered by the expedition

and of the dates on which they are seen, it appears that Palliser was mistaken in postulating this summer-winter migration for all the Plains Cree.

[70]MORRIS, ALEXANDER, The Treaties of Canada with the Indians of Manitoba and the North-West Territories, Toronto, 1880, pp. 77, 299.

[71]See MULVANEY, C.P., The History of the North-West Rebellion of 1885, Toronto, 1885.

[72]BURPEE, Journals and Letters, p. 256.

[73]PEESO, F.E., The Cree Indians (The Museum Journal, University of Pennsylvania, vol. 3, Philadelphia, 1912), p. 52.

[74]HAYDEN, F. V., Contributions to the Ethnography and Philology of the Indian Tribes of the Missouri Valley (Transactions, American Philosophical Society held at Philadelphia, for promoting Useful Knowledge, n.s., vol 12, article 3, Philadelphia, 1863), p. 243; McDONNELL, JOHN, Some Account of the Red River (About 1797), with Extracts from his Journal, 1793-1795 (In Les Bourgeois de la Compagnie du Nord-Ouest, Récits de Voyages, Lettres et Rapports Inédits Relatifs au Nord-Ouest Canadian. Publié avec une Esquisse Historique, Première Série, Quebec, 1889), p. 277; UMFREVILLE, The Present State of Hudson's Bay, p. 92; TYRRELL, David Thompson's Narrative, pp. 109, 321, 325, 336, 337.

[75]UMFREVILLE, The Present State of Hudson's Bay, p. 92.

[76]TYRRELL, David Thompson's Narrative, p. 322.

[77]HIND, Narrative of the Canadian Red River, vol. 2, p. 143; MARTIN, R.M., The Hudson's Bay Territories and Vancouver Island, London, 1849, p. 84; PALLISER, Papers Relative to . . . Explorations by Captain Palliser, p. 52.

[78]DENIG, EDWIN THOMPSON, Indian Tribes of the Upper Missouri. Edited with Notes and Biographical Sketch by J.N.B. Hewitt (Forty-Sixth Annual Report, Bureau of American Ethnology, Washington, 1930), p. 399.

The Mainstays of Plains Cree Economy

In 1858 Professor Henry Youle Hind, an eminent Canadian geologist, was commissioned to explore the lands between the Assiniboine and Saskatchewan rivers. Hind's travels across the Canadian prairies brought him in contact with the Plains Cree and of their life he wrote:—

> It may truly be said that they exist on the buffalo, and their knowledge of the habits of this animal is consequently essential to their preservation. . . .
> Next to the buffalo the horse is the mainstay of the prairie Indians. . . .
> Next to the horse, the dog is the Prairie Indians most valuable friend. . . .[1]

These three animals furnished the basis for, and indeed, almost the totality of the economic life. The buffalo was the source of a large part of the subsistence economy; the horse was a chief factor in the prestige economy; both horse and dog supplied the mobility demanded of a hunting population in a Plains environment.

THE BUFFALO

The importance of the buffalo may be gauged by the effect of its disappearance on the tribal life. In 1870, there were hundreds of thousands of buffalo in the Saskatchewan country; by 1881, there were only a few head, widely scattered.[2] When the herds abounded, the Plains Cree had lived in plenty, taking only the choice parts from a carcass, abandoning tons of meat to the wolves and coyotes. After the buffalo were gone, the tribe was always on the verge of starvation and subsisted largely on muskrat and gophers. They had been haughty and arrogant in their dealings with whites; they later besieged every trading post and settlement piteously begging for a ration of food. They had been well and even richly clothed; they came to depend on soldiers' cast-off garments for clothing. They had erected weather-tight and commodious shelters; they later lived in leaky sod and timber hovels. They had congregated in camps containing thousands; they were afterward isolated in small reserve groups. In 1860, an estimate of Plains Cree population placed their numbers at 12,500; in 1899, there were 6807 Western Cree.[3]

Despite its great economic importance, the buffalo did not loom large in the religious and ceremonial life. The Buffalo Spirit Power was considered very powerful, but there were several Spirit Powers equally or more powerful. In the Sun dance a buffalo skull was placed at the altar, but the dance itself was not primarily concerned with success in the hunt nor with increase of the herds. The ritual respect paid to the bear and the eagle was not given to the buffalo, nor was there any particular magic associated with the buffalo chase. The construction of a buffalo pound required supernatural sanctions, but any Spirit Power could give them.

The migrations of the herds regulated the tribal movements. When the buffalo, drifting southward, crossed the South Saskatchewan in June and July, the Plains Cree gathered in large encampments along that river. During the summer months many buffalo roamed the open plains between the Grand Couteau of the Missouri (roughly, the international boundary line) and the Qu'Appelle and Saskatchewan rivers. At that season many of the tribal camps were located in those plains. In the autumn when the herds moved northward into the woods along the Saskatchewan and Qu'Appelle valleys and into the hilly regions, most of the Cree camped in the wooded country. In late winter the buffalo were scattered in small groups. So were the Plains Cree. But, at all seasons of the year buffalo were obtainable within the territory of each band; hence a seasonal migration of the whole tribe was not economically necessary and did not occur.[4]

Hunting Methods

The techniques of procuring buffalo varied seasonally. In the autumn and early winter, when the herds were entering the wooded regions, the chute and pound method was used.[5] This procedure involved stampeding a herd into a corral and yielded the richest returns in meat and hides. The Plains Cree were perhaps the most proficient of the Northern Plains people in the use of the pound.

A pound had to be built under the supervision of a

shaman who had been given the power to do so by a spirit helper. Each pound could only be used through one winter; the following year a new one had to be built.

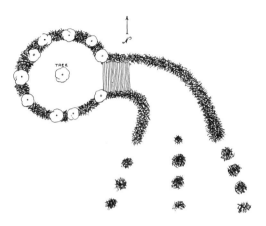

Fig. 5. Buffalo Pound.

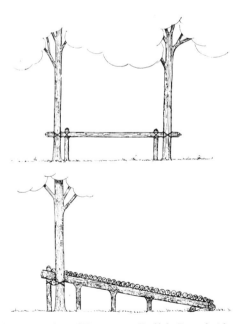

Fig. 6. Detail of Construction of Entrance to Buffalo Pound. Above, cross piece set in place; below, runway built leading up to and partially supported by cross piece.

The shaman who directed the construction and operation of a pound (Fig. 5), chose the site in a thicket; a circular area thirty to forty feet in diameter was cleared. The cut brush and felled logs were heaped up to make a wall ten to fifteen feet high. Loose boughs, interwoven between standing trees, furnished a foundation for the wall. A single tree was left standing in the center. The clearing and construction were done by the men. As *Maskwa* recounted this he commented, "That was the only time when men really worked."

The entrance was to the east, at a place where two sturdy trees grew about twenty feet apart. A log was lashed between the two trees (Fig. 6) at a level with the top of the wall. A runway leading into the pound was built from the ground up to this log. Wherever possible, the entrance was placed on the brow of a bluff, so that the drop from the runway to the floor of the corral was by so much the greater.

The chute which guided the herds into the pound extended obliquely from each side of the entrance. For perhaps a hundred yards out, the chute was constructed either by lashing saplings across standing timber or by piling up boughs to form a fence, at the end of which bundles of brush were set up about thirty yards apart. Each bundle was four feet high and stacked to lean inward, toward the opposite side of the chute. These bundles led out for a mile or more (ten miles according to *Maskwa*). Between the two widening lines of the funnel, a middle row of brush bundles was placed.

The chute took a sharp turn just before the entrance to the enclosure so that the onrushing herd could not see the corral until it was too late to stop. Men were stationed at this bend and at several places along the chute. When the buffalo approached, they jumped up, waved robes, yelled, and thus stampeded the animals up the runway and into the pound.

The tipi of the "maker" of the pound was placed beside the entrance. Here the shaman sang and smoked to invoke his spirit helpers. A buffalo skull, several cloth offerings, and two feathered crooks were placed underneath the runway. When buffalo were needed, the shaman invited several young men into his tipi. He gave them berries to eat, had each one blow on an eagle bone whistle, and then made a pipe offering. At night these young men went out to find buffalo. When they located a herd they surrounded it and drove it steadily toward the opening of the chute by slapping their folded robes on the ground or on the snow. The loud report startled the animals and they would move away from the source of the noise, but on perceiving no further danger, settled down to graze again. The young men would advance a little and send the herd on further with another report.

When the animals were close to the chute, a single horseman, mounted on a fast horse, rode out to guide them into the corral. He was able to do this by operating on the principle that the herd leaders would always swing toward a rapidly approaching rider in an effort to head him off. Thus, if the buffalo were running too far to the left of the pound, the rider galloped around and approached the leading buffaloes from their right. They would veer toward the horseman and, consequently, into the funnel. Once inside the chute the motion of the herd was accelerated by the violent movements of men stationed behind the barriers. In the pound the buffalo milled around clockwise and were shot with arrows. As the buffalo milled, daring young men would jump into the pound and pluck arrows from the sides of animals. All the arrows they could retrieve belonged to them.

Before the carcasses were butchered, the shaman ascended the wall of the pound and sang his power song, accompanying himself with a rattle. Then small boys undressed and climbed into the enclosure. They threw buffalo intestines over the branches of the central tree, imitating the call of crows as they did so. At the same time, little girls brought wood to the tipi of the shaman. For these functions, each girl received a piece of heart fat and each boy a buffalo tongue. The fatty tissue around the buffalo heart was peculiarly sacred. The person who cut it out of the carcass wailed as he did so.

The camp crier usually apportioned the buffalo, giving the fattest carcasses to the men who had worked on the pound. Often the original pound was filled with the accumulated débris and another had to be built adjoining it. If one pound proved unsuccessful, the group about it moved to an encampment whose pound furnished an ample supply of meat. All who were encamped in the vicinity of a pound were privileged to share in its yield, regardless of whether they had helped build it or whether they belonged to the band that had constructed it. Pounds were not used for any other animals.

Skinner's description of a pound states that the buffalo were enticed into the mouth of the chute by a man who could make the animals follow him.[6]

During the spring and summer, when the herds were moving southward in vast numbers, the concerted hunt was made. As soon as a large encampment was formed, scouts were dispatched to find buffalo. When one of them sighted a herd, he signaled by waving his robe. If he saw a great many buffalo, he threw up handfuls of dirt as well. The men in camp quickly saddled their horses and set out. If a man had more than one horse, he rode the pack animal out, saving the hunting horse for the chase. The warriors lined the hunters in a row so that each should have a fair chance and so that the herd might not be stampeded prematurely. At a signal from one of the warriors, the horses were given free rein and the hunt was begun. The riders singled out fat buffalo, pursuing and killing one after another until the herd had outdistanced them.

The chase is thus described by Robert Jefferson:—

. . . As each animal fell, its slayer dropped some article by which to recognize his property and again took up the chase. Bow and arrows, muzzle-loading guns—even flint locks—and a few rifles were the weapons. With these first-named, the Indians were quite dexterous, often, it is said, sending an arrow completely through the body of a buffalo. The arrows were carried in a quiver on the back, in such a position that the bearer, by throwing his right hand just over the left shoulder, could grasp an arrow. The drawing of an arrow, the fitting on the bowstring and the discharging are three movements merged into one, so perfect is their continuity. The guns, as discharged, are loaded again while racing:—a measure of powder poured into the muzzle haphazard, next a bullet rolled down the barrel from a store kept in the mouth, with a cap from a little circular arrangement on which they are stuck—and the hunter is ready for the next shot; no wads or paper or anything to keep each part of the load in its place. Of course the gun barrel must be kept in a semi-upright position till it can be aimed and discharged at the same moment. Many were the hands maimed, fingers blown off and other mischances by guns bursting owing to the bullet sticking in a dirty barrel.[7]

Whenever it was possible, buffalo were driven into places where they floundered and were easily taken. In summer they were guided into marshes; in winter, they were forced into deep snow or over ice. Sometimes a herd was stampeded over a cliff or a steep bank. The hunters did not plan such drives beforehand, but simply exploited the natural advantages of the terrain. Horses were used if they were available, but a great deal of buffalo hunting was done on foot.

Hind was an eyewitness to a kill, and graphically described it.

. . . the young Plains Cree threw off his leather hunting shirt, jumped on a horse, and hurried across the valley. Dismounting

56

at the foot of the bank, he rapidly ascended its steep sides, and just before reaching the top, cautiously approached a large boulder which lay on the brink, and crouched behind it.

The buffalo was within forty yards of the spot where the Indian crouched and (was) slowly approaching the valley. . . . When within twenty yards of the Indian the bull raised his head, snuffed the air, and began to paw the ground. Lying at full length, the Indian sent an arrow into the side of his huge antagonist. The bull shook his head and mane, planted his fore feet firmly in front of him, and looked from side to side in search of his unseen foe, who, after driving the arrow, had again crouched behind the boulder. Soon, however, observing the fixed attitude of the bull, a sure sign he was severely wounded, he stepped to one side and showed himself. The bull instantly charged, but when within five yards of his nimble enemy, the Indian sprang lightly behind the boulder, and the bull plunged headlong down the hill, receiving after he had passed the Indian, a second arrow in his flanks. . . . After one or two efforts to rise, the huge animal dropped his head and gave up the strife. The Indian was at his side without a moment's pause, cut out his tongue, caught his horse,—an excited spectator of the conflict,—and galloping across the valley, handed me the trophy of his success.[8]

The River People band did not practise the surround although they knew of its use by some of the eastern bands. Informants from the Calling River People told Skinner that horsemen would surround a herd, starting it milling, then ride in and slaughter.[9]

In the late winter and early spring, when only a few buffalo were to be found, various means of stalking were employed. A single animal would be tracked and followed until it was exhausted and abandoned the flight. Two men sometimes joined in a relay chase, alternately following the animal until it could run no more. Antelope were also taken by this method. Hunters crawled up to a herd until they were close enough for a sure hit. When there was snow on the ground, elbow length mittens were worn. Several men might drape a buffalo robe over a pole and approach a herd behind this screen. One of the hunters would bleat like a calf and attract the cows. A variant of this method is described by Skinner.[10] A man wearing a wolf hide pretended to attack another who wore a calfskin. The bleating of the dummy calf brought the cows and bulls to the rescue and within gunshot.

Hind mentions prairie fires set by Cree to divert buffalo from their course.[11] My informants stated that precautions were taken not to set the prairie afire since it caused great destruction of game.

Butchering and Food Preparation

During a concerted hunt, women followed the hunters and, as the buffalo fell, they butchered them and transported the meat and hides to camp. A hunter who killed an animal near the encampment sent his wife or a boy to bring in the carcass. Only if he had made the kill a long distance from home did he pack the meat himself.

In butchering, the carcass was turned on its back and the head jerked to one side to prop it up. The hide was removed along one side and then the head was tilted again and the skinning proceeded on the other side. The flayed hide was spread on the ground the meat heaped on it. The long sinews from the backbone and the shoulder were carefully extracted. The limbs were dislocated and cut off. A cut was made along the backbone and the ribs chopped off. The meat and marrow bones were folded in the hide, the internal parts wrapped separately, and all taken back to camp. Both meat and hides were the property of the women who could dispose of them as they pleased.

The choice parts of a buffalo were the tongue, shoulder, fat from the teats, and heart. The liver was often eaten raw. Sometimes a part of the muzzle and the kidneys were also eaten uncooked. Men drank warm blood so that they might not be perturbed at the sight of blood in battle. Old people sometimes cut out the teats of milking buffalo cows and drank the milk.

The first care of the women when meat was brought into camp was to dry it properly. A block of meat was cut spirally into thin sheets which were hung up to dry. In summer a drying rack made of two tripods joined by a number of horizontal poles was set up outside of every tipi. During inclement weather a drying rack consisting of four uprights which supported a platform was erected over the fire inside the tipi. When the strips of meat were thoroughly dry, they were tied in small bales or stuffed into rawhide sacks.

Pemmican (*pimɪ·hka·n* in Cree) was highly relished. Lean dried meat was pounded with stone hammers to a soft mass. Berries were added and melted fat poured over the mixture. Fish pemmican was also made.

Large bones were split open and pounded with a maul. The crushed splinters were placed in boiling water; the grease that rose to the surface was skimmed off with shell spoons and stored in buffalo paunches. It was called *oskanpimɪ·* (bone grease). Fat from shoulder and rump was placed before a fire and as it melted dripped into a hide container. This was called *sasıpmanpımı·* (frying grease).

Joints were roasted on a spit over the fire. Soups of many kinds were made. The usual meal consisted of a thick soup which contained pieces of meat, berries, fat, and Indian turnips. An old method of preparing food, usually used by men while on the warpath, entailed digging a pit which was lined with a green hide pegged to the ground around its rim. Meat and water were placed in the pocket and brought to a boil by adding hot stones. Meat was occasionally baked in a pit, although roots were more often prepared in this manner. A hole was dug in the tipi floor in which the food was placed. It was covered with hot ashes and left over night.

Storage

When there was a surplus of meat, a tipi-like storehouse was built. The three foundation poles were braced by lashing cross poles to the legs of the tripod. Upon this frame poles were laid in close order, covered with brush, and weighted with stones. Platform caches were constructed by utilizing the forks of two trees and two forked uprights. Poles were laid across these supports and on them a rectangular flooring was laid. Meat placed atop this structure was safely out of the reach of dogs and children.

Pit caches were excavated in hillsides. The bottom of the pit was lined with grass over which a flooring of sticks was laid. The meat was piled into the cache, covered with grass, and earth was heaped over the mouth of the pit.

Tanning

Tanning was exclusively women's work. The newly flayed hide was scraped clean of adhering fat and tissue while it was still warm from the animal. If the hide were not immediately worked, it stiffened and was difficult to tan. A straight, chisel-like tool with the cutting end serrated was used as a scraper. The butt was socketed in hide or canvas to which a wrist loop was attached. This implement is now made of a ten-inch length of gun barrel, one end of which is pounded flat. Formerly the cannon bones of buffalo or moose were utilized as scrapers. During the scraping process, the hide was pegged flat on the ground or laced to a four-sided frame which was set up vertically.

After the hide had been scraped, it could be laid aside until the tanner had time to work on it again. The next step consisted of removing the hair and thinning the hide down to an even texture. For this process the skin was stretched on the ground. The woman stood on it and bent over from the hips while using the adze-like fleshing tool of elk antler or wood. A metal or flint blade was bound on the inside of the short arm. Robes tanned with the hair on were thinned down on the flesh side only. All other hides were planed on both sides with this tool. According to Skinner,[12] deer and antelope hides were thrown over a log and a beaming tool, resembling a spoke-shave, was used to remove the hair.

The hide was then rubbed with fat and slightly heated so that the grease might penetrate. A mixture of liver and brains, taken from deer or buffalo, was applied. The skin was left to dry overnight. The next morning it was soaked in water and vigorously wrung. A smooth stone was briskly rubbed over it to insure a thorough drying. Finally, the hide was worked over a plaited sinew rope until it was soft and pliable.

Hide intended for moccasins was hung on a rod and smoked over a slow fire. Skinner states that the hide was sewn in the shape of a bag and suspended over the fire from a tripod or an inclined stick.[13]

By-products

Very few parts of the buffalo were not utilized. Every edible portion was used as food. The bones were used for arrowheads and arrow-straighteners. The skull was smeared with grease and lighted when wet weather put out ordinary fires. The tail and the bell were mounted on sticks and used as fly switches. The hair was twisted into rope. The sinew made bowstrings and sewing thread. The thick cartilage in the head was boiled for glue. The teeth were worn as necklaces and dress ornaments. The hooves were fashioned into ladles and spoons. The rough skin of the tongue furnished a comb. Buffalo chips offered the finest fuel to be had on the treeless plains.

THE HORSE

History

La Vérendrye, in 1738, mentioned that he had seen horses among the Cree. This is probably the earliest notice of Cree horses although an old Cree told David Thompson of the time when he had first seen a horse. Thompson dated the event about the year 1730.[14] Edward Umfreville, writing in 1789, stated that:—

> . . . it is but lately that they (horses) have become common among the Nehethawa (Cree) Indians.[15]

Horses were never as plentiful among the Plains Cree as they were among the Assiniboin and other Plains tribes to the south and west of them. Harmon, who lived in the Saskatchewan country from 1800 to 1819, said that the Cree and Assiniboin were alike in most things except language and horsemanship. The Cree had fewer horses and were not as adept in their use.[16] The information I gathered from living informants clearly indicates that even in the middle of the nineteenth century, they possessed relatively few horses. Eater-of-raw liver said:—

> When I was young [circa 1865] we had very few horses and used dog travois mostly.

Feather recalled that:—

> In my father's day [about 1840-1850] it was only an occasional Cree who had a horse. They used dogs. Later we got horses from the Blackfoot and most men would have three or four horses, sometimes as many as nine or twelve.

Fisher said, when I asked him whether he had ever participated in a concerted buffalo hunt:—

> No, I could not, because my family did not own a horse with which to chase buffalo.

These three informants were all from eastern bands of the tribe. The western bands evidently were better provided with mounts during the same period, although Fine-day, who is of the River People, made this statement:—

> My father came west as the Blackfoot were driven back, because there were more buffalo here. In his time [he died about 1860] they had only very few horses and used dogs more than we did.

From the evidences available, it appears that the Cree first became acquainted with horses in the early part of the eighteenth century. By the end of that century horses were no longer a rarity among them. During the last fifty years of the nomadic life, their stock was constantly increased through purchase and raiding. But, even in the closing decades of the buffalo era, the Cree were poor in horses as compared to the Blackfoot and Assiniboin.

Consequences of Acquisition

Plains Cree horses were used either as pack and riding animals or for hunting. Most families, though not all, owned several horses which drew the travois laden with household effects when camp was moved. But only a few men owned horses which were swift enough for the chase and trained to hunt buffalo. Fine-day stated that about one tipi in ten would have a good buffalo horse. A number of families would attach themselves to the owner of such a horse and followed him wherever he moved his camp. They shared in the buffalo he was able to secure by means of his horse. Since these families were dependent on the horse owner for food, they were naturally quick to carry out his wishes or orders.

The possession of horses facilitated a rise in social status. Prestige could be acquired through the bountiful bestowal of gifts. A horse was the very best and most praiseworthy gift that could be given. Since each present carried with it an obligation for the recipient to reciprocate, a man who gave away many horses often received as many in return. The old people and the poorer men to whom a man gave horses, could not reciprocate in kind but returned their fealty to the donor.

While horses could be obtained in trade, the most honorable and common means of acquiring them was by raiding the enemy. It was customary to replenish one's stock of horses and thus secure the wealth necessary to high social status by joining a war party. Early accounts make it clear that the unceasing hostility between the Plains Cree and their enemies was not due to any dispute over territory or struggle for trade advantages, but was largely the result of the continual raiding and counter-raiding for horses. A typical instance is related by Hind who tells that the Plains Cree and Blackfoot assembled at Eagle Hills, near the junction of the North Saskatchewan and Battle rivers. They arranged terms of peace and separated as friends.

> Some of the Crees, however, incapable of resisting the opportunity, stole some horses from the Blackfeet. They were pursued and three of them taken. . . . One only reached his tribe . . .
> Mis-tick-oos, when relating these adventures, raised the pipe he held in his hand and exclaimed, "This is what my Blackfoot friend gave me one day, the next he killed my young men; he is now my enemy again."[17]

The failure of the early traders and missionaries to establish peace in the northern plains country was due to the rôle of the horse in the functioning of the aboriginal social system. Among the Plains Cree, the horse was the standard of prestige value by means of which the status criteria of wealth, valor, and liberality could best be realized. The legitimate way of procuring horses, in terms of that social system, was to steal them from an enemy tribe.

In religious and ceremonial spheres, the horse was of slight import. Horse spirit power was not of the same magnitude as were Sun, Thunder, Bear, Buffalo spirit powers. There were no particular rites for the increase of horses. The one ceremony in which the horse might be expected to figure prominently, the Horse dance, was as much for Weasel spirit power as for Horse.

Care

Each man tenderly cared for and jealously guarded his horses. They were allowed to graze near the camp by day under the surveillance of their owners or of boys. At night, valuable horses were picketed to the tipi door. When there was danger of an enemy raid, the owner of a good horse would tie its halter to his foot or wrist as he slept in his tipi. Other horses would be hobbled by binding their forelegs with rawhide thongs. During the day a valuable horse would be picketed to a stake in some grassy place and allowed to graze. Corrals were not made.

In winter the hobbles were placed on the hind legs so that the horses could more easily paw away the snow. Fine-day stated that horses were kept from wandering in the winter by this device. A water hole was broken in the ice and some alkali salts, collected from certain marshes and ponds, placed around it. Once the horses tasted the salt, they would not stray away from the water hole. Fodder was not stored. When there was a deep snow, men cleared a space and cut some dried grass for their horses.

If a horse were ridden hard in winter, a robe was tied around its body until the animal had cooled off. On hot summer days, horses were led to a lake or river and water splashed over them.

No attempt was made to control the breeding. The natural increase of the herds seems to have been far below the rate which systematic breeding and care would have yielded. Some stallion colts were castrated. The horse was laid on its side and a round section cut out of the scrotum.

Fig. 7. Watching Over his Horses by Michael Lonechild.

The testes were squeezed through this hole and cut. The severed tissues were bound with sinew. Then the horse was run for a while. The testicles were thrown away. No ritual accompanied the process. Some colts died as a result of this operation. Horse meat was eaten, although horses were never purposely killed for food.

Wild horses were sometimes caught and broken to the saddle. But since they were difficult to catch and since most of them died soon after being captured, few additions to the tribal stock were obtained in this way.

When a hoof was worn to the quick, a cover for it was made from the thick hide at the head of a bull buffalo. The cover was shaped to fit closely over the hoof. A mixture of the horse's manure and water was placed in it and it was worn until the hoof grew out again.

Horses were trained to swim across rivers and even pulled rafts while swimming. A knot was tied in a horse's tail and a line fastened to it by which the raft was drawn. The horses used in hunting buffalo were trained to match their gait to the movements of the buffalo. If the rider were thrown, the horse instantly stopped.[18]

The care of horses was entirely the work of men. A woman could own horses and dispose of them as she liked, but her husband or father looked after them.

Riding and Transport Gear

Several styles of saddle were made. A common type had an elkhorn bow and cantle. The two curved pieces of horn were connected by side bars of wood. This frame was covered with hide. Another form utilized two forked sticks for pommel and cantle which were also joined by flat strips of wood and encased in hide. A simpler type consisted of an oblong antelope hide bag stuffed with antelope hair at each end so that a pad fell over each side of the horse.

Stirrups were made from a flat piece of wood, steamed and bent in a loop, fastened in place with sinew, and covered with green hide. The bridle was merely a length of rawhide thong or hair rope snaffled in a double loop around the horse's jaw. Whips were highly decorated. The stock was usually made of elkhorn to which a wrist loop was attached. Antelope hide thongs were passed through a hole made near the tip of the stock.

The horse travois was made by crossing two poles near the ends and binding them together with sinew and thongs. Two sticks were fastened transversely across the arms of the travois and a number of thongs tied across the parallel sticks. The load was borne on this carrier. The travois was fastened to the horse by a rawhide thong girth which passed around the belly just behind the fore legs and was fastened to each arm of the travois where it rested on the horse's back.

Horses were named according to their markings. Some of the names and their English equivalents were:—

> *wapastim*, gray or white
> *masinasowatim*, pinto
> *osawahtawakaı*, yellow ears
> *kakaskitewıhtawakaı*, black ears
> *wıpapastim*, dark gray
> *wapanuskago*, silver tail
> *nıpenakowes*, iron gray
> *kaskitewastim*, black
> *wapıhkwewatim*, bald face
> *wiyıpatim*, brown
> *mıhkwowewatim*, bay
> *apakocıcipiwai*, mouse-colored
> *wawaskecıwpıwai*, buckskin
> *musopıwaı*, moose-colored
> *omomeyescıcipıwai*, gray-black
> *osawasis kıwipıwai*, yellow mud
> *osawastim*, sorrel
> *wanokawec*, chestnut
> *mayawewatim*, shaggy haired
> *cıcıkıawatim*, roan (gray and brown)
> *pahpatewatim*, dappled

wapınakataı, white spot on belly
wapıckicokan, white hind quarters, black markings, small tail
wapohkatim, roan
kakaskitew, gray, dark hind quarters

THE DOG

Function

Much of the draught work was performed by dogs. They brought meat in after a hunt, carried firewood, and hauled household equipment on the march. Women cared for them and owned them. Although a woman who owned a number of canine pack bearers possessed a valuable economic asset, her property was not a freely circulating asset. A dog given or sold to a neighbor would promptly return to the tipi of its former mistress. Dogs were valued property, but inalienable property. Only when the Hudson's Bay Company men began to buy dogs to haul their sleds, did they acquire exchange value. The Company employees took them too far from their previous homes for them to return. When a dog was sold, the husband arranged the terms of the sale, but he had to secure his wife's permission and handed over the proceeds to her.

Unlike the horse and buffalo, the dog did play an important part in ceremonial practices, functioning as an accessory to rather than as an object of ritualism. Eating dog meat marked an occasion as extraordinary. Thus, a dog might be killed to provide food for an honored guest or to be served during a bundle transfer. In general, however, dogs were eaten in those rituals particularly associated with the Woodlands, as the purchase or renewal of medicines and the *mite·wiwin.* In purely Plains ceremonies, such as the Sun dance, it was neither essential nor important to serve dog meat.

A dog might be offered to a spirit power as a means of securing divine aid for a sick relative. It was strangled or clubbed and thrown into a spring.

Dogs were not used in hunting, although they were always eager to give chase. When a hunt was in progress near them, laden dogs had to be held, lest they run after the fleeing buffalo and so spill their burdens. Dogs were taken along by war parties to carry extra moccasins and other supplies.

Care and Training

Fine-day stated that Cree dogs looked like timber wolves and that he had once seen a bitch mating with a wolf. Sometimes the dogs would kill and eat a young colt. When allowed to run free they would try to separate a buffalo calf from the herd and make the kill.

Male pups were castrated by women. Hitched to a travois which was suddenly overturned the dog was pinned to the ground on his back. Two women spread his hind legs, a third cut open the scrotum and scooped out the testes with two fingers and threw them away. Then the dog was turned loose and no further attention given to the wound. The largest male dogs were left uncastrated for breeding.

Dogs were trained to work when they were only a few months old. They were placed in a thong harness until they became accustomed to it and then a travois was attached. The dog travois was similar in construction to the horse travois except that the baggage carrier on the dog travois was a netted oval frame. The harness consisted of a thong around the neck and another around the belly. When camp was being moved, dogs were tied one behind the travois of the other. If there were not enough travois available, the burden was packed on the back of the dog.

When food was plentiful, strips of meat were cut and the owner called each dog and fed it individually. They were trained to answer to their names which were usually descriptive of their coats or markings. Some dog names were:—

maya·we·watim, curly dog
kaskite·watcap, black eye
kaskite·wɩhtawikɩw, black ear
kaskite·wastim, black dog
kamamusɩnasat, black and white
pɩ·kwaskan, shaggy dog

The use of dog-drawn toboggans was taken over from the Company men. Fine-day stated:—

> In the summer, traveling is hard on the dogs, but in winter they can travel well. The Hudson Bay Company sent men around to us in the winter to buy pemmican and robes. These men had toboggans drawn by dogs. As soon as we saw the toboggans we all began to make them because otherwise we could only pack a little on a dog. We couldn't make the horsehair collars for dog harness that the Company men had. We made all the harness of thongs. We never drove dogs from behind as did the Company men, except when headed homeward. We had to lead them. The toboggans were made of two or three flat boards with sticks lashed across them. The bottom of each board was grooved to hold the lashing.

When the feet of a dog were cut by ice, small rawhide shoes were fitted over each paw. At night the dogs would howl three times, at sundown, about midnight, toward dawn.[19]

OTHER ELEMENTS OF ECONOMIC LIFE

Large Game

While many moose and elk were to be found in the hills, they were not extensively hunted, for these animals could best be taken by lone hunters or by small parties, and men were loath to leave the larger encampments. Another reason was that the lavish supply of buffalo made for a neglect of forest hunting techniques. Fine-day put it thus:—

> We depended mostly on the buffalo. This was because anyone could kill a buffalo but it took a good hunter to get moose or elk.

Stalking and running down moose and elk were the only hunting methods used for these animals. Deer were decoyed. The hunter put on a headdress with erect stuffed deer's ears. During the rutting season the males would see the ears moving and would approach. Moose and deer calls were not used to attract game. There were no drives or cooperative hunts, except for buffalo. Deer, moose, and elk hides were tanned in the same way as were buffalo skins.

The ease with which buffalo could be secured probably caused the atrophy of the Eastern hunting magic and hunting observances. There was little attempt to control game magically. If a hunter were unsuccessful over a long period he consulted a shaman to learn whether someone had bewitched him. The shaman might declare that some person had sent an intrusive object which was scaring off the game. After the object was extracted, the hunter was presumably able to secure game again.

The head and antlers of deer were customarily hung upon a bush after the kill, but apparently many hunters neglected to do it. Peeso declares that the skull of a large animal or a stone representing the spirit of the animal was placed near the fireplace.[20] I found no evidence of such a custom.

Pit traps were made for large animals. A large hole was dug in a place where the animals passed. The top was covered over with brush and earth.

Small Animals

A type of deadfall trap was used for wolves and coyotes. One end of a heavy log was supported by a stick to which bait was attached. The lower end of this upright was set on a short stick which was displaced when the upright was moved.

A deadfall to catch badger had the beam suspended at one end of a thong, the other end of which was attached to a trigger on which bait was placed. When the trigger was moved the thong released the beam.

Lynx were taken with snares. Twisted deerhide thongs were used for the noose which was hung from a tree so that in reaching for the bait, the lynx put his head through the loop. A fencing of small sticks made it impossible for the animal to reach the bait except through the noose.

Rabbit snares were similarly made or consisted of a forked stick planted fork down in the ground. The noose was attached to the two arms of the fork with strands of grass. Beaters went over a tract of land and the running rabbits plunged through the nooses and were held fast. A spring snare, attached to a bent-over sapling, was made for rabbits and prairie-chickens.

A sinew noose was placed over a gopher's hole. The other end of the line was held by the snarer. When a gopher appeared the line was jerked tight.

To snare prairie-chickens, willow sticks were arched and planted in the ground. A noose of horsehair was suspended within the arch. In "dancing," the chickens passed through the arch and were caught. Snaring of small animals and birds was done by women.

Wild fowl were killed in great numbers at the moulting seasons when they could not quickly fly from the water. Men armed with digging-sticks waded into ponds and lakes and struck them down. Women, also armed with digging-sticks, were stationed on the shores to get any of the birds that made for land.

The eggs were collected and eaten. They were placed in a shallow pit, covered with coals, and allowed to bake. As with game animals, the internal parts of birds were eaten.

Maskwa supplied the following list of birds that were eaten. Their common names in English are given:—

ıncip, mallard
kınatwanewıcip, pin tail
apictcınicıcip, black mallard
mısıkwayawewıcip, fall duck
nanatakwewıcip, going toward you, little teal
amiskocip, beaver duck, wood duck
pıtıkocip, black teal
wapaskatewicip, white breast duck, widgeon
kaskitecip, black duck

takwakıcip, late duck, fall duck
cıhkıhp, hell diver
wıskatcanıcip, stinking flesh, water heron
kahkakıwcip, raven duck (unidentified)
ayikaskitewcip, blackish duck (unidentified)
apıctcıcıpis, little duck (unidentified)
wehwewak, swans
kitcıkipusesak, blue geese
apictcinickis, laughing goose
otcıtcahkwak, wild turkeys
paspaskıw, partridge
pıhew, prairie-chicken
apictcıpıhecis, prairie hen
wapıhewak, white prairie-chicken
sakawhew, grouse (?)
apicıkahkakıs, little raven, magpie
opıpunacıw, chicken hawk
kɛhkɛhk, sparrow hawk
wıhtcikopıecıs, wıhtiko bird, (shrike?)
oho·, owl
mikcıw, eagle
apickwaı, near clouds, osprey (?)

Birds that were not eaten were:—

wakwah, loon
wanahkew, buzzard
tcahtcukıw, crane
kahkah, raven (young eaten)
ahacıw, crow (young eaten)
ohotcikinepikwecıw, snake hunter
pıskwak, night hawks
mahakos, small night owl
tcahtcakıw, pelican
pıtcıkıskısısak, wrens (?)
amowıpıecıs, bee bird, humming bird

Animals eaten were:—

badger	kit-fox
bear	lynx
beaver	prairie-dog
buffalo	marten
chipmunk	mink
coyote	muskrat
dog	otter
elk	porcupine
fisher	rabbit
fox	skunk
gopher	squirrel
ground hog	wolf
horse	wolverine

Snakes, ground squirrels, frogs, were not eaten. Insects

were not used for food. Mussels were sometimes eaten as medicine.

Fish

Fish were eaten as a change from a steady diet of meat. When poor hunting forced the tribesmen to subsist on dried meat, fresh fish were especially welcome. David Thompson stated that the Cree

> pride themselves with living by hunting animals, look on fish as inferior food and the catching of them beneath a Hunter.[21]

Some fifty years later Hind remarked:—

> The Plains Cree are not fishermen like the Ojibways, they did not know how to catch fish . . .[22]

The information I received both among eastern and western bands indicates that fishing with weirs or spears was regarded as good fun, although the sport soon palled. However, an ample supply of fish enabled fairly large groups to gather at seasons when they otherwise would have had to disperse over the countryside in search of game. Hence, fish not only added to the fare but also expanded the size of the camps and thus enlarged social opportunities. Hind's comment that the Plains Cree did not know how to fish may mean that they did not know how to catch lake fish. There can be no doubt that they caught river fish. In general, the tribe kept away from the lakes in their territory, rarely camping along lake shores, never fishing in lakes.

Practically all of the fishing was done in the winter and early spring. In summer a man might shoot at a sturgeon fin sticking out of the water, but no serious efforts to catch fish were made.

Weirs were constructed when, according to informants, the fish ran downstream in the spring. Two converging barriers of logs and stones were stretched across a stream (Fig. 8). At their apex a quadrupod made of four forked legs, interlocked at the top, was erected. Suspended from this stand was an inclined trough-like basket made by lashing together a set of parallel poles which had the bark stripped. One end of the trough lay below the surface; the other end was elevated above the water. The rush of the current swept the fish up on the poles. The water escaped through the interstices of the poles while the fish were pushed higher up the trough by a man who wielded a netted scoop. Sometimes men waded into

Fig. 8. Fish Weir, Poundmaker Reserve, Battleford, Saskatchewan. At the top is shown the construction of the entrance to the weir. Photographs by P.E. Goddard, 1911.

the river above the weir and threw stones into the water to send the fish downstream.

The successive steps in the construction of the weir were these.

Four forked poles set up in midstream and interlocked.

Two forked sticks driven into bed of stream and a curved pole laid across them.

"Sliding" poles laid against this rack. One end of poles resting on bed of stream and weighted with stones, other end of poles on rack. Curved stick bound on under side of poles to hold them in shape of trough.

72

Willow branches, stripped of leaves except at the top, bound with withes in trough shape, proximal ends rest on rack under the "sliding" poles. Distal ends elevated on another rack built for the purpose.

Platform on which fishermen stand made by placing logs across three supports. Runway to shore made.

Supports for barrier constructed by interlocking two forked poles near quadrupod and setting up one or two crotched poles near shore. Logs laid across fork of poles and on interlocked poles.

Logs six to eight feet long leaned against this frame, anchored in place by stones. Additional forked poles buttress frame of barrier.

Sweep, *wapahıkan*, made. Hoop of willow withe with netting in center.

Fine-day described a weir and its operation:—

> The whole camp would go to use a weir. There might be two tipis or as many as fifty or sixty. The weir was called *mitcskan* in the old days. Now it is called *askonan*. There were some places in the river that we came back to time after time. A new weir would be built every year, for the ice would carry the old one away.
>
> No matter who made the weir, all encamped around it got an equal share of the fish. The first night after the weir was built, three or four men were chosen [probably by the chief or leading man] to work it during the night. They hauled the fish to the shore and also passed them out. They were allowed to keep the best fish for themselves, but the men chosen were generally not stingy and gave everyone a fair share. All of the first catch had to be eaten. After that anybody could go and take fish from the weir.

There was no first fish rite beyond the ordinance that all of the first catch had to be immediately consumed. Unlike the buffalo pound, the construction of a fish weir did not require the supervision of a shaman. The success of the weir depended in large part on the swiftness of the current. If it were built at a place where the current was too slow, fish would not be carried into the basket.

The weir was usually operated at night. One man was stationed at the place where the fish came into the trough and dangled a stick in the water with which he felt the fish enter. At a signal from him, a second man swept the fish higher in the trough with a scoop; a third man clubbed them.

In winter, fish were speared at open places in the river ice made by inflowing springs. A fire was built on land and a birchbark torch set up close to the hole. The spear was made of a five-foot willow or saskatoon stick which was forked at one end, and which had both prongs sharpened. The spear was held near the butt end with both hands and plunged down almost perpendicularly. These open places in the ice were not individually owned and "a man would only be too glad to have a big bunch of people come together (to fish at a hole)." Holes were not chopped in the ice for fishing.

Double pointed bone fish gorges were known to be used by the Plains Ojibwa, but were not utilized by the Plains Cree. Fishhooks were introduced by the Hudson's Bay Company.

Much of the catch was split open, cleaned, and dried in the sun. When the fish were fat, the inner parts were rendered and the grease skimmed off. When eaten soon after being caught, fish were split open and set up near the fire on a stake. Dried fish was pounded, mixed with berries and fat, made into pemmican. Fish bones were not utilized for any purpose.

The principal fish eaten were:—

nipıkamekosak, gold eyes
osawaskwapesak, yellow head, northern pike, jackfish
mayumekwak, ugly fish
numewak, sturgeon
oka·wak, sharp points, pike, perch
nime·pıak, sturgeon-like, probably sturgeon sucker
cockonimepıak, small-scaled sucker, probably gray sucker
nona·tcikecisak, little sucker
kawayanucitik, hump back, mallock
inikinuceak, large fish, brocket
ukimawkinosew, chief fish
mıayak, chief fish
kamıhkwaskwanetcik, red tail

Vegetal Foods

Vegetal foods were extensively utilized. The meat soups which were the staple dish usually contained bits of roots and berries. The Indian turnip (*mistaskucımina*, grass berry) was the most important root food. The turnips were dug up by the women, peeled, and dried in the sun. After two days of drying, the roots were placed in a rawhide and pounded with a stone maul until reduced to a fine powder. The tough fibers from the center of the root were picked out and thrown away. The flour would keep for a long time. Unpeeled roots were strung on sinew lines and stored away. They were prepared in a shallow pit dug in the tipi floor. The roots were placed in the hole, covered over with coals, and left to bake overnight.

On July 17, 1858, Hind came upon a party of Plains Cree collecting Indian turnips. He says:—

> The botanical name is *Psoralea esculenta*. Many bushels had been collected by the squaws and children and when we came to their tents they were employed in peeling the roots, cutting them into shreds and drying them in the sun. I saw many roots as large as the egg of a goose, and among those brought with me to Canada are some of even larger dimensions. The Cree consume this important vegetable in various ways; they eat it uncooked, or they boil it, or roast it in the embers, or dry it, and crush it to powder and make soup of it. Large quantities are stored in buffalo skin bags for winter use. A sort of pudding made of the flour of the root and the mesaskatomina berry is very palatable, and a favourite dish among the Plain Crees.[23]

The roots were extracted with a digging stick. Each woman had one of her own and carried it with her constantly during the summer. It was made of a chokecherry or saskatoon berry stick four to five feet long. Near one end the wood was whittled away to form a knob. The other end was cut diagonally to make a sharp edge. The single plane surface so fashioned was whittled down on two sides so that the stick came to a sharp point.

Several other roots were gathered:—

askıwahkonak, earth peel
atcimwapitca, little dog teeth
mistikoskatask, wood carrot

Berries were the proper ceremonial food. As soon as they ripened in the summer, small groups of women and girls, often accompanied by a guard of several men, went out to pick them. The pickers had a cylindrical birchbark box slung around their necks and into these containers the berries were dropped. When a bush was particularly well laden, whole branches might be broken off and the fruit flailed on a spread hide.

Chokecherries were usually boiled and then crushed, pits and all, with a stone maul. The pulp was dried in the sun and packed into rawhide bags. Other berries were dried first and then crushed and packed away.

The following list gives the edible berries together with their common names in Saskatchewan:—

mısaskwatomına, saskatoon
takwahımina·na, pounding berry, chokecherry
ayoskanak, wild raspberries
otehimina, wild strawberries
manitomınak, manito berries, black currants

mıhkwapemakomina, red willow cherries
sasapominak, tart berries, goose berries
pasusawemina, pin cherries
nıpimına·na, high bush cranberries
musomina, mooseberry
atcikacımina, kinnikinnick berry, ground cedar berry
wapasko·mına·na, buffalo willow berries
nikikomina, blueberry
wısakımina, low bush cranberry
ınimina, man berry, bear berry
okinıak, rose berries
micokinıak, big thorn berries
atimostemina, dogfoot berries
oskısikomina, eye berry, dew berry
mahıhkocminana, wolf berry
mıhkomınsa, red cherries, mountain ash berry
meyıcimina, faeces berry, cactus fruit

Maple sugar (*ka·tcakıseikanipanik*) was collected in the early spring. Women did most of the work, but men helped. A short diagonal notch was cut in the trunk of a tree about a foot from the ground. To make the cut a knife was set in place and the blade was struck with a club. Below this gash a shorter, horizontal cut was made and a stick placed in it. The sap ran down the slanting cut on to the stick, whence it dripped into vessels made of whole buffalo horns or of birchbark, which were set on the ground.

The sap was collected from these cups and poured into a large container made by propping up a rawhide on several stakes so that there was a large pocket in the center. From this container the sap was transferred into a metal kettle and boiled over a large fire. When it was boiled down, it was placed in another metal kettle which was set over warm ashes. At this stage the sap was stirred with a wooden paddle, two feet long, until the syrup was of the proper consistency. To test this a little was placed on the snow; if it remained on the surface, it was ready. Shallow oblong birchbark boxes were greased with frozen fat and the syrup placed in them. The sugar which adhered to the sides of the kettle was then scraped off and placed in a buffalo bladder which, in turn, was placed in a rawhide bag. These scrapings were called *pısawihkahıkıw* and were sprinkled over meat as a condiment. The sugar was eaten as a delicacy, and as might be expected, was consumed largely by the children.

Wild honey was known and called "bee dung," but was never utilized as food. Aboriginally, salt was not used. The peoples to the east were known to have wild rice, but it did not grow in the Plains Cree country.

Annual Cycle

Throughout the year, the Plains Cree looked forward to the annual Sun dance encampment. Messengers bearing tobacco and invitations were sent out in the spring. Late in June or early in July the scattered sections of a band, or even several bands, converged to the preappointed places where the ceremony was to be held. The great encampment might hold together for two weeks or even longer, if there were buffalo herds in the vicinity. When the food supply ran low, the bands drifted apart, each slowly moving toward its own territory. Concerted buffalo hunts were made during this time. In midsummer roots were collected and a little later the people moved toward the low hills and valleys where berries were ripening. During August fresh buffalo meat had a poor taste. Many-birds said that this was because the buffalo ate wild onions at that time. Dried meat, berries, turnips, were then eaten.

With the onset of autumn, a few of the men separated from the larger group to hunt elk and deer. The Smoking Tipi ceremony was performed. As the weather turned cold, buffalo pounds were built and a successful pound was the nucleus for a large gathering of families. If any of the tribe had been induced by the Hudson's Bay Company to trap for furs, they struck out for the wooded places at this time.

The pounds were operated throughout the winter, but after it became very cold, in January and February, they yielded few returns. This season was the most difficult of the year and the tribesmen scattered in small family units into the more densely wooded country. Fishing was carried on and an occasional elk or deer was killed. Buffalo were hunted with varying success. During some winters more buffalo would be killed than could be used. In other years, the people were on the verge of starvation.

After the break-up of the river ice in the spring, fish weirs were built. At this time maple sugar was collected. The small groups moved to the open country as buffalo herds appeared. The groups grew in numbers until it was time for the Sun dance encampment.

Palliser's report indicates that the Plains Cree wintered along the North Saskatchewan between the Neutral and Beaver hills and spent the summer along the Qu'Appelle River and south of it. It is my impression that there was no such lengthy summer-winter migration. The eastern bands went into the woods near the Qu'Appelle Valley in the winter; the western bands ranged in the open country between the North and South Saskatchewan rivers in the summer. The seasonal migration was a very limited one. For the Sun dance celebrations both eastern and western bands usually converged to places along the South Saskatchewan River.

Property

Food collectively procured was collectively distributed. If ten men hunted buffalo together and only three made a kill, the three buffalo carcasses were evenly divided among the whole group. At the buffalo pound all those encamped nearby were entitled to a share of the meat, even if they had not helped construct the pound. Similarly all those who were at a fish weir received part of the catch.

The only means of prodding indolent individuals into aiding in the collective efforts was ridicule. Fine-day's comment was:—

> There were many men who were lazy and some who never even killed one buffalo. Their relatives would take care of them and other people would pity them and give them provisions. That is why there were so many lazy fellows. When they were needed to help with something their brothers-in-law would grab their arms and pull them over to where the work was being done. And all the time the brother-in-law of a lazy man would tease him and make fun of him when there were people to hear.

Foodstuffs that had been obtained by individual effort were not communally shared. Berries and roots were the property of the women who had gathered them. Small game fell into the same category.

There were no individually owned fur-trapping grounds, fishing places, or hunting locales. Rigid territorial lines were unknown. A band welcomed any other band of Plains Cree, Assiniboin, or Plains Ojibwa who might hunt in their territory when buffalo were abundant. If the herds failed, no other band would want to come into the area. Thus there were never any disputes over the occupation of land.

Material wealth was individually owned in the sense that each horse or dog or gun was the property of some one person. But in practice a man who lived near his father-in-law's tipi made free use of the elder man's horse. A woman who camped near her aunts or her mother took whatever she needed from their stores. When a man vowed to stage an expensive ceremony, all his close relatives impoverished themselves to help him. A chief might give away most of his possessions at a great ceremonial occasion and within a short time have as much wealth as before, due to the gifts of his kinsmen.

FOOTNOTES

[1]HIND, Narrative of the Canadian Red River, vol. 2, pp. 104, 114, 117.

[2]HORNADAY, WILLIAM T., The Extermination of the American Bison (Report, United States National Museum, for 1886-1887, Washington, 1889), pp. 504-505.

[3]WISSLER, Population Changes Among the Northern Plains Indians, pp. 9-10.

[4]For movements of the herds see HORNADAY, The Extermination of the American Bison, p. 424; HIND, Narrative of the Canadian Red River, vol. 2, pp. 106-110.

[5]HIND, Narrative of the Canadian Red River, vol. 1, pp. 354f., however, saw a pound in use on July 29, 1858.

[6]SKINNER, Political Organization, p. 525; for descriptions of pounds, see also JEFFERSON, Fifty Years on the Saskatchewan, pp. 91-94; HIND, Narrative of the Canadian Red River, vol. 1, pp. 355-359; PALLISER, Papers Relative to . . . the Explorations by Captain Palliser, p. 71; KANE, PAUL, Wanderings of an Artist among the Indians of North America from Canada to Vancouver's Island and Oregon through the Hudson's Bay Company's Territory and Back Again, London, 1859, pp. 117-118.

[7]JEFFERSON, Fifty Years on the Saskatchewan, p. 66.

[8]HIND, Narrative of the Canadian Red River, vol. 1, pp. 345-346.

[9]SKINNER, Political Organization, pp. 523, 527.

[10]*Ibid.*, p. 528.

[11]HIND, Narrative of the Canadian Red River, vol. 1, p. 337.

[12]SKINNER, Notes on the Plains Cree, p. 83.

[13]*Ibid.*, p. 83.

[14]WISSLER, CLARK, The Influence of the Horse in the Development of Plains Culture (American Anthropologist, n.s., vol. 16, Lancaster, 1914), p. 6; TYRRELL, David Thompson's Narrative, p. 328f.

[15]UMFREVILLE, The Present State of Hudson's Bay, p. 189.

[16]HARMON, A Journal of Voyages and Travels, p. 40.

[17]HIND, Narrative of the Canadian Red River, vol. 2, pp. 125-126.

[18]*Ibid.*, vol. 2, p. 114.

[19]Cf. WILSON, GILBERT L., The Horse and Dog in Hidatsa Culture (Anthropological Papers, American Museum of Natural History, vol. 15, part 2, New York, 1924), pp. 204-205.

[20]PEESO, The Cree Indians, p. 53.

[21]TYRRELL, David Thompson's Narrative, p. 165.

[22]HIND, Narrative of the Canadian Red River, vol. 1, pp. 414-415.

[23]*Ibid.*, vol. 1, p. 319.

Manufactures and Artifacts

CLOTHING

Men's Clothing

Men wore a breechclout of soft leather, hanging down, before and behind, over a narrow belt tied around the waist. Old men at the present time wear strips cut from a blanket, about eight inches wide and five feet long. The breechclouts used as a part of ceremonial costume are wider and longer, often ornamented with bead or quillwork on the pendant ends. Men had few compunctions about discarding the breechclout when swimming or sleeping. It was not removed, however, in the sweatlodge or while participating in a foot race. It was generally worn in camp, but it was no disgrace to be seen stark naked, except by female relatives toward whom a respectful attitude was due.

Men's leggings reached from the ankle to the groin and were attached to the belt by a loop at a place over the hip. Each legging was made of a single piece of hide doubled over. The seam on the outer side of the leg was on a bias so that the wide opening at the top narrowed down to fit the ankle closely. The two resultant flaps were finely slit to make ornamental fringes.

Shirts were worn by men on ceremonial occasions. *Maskwa* affirmed that no covering for the upper part of the body, save the buffalo robe, was ordinarily used, even in the coldest weather. For dances men wore, and still wear, heavily beaded or quilled shirts, usually of the poncho type, with an especially decorated triangular pendant at the throat and at the back of the neck.[1]

At the present time shirts and jackets are made of deer or moose hide cut in tailored coat style with separate sleeves sewn in. Mackenzie[2] describes a close-fitting shirt reaching down to the breechclout and belted with a strip of hide which was fastened behind with thongs. It is not certain, however, that the account refers to Plains Cree and not Woodland

81

Cree. Present-day informants tell of a loose-hanging knee-length coat for men, made of buffalo hide tanned in the hair. A peak hood was attached and sleeves sewn into the arm openings.

All men and women were equipped with a buffalo robe which was used in every season. Some robes were ornamented by a single strip of beadwork, perhaps four inches wide, extending across the hide from head to tail; others were painted with two rows of parallel figures. Two figures commonly used were an arrow and a form roughly like an hourglass with serrated ends (Fig. 9). The design was delineated with a buffalo hip bone which had been dipped in water. The arrows were painted in with a viscous black earth and then white clay was rubbed over the rest of the robe. The hourglass designs were filled in with a paint made of a mixture of blood and an unidentified red flower. Blood was also applied over the entire surface. Grooves to receive the paint were not incised. The ears and leg pieces were usually slit and painted red. The tail was often wrapped with porcupine quills. Noted warriors might inscribe pictographic representations of their battle exploits on their robes. Figures of supernatural characters were never drawn on robes, although they were occasionally painted on ceremonial shirts.

In wearing the robe the head part was grasped with the right hand and brought around to the left side. The tail part was thrown over the left shoulder, covering the left arm. The right arm and shoulder were thus left bare and free for action, while the left hand grasped the robe and held it in posi-

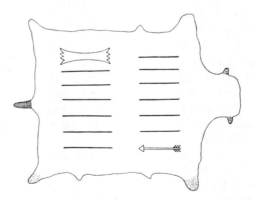

Fig. 9. Painted Buffalo Robe. The bars at right represent duplications of arrow design at lower right; the bars at left are duplicates of design at upper left. Stippled areas are painted red; cross hatching at tail indicates quillwork.

tion. While engaged in work requiring the use of both hands, men and women knotted the robe around the waist.

Women's Dresses

Women's dresses were made of two oblong pieces of hide or cloth, superimposed one on the other. They were sewn or laced together lengthwise, at the sides, except for a space of about eight inches at the top where the material was doubled to form an ornamental flap in front and back. The dress hung from the shoulders by two narrow straps and reached from just below the armpits to the middle of the leg. The lower border was ornamented with bead or quillwork and was often cut out in scallops. Fringes were also attached to the lower edge of the dress; these were sometimes wrapped with varicolored quills. Detachable sleeves with a cape-like extension hanging down the back covered arms and shoulders. This type of dress, both in cloth and hide, is illustrated and discussed by Wissler.[3] A belt, usually elaborately decorated, was fastened around the waist.

Women's leggings were simply oblong pieces of hide, covering the lower leg and gartered below the knee. Old women still wear these leggings. Modern ceremonial costumes include similar leggings of canvas, beaded over the entire surface, which are wrapped around the calf and held in place by short thongs attached to the legging itself.

Moccasins

Two styles of moccasins are now worn. The traditionally older type is cut in one piece and is sewn around the outside of the foot. The Plains Cree type is exactly the same as that minutely described for the Blackfoot by Wissler.[4] The other style, which is now more common, is said to have been introduced by half-breeds from the east. It is made of two pieces of leather, one forming the upper and sole, the other being inserted as a tongue piece. This type is Wissler's pattern No. 11.[5] Of late, young women have taken to wearing moccasins with long attached flaps which are wrapped around the leg and extend almost to the knee. This style is reputed to have been introduced by the Crow.

Winter moccasins were made of buffalo skin with the hair inside. Dried grass was stuffed into them as additional insulation against the cold.

Mittens

Fur mittens of supposedly aboriginal manufacture were

described by Fine-day. They were fastened together by a line which passed around the neck and were made with a separate thumbpiece.

Headgear

Men's winter hats consisted of a ring of buffalo hide, with the hair side outermost. A sinew was threaded along the upper edge and pulled tight to draw the cap to a peak. Another style of headgear was simply a fur fillet some six inches wide. A specimen in The American Museum of Natural History (50-5811) is made of dogskin. Coyote hide was also used for this purpose.

In summer, men wore a hat, or rather, a sun visor, made of a stiff rawhide rectangle. Two intersecting slits were cut near one end. The four triangles of hide so formed were pushed up so that the crown of the head fitted in the opening. The triangles were slit and the brim serrated.

There was a great variety of styles in ceremonial headdress. Eagle feather bonnets and buffalo horn caps were especially prized. These could only be made by persons so instructed in a vision and usually possessed magical properties involving immunity from wounds. The feather bonnets now worn in dances have a skull piece cut from an old felt hat, or a piece of hide sewn to fit the head closely. Wooden pegs are sewn on this base. Eagle feathers are split at the quill, slipped over the pegs, and tied in place with sinew. A single cord, to which the tip of each feather is attached, holds them erect. A strip of beadwork is sewn across the front of the cap and weasel skin pendants are attached on each side. A band of red flannel, on which more feathers are sewn, falls down the back.

Buffalo horn caps were similarly constructed with a leather skull piece. A horn was sewn at each side and the whole adorned with beadwork, weasel skins, and feathers.

Whole skins of birds, especially of the raven, and entire hides of small animals were used as ceremonial headgear in consequence of vision instructions.

The roached headdress worn in the Grass dance by many tribes[6] came into fashion when that ceremony was introduced. Hairs from porcupine and from the tails of deer are used and stand erect when the headdress is worn.

Elaborately beaded bandoliers were made by some of the eastern bands of the tribe, but were not in general use.

PERSONAL ADORNMENT

Disc earrings punched out of mussel shells were hung from the ear by short narrow thongs. Brass beads, strung on a wire ring, are now much favored for earrings. A child's ear lobes were pierced with an awl. Sinew or finely drawn lead was passed through the opening until it was large enough to receive the thong. Holes were sometimes pierced along the helix of the ear as well. No ceremony accompanied the ear piercing.

Round or oval mussel shell gorgets were fastened around the throat by a leather thong which was passed through two perforations at the center of the shell. The circumference was often serrated.

Necklaces were made of buffalo teeth, elk tusks, or bearclaws strung on sinew. Women's dresses were often ornamented with elk tusks and bearclaws in conjunction with a good deal of quillwork, beadwork, and some painting. The beads and spangles sold by the Hudson's Bay Company displaced many of the older forms of ornamentation at an early date.

Men plucked their facial hair between the thumb nail and index finger. Neither sex shaved nor pulled out pubic hair.

Hairdress was usually very simple. Both men and women parted their hair in the middle, and over each shoulder wore a braid, the lower part of which was wrapped with strips of hide, fur, or sinew. Dandies might lengthen their braids by weaving in horsehair. Women often tied the tips of the braids together in back; men occasionally tied them together in front. Some men wore a third braid falling down the back which, for some unascertained reason, was never combed out. This third braid might also be doubled and placed over the forehead. Only the very young and the very old let their hair hang loose. A boy observed by the writer had his hair arranged with two transverse parts. A braid was plaited from each quadrant thus formed. Warriors sometimes cut the front hair short, stiffened it with grease, brushed it up in an erect pompadour.

The rough side of a buffalo tongue was utilized as a comb. Red paint was often smeared along the part and daubed over the hair as well. An affectionate couple, or an unmarried man and his younger friend, would delouse each other, eating the catch. Baldness among older men was known.

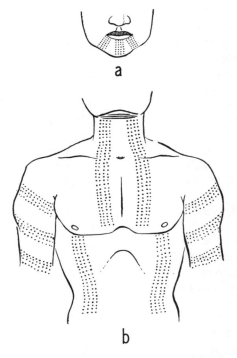

Fig. 10. Tattoo Marks. a, Women's lip-chin tattoo; b, Men's tattoo marks.

Tattooing was common for both sexes (Fig. 10). Men might have their arms and chests marked; women's markings are confined to three lip-chin lines and occasionally round marks on the cheeks and forehead. A common tattoo pattern for men consisted of two parallel lines extending from the under side of the chin to the middle of the chest at a level with the nipples. Two other parallel lines extended from the points below the nipples to the level of the navel. The arms were marked by a series of horizontal lines. Skinner[7] illustrates another pattern involving four lines radiating from each nipple across the chest. The lip-chin lines of women stretched from the middle and from each corner of the lower lip to the curve of the chin. Each stripe might consist of one to four individual tattoo lines. Realistic figures were never used in tattoo designs.

Fine-day described the tattooing process:—

A man has a dream which gives him the power to do tattooing although he may delegate the actual operation to someone who knows how to do it well. Much food is prepared and a large lodge set up. All the medicine bundles in camp are brought in. Then an old man goes around the camp and calls out, "Come early in the morning. When you are tattooed you will be all dressed up. At a dance all you will have to do is to take off your robe." They coax the boys to be tattooed. First they feed them well to fill out their skins. Everybody comes to watch. The boy lies down, naked to the hips. The tattooer marks out the design with a charcoal paste. Then he takes an instrument made of four needles tied together. Feathers are attached to the handle and inside the quills are little pellets which rattle as the instrument is used.

The man who received the power to tattoo in a vision begins to pray. He asks that the boys may wear the tattooing to an old age. Then he begins to sing and as he does the operator brings his needles down with short, rapid strokes. Then he takes an old piece of hide that has been thoroughly smoked and blots the blood. The singing continues until he has finished. The boy must not move until it is over. Then he is given some maple sugar to eat. Sometimes they ask the sweethearts of the boy to sit at his feet while he is being tattooed.

Skinner's[8] account adds that men might receive a vision command to be tattooed and that eight needles were used in the instrument. The pigmentation was furnished by the charcoal paste which entered the punctures made by the needles.

Face painting was an everyday occurrence during the period of large encampments. Women painted their cheeks; men covered the whole face. Red was the favorite color. Grease was first spread over the parts to be painted and a red substance, probably ocher, applied. Castoreum might be mixed with the paint as a perfume.

Ceremonial face painting was done in accordance with supernatural instructions. A part of many visions was the injunction to paint the face and body in a certain manner while carrying out the revealed procedure. Each sacred bundle had a particular style of painting accompanying its use.

Before a battle men would often daub themselves with white clay over which crushed, wet charcoal was laid. On returning from a war trip, warriors would blacken their faces with charcoal.

According to Skinner's information,[9] colored clays were pulverized, mixed with water, baked into small cakes. When wanted for use, the pigment was scraped off the cake and mixed with hot grease.

HOUSING

The only dwelling was the hide-covered tipi, constructed on a three-pole foundation. In setting up the tipi, three poles were laid on the ground and lashed together with what Wissler calls the "Cheyenne and Arapaho tie."[10] The poles were raised and the legs of the tripod extended. The rawhide line which tied the poles hung down and was staked to the ground inside the tipi. Upon this base thirteen poles were laid in counter-clockwise order. The total number of poles in the tipi frame varied with the size of the structure.

The cover was hoisted by being lashed to the last pole to be placed in position. It was drawn around the frame and pinned together between the door poles with peeled wooden pegs. Thongs were lashed across the door poles at a height of about five and seven feet to make foot rests for fastening the upper part of the cover. The pegs for fastening the cover above and below the doorway were about eighteen inches long, peeled of bark except for a section four inches wide near one side. The left edge of the cover had two holes to receive the pin, the right edge one. The pin was slipped into place in such a manner that from the outside of the tipi only the four-inch ring of bark was visible.

After the cover had been pinned together, the woman went inside and shoved the tipi poles out until the cover was taut. The bottom of the cover was fastened to the ground by driving short wooden pegs through eyelets in the cover itself, or through looped thongs fastened to it.

The doorway was an elliptical opening covered by a flap. The door flap was hung from two thongs fastened to the outside of the cover immediately above the door opening. It was made of hide stretched over a U-shaped willow frame. Two beaded bosses often covered the place where the door hangers were attached to the tipi cover.

The smoke-hole at the apex of the tipi was flanked by two projections of the cover, the tipi "ears." A pole was inserted in a hole in each "ear" and was shifted about to regulate the size and shape of the smoke-hole, and, consequently, the draught within the dwelling.

Twelve to twenty buffalo hides were used for a cover. An old woman skilled in cutting covers measured the hides and cut them to the proper shape. Then a feast was prepared and all the women of the camp were invited to partake. After they had eaten, they were assigned to sew at various places on the cover. A bone awl was used to punch holes through which sinew thread was drawn. According to Amelia Paget,[11] the ends of the sinew were not clipped, even if a piece ten inches long protruded. It was believed that the occupants of the dwelling would become mean and stingy if the threads were trimmed. The seams were on the flesh side of the hides. The side on which the hair had been was outermost when the tipi was set up. When the sewing had been completed, the cover was spread out and the seams flattened with awls.

Women made the tipi, set it up, owned it. Therefore, a man had to get his wife's consent to have a picture of his spirit helper drawn on the tipi cover.

A back wall of buffalo hide, similar to that used by the Blackfoot,[12] lined the sides of the tipi. Hay was stuffed between this screen and the tipi cover, providing insulation in winter and preventing draughts. In summer the bottom of the cover was rolled up on the poles to a height of about two feet from the ground.

Ten or twelve people usually lived in a single tipi. The fireplace was in the center, the place of honor being behind the fire, opposite the door.

D. A. Cadzow[13] witnessed the erection of a tipi in which the head of the household delivered an invocation just before the cover was raised. This was not often done.

An observer who lived among the Plains Cree in Montana noted that when a tipi was set up in a windy place, a four-pole foundation was used.[14] This was not corroborated by Canadian members of the tribe.

Some men were instructed in a vision to set up against their tipis a tall pole to the top of which was attached the hide of some animal or bird. Chief Sweetgrass, a noted leader, had the skin of a raven tied to the pole. When camp was broken, the pole was lowered and pointed in the direction of the march. The skin (50.1-5777) is now in The American Museum of Natural History. Horse tails were sometimes tied to the ears of the tipi.

While war records were sometimes painted on tipi covers, these more often bore representations of supernatural characters. Painted tipis were subject to special regulations: fire could not be taken out of them, nor could a menstruating woman enter them.

Several types of temporary shelter were made. One was constructed by stacking boughs in conical form or by leaning them against a convenient tree. In summer, women still do their work in a shelter similarly constructed of boughs, but laid over a three-pole foundation. Where boughs could not be obtained, rawhide was placed over the foundation poles.

Hunters erected a windbreak by stretching a robe between two upright poles. Men out on a long chase sometimes dug a hole in a river bank as shelter for the night. In winter a hole was scooped in a snowbank and its floor lined with buffalo chips.

A semi-cylindrical structure fashioned of a series of willow arches, connected by long rods at the top and sides, was set up when tipi poles were not available. The structure might also be hemispherical and built like a sweatlodge. The frame was covered with an ordinary tipi cover or with boughs. A smoke-hole was left open at the top in both types.

CEREMONIAL STRUCTURES

The sweatlodge was dome-shaped, about four feet high and six to eight feet in diameter. Six holes dug in a circle served as sockets for willow withes which were arched over and intertwined in opposite pairs. Robes, blankets, or tipi covers were laid over the frame. The covers were lifted to gain entrance. A circular hole was dug inside the lodge to receive the heated stones. A sweatlodge could be used only once. The frame was left standing and many may be seen on reserves today.

A house form used only for certain dances is the *sapohtowa·n*, which may be literally translated as "going right through tipi," i.e., long tipi. It is a long lodge with apsidal ends. Two tripods, made of poles forked at the top, were set up about twenty-five feet apart. The poles of each tripod were fastened together by interlocking the forks and not by lashing as in an ordinary tipi foundation. A ridgepole laid on the tripods was further supported in the middle by a pair of forked poles interlocked at the point where they joined the ridge pole. Two or three pairs of supports may be used. Ordinary tipi poles were laid against the ridge pole and in a semicircle around the two tripods. Tipi covers or brush were placed over the lower part of the frame; the upper portion remained open. A fire was built beneath the apex of each tripod. A space was left for the door at one end, usually toward the south.

A structure used only for certain dances was *wewah-tahoka·n*, literally, "joined together tipi." It was a tipi framework so large that two covers were needed to enclose it. No doorway was made; entrance was obtained by lifting the cover. For the Smoking Tipi ceremony, a special *wewahtahoka·n* was constructed. Four foundation poles were fastened together by interlocking their forked tops and binding with thongs. Additional poles were laid and two tipi covers drawn over this framework.

While the common tipi was erected by women, these ceremonial structures were set up by men.

HOUSEHOLD FURNISHINGS
AND UTENSILS

Beds were made of bundles of dried grass or rushes over which a buffalo robe was thrown. During warm weather, the robe alone sufficed. Pillows were rectangular sacks of rawhide filled with duck feathers.

Back-rests of peeled willow sticks were used by men of prestige only. In a specimen in The American Museum of Natural History (50.1-5697) a sinew thread is drawn through perforations at each end of every stick. A rawhide thong, laced around each stick, binds the willows together in the center. Back-rests were suspended from a tripod or from a four-pole base.

Spoons were made from the horns of yearling buffalo. The horn was cut from the carcass with a part of the skull still attached. It was boiled until soft enough for the bone to be worked out. Then the horn was warmed again and a wedge-shaped stone forced into a slit cut at the edge. The horn was repeatedly heated until the stone could be pushed far enough to lay the horn open. After the rough edges were trimmed smooth, the dull side of a knife blade was rubbed over the spoon to smooth and polish it. The tip was bent over to form a handle.

Mussel shells were also much used as spoons. Other spoons and ladles were roughly hewn of wood.

The parfleche was not made nor commonly used, although occasionally one would be acquired in trade. Rawhide bags were utilized for storing foods. They were usually made of a single piece of rawhide, doubled over, and sewn along two sides. The seam was more often along the two adjoining sides rather than along the parallel sides. A short projecting piece from one side of the bag served as a flap to close the opening.

Clothes, ornaments, and sometimes food, were kept in drawstring bags of tanned hide. These were made like the rawhide bags except that a strip of soft leather was sewn around the opening and gathered at the top to form an elastic mouth. Often a rectangle of deer legskins, untanned, with the dewclaws attached, was sewn on both faces of the bag. The skin from the head of the moose might be used in the same way.

Both bag types varied a good deal in size, averaging perhaps two feet wide and one foot deep. Only rarely were they painted, although quill and bead ornamentation was common. In addition to these two types, there was a great assortment of soft bags made for many different uses. Paints and medicine were carried in very small skin envelopes, which usually were completely beaded.

A favorite means of storing berries and, in later days, tea, was the whole skin of an unborn buffalo calf. The foetal carcass was removed through the mouth opening of its hide, the legs and umbilicus sewn up, and the skin worked between the hands until soft and pliable.

A buffalo paunch was utilized as a water container. When it was filled, a small stick was passed through perforations near the edge of the aperture to close it.

Bags woven of bark fiber are mentioned by Skinner,[15] but no corroborative evidence could be obtained. Basketry was unknown.

Birchbark containers were used for berries, roots, and even as water buckets. They were of the truncated pyramidal type familiar among the Northeastern Algonkin, the walls rising from a rectangular bottom to an oval opening. A willow hoop was fastened around the inside of the rim as a reinforcement against the splitting of the edge. Cylindrical birchbark vessels were employed in berrying. The container was slung around the neck. Shallow oblong bark vessels served as trays for cooked food. Paints, medicine objects, and perfume, were stored in small cylindrical bark boxes fitted with wooden stoppers. All bark was sewn with split spruce root and was sometimes ornamented with quillwork.

Makeshift dishes of birchbark were employed, but more often dishes were carved of wood. One type was made of a section of log split longitudinally. The inner plane was hollowed out and the outer surface whittled flat. Other wooden dishes were little more than discs cut out of small tree trunks.

Snow scoops were carved out of split logs. They were made in a single piece and had a straight handle which widened into a rounded blade. They were some four feet long and were about six inches wide at the edge of the blade.

During the last century, every man carried a bar of magnet steel from which a spark was struck to light a fire. A dim memory still exists of generating fire by twirling a stick between the palms on a bit of touchwood. More recently fire was made by placing flint on the inner bark of black poplar.

The flint was struck with a red stone until the sparks ignited the bark. After trade goods were introduced, gunpowder was dissolved in water and touchwood soaked in the solution. When the wood had thoroughly dried, it was possible to start a fire by enclosing it in a piece of cloth and striking it on a hard surface. Fire-making by means of a bowdrill is reported by Skinner.[16] Among the River People band this implement was totally unknown.

Men kindled the fires, but it was women's work to tend them and collect firewood. Branches for firewood were pulled down and broken off with rawhide thongs. Men on the warpath broke firewood between two stakes planted in the ground. When it was necessary to fell a tree, fires were built at the base until the trunk was burned through. Over the campfire a tripod about five feet high was erected, on which meat was laid to dry and from which cooking utensils were hung. Buffalo chips were much utilized as fuel. On wet days a buffalo skull was smeared with grease and set afire. The skull kept an even heat for a long time.

Every woman had as part of her household equipment several stone mauls and hammers. The maul used for splitting bones was roughly egg-shaped, its handle being about ten inches long. A lighter stone with a longer handle and sharp edges was used for pounding meat. Both types had a medial groove which was pecked out or abraded with a harder stone. To form the handle, a willow withe was twisted and bent around this groove. The two ends were bound together with green rawhide; the stone itself was not encased in hide.

One informant among the Calling River People band said that in the distant past the tribe had used clay vessels. Skinner[17] had similar information from the same band. The people of other bands, however, knew nothing at all about pottery.

The only weaving technique was that employed in making rabbitskin blankets. A rabbit was flayed by breaking through the skin at the tendons of the hind legs and the whole hide peeled back over the head. The hide was then cut in one continuous strip, three to four inches wide, and hung to dry for two days. It soon curled so that the fur was outermost on all sides. Four poles were lashed together to make a rectangular frame. A strip of hide was laced to the top of the frame and a line of perforations punched along its length. Similar strips were attached to the two vertical sides of the frame. The initial strand of fur was passed in and out of the top holes and then through one hole on the side strip where it

Fig. 11. Detail of Rabbit Robe Weaving. a, Upper bar of wooden frame; b, Perforated strip of hide or canvas through which initial rabbitskin strand is threaded; c, First strand of robe.

was looped back on itself (Fig. 11). The "simple loop" netting technique was used.[18] When one strand ran out, another was knotted to it. Recently another technique has been innovated. The strips of fur are simply passed in and out of a burlap sheet made of a number of old bags stitched together. Rabbitskin blankets were used as bed coverings rather than as robes. Clothing of this material was not made.

WEAPONS

The best bows were made of chokecherry wood. A straight shoot, three to four feet long and two or three inches in diameter, was whittled flat on both sides and smoothed with a stone. Two notches were cut at each end to receive the bowstring. Glue, made by boiling a buffalo hide until it was of viscid consistency, was applied to the back of the bow and lengths of stiff sinew embedded in it. When the glue dried, the sinew ends were trimmed.

The bowstring was made of long sinews, usually from the back of a buffalo. Skinner states[19] that the sinew was moistened in the mouth, divided into three strands, and twisted into cord by rolling on the thigh with the palm. Before being used it was dried, stretched, and straightened. Simple bows were made when lack of materials or time precluded the manufacture of backed bows.

Arrows were made of serviceberry shoots, about two feet long. The feathering consisted of three vanes laid parallel to the axis of the shaft and bound with sinew. The nock was in the same plane as the arrowhead. Bone or horn from deer and elk furnished materials for arrowheads. The heads were cut out with a knife and trimmed with a stone. Traditionally, a "yellow stone, like flint" was chipped to make arrowheads. The tang of the head was inserted into a cleft in the shaft and bound in place with sinew. War arrows were loosely bound so that the head remained in a wound when the shaft was withdrawn. Arrow poisons were not known although magical concoctions were applied to arrowheads to render them more efficacious. No information was secured on arrow grooves. A hole punched through the shoulder blade of a buffalo served as an arrow straightener.

The Mediterranean arrow release was employed. The bow was held almost vertically, except while shooting from horseback, when it was held in a horizontal position. Wrist guards were made out of a rectangular piece of hide to which two laces were attached.

Boys used a crossbow in play and were able to kill birds with that weapon. Two informants stated that crossbows were formerly used by men for large game. A flat stock was whittled out and the bow inserted in a hole made near one end. A groove for the arrows and a notch for the drawn bowstring were cut at the narrow top of the stock. Short feathered arrows were used.

A large bow with a knife or bayonet affixed to one end was used in warfare. When the enemy advanced to close quarters it was wielded like a pike.

Spears were used in battle only. They were never thrown, but were thrust with an upward, stabbing motion. They were about four feet long, ornamented with fur and feathers, and presumably tipped with horn or bone points, before iron heads were introduced.

Knives of aboriginal manufacture have been out of use for so long a time that only the tradition remains of knives made of the rib bones of large animals. Knife sheaths were made of a single piece of hide, doubled over and sewn together. The top part was turned over to make a cuff.

The most common type of warclub consisted of a stone encased in a hide bag attached to the end of a two-foot stick. The hide did not fit tightly around the stone and so furnished a flexible neck to the club. A wrist loop was fastened at the butt. Many warclubs were merely stout wooden cudgels into which knife blades or nails had been set. A solid wooden club with a large knob carved at the striking end was also made.

Shields were carried as much for magical as for practical protection and were usually decorated in accordance with vision instruction. They were bowl-shaped, ornamented with feathers around the circumference, and had a picture of some supernatural character on one or both faces. When carried they were slung over the shoulder by a thong. During a fight they were held at the top and braced with the forearm.

To make a shield, a round section was cut out of the

thick neck hide of a bull buffalo. It was heated and shrunk to the desired convex shape. Feathers were suspended from holes punched around the rim. Shields were usually carried in soft leather cases which had a fringed seam across the diameter.

Even during the last years of the roving life, the guns possessed by the tribesmen were of the muzzle-loading variety. Only a few wealthy men had rifles. Guns played a more important part in warfare than in the food quest. Bows were exclusively used in the buffalo pound, and for the concerted attack on a herd, the bow was almost as efficient as the gun. Only in stalking and tracking game did the gun give a decided advantage.

SMOKING UTENSILS

Pipes were made of a soft black stone taken out of the bed of the Battle River. A block of stone was hewn out with knives and two holes were bored in it to form a right angle. The stone around the holes was cut away until the finished pipe was produced. While being worked, the stone was kept wet. After being dried in the sun, the pipe was rubbed with fat throughout and gently heated over a fire. The melted fat was rubbed off with grass. The stone was then greased once more and polished with buffalo hair. Red catlinite, obtained in trade, was also used for pipes.

Most pipes were flat-bottomed and had a short piece projecting beyond the bowl in the same plane as the shank. This monitor type was evidently not the common one in Hind's day, for he illustrates a typical Plains Cree pipe of the platform variety, with a block beneath the bowl and a short keel-like piece extending along the bottom.[20] Pipes used in ceremonies were six to eight inches long. Those in ordinary use were smaller. Women's pipes were usually elbow-shaped. Incised lines or figures and lead inlay were common means of pipe ornamentation.

Pipestems were made from a straight saskatoon berry shoot. A suitable rod was split and longitudinal grooves cut down both halves. The two pieces were fitted together and bound with sinew. Aqueous matter from buffalo eyes was applied over the whole stem. Pipe tamps were pointed sticks, about a foot long, ornamented with quill and beadwork. Special boards were made on which tobacco was cut. They were usually ten-inch squares, studded with brass-headed tacks.

No traditions of growing or gathering tobacco exist. Bearberry leaves (*Arctostaphylos uva-ursi*) were gathered, tied in bunches, and dried over a fire. Before being smoked, they were crushed between the fingers and mixed with trade tobacco. In the days before trade goods were available, the leaves alone were smoked. The inner bark of red willow was also used for smoking.

Tobacco pouches were of tanned hide, about two feet long and six inches wide. A solid block of bead or quillwork covered the lower six inches of the bag on both sides. The rest of the bag was wrapped around this stiffened section. The opening was scalloped and had a line of beads around the edge. A four-inch fringe was attached to the lower end of the bag.

MUSICAL INSTRUMENTS

Whenever songs were sung some method of beating the rhythm was employed. If no instruments were available, the hands were clapped together to mark the time, or else a pole was placed on the ground and beaten. This was always done while playing the "Flathead" hand game. Drums were of the single-headed, tambourine variety, about eighteen inches in diameter. A flat board, three or four inches wide, was steamed and bent to form a hoop. The drum head, made of deer, antelope, or horsehide, was stretched over this frame and kept taut by several thongs drawn across the open face. The thongs were either part of the hide or were fastened to perforations in the circumference of the drum head. Sometimes holes were burned in the frame and through these the hide was laced. The place where the thongs crossed in the center of the open face was often bound with hide to make a hand hold. Drum snares of the kind used by the Northeastern Algonkin were not made.

The drumstick was a straight piece of wood, perhaps twelve inches long, wrapped with hide at the striking end. Drumheads were heated before being beaten to tighten the hide and so impart a good tone and resonance to the drum.

A man's spirit helper might direct him in a vision to paint the face of a drum with some design. Such a drum was beaten on sacred occasions only and was kept carefully wrapped and away from contaminating influences.

Water drums, hollowed out of a log section, were used in the *mite·wiwin*. They were not made by the Plains Cree, but were acquired from the Saulteaux. Before the drum was used the horsehide head was removed and water poured into the hollow to give greater resonance. The head was bound to the edge of the wooden cylinder with thongs. The drumstick made for this type of drum was curved and the tip of the stick was used as the striking surface.

In the Sun dance, a rawhide was spread on the ground and beaten with willow wands.

In the Plains Cree version of the Grass dance, a large, flat, double-headed drum was used. It was usually suspended horizontally from four stakes driven into the ground. Recently, such drums have come to be used in sacred ceremonies.

Bulb-shaped rattles were made of rawhide. To make a rattle, two pieces of green hide were cut out, each in the form of a circle with a projecting lip, and were sewn together, one over the other. Earth was stuffed inside and shaken out when the hide had dried in the desired shape. Pebbles and red willow seeds were inserted. A handle six inches long was fitted into the projecting mouth and bound in place with antelope hide thongs. No wrist loop was made.

Rattles, also, could be made and painted in accordance with vision injunctions. Such rattles were hung up outside the tipi before pebbles or seeds were inserted. Within four nights (the pattern number), the instrument would be heard to rattle when the wind shook it, even though there was nothing inside it. This was confirmation of its supernatural sanction.

Rattles were always employed by shamans while doctoring. In the Sun dance, the song leader shook a rattle, prefacing each new song with an interlude of rattling. Rattles were usually shaken with an up and down motion of the wrist and forearm. While doctoring, a shaman might beat the rattle against his body.

A special rattle, with dots burned in the hide over the upper half, was shaken to accompany songs sung during a thunderstorm. One of the Warrior societies had a ring-shaped rattle as part of its distinctive regalia. Another society, according to one informant, had a rattle made of a flat stick looped back upon itself. The loop was covered with buffalo pericardium. This type resembled the flat disc rattle of the Central and Eastern Algonkin.

The staff carried by the leader of the Masked dance was used as a rattle. It was a five-foot stick encased in an envelope of hide to which deer hooves were attached. The leader stamped it on the ground in time with the singing.

Beads, small bells, and cone-shaped tin pendants are now attached to practically all paraphernalia worn or carried on ceremonial occasions. They strike against each other and emit a soft rattle which accompanies every movement of the wearer.

Gourd and turtle shell rattles were not known. *Maskwa* described a rattle made of a wooden cylinder.

The long bones of eagles and other large birds were used to make the whistles blown by the dancers in the Sun dance. These were from four to ten inches long and were ornamented with quills, ribbons, and fur. A vent was cut in the bone and a small wooden peg fitted across the bone at the opening. Cedar pitch was placed over the peg. A flute was made by boring a hole through a ten-inch stick. The hole was bored from both ends, the diameter at the mouthpiece being smaller than that at the butt. A piece of birchbark fastened across the butt partially closed the opening. Finger holes were sometimes made, but were attributed by Fine-day to European influence.

A toy sometimes used as a deer call was made of a maple wood tube. A notch was cut at one end and a piece of wet sinew set into it so that the sinew extended down the length of the tube. Blowing into the mouthpiece caused the sinew to vibrate against the sides and made a loud call.

Women, to amuse themselves while on berrying trips, would blow against the edge of a leaf held between the cupped hands.

Buzzers were made out of a bone "from the inside of the hoof of a buffalo." A sinew was wound around the bone and two small sticks tied to the end of the string as hand grips. The sinew was twisted and as it was alternately pulled and relaxed, the bone spun around and made a buzzing sound.

Bull-roarers were used as toys only. A flat bit of wood was attached to the end of a three-foot stick by a thong about eighteen inches long. A groove was cut around the stick near its tip and the thongs were fastened to it so that the noose slipped around easily within the groove.

TRANSPORT DEVICES

Snowshoes were much used and gave the Plains Cree a great advantage in winter warfare over the Blackfoot who did not have them. Two kinds were known. The frame of the common type was in the shape of an elongated ellipse made out of two pieces of willow or chokecherry wood. The front

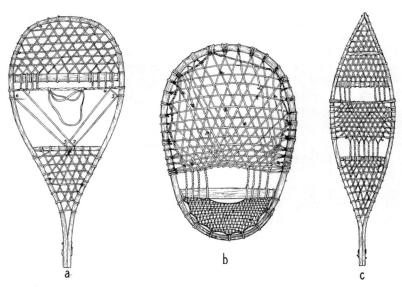

Fig. 12. Types of Snowshoes. a, Bent snowshoe. The central portion shows lacing procedure. Lacing begins at point 1; lace wound around frame at point 3; then to point 4; and so on. The upper part is called forehead, the center belly, the lower tail piece. The wooden crossbars are called movers because there is some play quickly developed in the slots into which they fit. b, Woman's snowshoe, thong for foothold not shown. c, Pointed snowshoe. The fore end turns up. The thong for the foothold is not shown.

end was pointed and turned up. The two pieces of the frame were lashed together in the rear and extended as a short tail piece. Three wooden crossbars supported the netting, which was passed through holes bored in the frame (Fig. 12). The other form was made of a single piece of willow bent to form an oval frame. No wooden crosspieces were used; the netting was wound around the frame and so afforded better purchase in slippery places.

A carrying strap was used by women when bringing in firewood and by men when carrying burdens on a war trip. It was simply a strip of tanned hide slung across the chest.

Water transport was limited to ferrying devices, for canoes were not made. Rafts were constructed by lashing poles across two large, dry logs. Brush and hides were spread over this frame. A hide boat was made by stretching hides, sewn together for the purpose, over two curved and crossed sticks.

TECHNIQUES OF ORNAMENTATION

The artistic achievements of the Plains Cree were largely

100

limited to bead and quillwork. Before the advent of trade goods, quillwork was used to ornament all articles of dress. The flattened quills were wound around two parallel sinew threads stitched along the fabric. The techniques discussed and illustrated by Wissler[21] as numbers 4, 5, and 17, were principally used.

Trade beads were soon substituted for porcupine quills although the technique of quillworking was never entirely displaced. In the most common beadworking technique, the beads were strung on a thread and laid along the surface to which they were to be attached. A second thread, passing between every bead or every two beads, was stitched over the first thread and fastened it to the fabric. Both geometric and floral designs are now used. It was the unanimous opinion of all informants questioned that floral designs were introduced from the east by half-breeds and that formerly only geometric patterns were used. There were no standardized design names. When it was necessary to refer to a particular design, each woman improvised a name that would be readily understood.

Beaded bands were made on a bow loom (Fig. 13). Ten strands of sinew or thread were laid across from end to end of a curved stick. Nine beads were strung and placed in the spaces between the warp threads. The beads were pressed down on the warp so that one bead lay between every two

Fig. 13. Bow Loom for making Beaded Belts and Bead Strips.

threads. The threaded needle was then brought back and passed through the beads again, but below the warp this time, and knotted at the end of the row of nine beads. Thus each line of nine beads was fastened to the warp by two threads.

Horsehair was much used for moccasin decoration. A hank of ten hairs was tacked to the leather by a stitch across the middle. It was doubled over and a single horsehair, usually colored, was wound around the doubled strands. At short intervals the colored hair was stitched to the leather. The finished product appeared as a thin round colored cord attached to the moccasin by invisible stitches. The horsehair line usually extended around the lower edge of the tongue piece.

A few instances of ribbon appliqué work were to be found, mostly among the eastern bands. But this technique was not common. Wood carving was not practised by this tribe although wooden images of supernatural characters were occasionally imported from their eastern neighbors.

Pictographic illustrations of battle deeds came into vogue only during the last years of the buffalo era. Representations of spirit helpers were often drawn on drumheads, tipi covers, shields, and other objects. The designs were first blocked out with charcoal. Red ocher and colored earths were mixed with grease and laid on with the spongy end of a bone. White clay was smeared over soiled garments to clean them and brushed off when dry.

Hide thongs served a multitude of uses, being the common means of clamping, fastening, and tying together both rigid and pliable objects. Thongs were cut from tanned or green hides in a continuous strip. The thong was tied to a stake, stretched, and pegged down when fully extended. The edges were trimmed to an even width. Three or four strands might be plaited together. Women prepared the thongs, but men did the plaiting.

Bark ropes were often utilized. They had a good deal of tensile strength, but became brittle when dry. The bark was stripped from a willow-like shrub in suitable lengths and three or four strips were plaited together.

Buffalo hair also furnished material for ropes. Hair from the mane was spread out and fluffed with the fingers. A bit was twisted to make a strand and inserted into a notch cut in the middle of a short stick which was rotated with the right hand while hair was added to the strand with the left. When the strand was long enough it was doubled and twisted. Two such lengths were twisted together to make a single rope.

Horsehair cords were used in snares set for small animals. Eight or ten hairs were rolled on the bare thigh to make a length of cord.

FOOTNOTES

[1]WISSLER, CLARK, Costumes of the Plains Indians (Anthropological Papers, American Museum of Natural History, vol. 17, part 2, New York, 1915), p. 51; WISSLER, CLARK, Structural Basis to the Decoration of Costumes among the Plains Indians (Anthropological Papers, American Museum of Natural History, vol. 17, part 2, New York, 1916), p. 103.
[2]MACKENZIE, Voyages from Montreal, vol. 1, p. cxlii.
[3]WISSLER, Costumes of the Plains Indians, pp. 71-75.
[4]WISSLER, CLARK, Material Culture of the Blackfoot Indians (Anthropological Papers, American Museum of Natural History, vol. 5, part 1, New York, 1910), pp. 128-129.
[5]*Ibid.*, pp. 144-145.
[6]WISSLER, CLARK, General Discussion of Shamanistic and Dancing Societies (Anthropological Papers, American Museum of Natural History, vol. 11, part 12, New York, 1916), p. 863.
[7]SKINNER, Notes on the Plains Cree, p. 76.
[8]*Ibid.*, p. 77.
[9]*Ibid.*, p. 81.
[10]WISSLER, Material Culture of the Blackfoot Indians, p. 113.
[11]PAGET, AMELIA M., The People of the Plains, Toronto, 1909, p. 94.
[12]WISSLER, Material Culture of the Blackfoot Indians, p. 106.
[13]CADZOW, DONALD A., The Prairie Cree Tipi (Indian Notes, Museum of the American Indian, Heye Foundation, vol. 3, New York, 1926), p. 21.
[14]PEESO, The Cree Indians, p. 57.
[15]SKINNER, Notes on the Plains Cree, p. 86.
[16]*Ibid.,* p. 81.
[17]*Ibid.,* p. 79.
[18]DAVIDSON, D.S., Knotless Netting in America and Oceania (American Anthropologist, n.s., vol. 37, Menasha, 1935), pp. 120, 123.
[19]SKINNER, Notes on the Plains Cree, p. 83.
[20]HIND, Narrative of the Canadian Red River, p. 140.
[21]WISSLER, Material Culture of the Blackfoot Indians, p. 55.

Social Life

THE BASIS OF BAND DIVISIONS

The bands of the Plains Cree were loose, shifting units usually named for the territory they occupied. Each band had its own range, but the limits were not clearly defined; sometimes a band traveled a hundred miles or more from its usual locality to join in a Sun dance or to hunt with some other band. Individuals, and even whole families, might separate from their group to follow another chief.

The most important consideration in the demarcation of band divisions was that all the members of a band lived in the same general territory. The prestige and power of the leading chief was also an important factor in the cohesiveness of a band. An influential leader attracted more families and held their allegiance better than a weaker man. Black-bear, a noted warrior of the last half of the nineteenth century, rose to chieftainship and welded a new band because of his abilities as a leader. Not only did families from several Plains Cree bands place themselves under his aegis, but a considerable number of Assiniboin and Plains Ojibwa joined his camp.

Another chief, *Tcimaskos*, was a noted pound maker. In winter, people from distant places would seek his encampment to enjoy the abundance of meat secured under his guidance. He was recognized as a paramount chief, even though his summer following was much smaller.

Kinship ties were operative in the transfer of band allegiance. A family which, for some reason, was dissatisfied with its neighbors, went to camp with relatives in another band. Young men traveled among the various bands a good deal and often married into and settled with a group distant from their own. But every band had a stable nucleus composed of the close relatives of the chief, who would not ordinarily leave his group.

Acceptance into band membership was a simple matter. Any person who lived in the encampment for some time and who traveled with the group soon came to be known as one of its members. Newcomers were ordinarily able to trace kinship with several people in the band and so established their status. When kinship ties were tenuous or non-existent, marriage into the band usually furnished an immigrant with the social alliances necessary for adjustment to the course of communal life. Thus the numbers of each band were constantly augmented by recruits from other bands of Plains Cree, or from other tribes. The eight bands listed above (p. 9ff.) were the principal groups of the tribe in the latter years of the nomadic life. Other bands were in existence, but were only minor groupings.

CHIEFTAINSHIP

Succession to chieftainship was often, though not necessarily, hereditary. If a chief's son were incompetent, some man of high prestige was acknowledged as successor. The number of chiefs was not fixed, nor was there any prescribed procedure for attaining the rank. A man became a chief by virtue of his accomplishments in battle, his ability as a hunter, his liberality, his capacities as an orator and executive. One who had not distinguished himself on the warpath could not be chief. But a brave warrior who was not also an industrious hunter and provider could hardly attain the highest rank. A chief had to give freely of his possessions to needy tribesmen and usually set the pace on the occasions for ceremonial gift giving. The chief was more a recognized leader or headman than he was an official.

Although an outstanding war record was the *sine qua non* for chieftainship, wealth and liberality were of great importance. To quote Fine-day:—

No matter how brave a man is and no matter how many horses he brings back (from raids), if he has nothing, he can't be a chief. It happened many times that a man would be brave and bring back many horses. But he would trade the horses for clothes and would be too lazy to get hides for a tipi cover and so he could never be a chief. When a young man showed (by his deeds) that he would be a chief some day the old men would go to see him and say, "Now young man, you are climbing higher and higher and are on the way to become a chief. It is for your own good (that we speak). It is not an easy thing to be chief. Look at this chief now. He has to have pity on the poor. When he sees a man in difficulty he must try to help him in whatever way he can. If a person asks for something in his tipi, he must give it to him willingly and without any bad feeling. We are telling you this now because you will meet these things and you must have a strong heart."

106

At ceremonies chiefs were expected to contribute a larger share of the feast than the other tribesmen. Visitors were fed and lodged in his tipi. This is still the practice.

In order to acquire the meat and hides and other material possessions demanded by the obligations of his position, a chief had to be an energetic hunter. When horses and dogs were led into camp loaded with meat from a hunt, the chief's wife dropped the choice parts in front of the tipis of the poor.

Not all of the burden of chieftainship was borne by the chief alone, for his relatives made contributions to his expenditures. A chief with many relatives had greater resources than one with few, he could be more lavish in his gift-giving and hospitality, and so acquire a greater reputation. His relatives, in turn, benefited by the prestige derived from kinship with a respected chief.

Men who had small, poorly furnished tipis and little surplus food were seated near the door in a council meeting and were not given a blanket or robe to sit on. Their inferior rank was indicated in this way and their opinions were little heeded.

It was incumbent upon the chief to maintain order and peace in his camp. Jealousy was a common cause of dissent and when it became known that one man suspected another of being intimate with his wife, the chief might approach the irate husband, ask him to lay aside his anger, and present him with a horse. Gift giving was the socially accepted method of mollifying an aggrieved person and in this way the chief eased troublesome situations. A modern parallel of this practice occurred on the Sweet Grass Reserve some ten years ago. A bitter quarrel broke out between two men over the disputed ownership of a heifer. The chief of the Reserve gave one of his own cattle to the man who claimed that his animal had been stolen. By this act the dispute was settled, the possibility of bloodshed averted, and the prestige of the chief was enhanced.

Moreover, a chief had to conduct his own affairs with the highest restraint. Sweet-grass, a chief whose name was given to one of the Reserves, once captured a very fast horse which he highly prized. The horse was high-spirited and proved hard to hold in check during the buffalo hunt. Rather than endanger the success of the hunt, Sweet-grass immediately traded it for an inferior, but docile animal.

Chief Big-bear, noted for his participation in the rebellion of 1885, was once wantonly assaulted and knocked unconscious by a drunken member of his band. In retaliation, Big-bear's daughter immediately ran to the attacker's tipi, slashed it, and bore off his possessions. When Big-bear was revived, he ordered all the man's goods taken back and decreed that no further retaliatory measures be taken. The attacker later tried to make propitiatory gifts, but he was never thenceforth able to regain his former prestige status.

Even if one of his relatives should be murdered, a chief was supposed to forego the blood vengeance which ordinary tribesmen would be impelled to take.

A band might have several chiefs, each of whom had his own following. One of them would be recognized as outranking the others because of seniority in age or, more important, because of his outstanding superiority. When several bands gathered in a large encampment, the chiefs would meet in one of the Warrior lodges. The hierarchy of rank among the chiefs would be tacitly recognized or, in any case of doubt, settled by a word or hint from a respected old man. The highest ranking chief sat directly behind the fire at the back of the lodge, the next highest on either side of him and so around the lodge with the least esteemed near the door. On such occasions the status accorded to a chief did not depend on the size of his following, but hinged largely on his war record. His fame as an open-handed person also was considered.

The Hudson's Bay Company disturbed the pattern of chieftainship in some degree. When a group arrived to trade at a post, the factors customarily presented the chief with several barrels of whiskey and a large amount of trade goods to distribute among his followers. Thus it became a matter of some importance to be recognized as a chief by the Company. Since the traders favored the peaceful industrious trappers and discouraged the aggressive troublesome warriors, in late years certain chiefs arose whose war achievements were not particularly outstanding.

A chief was not inducted into office ceremonially. When a chief died, he would most likely be succeeded by his son who would have the wealth and the support of kin necessary for the position. If the son lacked the necessary qualifications for leadership, some outstanding man was gradually accepted as the head of the group by tacit and common consent. Sometimes a chief voluntarily surrendered his position to a man who had outstripped him in battle achievements and in wealth distribution. There seems to have been little jockeying for position and few political rivalries.

The functions of chieftainship varied with the personalities who occupied the office. A strong, domineering man held his people closely in check, dictated their moves, tightly controlled the restive young men, and ordered his followers about. A less purposeful chief simply went his own way, offered advice now and then, submitted all controversial matters to the council of prominent men.

The council was an informal affair. When an important decision was to be made, the chief's crier summoned the leading men by name, told them what was to be discussed, and invited them to go to the tipi where the meeting was to take place. The chief briefly laid the matter before them and then each spoke. The youngest spoke first, those of higher rank last. Every man told why he held a particular opinion. After all had spoken, the chief made the decision. Thereupon the crier announced the decree to the camp.

Every band encampment had one or two criers, *oca·kit-ostamakew*, who went around the camp circle calling out the news of the day, the chief's orders, and other matters of public interest. They were usually men who had good war records, but were too old to participate in fighting any longer. They were chosen by the chief and received many gifts from him and from the leading men in the band. The men of high status saw to it that the criers were well dressed and plentifully supplied with food.

In the chief's absence his crier had what may be called the power of attorney over his possessions. Those who sought the chief's bounty, put their requests to the crier. Should the chief be absent, the crier gave whatever was needed to the supplicant. The crier also acted for the chief in keeping order in camp. If an angry man took a gun to kill one of his tribesmen, it was the crier's duty to disarm him. Because of the dangers of the position, men who suspected that they were to be chosen as criers would leave camp and hide until another had been selected. Fleeing from appointment to office was perhaps also a way of demonstrating personal modesty.

Not the least of the crier's functions was to announce publicly the giving of a gift. Since liberality was an important criterion of prestige, the crier was the agency for transforming generosity into a status asset. In many camps there were two criers.

An official distinct from the crier was the chief's caller, *otepwestamakew*. He, too, was an old man of prestige and received gifts from the wealthy men, so that he might not endanger the dignity of his position by being poorly clad. It was his duty to summon by name any men whom the chief invited to his tipi. The caller never went about the camp in performing this function, but always stood at the door of the tipi and shouted so that the men invited could hear. The offices of crier and caller were never vested in the same man. The office of chief's speaker was not known.

When the whole band came together during the summer, the chief and the council chose an old man to be camp leader. He had to be one with powerful spirit helpers to guide him. He traveled at the head of the march when camp was broken and selected the camping sites. If any misfortune befell the band, or if he were not successful in locating good hunting grounds, another old man would be chosen in his stead. Fine-day stated that a council meeting was held on one night during each waning of the moon throughout the summer. The camp leader held office for one moon only and a new one was chosen at every council meeting.

Attached to the household of the chief were several young men who cared for his horses and hunted for him. These were orphans or boys whose relatives were poor, and who voluntarily came to live with and work for the chief. They were treated as members of the family, provided with clothes and food, and were able to use the chief's horses. From the chief they received informal training in hunting and warfare. These workers, *otockinıkıma*, were to be found in the tipis of most men of high rank.

RANK AND SOCIETIES

Next to the chief in prestige status were the *kıhtockinikiwak*, Worthy Young Men, and the *okihtcitawak*, a term which may arbitrarily be translated as "Warriors" and which is possibly of Dakota origin.[1] A young man who became known as a brave fighter and a daring raider came to be called a Worthy Young Man. There was no formal investiture of the title, nor were there any rigidly defined requirements for this rank. It was applied to anyone who had accomplished brave deeds in warfare. One man might not achieve the name until he had participated in many raids, another might distinguish himself sufficiently in a single skirmish. The old men of the band were usually the first to refer to a man by this title. They would be quick to give the name to the son of a chief, while a young man of inconsequential parents would have to demonstrate his ability and valor beyond any doubt.

The men bearing this title were not organized nor did they have any obligations beyond those of fortitude and liberality incumbent upon any person of prestige. As men of some distinction they were expected to keep open house and feed visitors and guests frequently. In the case of an enemy attack, they had to be among the first to defend the camp and to pursue the marauders.

The Warriors were organized into societies and had definite duties. A man became a Warrior when he was formally invited to sit in the Warrior's lodge and to participate in the dances. Warriors were on a higher prestige level than the Worthy Young Men. In practice, however, most Worthy Young Men were soon asked to join the society. Since membership in the society entailed considerable expenses, Worthy Young Men did not usually become Warriors until they had acquired a number of horses, hides, and other material possessions.

Each band had only one Warrior society which had its unique insignia, songs, and dance. An existing society, or a previously unorganized group of distinguished men, might purchase the right to perform a certain dance from the Warriors of another band or even from a society of a different tribe. The following account illustrates how the Plains Cree acquired the Buffalo Dancers' society.

The Buffalo dance was bought from the *Pwatuk*, the Dakota, by a group of Warriors who were of the West People, the River People, and East People.[2] The bargain was made when the Plains Cree and the Dakota were camping together along the South Saskatchewan River, southwest of where Saskatoon now stands. The Dakota came from a place called the Red Sand Hills. I was only a boy then. It happened shortly after Sitting-bull killed three white men, about four years before his big fight with the Americans.

The way it was done was this: The Plains Cree came up to the Warrior's lodge of the Dakota. The Pipestem Bearer of the Cree (an official in whose charge the sacred pipestem was entrusted) led the way, pointing the unwrapped stem toward the Dakota. His tribesmen followed, carrying many clothes and leading many horses. They piled the clothing in front of the Dakota Warriors' lodge and tied the horses to the tipi stakes. The Dakota came out carrying clothes over their shoulders. Each one of the Dakota went up to the pipestem, raised his arm outstretched before it, passed his hand along the stem from butt up to mouthpiece, and then down over his forehead and chest. With the same motion he took the clothing from his shoulder and placed it under the pipestem which was being held up by the Bearer. This continued until the Bearer slowly laid the stem on the pile of clothing, signifying that enough had been given and that the bargain was concluded. The Dakota gave clothing to the Cree because they were buying back the right to perform the dance themselves. They gave the Plains Cree about as much clothing as the Plains Cree gave them, but the Cree had also given many horses.

When the transfer was completed, the Dakota took the Cree into their lodge and taught them the songs and the dance. They had the tipi partly open and everyone was invited to come and look. I saw two big buffalo heads, one painted red on the muzzle and the other painted black. They were laid on a red cloth. Around them were smaller heads. The Cree sat in a row on one side, the Dakota on the opposite side. They did a lot of praying. When they sang the following song, "My father gave me the buffalo bull," the dancers would stand, put on the buffalo heads, and dance.

That same year the East People Band bought the Big Dog dance from the Paddling Men Band of Stoney.

A similar account reveals that the Plains Cree were vendors as well as buyers of society dances:—

The *Opwasimu*, Stoney, saw the Rattlers dance and wanted to buy it from the Plains Cree. Their Warriors collected a lot of clothes to give to the members of the Rattlers society. They came up to the Plains Cree in a body, led by one of their number bearing a sacred pipestem. The Plains Cree could not refuse them but stipulated that they would not sell all of the dance and so they, in turn, brought out many gifts and piled them under the pipestem. They did not give as many things as they had received. Then the Plains Cree Warriors taught the songs to the Stoneys. They did not teach them all the songs, only certain ones, and even those they could still use themselves.

The Plains Cree Rattlers had themselves bought the dance from other Warriors, but I don't know from whom.

An interesting sequel to this event followed.

Once, while the Rattlers were singing and dancing, some Stoneys who had bought the dance came into the lodge. They entered with bared knives and jumped about saying that they were going to cut up the Warriors' tipi. They thought that the Cree had stolen their dance. The chief of the Stoneys grabbed the robe of the old man who was teaching the songs to the Warriors and was going to cut it up. The old man said, "Wait a while." Then the Cree Warrior Chief arose and counted coup. "Once I grabbed a Blackfoot chief as he was coming out of his tipi. I stabbed him and threw him down beside the fire which had been used by the women in tanning hides. Now you (he said to the Stoney chief) will have to lie near the fire all night unless there is someone who can recite a greater deed and who can save you in that way." No one could tell a braver deed and so the Stoney had to lie near the fire all night, half roasting all the time. In the morning they gave him the blankets he had lain on because he had taken it all good-naturedly and because the Cree chief had proved that he was greater.

The name of the Stoney chief was *Kawahkatosuwipwat*, Skinny Stoney. When he came into the lodge he was not angry, but was only carrying out his duty since he thought that the Rattlers were in the wrong. But before he laid hands on the old man he should have made a speech reciting his war deeds. The old man said to him, "We didn't sell all of the dance to you, only half." I saw this myself.

The Warriors' lodge was erected in the center of the camp circle when the band came together in the spring. The societies did not function during the winter, except on those rare occasions when plentiful food and fuel made a large winter encampment possible. Their lodge was an enlarged ti-pi and was erected by the wives of the Warriors. One pole was taken from each tipi in camp until there were a sufficient number, and two tipi covers were requisitioned from house-holds in which additional covers were available.

Warriors, especially the unmarried ones, spent much of their time in the lodge, eating, sleeping, dancing. Back-rests were used in the lodge as prestige symbols, for they were not ordinarily to be found among household furnishings. The members were seated in the order of their prestige, the place of honor behind the fire being reserved for the Warrior Chief.

This official was chosen by the Warriors; his authority was confined to those activities performed by the Warriors as a group. He led the dances and directed policing operations. The Warrior Chief was distinct from the Chief proper, al-though a Warrior Chief often became Band Chief. Since the societies had no functions in warfare, the Warrior Chief was not also a war chief. But he was always one of the boldest and ablest of the fighting men. In general, those qualities prerequisite for chieftainship also appertained to the leader of the Warriors.

While it was usually the bravest men who were taken into the society, a man without a war record might be asked to join if he were a good hunter and had many horses. No for-mal initiations were held. The members discussed a desirable candidate, if they all agreed, he was invited to eat in the lodge where he was lectured on his obligations as a Warrior and thenceforward was a full-fledged member. In honor of the occasion he usually distributed gifts to the old people.

There were two *oskapewisak*, "servers," in every soci-ety. They were Warriors who had grown too old to engage actively in hunting or fighting. They served food to the members and performed the menial work of the lodge. In serving, they used pointed sticks, about two feet long and painted red. Sometimes they placed bits of meat in the mouths of the Warriors with these sticks. The servers also acted as criers, summoning the members, and announcing the proclamations of the society to the camp. Just as the chief's crier could dispose of the chief's belongings in his absence, so could the servers distribute the possessions of the Warriors in the event of their absence during an occasion which warranted the distribution of gifts.

Fine-day was chosen to be a Warrior at a time when two members of the society were appointed as servers.

I once was at a meeting of the Rattlers. I was a Worthy Young Man, but was not yet a Warrior. The Warriors were talking about the men who were to be chosen as servers and so I didn't know that I would be involved. Many people were present for there was to be a dance that night and people came to watch. The two who were to be chosen as servers were sitting in their places near the chief, according to their ranks as Warriors.

During an interval in the dance, a chief got up and made a speech about how he had rescued two Cree from death and how he had dragged a wounded man from near the Blackfoot fortification to the Plains Cree side. When he finished he took one of the older Warriors by the arm and led him in front of the singers (i.e., to the center of the lodge). He did the same with the other one. We all stood up and danced in place.

Then the chief took me by the arm and led me from where I had been sitting near the door to one of the places vacated by the older men. I knew I was taken to be a Warrior. I had on the red flannel leggings that we wore then and a good blanket. I took them off and gave them to the man whose place I had taken. The other Warriors also gave gifts to the two men.

When the newly chosen servers thought that they had received enough, one of them said, "That is enough, my friends. I am very thankful for what you have given me. Don't let me yell too long for any of you when I have to call. Let me call only once and then come. I will be as a child to the Worthy Young Man who is taking my seat. Let him not be ashamed to send me anywhere he likes, for water or for wood. I will do the work as best I can. I will be kind to you, and try to be kind to me." The other server spoke in the same way.

Then an old man said to those of us who had just been taken as Warriors, "From now on your homes and your possessions are not your own. From today, these two old men, the servers, are the owners of your goods. If a poor person comes for help and you are not at home, these men may give away your things. You must look after all the people. If their moccasins are torn you must supply new ones. Any clothing you

114

may have must be given to those who come for help and who need it. If you see an old person stranded while camp is moved, you must get off your horse and put him on. Then the horse is his."

And I did give away a lot of clothing as a Warrior should.

Old people or widows who were in need would kill a dog and bring it to the society lodge. The Warriors feasted on the dog meat and then gave the donor whatever was requested. During the dog feast a Warrior would sometimes display his bravado by having a new robe passed around on which the others wiped their greasy hands. Then the robe was tossed out of the lodge for anyone to pick up and keep.

The one important function of the society beyond dancing, feasting, and providing for the needy, was policing the buffalo hunt. When the Cree were gathered in large encampments, individual hunting could not be tolerated lest the game be driven away from the vicinity in a short time. When a herd was sighted, the Warriors went on guard to see that no one disturbed the buffalo before adequate preparations for the hunt were made. When all the hunters were ready, they were allowed to approach the herd slowly until the signal for the charge was given.

If a man evaded the Warriors and tried to make a kill before the proper time, they immediately advanced to the offender's tipi, slashed it to bits, and destroyed all his possessions. This was also done to a hunter who had unintentionally stampeded the buffalo because of an unmanageable horse.

If the transgressor took his punishment composedly, four days later the Warriors gathered and each contributed some article, until ample restitution had been made for the guilty man's losses. Indeed, the gifts often amounted to more than had been destroyed. An offender who showed any anger while his tipi was being demolished, or who tried to defend his possessions in any way, received nothing in return, and had to bear his loss.

A young hunter named Little-man, once rode out to kill a buffalo before the proper time. When the Warriors noticed that the herd had been disturbed, they searched for the culprit. They caught Little-man, stripped him of all his clothes, even his breechclout, and cut them to pieces. They did not kill his horse, because it was a valuable animal which none could replace. Had a Warrior slaughtered the horse, he later would have had to present Little-man with a mount as fast or faster than the one killed. The foretop, mane, and tail of the horse were docked. When restitution was made, the man who had cut the mane and foretop presented Little-man with a robe and a horse; the one who had clipped the tail gave a coat and a horse.

Little-man was of the Parklands People whose Warriors had the "Cold" lodge. The Cold Warriors in the punitive party gave the honor of destroying Little-man's clothes to the others who were of the Hairy Legs and the Rattlers. The Hairy Legs, as a matter of courtesy, gave the privilege to the Rattlers and the Warriors of that society destroyed the culprit's possessions.

While his clothes were being slashed, Little-man proved his worth by standing aside and laughing at the procedure. He was an unmarried young man and so the tipi in which he was living was not molested, since it was not his own. Had he been caught while coming into camp with the meat of an illicitly slaughtered buffalo, the household effects of the family with whom he was staying would have been destroyed. For his deed would then be construed as having been done for the benefit of the household, and not perpetrated out of sheer foolhardiness.

The ideal of behavior during punishment is revealed in this anecdote:—

A young fellow was riding his brother-in-law's horse to the chase. The hunters always rode in a line abreast until the leader fired his gun and then they gave the horses free rein. They were just beginning to gallop, when the young man's horse broke ahead. The leader had to fire his gun (i.e., gave the signal prematurely) and they had a long chase. The Warriors decided to cut up the brother-in-law's tipi, since he was the owner of the horse which had spoiled the hunt.

That evening, the server fired his gun and called the Warriors together. It was the custom that when a tipi was to be stripped, the group stopped at a short distance and then made a rush for it. As they paused, the tipi owner came out with a pipe and a long rope of tobacco. He offered the Warriors a smoke. "If any of you take a fancy to the pipe, keep it. I am thankful that you didn't destroy my tipi right away. While you smoke this pipe you will give my wife and children a chance to get out." The Warriors took the pipe and sang a song in which they named the man. The song was the one which was sung in gratitude on receiving a gift. They smoked and then went up to the tipi. One of the Warriors told of a time when he struck an enemy and then he made the first slash in the tipi cover. The owner of the tipi had many things and they wrecked everything. Four nights later they gave him even more than had been destroyed.

William Cameron,[3] while a captive of the Plains Cree in 1885, witnessed two Warriors slash the coat of a man who had killed cattle belonging to another Indian.

The Warriors guarded the line of march when camp was being moved and hurried the stragglers so that they might not fall too far behind. The number of Warriors in any society was not fixed and large bands had many more Warriors than the smaller bands.

Skinner[4] enumerates certain insignia as distinctive of Warriors, but the badges described are those connected with the general symbolism of battle and did not identify a man as a member of any particular society. They were worn by all men who had performed the deeds which the various tokens symbolized.

Since the names and regalia of the societies often changed through purchase and accretion of new elements, it is difficult to correlate each society with a particular band.

The River People Band did have the Rattlers society. The only distinctive regalia of these warriors were small ring-shaped rawhide rattles carried by the dancers.

The members of the Big Dog society carried sticks about two feet long which were completely covered with feathers, beads, and quills. Small metal cones were hung from the butt and rattled when the stick was shaken. This dance is said to have been bought from the Assiniboin and belonged to one of the eastern bands of Plains Cree.

The Buffalo Dancers society wore a headdress made of the entire head of a buffalo. In dancing, they crouched over and rapidly lifted their knees. The purchase of this society from the Dakota has been described above.

The Prairie-Chicken society, also called Hairy Legs, belonged to the Warriors of the Upstream People Band. The "Cold" society belonged to the House People Band. The "Ghost" lodge, *tcɪpahkanak*, probably was in the Calling River People Band. The Kit-Fox society was found among one of the western bands.

When several bands were camped together, each Warrior lodge was pitched near the center of the camp circle, opposite that segment of the circle occupied by its band. The tipi of the band chief stood between the Warrior lodge and the arc of the camp circle. The tipi of the Warrior Chief was placed directly behind that of the Band Chief.

During large encampments, a great deal of dancing and ceremonialism went on, and there was a friendly rivalry among the various Warrior lodges. One informant thus described the competition:—

The *okihtcitaw* were brave men and they liked to laugh and to have fun. Sometimes two of the Warrior societies, say the Rattlers and the Big Dogs, each had a dance. The sides of their tipis would be raised to let the people watch. Suppose it happened that most of the people were watching the Rattlers and only a few were looking in at the Big Dog lodge. Then the Big Dogs would get one of their members who had taken a woman captive and one who had taken a drum from the enemy. With

117

these men leading, the Big Dogs would go over to the Rattlers' tipi. They would dance there for a while and then their two men would say, "We have captured a woman and a drum from the enemy, give us your women and your drums." Everybody would laugh, the drums would be surrendered, the women who had been watching escorted away, and all the spectators would go over to the Big Dogs' tipi. Now the Rattlers would have to get someone who had done a greater deed to retrieve their drums and the women. If no one among them could do it, they might get some qualified man from another Warrior lodge.

When the Warriors sang and danced at night, their wives and daughters helped them sing. The women did not dance. A young girl would have her mother or grandmother along to chaperon her.

Under the heading *"Okitcitau* Rivalry" Skinner[5] notes that youths were tormented by making them lie next to a fire until their friends could find someone to count coup and release them. I obtained no corroboration of this custom.

The Warriors usually danced in place with a rhythmic bending of the knees. Sometimes they danced around the center of the lodge, posturing and maneuvering as though in battle. Each lodge had its own songs, some of which had been acquired in the original purchase, some contributed by members. A Warrior might receive a song in a vision and teach it to his fellow Warriors. From then on the song was the property of the society and could be sung by any of the members.

A ceremony called Sitting Up Until Morning ($\epsilon \cdot wap\text{-}ana \cdot p\iota htcik\epsilon hk$) was performed when there were several Warrior lodges in a single encampment. The Warriors of one society issued invitations to the wives or daughters of the members of other societies. The women came into the lodge and helped in the singing. The men danced for a while and the rest of the night was spent in telling tales. At dawn, the men washed and painted the women's faces, combed their hair, and gave them a gift. When the women returned to their homes, their husbands or fathers often gave a return gift to the man. No sexual license was permitted during this occasion.

Fine-day gave this account of the proceedings:—

One of the Warriors who had taken an enemy woman captive would go around to the tipis of the other bands. He would stop in front of the tipis of Warriors and Worthy Young Men, look in, beckon to the women. "Come here, I want you." Soon he had many women and girls following him.

It sometimes happened that when he called a Worthy Young Man's wife, her husband might say to him, "Wait out-

118

side a bit." The inviter waited and soon the Worthy Young Man would bring out a gift of something very nice, perhaps clothing for him. This was for the honor paid to the man in taking his wife. Of course, not every man could afford to do this.

The inviter led all the women to the Warrior tipi. He stood at the doorway and said, "Go right in." They did, and then he followed them.

The dance started as soon as the sun went down and when the women came in, the Warriors were already dancing in their places. On the side where the women sat, the tipi cover was raised so that people might watch the dance. The women did not dance, they only sang the songs. Stories were told. When morning came, the servers took the women and sat one down in front of each dancer. If one of the dancers happened to have a relative among the women, he asked a friend to tell the server not to give that woman to him. Each man combed a woman's hair, washed, and painted her face. Then he gave the woman a present because he had kept her up all night. If the man didn't have a nice suit of clothes, he might give the woman a horse. When this was done, the women went home.

There was no sexual play at all with the women. If one of the Warriors made advances to the woman whose hair he was combing, she might get up and make a speech saying that the man had asked her questions. After the women left, the other Warriors would tear up his clothes and his tipi. This did occur twice, but I never saw it myself.

Coming-day added this information:—

When the women went home, their husbands told them to go to sleep. "But don't sleep very long. When you get up cook the best you have and bring it to *kinapem* (your husband; i.e., the Warrior who had painted her face)." In this way the man would show that he was not jealous and that he was as strong hearted as the other man (who had demonstrated his courage in giving a valuable gift). The husband might even tell the woman to give her best moccasins to the Warrior. Then the woman would take a vessel of food and go into the dancing lodge. There she would put the moccasins on the feet of the man who had combed her hair (cf. marriage customs), and would give him the food. Then she would go back.

It was as though the Warriors from the different societies were competing to see who would give away the most.

This last statement is the clue to the nuclear purpose of this ceremony. It seems to have been essentially a mechanism for that conspicuous distribution of wealth which was a means of attaining prestige.

Another aspect of the gift giving in this ceremony was related by Coming-day:—

There would be some young fellows in the lodge who would

try to go away when the women were brought in because they didn't have anything to give them. But the Warriors didn't let them go. They gave a woman to each of these poor young men. When gifts were presented in the morning, some Warrior would give the best robe he had to one of these boys, saying, "Give this to your wife." Sometimes a Warrior sent the server to bring something from his tipi for the young man and the Warrior's wife might give one of her finest dresses. These poor young men often gave the richest gifts, because everybody helped them.

Aiding a young man in this was redounded to the donor's glory. It is probable that not any young man would be helped, only those who showed promise of becoming men of high status.

To recapitulate the difference between the two status titles, any man who had performed valorous deeds in battle was called a Worthy Young Man. Most Worthy Young Men joined the Warrior society, although a few did not. One reason why some men did not join the society was because they did not want to be conspicuous—as every dancer in the Warrior lodge must be. Although most Warriors were also Worthy Young Men, a few were invited into the society because of their hunting abilities and their wealth. Even an adolescent boy might be allowed to dance with the Warriors, if his parents had distributed many gifts on the occasion when he first danced with the group.

Both the Warriors and the Worthy Young Men maintained prestige by demonstrating their dissociation from sentiments held by common people. They had to part with their material possessions freely and willingly; they were expected to be above sexual jealousy; they took it upon themselves to prepare corpses for burial, an unpleasant and dread task. When a Worthy Young Man died in battle the usual manifestations of mourning were foregone because he had willingly courted death.

At the present time the term *okihtcitaw*, Warrior, is applied in two senses. It denotes one who gives many gifts in the modern Grass dance, an extension of the Warrior's obligations of liberality. It also means one who is a fool, or is fool-hardy, from the Warriors' traditions of reckless bravery.

One of the Blackfoot societies was a boys' group called "Mosquitoes" which functioned as a true society organization.[6] Among the Plains Cree the term Mosquitoes was applied to any group of boys who happened to be out herding horses together. To vary the monotony of their task the boys would prepare to raid their camp. They would daub mud over the horses so that their owners might not recognize them and later reprimand the boys. Mounting the fastest horses, they dashed into camp. When they were seen coming, a great hubbub arose. Everybody yelled, "The Mosquitoes are coming." The women scurried to hide any food that might be exposed, for the boys' purpose was to snatch and carry off any edibles they could seize. Old men armed themselves with switches and pretended to strike at the boys as they rode past. Then the Mosquitoes retired and ate their loot. The raid was an occasion for high hilarity. It is to be noted that the Cree Mosquitoes did not constitute a society in any sense, and that the age-grade feature was lacking from the Cree society system.

CAMP LIFE

When the leader of the march had selected a camping site, the women unloaded the travois and set up their tipis. If the group consisted of only a few families, no particular arrangement of the tipis was followed. In large gatherings, a camp circle was formed with an open space to the south. The site was usually chosen for the availability of wood and water. As soon as the tipis had been set up, the women collected firewood and drew water. In summer, fires were kindled outside the door of each tipi and a tripod placed over them from which cooking vessels were suspended. In winter the fires were built inside and a rectangular drying rack placed over them.

Latrines were not made. The nearest copse served the purpose. When the camp was near a river, both men and women bathed during hot weather. Separate places on the stream were used by each sex.

Behind many tipis small tripods were set up on which sacred bundles were hung.

At dawn and at dusk old men called out. Fine-day recalled that:—

> An old man would get up just before daylight and cry out, "If the sun finds you working when he comes up, you will live long and be healthy." Any old man could do this. If one got up before the others, those who slept later didn't bother to call out. But it took a powerful old man or a big chief to call out in the evening, "Get my grandchildren ready to watch the sun go out of sight." All the children watched the sun go down. When the children fell asleep, sweetgrass smudges would be made so that they would have good dreams. This was done only when there was a large camp.

CRIME AND JUSTICE

Criminal acts were usually perpetrated in the heat of anger or jealousy, and in later times, during drinking bouts. Murder demanded blood vengeance by the relatives of the murdered man. If the avengers succeeded in putting the culprit to death, his family in turn would seek revenge. Disastrous blood feuds were averted by the intercession of Worthy Young Men.

The Worthy Young Men who were related to the participants in a feud forcibly escorted their relatives into a tipi. There the Sacred Pipestem was unwrapped. In the presence of this sacrosanct object, all quarrels had to be relinquished and resolved. The stem was pointed toward each of the vindictive relatives. When the Sacred Pipestem was presented to a man in this way, he was obliged to pass his hand along the stem and then over his face and chest. This gesture indicated that the angry man, compelled to do so by the presence of the Pipestem, relinquished his anger. The awe in which the stem was held was enough to abate the greatest heights of impassioned rage.

A payment of horses sometimes commuted blood vengeance. On one occasion, three brothers attempted to hunt, against the orders of the Warriors. When the Warriors rode out to stop them, one of the brothers fatally wounded a Warrior. The three turned and fled, but during an exchange of volleys one brother was wounded and later bled to death. The two surviving brothers were caught and overpowered. To avoid further bloodshed, an exchange of blood payments was arranged. The brother who had killed a Warrior gave the dead man's relatives two horses and the Warrior who had shot one of the brothers gave his family a fast horse. Skinner[7] notes that eight horses or an enemy's scalp constituted the usual blood money demanded by the parents of a murdered person. My informants did not know of this specific levy.

Murderers who were palpably in the wrong often fled to another tribe and did not return for many years. When they did return, the lapse of time had negated the necessity for vengeance and no blood money was paid. When the Sacred Pipestem was used to settle a quarrel or a feud, there was no necessity for the payment of blood money although the arbitrator often urged an exchange of gifts.

Justifiable homicide was recognized. Fine-day told this tale: —

Once I was playing the hoop and pole game in the center of

the camp circle when a respected young man named Small-hand, walked across to go into the Warriors' lodge. His wife was following him shouting bad things and abusing him. She was a bad wife. He took the cover from his gun and threw it behind him saying to her, "If you step over it, I'll kill you." She did, and he killed her.

The dead woman's eldest brother called his three other brothers to hold counsel. He said, "Our brother-in-law hurt us and has made us cry. Yet our sister deserved to be killed because of the way she treated him. The best thing we can do now is to ask our brother-in-law to eat in our tipis and to have our wives look after his moccasins. He was kind to our sister and it was all her fault."

They invited him into their tipis, told him not to be ashamed before any of them, and thanked him for his kindness to their sister up until the time the fatal shot was fired. They kept him all summer. And all summer he was sore hearted because he had made his brothers-in-law lonely and they had treated him with kindness.

In the fall he made a war trip to the south. Twenty-five men went out to get horses. Before they reached the enemy country Small-hand told them what was in his mind. "I came on this trip, not to return alive, but to do something worthy for my brothers-in-law. When I was in the Warriors' lodge after I had killed my wife I determined to sell my life dearly. If they would come to kill me, I would get some of them also. When they spoke to me kindly, I grew very sad and that is why I want to repay them."

After he had spoken, one of the men said, "You had better forget about it and stop talking about being killed." Small-hand replied, "I don't mean to go out and get killed; but if there is any fighting I will not be afraid. I'll do something really worth while for my brothers-in-law." Small-hand succeeded in taking some horses, but when he went back to get a Blackfoot scalp he was killed. When the war party came back to camp, the horses he had taken were given to his brothers-in-law.

Theft was rare and was usually the consequence of a thoughtless act by a young man. When a boy's father discovered that his son had taken something belonging to another, the parent would immediately return it to the owner.

Tampering with or wantonly appropriating sacred things was not punished by any mundane agency but inevitably incurred swift and sure supernatural penalties. A man who painted a design on his tipi cover without securing authorization for his act in a vision, soon after suffered death or the loss of a relative. Many stories were told of half-breeds who took cloth that had been left as an offering to the spirit powers. Death and woe did not fail to come upon them.

On occasions when there were numerous gift exchanges, a man might promise to give some gift at a later date. If he failed to fulfill his contract, his relatives, especially those who stood in a joking-relationship to him, teased and mocked him until he settled his debt.

Case examples of the manner in which the chief and the men of high rank in a band averted quarrels and ill-feeling have been previously cited. It was their obligation to keep peace and order in camp, to step between quarreling men, to use force, persuasion, gifts, and the influence of the Sacred Pipestem in restoring harmony.

KINSHIP

The basic principles of the kinship system are these:—

1. Each member of the second descending generation from ego is called *nosisim*, grandchild.

2. All in the second ascending generation from ego are *nohkum*, grandmother, or *nimusum*, grandfather.

3. There are differing terms for speaker's elder brother and younger brother, for the speaker's elder sister and younger sister. Siblings who stand in other relationships to ego are not differentiated according to age.

4. The dominant classificatory principle is that of cross-cousin marriage; although this type of marriage was not commonly practised.[8] Thus the term for daughter's husband (male speaker) is the same as that for sister's son. Other equivalences which illustrate the principle are the terms[9] for father's brother's wife and mother's sister, for wife's father and mother's brother, for sister's daughter's husband and son. While the term for cross-cousin is not used for ego's wife, it does have the connotation of "sweetheart."

One qualification to this rule must be made. In many instances there are two terms which may be utilized:—thus, sister's daughter's husband may be called *nikosis*, son, or another term may be applied to this relative. It is *ntosim*, which is now used specifically for cross-niece's husband. Lacombe[10] defines this term as "brother's son" which is consistent with the cross-cousin marriage principle, although the term is not at present used for that relationship. It seems as though a set of extraneous terms had been added to a consistent system based on cross-cousin marriage. In some cases the "extraneous" terms have entirely supplanted the "older" terminology.

5. Children of female cross-cousins are called by the terms for son and daughter. Children of male cross-cousins are called by the terms used for sister's son and sister's daughter.

124

6. Children of male siblings are called son and daughter.

7. Parallel cousins may be called by the terms for sibling or by a special term for this relationship. Children of male parallel cousins are called son and daughter. Children of female parallel cousins are called sister's son and sister's daughter.

8. The term applied to an affinal relative is also used for his siblings of the same sex. Corresponding terms are used for his siblings of the opposite sex. Thus, sister's husband's brother is called *nictaw*, the term applied to sister's husband. The primary meaning of *nictaw* is, male cross-cousin; hence, the term for sister's husband's sister is *nıtim*, female cross-cousin.

9. When kinship terms were used vocatively, there was a tendency to employ terms of closer kinship than would otherwise be used. This was done through the equating of siblings; for example, father's brother would be called father, mother's sister would be called mother.

My interpreter, Solomon Bluehorn, called Fine-day "grandfather," but called Fine-day's wife "mother." Solomon explained, "My father called Fine-day, *nohtcawes*, 'father's brother,' and so I call him grandfather. But the old woman is my mother's sister and so I call her 'mother' now that my own mother is dead."

The primary meanings of the thirty Plains Cree kinship terms are given below. The terms in parentheses are equivalent appellations. Thus the relationship, male cross-cousin, may be expressed either by the term second on the list, *nictaw*, or by the term *nictac*. All terms must have a personal pronoun prefix; *ni-* or *n-* mean "my."

1. *nimis*, elder sister
2. *nictaw*, male cross-cousin (also, *nictcac*)
3. *nıtim*, female cross-cousin (also, *nıtcimus*)
4. *nisis*, mother's brother
5. *nisikos*, father's sister
6. *nohtcawıs*, father's brother
7. *nikawıs*, mother's sister
8. *ntawemaw*, female parallel cousin
9. *nitciwam*, male parallel cousin
10. *nisım*, younger brother; younger sister (younger sister is also *nis mis*)
11. *ntɛhkwatim*, sister's son
12. *nictim*, sister's daughter
13. *ntosim*, sister's daughter's husband (also *nikosis*)
14. *nikosis*, son
15. *nosisim*, grandchild
16. *ntanis*, daughter

17. *ntosimiskwɛm*, sister's son's wife (also *ntanis*)
18. *nistɛs*, elder brother
19. *nohkum*, grandmother (paternal or maternal)
20. *nimusum*, grandfather (paternal or maternal)
21. *ntɛhtawaw*, parents (male and female) of child's (male or female) spouse
22. *ninahakicim*, brother's daughter's husband (also *ntɛhkwatim)*
23. *ninahakaniskwɛm*, son's wife (also *nictim*)
24. *ntaniskotapan*, great grandchild (also *nosisim*)
25. *nictac*, male cross-cousin (also *nictaw*)
26. *nɪwa*, wife (also *nɪwɪkimagan*); (*ninapɛm,* husband)
27. *nimanatcimahakan*, wife's parent (male and female) (also *nisis, nisikos*)
28. *nɪtcimus*, female cross-cousin (also *nɪtim*)
29. *nohtawɪ*, father
30. *nikawɪ*, mother

Additional terms are *nitayim*, co-wife, and *nikocak*, co-husband. Wives of father, other than mother, are called *nikawis,* mother's sister. Stepfather was *nohtcawɪs,* father's brother.

Strict mother-in-law avoidance was observed; nor could a man speak to his father-in-law except under one condition. If on returning from battle, a man presented his father-in-law with a scalp which he had taken, the taboo was raised. Thenceforward, he could speak with his father-in-law. A woman was very close to her mother-in-law, but could have nothing whatever to do with her father-in-law. In case of dire emergency, as when a woman wanted to warn her father-in-law of an enemy raid, she might turn her back to him and speak so that he could hear.

These restrictions extended to the siblings of the married person. A man's sisters could not speak to his father-in-law although they could speak to his mother-in-law. A woman's brothers might not speak either to her mother-in-law or to her father-in-law.

Siblings of opposite sex avoided each other. Coming-day said of the avoidance custom:—

A girl must never speak to her own brothers and a man must never talk to his sisters. When your sisters are young, you can play with them, but when they are about ten years old you must quit. Your sisters look after your moccasins and clothes, but they never talk with you. If necessary, you might say one or two words to your sister, but she would never reply. Suppose you came home hungry and only your sister is there. You can let her know that you want something to eat. She prepares the food and leaves the tipi. If another girl is present she can stay until you finish eating. The first time I ever talked with my

126

sisters was when I visited their reserve not long ago and they were very old.

A joking-relationship existed between grandparents and grandchildren. A man constantly teased and made obscene and derogatory remarks about his male cross-cousin, his brother-in-law, his male parallel cousin. To a lesser extent he was familiar with his female cross-cousin. A woman joked with her male cross-cousin and with her grandparents.

Among the River People band cross-cousin marriage sometimes occurred, but the practice was not common. Fine-day stated, "The Calling River People marry their cross-cousins, the River People do not." The one informant of the Calling River People band from whom kinship data were obtained, had married his cross-cousin. This custom was probably common among them, but not compulsory.

It often happened that a person who had lost a close relative would adopt someone who resembled the deceased in appearance. This was done by Fine-day.

> I took a man from Pelican Lake for a son because he resembles my eldest boy who is dead. He comes here every once in a while and I generally have a horse for him. Sometimes he brings me moose hides and meat in the winter. When I first took him for a son, I told him and gave him a horse. I didn't expect anything in return. If he is poor he doesn't have to give me anything. I am getting old and cannot do everything myself. When I built that stable he helped me.

Destitute old people were sometimes adopted into younger families. When Coming-day's daughter and son-in-law died, he and his wife were without close relatives. Chief Swimmer took them to his house, fed them, and treated them as his parents.

There was no adoption ceremony. Gifts were usually exchanged to mark the inception of a new relationship.

GAMES

Games were played at all seasons of the year, but especially whenever there was a large encampment. Then young and old competed throughout the day and sometimes through the night as well.

Men's Games
Striking the Bow (pakama·pekihtcitcıkwanıw). This was a very popular game and was usually the first to be played when a group of men congregated. Four players participat-

ed, two on a side. Each player had four arrows. A bow was braced against the ground and an arrow sharply struck against the bowstring. The arrow bounced off and served as a marker where it fell. The object of the game is to strike an arrow against the bow and have it fall across the feathers or head of the arrow marker. When one player succeeded in doing so, he and his partner received one arrow each, and he continued to try until he had missed four times. A player of the other side then tried. The play went on until the quivers of one side were emptied.

Shooting Arrows (e·pɪmutahkwatahk). The shooting arrows game was played in summer with two men on a side. One arrow was shot far out. The object of the game was to lean an arrow against this target. Each man shot four arrows. If none scored by touching the marker with his arrow, the player whose arrow was closest planted one arrow in the ground as a tally stick. The player who got four tallies won. He and his partner collected the arrows that had been bet on the outcome of the game. If one of the players made a direct score, he collected the arrows that had been shot as well as the stakes.

Rolling Game (tɪhtipintowan). This is the familiar hoop and pole game. It was played in the spring after the snow had melted, but while the ground was still hard. The hoop was a netted wheel, about a foot in diameter, made of a willow twig bent into shape and netted with rawhide thongs. A circular opening was left in the center. Each player was equipped with a dart, a three-foot pointed stick with a small projection near the tip.

Six or eight men played on a side. Each side lined up in turn and a player of the opposing side sent the hoop rolling past them. They threw their darts at it. When a player made a hit, he seized the hoop and ran after the players of the opposite side. If he succeeded in hitting one of them with the hoop, that player retired from the game. It seems that one player from the side of the man who had scored also retired from the game, although this is not certain. The last man to be touched with the hoop lost the game for his side.

A hit through the center opening was called "heart"; if the dart caught in the mesh it was called "claws."

Hoop Game (ɛ·tcihtcɛpintcoecihk). The hoop used in this game was made of several willow withes bent into circular form and wound with strips of buffalo willow bark. Each side of one to four men stood about thirty yards apart, facing each other. The hoop was thrown so that it rolled between them. The players shot at the rolling hoop with bows and small, blunt arrows. If one side registered a hit (the arrow had to stick in the hoop to count), the hoop was set up against a peg. The scoring side shot at it and if a hit was made, each man on the losing side shot over an arrow to the scorers.

Hand Game (mitcıhtcıhk) or Double Stick (kanıcwackwahk). This version of the hand game was played by two men or, rarely, by two women. It was played with a bone and a bullet as hiding pieces, although beads, twigs, and other small objects could also be used.

The players sat facing each other. At the beginning of the game each took one of the hiding pieces. They guessed in which hand their opponent had hidden the piece. When one player guessed correctly and the other incorrectly, the former took both hiding pieces and began the game.[11] He held his hands behind his back or under a robe and hid the pieces. He could place one in each hand, two in one hand, one on the ground and one in his hand, or both on the ground. He slowly withdrew his clenched fists from beneath the robe, crossed his arms, holding a fist over each arm. All the while he sang a taunting gambling song. His opponent watched his moves narrowly and then made the gesture which indicated his guess. The primary object was to guess in which hand the bullet was held. With the same gesture, the guesser also indicated where he thought the bone was. Points were gained by a player only when his opponent guessed wrong. A tally stick was stuck in the ground for each point gained. A player who won a point did not set up a tally stick for himself if his opponent had any set up. Instead, he took down one of his opponent's sticks. The play continued until one player had won an inning by setting up four tally sticks. The number of innings in the game was determined by the wagers. Thus, if a man bet a horse against a coat, he might stipulate that his opponent had to win eight innings to get the horse, while he need win only four to get the coat.

The guessing gesture consisted of pointing the index finger to the side on which the guesser believed the bullet to be held. The thumb indicated where the guesser believed the bone to be. When a voiceless linguo-labial trill was sounded as the guessing gesture was made, the signal was reversed.

When a player guessed where both the bullet and the bone were hidden, the pieces were passed over to him and it was his turn to hide them.

This game is still played. It is not as popular as the following variety of the hand game.

Bone Game (oskanihk or *micɩka·tcikanihk)*. This is now the principal gambling game. It is said to have been learned from the Flathead by the Plains Cree who fled from Canada after the rebellion of 1885. When they returned, they introduced the game to the rest of the tribe.

Four men or more played on a side. The two sides sat facing each other. A log placed in front of each side was beaten in time to the singing. To begin the game, one man on each side was provided with two short bones or sticks; one of each pair of bones was marked with a black band. The two opponents manipulated the bones and each tried to guess in which of his opponent's hands the unbanded bone was hidden. When one guessed correctly and the other incorrectly, the scorer's side took both pairs of bones and the game began.

Each group had a captain or leader who guessed for his side and chose two of his men to hide the bones. He chose them anew every time his side received the bones and might also delegate one to do the guessing for a time.

The two men who had each a pair of bones shifted them from hand to hand behind their backs or under a coat or blanket. They swayed and waved their arms with slow, deliberate, taunting motions. They and all the men on their side kept singing, their opponents remained silent. When they finally came to rest, with arms crossed and a clenched fist over each arm, the guesser made the gesture which indicated his guess. If he guessed where both unbanded bones were, his side took the bones. If he guessed where one unbanded bone was, his side took one pair of bones and their opponents set up one tally stick for themselves. The opponents continued to hide one set of bones until the leader guessed in which hand the remaining unbanded bone was placed. If the leader did not correctly indicate either of the banded bones, the opposing side scored two points. Thus a side could score only when the opposing leader guessed incorrectly.

The gestures of guessing were similar to those described for the preceding game. In the tabulation below, the bones are represented as in the hands of two men seated side by side; crosses indicate the banded, circles the unbanded bones.

Arrangement:	Gesture	Result
OXXO	Thumb and index finger outstretched, other fingers flexed	Correct guess: guesser's side takes both pairs of bones
OXXO	Index finger pointed to right; all others flexed	Guesser's side takes one pair of bones; opponents score one point
OXXO	Hand edgewise down middle	Guesser wrong; opponents score two points
XOOX	Hand edgewise down middle	Correct guess; guesser's side takes bones
XOXO	Index finger pointed to right; all others flexed	Correct guess; guesser's side takes bones
XOOX	Thumb and index finger outstretched, others flexed, plus linguo-labial trill	Correct guess; guesser's side takes bones

Ten tally sticks were used. To win a game, one side had to capture all ten sticks. Bets were made between individuals on the opposing sides.

Gambling songs were usually sung to nonsense syllables, although certain standardized and sometimes improvised words were also used. If a drum were available, it was used by the side which was hiding the bones. The movement of the prone hand forward, used by some tribes as a guessing gesture, was made just before the final gesture was made.

Shaking Game (pakecewıakan). This was formerly a favorite gambling game, but has not been played for many years. It was played with a wooden bowl and four kinds of counters. The counters included two lynx claws painted red on the inner surface, two metal slugs cut out of an old kettle, an eagle's claw, and four prune pits. The prune pits were cut flat and painted black on one side.

The player placed his hand over the mouth of the bowl and shook the counters. The highest score was made when the eagle's claw stood on end, or when both lynx claws showed red, or when the copper slugs were touching, or when all

131

the prune stones showed black. Other means of scoring points are not now remembered. Women played this game also.

Stake Game (itcımatwahto·k). A snow bank was piled up and a stake set in one vertical side so that it projected about two feet. Pointed willow wands, three or four feet long, were thrown at it by the players. Sometimes arrows were thrown also. The player who hit or came nearest to the stake won.

Sliding Game (tcoskumina·n). A five-foot strip of snow was brushed off to make a sloping surface and then iced. Twelve holes were made in the lower end, each of which had a different scoring value. Marbles were made by rounding tips of buffalo horns. The marbles were rolled down the slope and scored points when they came to rest in one of the holes.

Moccasin Game (maskicinetowewin). Culin[12] cites a description of a true moccasin game under this name in which an object was concealed in one of four moccasins. The opposing player attempted to guess where the piece was hidden. Fine-day gave this name to a sleight-of-hand trick in which seven bullets were made to disappear and were then found in a moccasin placed in front of the manipulator. The bullets were concealed in the palms of the manipulator's hand and quickly rolled into the moccasin.

Games Played by Men and Women

Stick Dropping Game (ıtcikahkwe·hk). A gambling game was played with four flat sticks, ten to fourteen inches long and about one inch wide. Each stick had a design burnt on one face, the obverse was blank. Each design was marked on two sticks. Thus two sticks might be marked with a snake, two with a conventionalized frog character, etc. The sticks were held up by their ends and dropped. Points were scored as follows:—

Position	Count
All marked sides up	4
All blank sides up	3
Two snakes up	2
Two frogs up	2

The number of points necessary to win a bet was determined by the players.

Stick Striking Game (tipaskwo·namatowin). This game was played by two persons with twenty-one peeled willow twigs, each about eighteen inches long. The bundle of sticks was rolled between the palms by one player and then divided

132

into two bundles, one held in each hand. The two were crossed and presented before the opponent who chose one of the bundles. The object was to choose the bundle with an even number of sticks. If he picked the one with an even number, his opponent divided the sticks again. When a player had picked the even bundle three times in succession, he took the whole bundle, and with a stereotyped gesture, pretended to kiss the sticks and placed them at his (or her) breast as though to suckle them. Then he picked up a handful of sticks and if he had an even number, he won the wager. The sticks exchanged sides when an odd bundle was chosen. Fine-day interpreted the kissing and suckling motions as a means of teasing one's opponent.

Culin[13] describes two stick bundles collected from the Plains Cree, one containing twenty-nine twigs, the other twenty-five. The collector of the latter bundle stated that the game was played by a number of men and women divided into two parties. When the guesser chose the odd bundle, the play passed to the opponents.

Skinner[14] mentions still another method of playing the stick game in which there were two players on each side and the object was to guess which one held the odd-numbered bundle. The side that guessed successfully four times won.

Playing with a Ball (epa·pa·towɪhk). This was played with a hide-covered ball, about five inches in diameter, stuffed with buffalo or antelope hair. Four to six players were on each side, usually composed of the followers of one chief. Each player was equipped with a curved stick, resembling a modern hockey stick, with which the ball was driven. It was not permissible to touch the ball with any part of the body. At the ends of the field, sticks were placed in the ground as goal line markers. The goals were one hundred to one hundred fifty yards apart. The game was won when one side succeeded in sending the ball across their opponent's goal line. There were no rest periods; the game continued until one side had won. Both men and women played, but never together.

Tossing the Ball (ekwackwackwintowɛhk). In this game a ball was batted back and forth between two players or around a circle of players. When one player tired or missed the ball, another stepped in to take his place, perhaps saying to the group, "Your eyes will be dry (i.e., from close watching) before I miss."

Stringing the Bone Cups (tapa whan). This is the familiar cup and pin game. Eight or nine phalangeal bones were strung on a thong with a wire or wooden pin at one end and a

133

buckskin flap at the other. The flap was pierced by a number of holes and the object of the game was to catch the pin in one of the holes or through one of the bones.[15] This game was played mostly by women.

Boys' Games

Bouncing Stick Game (kwaskweco·cimewin). A throwing stick was made by scraping a buffalo horn thin and fitting it over the end of a four-foot saskatoon wood stick. Fat was packed inside the horn and frozen solid to hold the shaft in place. The stick was slender enough to bend under the weight of the head. The throwing stick was called *cocimenak*. The object of the game was to throw the stick farther than one's opponents along a smooth stretch of hard snow. The stick was grasped at the butt, whisked around vertically, and released with an underhand motion.

Sliding Stick (cocimewin). A four-foot stick was whittled flat at one end to afford a finger hold. A mound of snow was made and the stick was whirled and bounced off the mound. The player who sent his stick farthest won. A variant of this game, in which the dart had to be thrown through several snow barriers, is listed by Culin.[16]

Tops. Boys played with small tops made of wood, stone, or horn which they spun by beating them with a whip.[17]

Slings. Slings were made of a small square of hide to which two long thongs were attached. A favorite pastime for youngsters was skipping stones over the surface of a river.

Gliding Stick (pakitcaman). Hardwood sticks about two feet long were whittled flat on one side and had a snake or duck carved on the other. A zigzag road was beaten down a hill and the sticks sent down this path. The stick that slid farthest won.

According to Culin's[18] information several barriers were placed across the iced track. Considerable skill in handling the stick was needed to make it pass through the barriers.

Women's Games

Testicle Game (opwe·piticiweqehk). This was played with a double ball made of two bags of deerskin stuffed with buffalo hair and connected by a strip of hide (Fig. 14). Four to eight women played on a side. The players were equipped with sticks two to three feet long, and curved at the end. Two tipis on opposite sides of the camp circle were selected as goals. The game started in the center of the field when one of the players threw the ball in the air. The ball could not be

Fig. 14. Three Stages of the Woman's Shinny Game, Poundmaker Reserve, Battleford. Photographs by P.E. Goddard, 1911.

135

touched with the hands or feet nor could it be carried on the stick. It was advanced by being passed from one player to another. The players tried to knock the ball off their opponents' sticks. When the ball had been passed beyond the goal, the scoring side won.

Culin[19] illustrates both ball and stick and includes a statement that the goals are usually about a mile apart.

Shooting Women's Arrows (εpımatıkanatahk). Two digging-sticks were set close together. The players stood several yards off and tried to throw their digging-sticks so that they fell between the two upright sticks. The sticks were thrown with an overhand motion.

When camp was being moved, young girls often went along throwing their digging-sticks at some target to see who could come closest to it.

Contests

Contests of strength and endurance were often held and large amounts were bet on their outcome. Wrestling bouts were of several types. Ordinary catch-as-catch-can wrestlers tried to break through their adversary's guard to secure a firm hold on his abdomen. The loser was the first man to be down on the ground full length. Two falls were necessary to win a bout.

In "head over heels" wrestling, the contestants lay on their backs next to each other, with their heads in opposite directions. They locked adjoining legs and arms. Each tried to turn the other over.

In "back wrestling" the opponents kneeled back to back and were bound by a loop of rawhide thong passed around their chests. Each pulled forward, trying to force the other over backward.

Yet another way of wrestling was to lock fingers at arms' length. Each contestant tried to pull the other forward. Cameron[20] describes a type of wrestling in which the contestants sat facing each other, knees bent, and the soles of the feet opposed. They grasped a stick which was held between them and at a signal each tried to pull the other over.

Foot races were very common and were usually over courses several miles long. Short sprints were not often run.

Riddles

Riddles were apparently unknown but tongue twisters

were often repeated with much merriment. A typical one is:—

ayapatcinacεhk over hilly country	*nipaspas* by walking	*kitasis* the muscles
kitanεhtan slip from the calves	*konta* for nothing	*ayapatcinacεhk* over hilly country
peyakwanohk in one place	*nipaspas* your loin	*kitcitcas* ligaments
ka·yetan break from walking		

The meaning may be translated as "The muscles are stripped from the calves when walking in hilly country. You keep walking, but stay in one place though your thigh muscles are breaking."

String Figures

String figures were made but none of the forms could be remembered by my informants.

FOOTNOTES

[1] Cf. LOWIE, ROBERT H., Plains Indian Age Societies: Historical and Comparative Summary (Anthropological Papers, American Museum of Natural History, vol. 11, part 13, New York, 1916), p. 910.

[2] Despite this testimony that Warriors from three bands had collaborated in purchasing a dance, the same informant and all others who were questioned, stated that each band had only one Warrior lodge.

[3] CAMERON, WILLIAM BLEASDELL, The War Trail of Big Bear, Boston, 1927, pp. 139-140.

[4] SKINNER, Political Organization, p. 519.

[5] *Ibid.*, pp. 520-521.

[6] WISSLER, CLARK, Societies and Dance Associations of the Blackfoot Indians (Anthropological Papers, American Museum of Natural History, vol. 11, part 4, New York, 1913), p. 420.

[7] SKINNER, Notes on the Plains Cree, p. 72.

[8] HALLOWELL, A. IRVING, Was Cross-Cousin Marriage Practised by the North-Central Algonkian? (Proceedings, Twenty-Third International Congress of Americanists, New York, 1930), pp. 519-544; HALLOWELL, A. IRVING, Kinship Terms and Cross-Cousin Marriage of the Montagnais-Naskapi and the Cree (American Anthropologist, n.s., vol. 34, Menasha, 1932), pp. 171-199; MICHELSON, TRUMAN, Some Algonquian Kinship Terms (American Anthropologist, n.s., vol. 34, Menasha, 1932), pp. 357-359.

[9] All terms are for male speaker.

[10] LACOMBE, Dictionnaire et Grammaire, p. 666; Lacombe's terminology is not markedly divergent from that given here except for his terms for father's brother, *N'okkumis* and mother's sister, *N't'osis*.

[11] For a graphic account of this game see CAMERON, The War Trail of Big Bear, pp. 147-149.

[12]CULIN, STEWART, Games of the North American Indians (Twenty-Fourth Annual Report, Bureau of American Ethnology, Washington, 1907), p. 342.
[13]*Ibid.*, p. 230.
[14]SKINNER, Notes on the Plains Cree, p. 81.
[15]Cf. CULIN, Games of the North American Indians, p. 535.
[16]*Ibid.*, p. 403.
[17]*Ibid.*, p. 734.
[18]*Ibid.*, p. 403.
[19]*Ibid.*, p. 652.
[20]CAMERON, The War Trail of Big Bear, p. 156.

The Individual Life Cycle

BIRTH

No particular taboos were imposed during pregnancy. Several informants stated that a pregnant woman took care not to strain or over-exert herself, but that no prohibitions of a supernatural nature were observed. During childbirth, the woman kneeled against a chest-high support, made by lashing a pole across two forked uprights. Three women usually attended at birth. The head midwife stood behind the mother and massaged and supported her. Another received and cared for the newly born infant and cut the navel cord with a knife. The third was a younger woman who assisted the other two. The afterbirth was wrapped in an old piece of hide and hung on a tree in the forest. This was done to prevent it from being eaten by dogs. To induce an easy discharge of the placenta, a vessel of hot water was placed under the woman as she knelt.

The navel cord was cut at a point one hand grip and one thumb's breadth from the child's abdomen. The downy inside of the prairie puffball *(Lycoperdon Gemmatum Batsch)* was packed over the infant's navel and held in place by a bandage. The knife with which the cord was cut was not used again until the navel had healed over. The cord was later placed in an ornamented bag which the child wore around its neck.

The child was not bathed after delivery, but was dried with dry rotted wood or moss. Leather from the top of an old tipi cover, soft and well smoked, was used to wrap infants. Mother's milk was squeezed on the child's eyes. The baby was not nursed until two days after birth. Until that time, the infant was permitted to suck a piece of hard fat pointed at one end.

There were no special twin beliefs. The twin born last was considered to be the elder.

Several days after birth the child was placed in a moss

bag made by folding an oblong piece of hide or cloth lengthwise and sewing one end. It was stuffed with dried moss, with rotted and crumbled wood, or with pulverized buffalo chips mixed with cat-tail down. Two perforated strips of hide were sewn on each side of the long opening and laces were drawn through them. When a child urinated or defecated in the bag, the moss was shaken out and a fresh supply of absorbent stuffed between the child's legs. Children were, and often still are, kept in the moss bag until they are able to toddle about.

Cradleboards were also used but, within the memory of the oldest informants, were purchased from the Hudson's Bay Company. These may not have been made before the advent of traders, for Mrs. Paget states: —

> Some of the Indian women used a cradle to lie their babies in, and in the old days the women who had these were looked upon as possessing a luxury.[1]

The trade cradleboards were rectangular and had a forward projecting arc of wood at the head. A U-shaped wooden rim set upright on the face of the board some four inches from its margins, served as a holder in which the child, wrapped in the moss bag, was placed and lashed to it.

NAMES

Not long after a child was born its parents prepared a feast. They invited a number of people and especially an old man known to have powerful supernatural guardians. Female children were usually named by some old woman renowned for her supernatural prowess. When the company assembled, the father formally asked the old man or woman to name the child and at the same time presented the shaman with a filled pipe and some cloth to offer to the spirit helpers. The old man lit the pipe and then prayed aloud to *manito* and to the power who had inspired the name to be bestowed. After the shaman had spoken he sang one of his power songs. Then he asked for the child, took it in his arms, and pronounced its name. The name was derived from an incident or a character in one of the shaman's visions. He asked the spirit guardian from whom the name had come to protect the child.

Then the infant was passed from arm to arm around the tipi.[2] As each person took the baby, he held it for a moment, addressed it by name, and added a wish for its future happiness. The child thus was passed around to all the guests until it reached its mother. Then the food was eaten and the ceremony so concluded. Skinner[3] states that the naming occurred when the child was about a year old and that four old men were invited to conduct the ceremony.

A special relationship existed between a person and the man who had named him. The two called each other *nikwɛmɛ,* and seem to have maintained something of the grandparent-grandchild relationship. In the ceremony accompanying the painting of a tipi cover, the man who had named the owner of the tipi led the procedure.

If the child fell ill, its parents might call in a shaman other than the original namer to bestow another name. The former name was not abandoned and the child thenceforward was known by both names. The motive for renaming was not because the first name was unlucky, but that the child might receive additional supernatural aid with another name and namer. Adults could not change their names in this way. A grandfather could give one of his own names to his grandson in order that the boy might inherit some of its supernatural potency. The old man would let it be known that only the child was to be called by that particular name.

Nicknames based on personal attributes and foibles were freely given and commonly used. Fine-day recalled that:—

> Children would sometimes give each other nicknames in play and they would stick. I had a very good friend whose name was really Redthunder. When we were small we used to call each other *nikowa·t.* We would say, *"nikowa·t,* let's go somewhere." This is not a Cree word at all and means nothing. But it stuck to my friend and that is what he was always called. He was killed by the Piegan and the place where the battle occurred is known as "The Place where *nikowa·t* was killed."

Great fighters might name a child after one of their exploits in battle. Thus Chief *paɪpwat* named his infant son, Dragging-him, because he had once dragged a Blackfoot out of an entrenchment to the Cree lines in order to scalp him. But it was not usual to give such names and it was still rarer for a father to bestow a name on his own son.

A man who had performed a noteworthy deed or had had a remarkable experience in battle might be called by a name commemorative of the event. One such name was Strike-him-on-the-back, given to a warrior after a Gros Ventre had crept up behind him and brought a bow down on his back. A name of this kind was not formally bestowed, but was a matter of popular usage.

Sometimes a child was named for an unusual occurrence.

Soon after Many-birds was born, her mother had propped the cradleboard against a tree and had gone off to attend to some task. When she returned, a great flock of birds had settled around the child and on her cradle. Because of this incident the child was known as Many-birds.

An eldest son often inherited his father's name, especially if the father had been a man of distinction. Again the name was not formally bestowed. The people of the camp simply called the son by his father's name.

It was considered impolite to ask a man for his name. Mrs. Paget[4] ascribes the taboo against mentioning one's own name to the belief that the supernatural guardians from whom the name originated would be offended if the names were pronounced. However, a name that originated from a battle deed or from a peculiar incident could be freely uttered. It was disrespectful to refer to a dead person by name. An exception was made in the case of famous fighters whose names were recalled and pronounced long after their deaths as a means of perpetuating their glory.

The terms for various ages of man were:—

oskawasis, infant
tcahkopitcawaconic, child in cradleboard
pamtactimu, crawler
nipawew, stander
otcectiw, takes a step
pimuhtew, walker
pimpuhtaw, runner
mapecic, boy
iskwecic, girl
oskinikiwiginis, boy of ten or eleven
oskinikiskwesis, girl of ten or eleven
kicapewia, boy at puberty
kicickwekiw or *oskwekiw,* girl at puberty
oskinikiw, boy about fourteen
oskinikiskwew, girl about fourteen
kɛhteoskinikiw, youth of about twenty
kɛhteoskinikiskwew, unmarried young woman
kɛhteyatciw, young married man
kɛhteyiwiw, young married woman
kɛceyinu, elderly man
notokwea, elderly woman
kawikehkaw, very old person
nipahikɛhkan, already dead, senile

CHILDHOOD

The period during which children were nursed varied. Some women weaned their babies when they were about a year old; others kept them at the breast much longer. A child of four or five on a present-day reserve was seen to reach under his mother's dress for the breast and put it to his mouth. The fact that intercourse was supposed to cease until the child was weaned was a factor in curtailing the nursing period.

When a child was weaned, it was given a tough piece of meat to suck and put to sleep with a woman who was not its mother. The woman slept with a paunch full of soup next to her body. When the child awoke, she fed it the warm soup with a mussel shell spoon.

A broth made of the scrapings from a buffalo hide was the first non-milk food given to infants. Later, a soup made of blood and berries was fed to the child. Mothers also chewed meat and vegetable foods thoroughly and placed them in their babies' mouths.

Lullabies had distinctive melodies and were usually sung to nonsense syllables.

As soon as a child was able to run about, a navel cord bag was tied around its neck so that it hung down the back. The bag, finely decorated with beads and quills, was about four inches long. It had two compartments; in one the cord was stored, the other was filled with tobacco. An old man or woman might call the child and take a pipeful of tobacco from the bag. Before the old person smoked the pipe, he would offer it to his spirit helpers and ask them to grant good fortune to the child. In this way the parents assured a continual round of supplication for their child. Not all boys and girls wore these bags for only the wealthy could afford to keep them filled with tobacco. When the child reached puberty, the bag was discarded. Boys abandoned it in the woods when on a hunting trip; girls laid it on the ground when they went out to collect firewood.

Children wore little or no clothing. Boys ran about naked until they were about five years old, when they were given a breechclout. At the same age girls were dressed in garments similar to those worn by adult women. During a rainstorm children were stripped and sent out to get wet. Whenever the band camped along a river, the children spent much of their time swimming. They soon learned to use the dog paddle stroke and to float on their backs. The best swimmers among them swam with an over-arm stroke.

They were never beaten and rarely reprimanded. One informant related that as a child he habitually threw himself on his back and yelled if he disliked his food. The habit was broken when his parents placed a vessel full of water behind him. As he went over on his back, he got wet and when everyone laughed he also laughed.

Even during the most sacred rites children were accorded perfect liberty. An extract from my journal relating to a Sun dance witnessed in 1935 reads:—

> A youngster, a little over two years old, came wandering into the Sun dance lodge. He stopped near the circle of singers and stood there for fully fifteen minutes gazing about him. He sucked his thumb for part of the time and was quite stolid throughout the period. Four drums were pounding away a few feet from him and some twenty dancers bobbing and piping.
>
> Children often wandered in and out of the lodge. At one time during the dance, two boys of about four engaged in a battle, throwing stones and chips at each other. One would run up and pound his adversary with a twig at intervals. I was a bit perturbed, being in the line of fire. But no one else seemed to care; eventually the boys ran out to play elsewhere.

Children spent a great deal of time with their grandparents and relatively little with their parents who were preoccupied with adult tasks and cares. Once, in telling how the souls of the dead sometimes visit the earth, Fine-day incidentally said, "The old people come back to see their children and especially their grandchildren, for the Cree love their grandchildren even more than their own children." When asked for an explanation, he replied that when a person grows old he has more time to spend with the children and so grows very fond of them.

Sex knowledge was not formally imparted, but was acquired by boys and girls largely through observation and the talk of their contemporaries.

A boy often attached himself to a young man who was a good hunter and a brave warrior. The two were constant companions and called each other, *niwıtcewahakan*, "he with whom I go about." The young man taught the boy how to hunt and fight and was proud of his protégé, since the boy's attentions symbolized his own merit.[5]

When there was a large encampment, boys of different band divisions would play together and become close friends. When camp was broken, one of the boys might go off with his friend's family. After a time the two would go to live with the other household. The boys exchanged gifts and each received many things from the other's parents. If one died, the parents of the surviving boy sent him to live with the parents of his deceased friend for a while. The boy considered both households equally his own. When two such friends grew up and went on the warpath, they shared all dangers. If one were killed, the other was also usually killed. The relationship term they used was the same as that given above, *niwɪtcewahakan.*

PUBERTY AND WOMEN'S OBSERVANCES

Girls were secluded for four nights at their first menstruation. A small tipi was set up at some distance from the encampment and there the girl remained with an old woman. The pubescent was kept busy chopping wood, sewing, and preparing hides. At night, the old woman would tell her tales and perhaps relate some didactic anecdotes concerning sexual matters. Before the girl was allowed to step out of the tipi the old woman made sure that no men were in the vicinity, for should she look on a man, he would be liable to lose his supernatural guardians. The girl used a pointed wooden stick to scratch her head. During her seclusion, she was given very little food to eat and was expected to cry a good deal. This four-day period was regarded as the most auspicious time in a woman's life to receive a vision. Women did not otherwise engage in a vision quest and might experience visions at any time.

On the fourth night the women of the camp gathered and went out to the girl's shelter. Four old women who had strong spirit helpers[6] piled up the wood that she had chopped and then prayed that the girl have a good life. Then they pushed the pile over and each woman carried off some of the wood. They led the pubescent to her father's tipi. Four sweetgrass smudges were kindled, two outside the door, two inside. The girl stepped over them one by one; and as she straddled each smudge, two women inside the tipi prayed to their spirit helpers. The assembled men and women followed the girl in. A feast was served and the woman who was leader offered up a pipe to *manito·* and to her own spirits. After the feast, the girl's parents distributed gifts to the guests.

There were no corresponding puberty rites for boys although the vision quest was usually undertaken about the time of puberty.

During menstrual periods a woman slept away from her usual place at her husband's side. She left the tipi only when its cover was painted with a supernatural design. The wives and daughters of men who had important medicine or sacred bundles in or near their tipis slept elsewhere during catamenia. The presence of a menstruating woman was believed to defile a religious ceremony and she was forbidden to come in contact with any religious paraphernalia. If a menstruating

145

woman were among the onlookers at any ceremony, the supernatural powers would take offense and bring about an untoward occurrence.

This did not prevent the women from acquiring supernatural powers; and some of the most respected shamans were women. However, they could not lead or vow to perform important ceremonies. Thus, a woman who wanted to give a Sun dance would have to induce her husband to make the vow. If she had been given a song in a vision, she taught it to her son or her husband and he would sing it during the ritual. Women had no officially recognized voice in political and social affairs.

MARRIAGE

Marriage was a simple procedure. The father of a marriageable girl took a gift, usually horses, to the father of a young man whom he considered to be a good match for his daughter. Commonly enough, it was the man's father who initiated the proposal. If the parents agreed to the marriage, the bride's people made a new tipi. As it was being erected, the groom came into the bride's tipi and sat down beside her. She presented him with a new pair of moccasins; his acceptance sealed the marriage. The two then moved into a new tipi furnished with the necessary equipment by the bride's family. The newly married couple usually lived near the husband's parents although this was not an inflexible rule. Skinner's information from an eastern group states that residence was matrilocal and that the bride was herself sent with the marriage proposal.[7]

Parents preferred to choose husbands and wives for their children from among their own band. The potential merits and faults of young people were gauged by the character of their family; its ability to reciprocate with suitable gifts was an important consideration. Hence, it was important to know the family thoroughly before setting up an affinal relationship.

While parents customarily selected their child's spouse, courtship and love affairs leading to marriage were not unknown. A man would lie in wait for a girl whom he liked while she was berrying or on her way to fetch wood or water. He would try to engage her in conversation; if she were willing to talk with him, he knew that his suit was well received. After several such conversations, either the boy or the girl, or both, might ask their parents to make the marriage arrangements.

Quite different from this pre-nuptial courtship were the love-making escapades of young men. An unmarried young man would forewarn a girl that he intended to visit her at night and would steal up to her tipi. Having previously ascertained on which side of the tipi the girl slept, he would reach under the cover and gently wake her. When she felt her lover's hand she took his fingers and played with them. This finger play was the prelude to more intimate caresses. If her parents became aware of his presence, they would drive him off. No other punishment was inflicted.

Unmarried young women were always chaperoned and escorted when they went out of camp. If a young man came upon a girl alone, she was fair game for him. Apparently, women rarely repulsed such advances and never made an outcry. To discourage these attempts women sometimes tied thongs around their thighs and over the pubic region.

Virginity was not of such great concern among the Plains Cree as it was among some of the neighboring tribes. A bride who was also a virgin was prized, but if she were not, it made no great difference. An unmarried girl who gave birth to a child was married off to an elderly or poor husband if the father of the child were unwilling to marry her. If she thereafter comported herself with modesty and dignity, no stigma was attached to her or to the child.

After marriage there was a good deal of gift exchange between the affinal families. The groom was obligated to contribute as much as he could to his father-in-law. If a man's parents were dead, he had to live with and support his wife's parents. In the words of one informant, "A man is never finished with giving horses to his father-in-law." The brother of a woman also received many gifts from her husband and had an important voice in arranging his sister's marriage.

Coming-day gave this account of the marriage procedure:—

> A man had to be a good hunter and had to have a war record in order to have a good standing in marriage. As long as he had a good name it didn't matter if he had few relatives. The people with daughters of marriageable age looked for such a young man and gave their daughters to him even if he were poor. He might not be good looking and she might not want to go; but she must obey her parents and especially, her brother. Brothers and sisters didn't speak to each other, so if a brother sent word to his sister, she had to obey immediately.
> So it was with a man who had a son. When the boy grew up the father would watch for a girl who was not crazy (i.e., loose

or frivolous) and who was a good worker. If the parents agreed to a match, they told the young people to live together. They did so, even if they never had seen each other before.

After they were married, the man's father would give the girl's father some clothing and a horse. The girl's father reciprocated with gifts. The young couple went back and forth between his and her parents. The husband might be mean and the girl would return to her parents. The father of the girl would send her back with clothing and horses to shame her husband into being kind to her. By that means many young men were stopped from being cruel to their wives.

We have here an example of the manner in which the giving of a gift brings social pressure to bear on the miscreant.

Men of rank often had two or more wives. Because of the obligations of liberality and hospitality borne by men of high status, the household work in their tipis was burdensome. The wife of such a man often asked her husband to take another spouse to aid in the work. The senior wife usually directed the others, but she and her children had no special prerogatives. The additional wives might be sisters of the first, but not necessarily so.

Women were usually married three or four years after they had reached puberty. Men did not marry until they were about twenty-five. Young men often sought to avoid marriage, for they then had to settle down and work hard to provide for their wives and their parents.

Elopements occurred; the couple went to another camp to avoid parental opposition. After a while they returned, and if they appeared well mated they were accepted as man and wife.

Adulterous wives might be beaten but the most highly regarded procedure was quite otherwise. A brave man, upon discovering his wife's infidelity, gave her to the lover. The lover, in turn, was obliged to reciprocate with a gift of a horse. Thereafter, the woman was the other man's wife and the two men formed a special relationship involving the exchange of gifts. Fine-day related this incident:—

> My mother's brother once caught a man with his wife. He gave her to the other man. Later, he told us, "That was the only way I could get over it. It was a hard thing to do. I didn't sleep for four nights; but if I hadn't done it, I might have decided to kill that fellow. I loved my wife. She didn't love me or she wouldn't have done such a thing. Afterward I got over it and I never think about it any more."

148

WIFE EXCHANGE

Wife exchange operated on a similar basis. A young man might become infatuated with the wife of another. He proposed an exchange of wives to the woman's husband. If the husband considered him worthy he consented and the exchange was made from time to time. The two men became close companions and gave each other many presents. The men called each other *nikocak,* "fellow husband" or *niwɪtcewahakan,* "he with whom I go about." The women used the term, *nita·yim,* for each other. This relationship reflected considerable honor upon the participants, for only the most stout-hearted of men could become intimate companions of their wives' paramours.

A story told by Coming-day illustrates the wife exchange procedure. It was told as a humorous tale because the central character is an old man who desires to be known as a brave man although he is really not up to it.

> *tetepwatat* was an old man who had a blind wife. His father's brother's son was an unmarried young man. To his wife *tetepwatat* said, "Old woman, I want to take my cousin for a fellow-husband." Thus, he told his wife to sleep with his cousin so that he might become his very good friend. "No, you will get angry and beat me." "No, I have made up my mind to do this thing and I won't get angry. I can't get angry anyway, because I am already related to my cousin. I have always envied two men who go together, eat together, move camp together. People point them out as fellow husbands." Finally, the woman consented.
>
> In the evening when the old woman was preparing a meal, *tetepwatat* called in his cousin and gave him something to eat. Then he filled a pipe. "Here, cousin, take this pipe. Do as I shall tell you. My cousin, the reason I have called you here is that I have always liked to see two men go together and love each other as fellow husbands. I am willing that you sleep with this old woman of mine tonight. I'll sleep elsewhere." The other man knew that *tetepwatat* was not good tempered. "Cousin, even the bravest in camp have no control over themselves when it comes to that. It is very hard." "Cousin, I have thought of it for a long time. I have told this old woman. I have made up my mind not to get angry and I expect you to comply with my wishes." "All right, but as soon as I know that you are becoming angry, I'll stop (the relationship)."
>
> That evening the two sat in the tipi talking, telling stories, smoking, till late at night. Then *tetepwatat* said, "Cousin, it is late. I will go to the Warriors' lodge and sleep there. In the morning I'll come back. Don't go home until I come and we'll

eat together. Old woman, get the bed ready so that you and my cousin may sleep."

When *tetepwatat* came back to the tipi in the morning he looked up and saw no smoke coming out. They were still asleep. He took a piece of wood and knocked at the door, clearing his throat at the same time to let them know it was he. "Hm, hm, my cousin. You are not sleeping?" "No, I am awake." *tetepwatat* went in and started the fire. He sat at the visitor's side of the tipi and said, "Old woman, get some water so that my cousin may wash. When people are sleeping sometimes they don't know where they put their hands."

They ate and talked. Then the cousin went home. The old woman said, "Your cousin has left some clothes for you." *tetepwatat* took the clothes, which were very fine. "My cousin must think a lot of his body to give such good clothing." (i.e., his gifts reflect honor on himself.)

Then *tetepwatat* turned to his wife. "Did you and my cousin have each other for lovers last night?" "O, so that's what is on your mind, to ask me questions like that." "Women who do it tell their husbands everything." "You told me to do it and you told him to do it. We did." "All right, all right, I can't get angry because you told me. One more thing, is he a better man than I am?" "Yes, he is." Then *tetepwatat* rubbed his chest as though he had been hurt, but he didn't allow himself to get angry.

A ceremony involving sexual confession was noted by Skinner.[8] No trace of such a ritual could be found among the River People.

If a couple proved to be incompatible, either the man or the woman returned to the tipi of his or her parents. The one who remained cared for the children and kept the household effects. After a time both were free to marry again.

DEATH, BURIAL, AND MOURNING

Several forms of burial were practised. Most commonly a grave about five feet deep was dug and the bottom lined with a robe. Two horizontal slots were cut in the long sides of the grave about a foot below the surface. After the corpse was placed in the grave, sections of tipi poles were tightly fitted into the slots. A robe was placed over the poles and a rawhide pegged down over the excavation. Earth was heaped over the rawhide.

Sometimes a kind of burial chamber was prepared. This was most often done in winter when the ground was frozen too hard to excavate. A place was cleared where two trees grew about four feet apart. Between the trees a flooring of sticks about seven feet in length was laid down. Over this surface a grave house of logs was built. The standing trees support the long walls of the burial box. The timbers were notched and fitted together in log cabin fashion. After the body was lowered into the chamber, a flat roof was placed over it and covered with rawhide. Brush was heaped over the whole structure.

Tree burial was also a winter practice. A platform of poles was built across the forks of a large tree. The body was wrapped in a robe and placed on the flooring. Several rawhides were wrapped around the platform and corpse and the whole was tightly bound with thongs.

Another form of interment was practised only when the deceased had requested it. A tipi was pitched on a hill and the body placed in it, reclining against a willow backrest. A low stone wall, perhaps three feet high, was built inside the tipi around the corpse.

Occasionally, a tipi was pitched and left standing over a grave. This was done because a dead person's tipi had to be disposed of and placing it over the grave was a ready means of doing so. The Calling River People, now on the Crooked Lake reserves, erect small gable-roofed board houses over the graves at the present time. Skinner[9] describes the grave house as "a little canvas-covered tent roof." Food and tobacco offerings are placed inside these houses from time to time after the death. The other bands of Plains Cree have never built these grave houses.

A tale which relates how several women were killed by the Blackfoot includes a description of their burial. The bodies were placed in a cave excavated in the side of a cutbank. The mouth of the cave was closed with tipi poles and earth and stones pushed down over it. Hayden[10] mentions burial mounds in the Plains Cree country, which were made for the mass burials following the smallpox epidemic of 1776-1777.

Soon after death had occurred, the face of the deceased was painted, his hair combed, and the body clothed in the finest garments. A lock of hair at the crown of the head was brushed up and bound with sinew. The legs were bound together with the knees slightly flexed. When rigor mortis had set this position, the bindings were removed. The hands were folded over the chest, palms down.

When the corpse was placed in the grave, a filled pipe was laid between the left arm and the body. A birchbark container full of grease was also interred. The head, resting on a pillow, was always toward the north. Men did all the work connected with burial, except that of preparing the corpse of a woman.

The data published by Skinner differ in several respects from the burial customs noted by the writer. Skinner[11] states that all of the personal property of the deceased was buried with him, that the corpse was placed in the grave in an upright position, that a feast was given immediately after the burial and again a year later. These traits were not practised by the River People Band.

If the death occurred in the evening, people gathered in the tipi where the corpse lay and remained through the night. They consoled the mourning relatives and told stories to distract them. It was one of the obligations of men of status, whether Chiefs, Warriors, or Worthy Young Men, to make the funeral preparations and to assist in the burial rites.

In the morning these men had their wives prepare a meal for all those who had been in the mourners' tipi. When they had eaten, one of the men who had dragged an enemy out of his tipi or who had a similar deed to his credit rose. He stood at the back of the tipi and counted his coup, "I attacked the enemy, killed one of them and dragged his body out of the tipi to scalp it. Now I am going to pull this dead body out." The sides of the tipi were raised, the corpse placed on a robe and pulled out from the side. The mourners gathered around the body. The closest relatives of the dead person began to wail and then all the others followed their example.

Four men carried the body on a robe and led the procession to the burial place. The whole camp followed them, everyone wailing. At the grave, the body was let down on the ground and a Warrior counted coup again. He told how he had been in a fight and had taken a scalp. Grasping the braid on the head of the corpse, he cut it off saying, "And this is the way in which I cut that scalp." The braid was tied to the end of a stick set upright in the ground at the head of the grave. Before the body of an important man or woman was lowered into the grave, all those present filed past the corpse and kissed it. Informants stated that this custom was followed in pre-reserve days. However, it may have been introduced by the half-breeds. After the burial was completed, the people went back to camp.

In mourning, the close relatives of the deceased unbound their hair and wore it loose. They wore no other clothing than a robe and cut gashes in their forearms and legs. The mourners were the parents, siblings, spouse, children, and parents' siblings of the dead person. Close friends and grandparents showed their sorrow by letting their hair hang uncombed. They remained in mourning until some man of prestige or, for women mourners, the wife of such a man, told them that it was time to cease mourning. This person combed and braided the mourner's hair, thus officially terminating the mourning period which usually lasted four days.

On the fourth night after the death, a feast was prepared by the relatives. The man who had cut the braid from the head of the corpse went to the grave and brought the braid into the tipi. He was seated in the place of honor with a little of each kind of food prepared for the feast before him. The stick bearing the braid was set up at his side. A pipe was filled and given to him. He took four puffs and then pointed the stem upwards to *kice·manito·*, the Great *manito*. After addressing a prayer to the Creator, he successively pointed the pipe to those spirit powers whose duty it was to care for the souls of the dead and petitioned their aid.

The pipestem was first pointed to the north where dwelt Touching Spirit (*tcahkapewatayohkan*), who directed the wandering soul in its course. In the same direction lived Touching Spirit's sister, Old Woman Spirit *(notokwewata-yohkan),* who taught the soul how to comport itself and kept it from looking back in its journey. Then the stem was pointed to the south to Old Man *(kice·yinɪw)* who kept the souls in his Green Grass World where they remained eternally. Below the ground was Ghost Stone *(tcɪpaɪyusinɪ),* a spirit power which guarded the soul.

After the pipe had been pointed toward these spirits, it was passed around the tipi and each man puffed at it. When it was smoked out, one of the mourners cleaned it and propped it up before the leader of the ceremony. Meanwhile, the leader offered food to the same spirit powers. His prayers asked that the braid become imbued with the soul of the deceased so that, on occasion, the soul might revisit the earth.

Then two servers passed food around in a clockwise direction and always turned in the same direction. They served all the food that had been prepared, being careful not to spill any lest the powers be offended. The server who finished first waited until the other had completed his task and then broke some sweetgrass over the fire, saying, "It is all finished and ready now." The leader then prayed to *manito·* again, asking that the people be given His blessing.

Then all ate. If anyone could not eat the whole of his portion, he took whatever was left to his home. The server who finished his meal first placed some sweetgrass on the fire, passed a pipe through the sweetgrass smoke, and handed the pipe to the leader who offered up the pipe and again prayed that the spirit of the deceased enter the braid. Then the pipe was smoked around and returned to the server who passed it over the sweetgrass smudge and once more handed it to the leader who held the stem vertically above his head, prayed to the spirit powers, and lowered the pipe three successive times. As he lowered the pipe for the fourth time, he laid it on the ground, the stem pointing toward the door. This signalized the conclusion of the ceremony and the spectators filed out of the tipi.

When none remained, except the leader and a few old people, the braid was untied from the stick, wrapped in cloth or hide, and bound with thongs. A bit of tobacco was placed next to the hair. The wrapped braid was placed in the Carried on the Back Bundle *(nayahtcikan),* together with the braids of other deceased members of the family.

These bundles were sacred family possessions and were carefully guarded. When camp was moved the women carried them slung across their backs. The bundle hung up beside the bed of the head of the household at night. Sometimes toys or clothes of deceased children were included in them.

It often happened that the supply of tobacco in camp would be exhausted. At such times a feast was prepared, pipe offerings made, the bundle unwrapped, and tobacco "borrowed" from it. When a fresh supply of tobacco was available, the amount taken from the bundle was replaced.

Whenever camp was pitched near a grave, a feast was given by the relatives of the person who had been buried there. The grave was cleaned of plant growth and the site generally tidied. Since the establishment of cemeteries on the reserves, this feast is given annually and all the graves cleaned at once.

The personal property of the deceased was given away. While there was no overpowering fear of death and of corpses, it was felt that the possessions of a dead person always reminded the relatives of their loss and so unnecessarily protracted the mourning period. For that reason, according to informants, the things used by the deceased were usually not kept by his family. When a man died, the widow gave his clothes to an old man who distributed them to men in camp of the same age as the man who had died. The wives of the recipients gave women's clothes to the widow. The tipi was abandoned, or more often, exchanged for another. The eldest son took charge of the horses inherited and distributed them among his brothers and sisters. At least one horse had to be reserved for the widow, so that she might not have to go on foot when camp was being moved. The elder brother kept the horses allotted to his unmarried brothers until they were married. Young men were considered to be irresponsible and would only squander their possessions. The married daughters of the deceased inherited none of the horses, but their brothers were obliged to assist them if they and their families should be in need.

Fast horses or the favorite horse of the dead man were not used in hunting until some time following the death. Their tails and manes were cut short as a token of mourning. Great danger was attached to using a dead man's weapons or horse in battle. After the weapons or the horse had once been through a fight, however, the danger was lifted and good fortune attended those who used them. No danger was involved in using the horses or guns of dead enemies.

When a woman died, the widower gave away all her things and expected nothing in return. The dogs were not disposed of, since they were accustomed to the household and would not remain with another family. The moccasins made by the dead woman were put away until the widower or one of his relatives went off on a war trip. They were worn on the journey and thrown away in the enemy country. The purpose of this action, according to one informant, was simply to discard the mementoes of the dead women in a distant place.

After a widow's death, her possessions were given away if her children were young. If she had mature daughters, they put her clothes aside for a while and later wore them.

FOOTNOTES

[1]PAGET, The People of the Plains, p. 122.
[2]See Appendix p. 366, for further account of the naming ceremony.
[3]SKINNER, Notes on the Plains Cree, pp. 68-69.
[4]PAGET, The People of the Plains, p. 109.
[5]MANDELBAUM, DAVID G., Friendship in North America (Man, vol. 36, no. 272, London, 1936), pp. 205-206.
[6]As evidenced by the songs and curing ability possessed by the woman.
[7]SKINNER, Notes on the Plains Cree, p. 72.
[8]SKINNER, Political Organization, p. 540.
[9]SKINNER, Notes on the Plains Cree, p. 75.
[10]HAYDEN, Ethnography and Philology of the Indian Tribes of the Missouri Valley, p. 243.
[11]SKINNER, Notes on the Plains Cree, pp. 74-76.

Religion and Ceremonialism

SUPERNATURALS

The concept of a single all powerful creator was dominant in Plains Cree religious ideology and ceremonialism. Every prayer for supernatural aid, every ritual addressed to divine powers, had to begin with an invocation to *kıce· manito·,* Great *Manito.* All the phenomena of the universe are considered to be under His control and everything was created by His will. He was not personalized, nor given any definite abode other than a general empyrean locale; He did not appear to men in visions. Moreover, He was conceived as being too great, too awesome, to be asked directly for His blessing.

The intermediaries between the Creator and man were the spirit powers, *atayohkanak.* Their number was legion, for they possessed every living thing. For example, there was a bear spirit power, a horse spirit power, a hummingbird spirit power, a spirit power of the maple tree. In addition, there were folkloristic characters such as the trickster, *wısa·hkɛtcak,* who were also spirit powers. Non-organic objects, too, might be spirit powers and one of the most important of all was "stone." Natural phenomena, thunder, wind, the sun, were among the mightiest spirit powers; an individual spirit might be localized in a pebble of unusual shape. Occasionally, a spirit power no one had ever heard of before would reveal itself. Thus a man once called upon "Iron Capped Eagle" for aid, another mentioned "Two Legged Buffalo" in his prayers.

When a spirit power appeared to an individual in a vision, it became that person's *pawakan*, his supernatural guardian, or better, his spirit helper. The power did not guard and protect a man against all contingencies, but rather aided him in definite, prescribed situations. When a spirit power revealed itself, it enumerated to the visioner the blessings to be conferred upon him, and the feats he might accomplish under its aegis.

157

The spirit powers resided in their namesakes, but were not confined to them. The spirit power of bear dwelt in every bear, but was also present somewhere on high, where lived all the powers. Moreover, there was a concept of a greater bear power, overlord of the other bear spirit powers, who was called "Great Parent of Bear." The greater spirit powers were never seen, but they controlled those which did reveal themselves. Similarly there were masters of Moose, Horse, and all other spirit powers.

SOUL AND AFTERWORLD

Quite apart from the spirit power concepts were the ideas concerning the life force in man. This force was present in all living things and was called *ahtca·k,* which we may translate as "soul." The soul entered the body at birth and left at death. It resided along the nape of the neck. Only when danger threatened did a man feel the presence of his soul along the back of his neck.

During a vision the soul could leave the body and travel about with the spirit helper. It was the soul that experienced all contacts with the supernatural visitor. After death, the soul wandered about aimlessly for four days, then traversed the Milky Way, and entered the land of the dead. In the Green Grass World *(oskaskogi·waski),* men, women, and children, all lived a carefree life.

Although souls might return to earth on occasion, especially during the ceremony for the Carried on the Back Bundle, they did not appear in visions nor were they able to bestow power on men. No offerings were made to departed souls. When prayers were addressed to them during the ceremony, or at the cleaning of a grave, they were asked to petition the higher powers to render aid to mortals. Sometimes souls returned to earth and haunted the habitations of men. The soul of a man who had died before he could fulfill his promise to give a Sun dance haunted the camp of his son until he gave the ceremony. The failure to provide a suitable funeral feast might cause a soul to linger until the feast was finally given. Such souls made their presence known by weird noises and were called *tcɩpayak,* ghosts.

Unpleasant things, vicious animals, thorned bushes, diseases, arose from *matcɩ·manito·,* Evil *Manito.* His spirit powers were Cougar, Lynx, Snake. They could grant certain abilities to a man, but exacted the life of his wife or child in payment. Currently, the Evil *Manito* is modeled after the

Christian devil and the whole concept of evil power may possibly spring from missionary influence.

The term *manito·* primarily referred to the Supreme Being but had also many other usages. It was applied to manifestations of skill, fortune, blessing, luck, to any wondrous occurrence. It connoted any phenomenon which transcended the run of everyday experience.

THE VISION QUEST

When a boy approached puberty, his father or grandfather might send him out "to fast." Not all boys sought visions, but many did. The boy and his father went to some lonely place, carrying with them cloths for offerings and a filled pipe. The place chosen was often atop a high hill, although any secluded spot might be chosen. Some boys entered a bear's den, others would repair to a tree overhanging a river, some stayed on a raft, a few remained on an unsaddled horse for the duration of the quest. It was believed that a boy was more likely to be visited by the horse spirit if he sought a vision on horseback and would have a better chance of seeing the buffalo spirit if he pillowed his head on a buffalo skull. But there was nothing inevitable about this, and sometimes a youth who slept on a buffalo skull or who remained in a bear's den would know many spirit powers but not the buffalo nor the bear.

The boy stripped to his breechclout and daubed himself with white clay. A brush shelter was constructed and the offering cloths hung on it. A buffalo skull was commonly placed inside the shelter. The father offered up a pipe and then went back to camp.

For several days and nights thereafter, the boy wept and prayed and fasted, continually concentrating upon his desire for supernatural visitation. He might take it upon himself to stand all through the day, or to look into the sun, or to perform any other feats which would hasten the vision, for the spirit powers came to a person because they knew of his suffering and pitied him. Therefore, the greater tortures a boy underwent, the more certain was he of attaining his purpose.

While the boy slept, he might see a person coming toward him. It was the power that was to be his spirit helper. The visitor identified himself, often by momentarily changing into the guise of its namesake. The boy was led to an assemblage of spirit powers, all in human form, who sat around a great tipi. There the youth was told the gifts that had been granted him. Very often he was informed that he would be able to cure the sick. The procedure he must follow and the song to be used were then revealed. Some youths had conferred upon them the right to perform a certain ceremony, perhaps the Sun dance. Others obtained the ability to construct a buffalo pound. A much desired blessing enabled a man to lead a war party. In every case, the visioner was taught a song which had to be sung when the vision capabilities and prerogatives were being exercised.

Upon awakening, the boy went back to camp. He did not immediately relate his vision, and his experience might not become known until he was called on to cure or to lead a ceremony in middle age. Often the quest was repeated, either because of instructions to do so in a previous vision, or in an effort to secure additional power, or because of failure to receive a vision on former attempts. A man might have several spirit helpers, each of whom taught him a song or gave him certain capabilities.

Girls never deliberately sought visions but were apt to acquire power during menstrual seclusion. The spirit helpers usually, though not always, appeared to women as females, to men as males. Skinner[1] noted "a course of training given [to children of both sexes] to inure [them] to the hardships of the puberty fast." Nothing of the sort occurred among the River People. Visions might come unsought. Fine-day made the following remarks:—

> The spirit powers may come to you when you are sleeping in your own tipi when you are young. If you want to be still more powerful then you go out and fast. The ordinary dreams you have while sleeping are called *pawamuwin*. They are not worth anything although sometimes you dream of things that are going to happen.
>
> You can tell a power dream in this way. You are invited into a painted tipi where there is only one man. The crier, who is the Raven Spirit, calls, and many come. I myself knew right away that they were spirit powers. I sat and thought to myself, "That is Horse, that is Buffalo spirit." The one that invited me said, "That's right."
>
> I was called many times and they always told me the same thing — that I must do more fasting. Each time they invite me to a different painted tipi. Often after I wake up I wonder why they didn't tell me anything. I had nothing to do with girls when I tried to dream. [Men were not as likely to receive visions as boys because they had been contaminated by intercourse with women.]
>
> Finally, they told me that this would be the last time. They want me to go and fast for eight days. One of them said, "Try hard to finish these eight days, for that will be all." I gathered

as many offerings as I could. It was during the moon just past [July] and there was plenty of food in camp so I knew the people wouldn't move for a while.

I promised to stand and face the sun all day and to turn with the sun. Only after sunset would I sit down. I had heard that this was the hardest thing to do and that is why I resolved to do it out of my own mind. I thought that I could help myself a little in that way. [By making himself suffer more, he would secure greater blessings.] The sun wasn't very high when I got tired. I suffered all day. I tried all kinds of ways to stand, but I was played out. I raised my hands and cried; I could hardly finish. The sun went down and I just fell over. That was the first day.

The next morning I got very thirsty. I was not hungry but was thirsty all the time. On the fourth night my brother came with horses to get me. I told him I would stay. He came again on the sixth night but I said I would remain for two more nights. He said, "From the way you look, I may not find you alive."

All kinds of different spirit powers came to see me every night. Each one who invited me gave me power and songs. Then one gave me the power to make the Sun dance.[2] That is how I got power and how I know many songs. Pretty nearly every night now I sing some of those songs.

The supernaturals sometimes deluded the visioner, promised him certain boons and forsook him when he attempted to carry them out. Fine-day continued:—

When the Sun dance was given to me, I thought I knew how to make water come out of my whistle to give to the thirsty dancers. I tried it secretly. I painted my face and blew the whistle as I should, but I didn't go up to the center pole [as the spirit had told him to do]. Suddenly the whistle was blocked, I thought surely water was coming. Then it cleared. No water. That is one time when the spirit powers fooled me. Maybe if I had had faith and gone up to the center pole I could have done it. Maybe.

It was not entirely an unmixed blessing to be under supernatural tutelage, for a man might displease his spirit helpers, perhaps by violating one of their ordinances or by reneging on a promise made to them. If a person promised to give a cloth offering to the Horse spirit power and then failed to do so, a horse would kick him or harm him in some other way. The men and women who had never had a vision and who possessed no spirit helpers were under the guardianship of kıce·manito· alone.

A man's spirit helper might impose a food taboo. Thus a noted shaman was prohibited from eating dog flesh by the Dog spirit power. However, not every man who had the Dog

161

spirit power was forbidden to eat of the dog. Commonly a doctor would be enjoined to give to his patients a bit of the food tabooed to him.

SHAMANISM

Since many individuals had supernatural power bestowed upon them, shamanism was not confined to the few but was practised in varying forms and degrees by a good part of the tribe. Certain people were known to have especially strong powers because of the results they had effected, and they were called on more often than others to invoke their spirit helpers.

The prime blessing which could be granted in a vision was the ability to cure. When a person fell sick, his relatives sent gifts of clothing or of horses to a doctor. A number of cloths were sent along with this gift, which were to be offered by the shaman to his spirit helpers. Gifts for the shaman's wife might also be sent, for an old couple often cooperated in curing. There were many women doctors. If the gift were accepted, the shaman soon came to the side of the patient. He made a pipe offering and called upon his spirit helper to vouchsafe the assistance promised in the vision. The shaman repeated the circumstances of the dream, told when and where it was received, and notified the powers that he was about to demonstrate the procedure revealed to him. Thus the doctor publicly asserted his right to undertake the cure by reminding the spirit powers that he was upholding his part of their pact and that it was incumbent upon them to fulfill their promises.

The shaman then sang his power songs to the accompaniment of a rattle. The singing was usually carried on by several assistants as well as by the shaman himself, and continued throughout the treatment. Drums were rarely used in doctoring.

The shaman commonly performed magical acts which further established his supernatural connections in the belief of his patient and of the onlookers. One doctor might make a whistle disappear and reappear; another might plunge an arrow into his chest; yet another might walk barefooted over hot coals. That the shamans themselves took a thoroughly practical attitude toward these feats was evidenced when Fine-day told me that another shaman had once taught him how to take live coals into his mouth. The heat of the coal frightened him, however, and he was not able to follow the

162

instructions. Officially, however, all these feats were performed in accordance with directions imparted in a vision.

After offerings had been made, prayers uttered, tricks displayed, the singing rose to a crescendo and the shaman came close to the patient. Holding his mouth a few inches from the sick person's skin, he blew over the patient's body. With a sudden movement he placed his mouth over the affected part and sucked out the cause of the illness. Sometimes a tube, made of a section of horn or of a piece cut out of a gun barrel, was used in sucking. Then the shaman spewed out the matter that he had withdrawn from the patient's body.

The shaman usually displayed a yellowish, foul smelling substance as the cause of the trouble. Often, however, the illness came from an intrusive object sent by a malevolent shaman. Should such an object be extracted, the doctor placed it on his open palm and showed it to the spectators. It might have the shape of some strange insect, or it might resemble a piece of flint, or perhaps be only a bit of a twig. These objects were sent by shamans who were jealous or resentful of some person's accomplishments. Swimmer related that a *pitcitcihtcikan,* literally "something moving," had been sent into his leg by a rival whom he had beaten in a footrace. A woman informant, Lives-in-a-bear-den, said that such an object had entered her when she and her husband had had an unusually favorable trapping season. Someone had envied their catch and had made use of his powers to bring them to grief.

In sending the object, a maleficent shaman held it on the palm of his hand, addressed his spirit helpers, and blew the *pitcitcihtcikan* toward the victim. The evil thing was whisked away and entered the body of the unfortunate recipient, there to remain until the person died or until a shaman succeeded in extracting it. Only a shaman whose spirit helpers were stronger than those of the sender, could remove the intrusive object. Once it was extracted, the shaman who sent it had not long to live.

While it was a serious matter to run foul of an evil shaman, there was no overwhelming nor all pervasive dread of sorcery. Three informants freely and calmly told me how they had become ill because of an intrusive object and described the curing ceremony and its effects. In the case of Coming-day, the sorcerer had succeeded in blinding him. The other two had recovered immediately after the extraction of the object. The evil powers of the Woodland tribes were more greatly feared than those of one's own tribesmen. Plains dwellers had little traffic in sorcery.

Another way in which an object or evil medicine might enter the body was through the use of sympathetic magic. The shaman might mould a figure of a man in clay, or cut out hide in the shape of a person. The intrusive object was inserted into that part of the body which was to be affected, or, in the case of the hide figure, medicine was placed over that part.

Love medicines might be used in a similar way. Fine-day recalled this incident:—

> I have often heard of love medicines, but I saw only one man use them. He had two wives. One was a young girl who did not like him and who kept leaving him. He went to an old man who had that medicine. "I'll have a dog cooked for you to give a feast to your medicine."[3] He also took off his clothes and gave them to the old man.
>
> The owner of the medicine said, "Yes, she'll come back if the medicine is still strong." He spread out the medicine. We boys who were there were told not to look. But I did. The owner cut two figures out of bark, one a man, one a woman. He sang his medicine song. He put some medicine on a little stick and touched it to the heart of the male figure, then to the heart of the female figure. "If the medicine is good, she'll be back tonight. We'll sing a little while tonight." They stopped singing about midnight.
>
> While the girl was sleeping that night she woke up thinking of the man. She had to go to him. She never left him again. Sometimes women bought love medicines also.

Love potions were a Saulteaux specialty, although a few Cree made them. One of Skinner's informants[4] said that

> the Plains Cree have many powerful love-medicines which other Indians buy from them.

However, this informant came from the Calling River People band, who were nearest the Saulteaux.

To ward off baleful influences, amulets were worn or carried. They were composed of some small object encased in a beaded envelope. The nature of the enclosed object depended on the vision instructions received by the maker. One man might be told by his spirit helper to use a bear's claw as an amulet. Another might carry a small bone. For fifty years, Fine-day wore two leaden gun shot, strung on a sinew, around his neck. *Maskwa* still carries a tiny bag filled with a mixture of certain roots which one of his spirit helpers had taught him to concoct. Often the old man who named a child made an amulet for the baby which was always worn thereafter.

Most shamans also administered herbal medication to their patients. While the shamanistic procedure described above emanated from vision experiences, the knowledge and use of plant medicines was almost always purchased or inherited. The medicinal ingredients were kept wrapped in little packets and were stored in the whole hide of a small animal. The hide was similar to that used in the *mite·wiwin,* and indeed many medicines were obtained by transfer in that ceremony.

Although the fame of "Cree medicines" was widespread, the writer's informants asserted that the Plains Cree had originally received most medicines from the Saulteaux (Plains Ojibwa). *Maskwa* told of a Plains Cree who went on an expedition to the east for the express purpose of securing medicines. He took with him two horses loaded with fine clothes. The Saulteaux were especially glad to get the horses, for they had very few. They took him into their *mite·wiwin* lodge where they taught him the use of many plants for medicinal purposes. Whenever it was possible, Saulteaux practitioners were called in to treat the sick.

The Plains Cree regarded the Saulteaux and the Wood Cree as "bad medicine" men who fought by magical means rather than by strength of arms. Hence, care was taken not to offend visitors from these tribes and their company was not sought.

The following tale of a shamanistic contest illustrates the attitude toward the Saulteaux. It was told by Pierre La Cree whose father was Saulteaux, his mother Plains Cree.

> My mother's brother was a man with many visions. He was of the West People band. When he was young he was a Catholic. As he grew up he discarded Christianity and as soon as he did, the visions appeared to him. He dreamed about everything: all that flies in the air and all that crawls on the earth. He dreamt that they all took pity on him. His name was Beautifulfeathers.
>
> In the fall of the year there would be a great encampment at the trading post near Edmonton. One year he was camping there. There was an old Saulteaux who had caused a lot of trouble through bad magic. When the Cree saw him they said, "Here's where we have trouble." Sure enough, before long a man came around announcing that the Saulteaux was challenging the Cree medicine men to a contest in his tipi. They all had to go lest the old Saulteaux work even more harm on them if they stayed away.

Beautiful-feathers waited until the last when the Saulteaux's large tipi was full of men. He entered and took a seat near the door. Next to the Saulteaux was a barrel of whiskey, a case of twist tobacco, ammunition, and a brand new gun. These were to go to the winner of the contest.

The Saulteaux began by lighting the pipe and passing it on. But when the next man took it, a snake head darted out of the stem. The man passed it on and so it was passed around until it reached Beautiful-feathers. He just took the snake's head between his teeth, drew it out, threw it away, and smoked the pipe. Then the pipe was smoked around.

"Aha," said the old Saulteaux, "Things are beginning to become interesting. Young man, you and I are going to play a little. You begin, young man." But Beautiful-feathers said, "No, old man, you are the challenger, you begin."

Then the Saulteaux put his thumb in the rifle barrel, ripped it open, and handed it over. Beautiful-feathers grasped the barrel, drew his hand up, and the gun was whole again.

"Aha," said the Saulteaux, "things are interesting." He took an eagle feather, smoothed it, and said, "Young man, watch out." He hurled the feather at Beautiful-feathers who caught it. Beautiful-feathers also smoothed the feather and said, "Old man, watch out." He hurled the feather and it pierced the old Saulteaux until only the tip was showing.

The old Saulteaux fell over, but he had provided four singers for just such a time. One singer began and the old Saulteaux stopped bleeding. The second joined in and the Saulteaux began to breathe. When the third and fourth sang, he was all right. Then he rolled the whiskey, the tobacco, the gun, outside of his tipi and said, "Young man, you win." When the Saulteaux went back to his country, he died.

I could tell you of the things my mother's brother did for two days and two nights.

Berdaches usually became noted shamans. When asked whether he knew of any transvestites, Fine-day said:—

They were called a·yahkwew. It happened very seldom. But one of them was my own relative. He was a very great doctor. When he talked his voice was like a man's and he looked like a man. But he always stayed among the women and dressed like them. He was a great gambler and when he lost all his clothes he made others for himself. He was a good worker and would go digging wild turnips with the women.

His father got sick and died. He cried a lot and said, "Although I knew I could save a life I was ashamed to doctor my father."[5] Some time later his little brother got sick. He got someone to make two drums for him. He made his own rattle. Before it dried he put marks on it and then hung it up. He put nothing inside, but four nights later it rattled in the wind. He took it down.

His brother was pretty weak and had lost consciousness. He got someone to call the old men together to sing with him. They had a big tipi where there was a lot of wood along the river. Pretty soon you could smell the sweetgrass. You saw a big fire, the sound of the rattle, and then you could hear his voice sounding very loud as he prayed. The drums beat at the same time.

I was not inside the tipi, but we could hear him stand up. He stood on the fire. Then he started to blow his sick brother. His blowing made a loud whistling noise. The young fellow began to feel better. Then he sang and blew on him again. Then he sucked at him where he was sore, "This is what has been hurting you. You will be all right now." When he was finished he said, "I will have another name now. They will call me *piecuwiskwew,* thunder-woman. My brother's name will be *piecuowasis,* thunder-child." He doctored the boy for four nights and saved him.

We called the boy Thunder-child from then on, but we called him *a·yahkwew* still for that's what he was. He had another name, *oskas·ewis,* Clawed-woman. He wanted to be called *piecuwiskwew,* because Thunder is a name for a man and *iskwew* is a woman's name; half and half just like he was.

He never took a wife, nor did he bother the women or the men. We never teased him or made fun of him. We were afraid to, because he was a great doctor.

Once an old man brought him some clothes and a horse to doctor a boy who had fallen from a horse. He took them right away. He called for my father to sing with him. Again he made a big fire. He took his dress off, just wore a breechclout. I heard the sound from the outside as he stood on the fire. He blew at the side of the boy and called for a wooden bowl. "He has got matter inside of him, but not in his lungs." He sang again, he held his hands over the sweetgrass and tapped one hand over the other. Suddenly, you could see bearclaws sticking from his palm. He laid the boy on his belly. He stuck the bearclaw in the boy's neck. Then he sucked out a lot of matter and spit it into the bowl. He rubbed his hands over the wound and though it was daylight we couldn't see any marks on the boy where he had been stuck. "I've got pretty nearly all the matter out. But there is some left. I don't want to take it all for fear that I'll hurt the boy. I'll take the rest out this evening." In the evening he went back and took more out. He saved that sick boy.

He saved a lot of people. Sometimes he would doctor them only once and they would be well. He got lots of horses that way. Even those who had only one horse would give it to him so that he would doctor.

But he himself got sick and no doctor could save him. Once he lost all his clothes gambling and he borrowed some to wear from a woman. She gave him a dress that was not clean — that she had worn while menstruating.

He got very sick and asked someone to put up a conjuring booth. They finished it before sundown. Then they carried him out on a blanket to a little hill some distance off. Two young fellows wrapped him in a buffalo hide and tied him all around.

167

Then they laid him with his head toward the booth. My father started to sing *a·yahkwew's* songs. It was getting dark. As soon as the young men tied him they ran to the booth as fast as they could. But before they got there, he was inside.

Then you could hear the different spirit powers talking. An old man asked them why *a·yahkwew* was sick. "You knew, *a·yahkwew*, that the clothes you put on would hurt you. We try to do everything we can to save you, but we can't. What you call *pawakanak*, spirit helpers — that's us. But we are afraid ourselves of what you have done."

He suffered for a long time before he died. He was not old when he died. He had a dress with the picture of a flying porcupine done in quillwork on the back. He had made that himself and never gambled for it. They buried him in this dress.

Failure to effect a cure might be ascribed to several causes. As in the case above, the death of the sick person

Fig. 15. Fine-day near Center Pole of Sundance lodge. Little Pine Reserve, 1935.

might be caused by a transgression so grave that the spirit powers themselves were helpless. More often, the doctor, on seeing a patient sink dangerously low, announced that the malevolent influences had been at work too long before he had been called. The friends of the sick person might say that the shaman's spirit helpers were weak or perhaps that he had made an error in the ritual revealed to him.

Certain surgical and medical techniques were used for specific ailments. They were often based on practical experience and used in conjunction with the common shamanistic procedures of singing, blowing, and sucking. Setting broken bones was described by Fine-day in these words:—

> I was once chasing buffalo when my horse fell and broke my leg. When they took me home an old man sat me on a pillow and drove a stake at my crotch and another a little beyond my foot. He pulled my leg out, patted the bones into place, then put medicine around my leg. He took sticks, laid them parallel to each other and bound them together with three cords, one at each end, one across the middle. He wrapped these sticks very tightly around my leg. They stuck out beyond my foot and he fastened them to the two stakes. I had to stay that way for four days and four nights.
>
> Since it was done to me, and I saw how to do it, I have set six broken legs. It is not necessary to dream of it in order to be able to set a broken arm or leg. You must watch how it is done and also be brave enough. Some of those whose legs I set fainted. That made it easier for me to do it right.
>
> For broken ribs they would cut the skin open with flint and rub medicine in. They also made them sneeze with the powdered petals of a yellow flower (mustard).

Blood letting was frequently practised. The lancet was made of a sharpened piece of metal or flint set into a short stick and tightly bound in place. The lancet was held over a vein and flicked with the index finger so that the blade made a quick, sharp incision. For pains in the upper part of the body the arm was tied above the elbow until the veins swelled. Then a vein at the elbow was cut and a little blood let out. To stop the bleeding the arm was simply doubled until the circulation was reduced. For pains in the abdomen a vein over the ankle was tapped.

Men who were bitten by mad wolves or mad dogs were tightly wrapped in buffalo robes until they were completely encased. A smudge fire was made and the victim rolled in the fire and made to inhale the smoke. The combined smoke from the fire and from the singed robes caused him to vomit and this was believed to help in the cure.

Those stunned by lightning were wrapped in a robe and tossed in the air with another robe.

Frost bitten hands or feet were pricked with a sharp bone. Medicinal alkaline salt or snow was rubbed into the scratches and packed around the frozen part.

Wounds were washed with buffalo hair dipped in water in which certain medicines had been dissolved.

A bit of a man's foreskin would be cut off as a cure for intestinal worms.

Raw buffalo liver dipped in gall was considered to be a specific for tuberculosis.

Weather control was known, but was not often attempted. The shaman simply sang his power songs and asked his spirit helpers to bring on more favorable weather.

There were few hunting medicines. Those in use were mainly for the purpose of luring fur-bearing animals into traps. In all, there was remarkably little concern with the supernaturals in the procuring of food.

A shaman's ability to cure might bring him considerable fame and respect, but it did not particularly enhance his social status. A man could never become chief merely because he was a noted doctor. However, every man of prestige was believed to have powerful spirit helpers, else he could not have won his fame on the field of battle.

BUNDLES

Another type of sanction which might be imparted in a vision, was the ability to make bundles containing war equipment to protect the wearer from wounds and from other hazards of battle. Favorite devices were feather bonnets, buffalo horn bonnets, the whole hide of an owl or an eagle sewn on a cape-like garment, bear paws worn around the neck, figured shirts, and painted shields. These were kept carefully wrapped in many layers of cloth or hide. They were hung on a tripod behind the tipi of the owner and guarded against contact with contaminating persons. Any article which had been designated by a spirit power as being magically protective would be kept in this way. Thus, one man's spirit helper had told him in a vision to make a decorated lance, and had promised that he would not be wounded if he carried that lance into battle. The vision seeker made the weapon and used it in a raid. Since he took part in a skirmish and emerged unhurt, the lance had proved its worth and was thereafter highly prized.

The generic term for sacred bundles is *wıskwe·hpita·kan,* "kept in a clean place." Each bundle had its own descriptive name. One containing a bear's paw was known as "chief's son's hand," the term, chief's son, being a circumlocution for bear. Whenever such equipment was used in battle, a cloth was added to the bundle as an offering to the powers for the use of the device. When bundle contents were worn on ceremonial occasions, a cloth had to be given to the bundle just as when they were worn in battle.

The bundles contained little more than the single article of war equipment encased in many layers of cloth. Sweetgrass and tobacco and small charms, such as peculiarly shaped pebbles, might also be enclosed. These bundles were never used in curing and were unwrapped only when the gear was to be worn in battle or in a dance. Some men were known to wear their war-bonnets or capes on the hunt, but this was exceedingly rare.

When a bundle had demonstrated its efficacy by protecting the wearer during an encounter, it was highly valued, and young men setting out on the warpath sought to obtain it. They would present gifts to the owner and would ask him to transfer the bundle to them. If he were willing to part with it, either because his own fighting days were over, or because the gifts were very attractive, the transfer would be arranged. The bundle was unwrapped; the war gear was handed over to the purchaser by the former owner, and the songs and procedure that went with the bundle were taught to the new owner. Each bundle had its own song and particular ritual procedure which were imparted in the vision and without which it was valueless.

A bundle which had been made by Big-bear, a chief of the River People band who led them in the rebellion of 1885, is now in The American Museum of Natural History (50.2-3739 A-M). It is the "Chief's Son's Hand" mentioned above. The charm itself is simply the tanned hide from a bear paw, with the claws attached. It is sewn on a square collar of scarlet flannel, and was worn as a neckpiece. Big-bear was visited by the Bear spirit power who told him to make the bundle and taught him a song. The words of the song are "My teeth are my knives; my claws are my knives." Before he unwrapped the bundle, Big-bear would dig a hole and scoop out some clay which he would plaster over his face and streak with outspread fingers in imitation of bear scratches.

When any bundle was unwrapped, pipe offerings had to be made. When Big-bear's bundle was opened a filled pipe

171

was passed through sweetgrass smoke, then held with the stem pointing directly upward. Great *Manito* was addressed and asked to notice that a pipe offering was being made as he had directed. Then the pipe was lit; four puffs were taken, and the pipestem rotated in a counter-clockwise direction so that the mouthpiece described a complete circle. Then the stem was held up again, somewhat lower than before, and the Great Parent Bear spirit was addressed and told the reason for unwrapping the bundle. The cloth to be added to the bundle as a payment offering was mentioned. The pipe was rotated once again and the stem pointed to the forks of the South Saskatchewan and Red Deer rivers, the place where the vision appeared to Chief Big-bear. The Bear spirit which visited Big-bear was addressed and the circumstances of the vision were recited. The pipe was rotated again and pointed to the ground. It was held over four places on the ground as though being pointed to the four legs of a bear or of a bear hide. The Great Parent of Bear was again addressed. No explanation could be given for the four-fold pointing save that such were the vision instructions.

The pipe was then passed around to the men who were watching the ritual and berries, a favorite food of the bear, were eaten. Women could not be present during the procedure. When the charm was rewrapped, a similar pipe offering was enacted. A new cloth was placed as the innermost wrapper, and the bundle tied up again. One end of the bundle was doubled over and fastened with thongs; the other was allowed to hang free. When the bundle was suspended from its tripod, the tied end was hung uppermost.

One sacred bundle was in the nature of a tribal palladium rather than an individual's means of protection. It was the *oskitcɪ·,* Pipestem bundle, which was said to have been given by Great *Manito* to Earth Man, the first human being. The successive owners of this bundle did not receive it through purchase or revelation, but were chosen for the honor by the band council. Its ownership entailed obligations of fearlessness, liberality, and equanimity; men chosen for the office often ran away in an attempt to evade the responsibility.

The bundle contained a pipestem three or four feet long, elaborately decorated with quills, beads, fur, and feathers. Sweetgrass, tobacco, and an ornamented pipe tamp were also included. The pipestem had no bowl; in fact, the stem was not used for smoking. Some sacred pipestems were not perforated through their length. As in other bundles, a new cloth was added whenever the stem was unwrapped. The bundle was kept on a tripod outside the tipi.

No intemperate action could occur in the presence of the Pipestem and in this quality lay its peculiar potency. If two men were engaged in a quarrel, no matter how serious, they were bound to desist when the *oskitcı·* was presented to them. A man bent on avenging the death of a relative could not continue in his purpose if confronted with this Pipestem. When peace was to be made with a hostile tribe, the Pipestem Bearer led the way. When the enemy saw the pipe, they recognized it and respected its sanctity.

The owner of the bundle had to intervene in all intertribal disputes, a duty often hazardous when the men were beside themselves with anger. The Bearer himself could not engage in quarrels no matter how greatly he was provoked and in all things his conduct had to be exemplary. When he felt that he could no longer sustain the obligations incumbent upon him, he might, with the advice of the council, pass it on to a younger man. The new owner gave many horses to the one from whom he received the bundle. There might be as many as three or four such bundles in a band.[6]

One *oskitcı·* still exists on the Little Pine Reserve and was shown to me. The unwrapping ritual was performed by Night-traveler. Very few men dare tamper with anything as highly charged with supernatural power as is the Sacred Pipestem bundle, but Night-traveler, by virtue of his visions and his battle exploits, considered himself equal to the task.

The procedure, in essence, was not markedly different from that performed for the bundle described above. The Pipestem bundle was laid out on a clean blanket; a number of old men were invited by name to witness the proceedings. A pipe was passed around the company and then some sweetgrass was kindled. Night-traveler washed his hands in the smoke, then drew them over his arms, face, and forehead. This was done four times. Then he placed his hands in the smoke again, passed them over the bundle and, with a single movement, held his hands up and addressed the Creator, telling Him why the *oskitcı·* was to be unwrapped. He offered four separate prayers, punctuating each by dropping his hands down along his body, over the bundle, and raising them up once more.

After this, a filled pipe was passed through the sweetgrass smoke, held up to Great *Manito*, then pointed to a spirit power. The pipe was passed around, and as it was being smoked by each man, the bundle was untied and the stem exposed to view. There were three wrappers of cloth. The stem itself was about four feet long, completely covered with blue beads and with red and white feathers. Weasel skins hung from each end and at the center a row of four feathers was suspended.

The stem was passed over the smoke and held before one of the old men. The old man emulated Night-traveler's procedure in drawing the sweetgrass smoke over his body and then passed his hands along the pipestem. As he did this he kept repeating the ceremonial word for thanks, "ha*i*." He uttered a short prayer and then the pipe was presented to another man. So it went around the company. After all had prayed to it, the stem was rewrapped and berries were eaten.

D.A. Cadzow[7] collected a Sacred Pipestem for the Museum of the American Indian and wrote an excellent description of the stem and its uses. His information differs from mine in a few respects. He quotes Skinner's statement that there were only two such stems in possession of the tribe. It is certain that there were many more than that. The old woman from whom the bundle was purchased had wanted to dispose of it and was traveling from reserve to reserve to "gain authority from old men of a certain secret society" to transfer the bundle. This quite probably means that she was seeking the advice of certain powerful old men, for "secret societies" did not exist.

According to Cadzow's data, there were several Pipe Bearers, each appointed for a term of four years. This is at variance with my information that only one man was Bearer and his term of office was not definitely set. Cadzow also writes that the *oskitci·* played an important part in the Sun dance. This is not so. My informants were not clear as to whether a man could receive the right to make a Pipestem bundle in a vision. Cadzow affirms that "the stem could be made only by a man who had dreamed the right to do so."[8]

The only other type of bundle known to the Plains Cree was the "Carried on the Back" bundle, previously mentioned in the section on Death, Mourning, and Burial. It was not endowed by a spirit helper and was used in only one ceremony, The Round dance. This bundle was a precious family possession, however, and contained the hair braids of deceased relatives. Women carried these bundles on their backs when camp was moved, hence the name. Every family had one and they were inherited along paternal lines.

VISION PREROGATIVES

In addition to curing and bundle-owning capabilities, other rights could be granted in a vision. The power of divining might be bestowed upon a visioner. It was usually given as the ability to foresee the enemy. This was an important qualification since the leader of a war party was expected to know where the hostile camps were located and plan the attack accordingly. This knowledge came to the leader as he sang his power songs while on the warpath.

The ability to operate a conjuring booth was another type of divining power which could be obtained from a spirit helper. The *koca·pahtcikan,* the booth, was constructed inside a tipi. Stout logs, four or five inches in diameter and about six feet long, were implanted in the ground to a depth of two feet and reinforced by two hoops made of willow withes. Robes and hides were bound around this frame which was so firmly built that a strong man could hardly shake it. The finished booth was about four feet in diameter and four to five feet high.

When the divining performance was to take place, the shaman stripped to his breechclout. The procedure always took place during the night. A pipe offering was made and two men bound the diviner with thongs. They placed his hands behind his back, palms out, and tied together the similar fingers of the opposing hands. Then the shaman knelt and bowed his head to the ground. A thong was fastened around his neck and tied about his ankles. Many turns were taken around his body until he was very tightly trussed. A rattle was stuck in the thongs on his back and he was placed against the booth. Some diviners entered the booth without human help, according to tales. Jefferson, however, states that the shaman "was inserted through the top as gently as might be."[9]

Then the fire was stamped out and a man with a drum began to beat. The tipi was always packed with onlookers, who helped sing one of the diviners' power songs. Soon the thongs which bound him came flying out of the top of the booth, each loop in turn still in place as though the shaman had slipped right out of them. The structure began to shake more and more violently, ringing bells which were attached to the top of the poles. Voices which identified themselves as various spirit powers were heard, sounding as though they had hurried to come in response to a summons. An old man put questions to the spirit powers and they answered. They might be asked to diagnose an illness, to tell whether it was auspicious to start on a particular journey, to report the welfare of distant relatives. When all the questions had been asked and answered, the fire was rekindled. The posts which had been driven deep were now loosened. One was extracted and the shaman came out of the booth.

Only a few shamans among the Plains Cree could manipulate the conjuring booth. They were not affiliated in any order or society although Skinner[10] implies that they were.

Baptiste Pooyak, a well-read Indian and a devout Christian, told of a conjuring booth performance he had witnessed in 1903. The shaman, Owl-thunder, had made it to ascertain why a patient of his had fallen ill.

> Two men tied Owl-thunder outside the tipi. After they tied him, they ran back into the tipi, a distance of about ten yards, but Owl-thunder was in the booth before they entered.[11] Soon the ropes were thrown out at the top. I saw that the knots had not been untied. It was as if he had slipped right out of the bonds. The booth shook. There were bells on it somewhere and they rang. We could hear all kinds of animals and birds — and also Old Woman spirit power. Then Thunder spirit power was asked, "Why is this man sick, Thunder?" [The reply was], "He had many horses. He refused to lend one to *kumustusumit,* Cattle Owner, and that man sent a *pıtcitcıhtcikan* (an intrusive object) into him."
>
> Many other questions were asked. White-calf had lost two horses. He asked where they were. "Directly south of your house there is a small slough with willows all around it. They are feeding there now. In the morning they will be a little west of there." The next morning I myself went there to look. There were the two horses that had been lost for a week. White-calf later promised to give a cloth to Owl-thunder [as an offering to Owl-thunder's spirit helpers].
>
> Another man had married a young girl and he asked if the child she bore were his. The answer was, "Yes [you are right] that is not your child; it is the child of your testes." We all laughed.
>
> Then we saw sparks fly upward. It was the spirit powers leaving. Owl-thunder came out and the fire was built up.

Certain methods of divining did not require vision sanctions. One might see his future state by peering into the coagulated blood of a badger which had been left in the carcass over-night. Coming-day furnished this account of badger blood divining.

> If you kill a badger, lay it on its back. Take the entrails out, but leave the blood in, and you can tell something the next morning. If a man looks into it he can see himself there. I knew of four young men who did it. One saw a black faced man, just

skin and bones. He died after a long sickness. Another saw a very old man with many wrinkles and hair white as snow. He lived to an old age. One saw a man who had been scalped. He was killed in battle shortly afterward. The last saw a young man with his eyes closed. He died at an early age.

These men were all young. The old men told them not to do it, for it is the one certain way of knowing how you would die. The old people thought it would worry the young men and disturb them. This badger blood looking was discovered accidentally once when a man was out hunting.

Information on scapulimancy and water scrying was given by Fine-day. He was not certain as to whether these were learned or vision-revealed techniques.

I knew an old Saulteaux who could foretell the future by beating the shoulder blade of an animal and reading the cracks. I never saw any Cree do this.

The Plains Cree did tell the future by looking into water. On the warpath each man would carry a cup [for drinking]. On one trip the leader filled his cup half full of water. Then he talked to *Manito*. The men built a big fire. The leader kneeled, pulled a robe over his head, grasped it on both sides so as to shade his eyes. He peered at the water intently — gazing from different angles continually. He asked, "Does the fire shine brightly on the water?" The men answered, "Yes." When the fire died down he told them to build it up again. Finally he said, "Tomorrow, the enemy will discover you while you are hunting buffalo." What he said came true. I never saw this done except in war but it may have been done for the hunt, too. It was called *wapɪ·munɪpɪ,* Mirror Water. It sometimes didn't turn out as the seer had predicted, but pretty often it did."

A vision prerogative which carried with it considerable prestige was the privilege of constructing a buffalo pound. A man had to have supernatural guarantees that he would be able to entice buffalo into a pound before he could build one, for its success depended on the aid of the shaman's supernaturals. It is noteworthy that the making of a fish weir did not require vision authorization.

Not all of the capabilities obtained through vision contacts could be transferred. We have already noted that a bundle could be passed on and would protect the new owner as it did the visioner. The knowledge of various herbal medicines was considered to have been originally given through visions, but was almost always acquired through purchase. The ability to doctor, however, was not entirely transferable. Shamanistic curing tricks and procedures were certainly taught by one shaman to another, but the right to undertake a cure had to be sanctioned in a dream. A man could scarcely become a noted doctor unless he himself had experienced a supernatural visitation. The material details connected with the construction of conjuring booths and buffalo pounds were undoubtedly acquired by novices from experienced men, but the novices generally asserted that they had received supernatural fiat to undertake these tasks.

A vision prerogative that was often passed from father to son was the right to give a certain vowed ceremony. All the sacred ceremonies were performed in fulfilment of vows made in order to secure supernatural assistance for a sick relative or for one's self. A man usually vowed to give a ceremony which he had a right to conduct. If the vower did not have this right, he was obliged to obtain the services of a man who had the necessary vision sanctions and who led the ceremony.

When a spirit helper told its beneficiary that he would be empowered to give a ceremony, say the Smoking Tipi, the songs which he would use were given to him. The details of the ritual, however, had to be learned laboriously from men who had participated in many Smoking Tipi ceremonies.

Ordinarily, any spirit power might assign a ceremony. For example, the right to give a Sun dance might come from Sun, or Buffalo, or Thunder, or from other spirit powers. This was true for all vision experiences. There was little specialization of function among the supernaturals. A few rituals were given for, and imparted by one particular spirit. Thus the Give Away dance was an offering to Bony Specter and the privilege of staging this dance was given only by that spirit power.

BELIEFS

Stories were told of encounters with dwarfs, *memekwe · ciwak,* who lived in river banks and sand hills. The chipped flint arrowheads which were found in many places were believed to have been made by these dwarfs. While these creatures did not appear to men in visions, they could grant powers and did function as spirit helpers. A story told by Coming-day illustrates the beliefs concerning them.

About twenty years ago he who told this story died. South of Unity there is a lake called "Where They Saw Children." South of the lake about a mile is a sand hill. That is where he saw them.

They were camping near there at "Little Round Valley." It was fall and they had a little snow. Well-dressed-man took his

178

gun and went to hunt buffalo. He saw a wolf and shot it. It was almost white. He remembered that once he dreamt that if he wore a white wolfskin in battle, no bullet would go through him. He skinned it, claws and all. He spoke to his spirit helper. "You told me to wear your blanket. I hope you didn't tell a lie." He tied a thong to the nose and dragged the carcass along to wash the blood off in the snow.

As he went by the sand hills he heard something. He saw a little man standing a short distance off. It smiled at him. He saw that. The sand hill was like a house and the little man was standing at the door. The door opened and another came out and leaned against the door post. He looked so hard [intently] at the little men that he didn't look inside. They were dressed like white children, wearing boots and dark clothes, hats with a visor; they had curly hair. Their eyes were hollow and their mouths came out like snouts.

One came up and looked at the wolf skin.

"Give it to me."

"No, I can't."

"You had better."

"No, I can't. I am taking it to fix it as I want to."

"Well, we'll wrestle for it."

"O no, I never wrestle." The little one asked four times. At last Well-dressed-man consented to wrestle. He put his gun down. He took his coat off. He tightened his belt. The little fellow took his cap off. Well-dressed-man had a good look at him. They wrestled. The little man had short arms, so he couldn't grab Well-dressed-man around the middle, but he squeezed him and his arms felt like bands of iron.

[Here Coming-day switched to the first person and the present tense.] I lift him up thinking to throw him. I swing him, but he stands up again. Sometimes he grabs me to throw me, but I always landed upright. He couldn't throw me. I began to sweat. The little man at the door laughs. I am just about exhausted when I trip him and put him to the ground. The other laughed. "It serves you right. You got beaten." The little one said, "I stumbled over your leg, that's why you beat me." After we got our wind, we tried again. I feel his arms again. Just as I am about all in I trip him. The one at the door post has a good laugh.

[The dwarf said] "I guess that's enough. You beat me twice, but only because I stumbled over your leg." He looked in his pockets and took something out. He handed it to me — it was an arrow-shaped stone. "Keep it as long as you live. It will never be evil. In case your friends get sick you will be able to cure them with this. If there is any war I will take care of you. That which I give you will make your body as hard as the stone. You will never be killed. That's all I have to tell you." He took his cap and went back. Before he entered he turned and said, "Whenever there is sickness think of me. I'll be with you right along. Think of the place where I am." I saw the door close and at the next look there was nothing there but sand. I never saw them again after that.

He [Well-dressed-man] was a brave man and never got

179

wounded. He was the only man I ever knew who saw them. The thing he got is called *pekpekaha·*. I saw it twice. He would show it before he told that story. He kept it in a bag around his neck.

Some shamans affirmed that they had visited the land of the dead. One claimed that he had brought back the Cree syllabic writing from the spirit world. This system was actually invented in 1841 by James Evans, a missionary.[12] Fine-day gave this version of the event:—

A Wood Cree named Badger-call died and then became alive again. While he was dead he was given the characters of the syllabary and told that with them he could write Cree. Strike-him-on-the-back learned this writing from Badger-call. He made a feast and announced that he would teach it to anyone who wanted to learn. That is how I learned it. Badger-call also taught the writing to the missionaries. When the writing was given to Badger-call he was told "They [the missionaries] will change the script and will say that the writing belongs to them. But only those who know Cree will be able to read it." That is how we know that the writing does not belong to the whites, for it can be read only by those who know the Cree language.

In another case, the resurrected man had seen a peculiar food served to the denizens of the spirit land. He initiated a dance in which he served food similar in appearance to that he had noticed in the "green grass world."

A third case of a visit to the land of the dead was related as a personal experience by an informant. He had brought back no message.

It is to be noted that all the necessary elements for a revivalistic uprising, such as was the Ghost dance, were present. A strong personality might easily have proclaimed that he had visited the dead and had received encouragement from them to drive out the whites. However, no such personality appeared.

Several years ago a shaman at Moose Mountain, *Pa·tca-pıc* by name, initiated a cult that contains elements of the old shamanistic practice and of Catholic ritual. It has spread to two other reserves, but has not acquired much influence.

The behavior of animals was considered to be an index to weather changes. Some of the weather omens that were recognized are these:—

When loons are heard to call as they are flying, it is a sign that rain is coming.

When dogs are seen to play during bad weather, good weather will soon follow.

Horses shaking themselves during a storm indicate that the storm will soon cease.

When coyotes call in short yelps, a strong wind will follow.

The call of ground squirrels means that rain is coming.

The accidental defilement of a sacred object was considered an evil omen. If a sacred bundle happened to fall to the ground, the wrath of the spirit powers would follow. During one Sun dance an image of an eagle which had been attached to the center pole came loose and dropped. The pledger built a great sweatlodge for Eagle Spirit Power soon after the dance and thus averted the evil consequences.

FOOTNOTES

[1]SKINNER, Notes on the Plains Cree, p. 70.
[2]See p. 363, Appendix, for an account of this vision.
[3]Generally, medicines were used with little regard for the spirit powers. However, if a dog were offered to the spirit power of the medicines, their effect would be more certain. The purchaser and the owner of the medicine would benefit thereby, since the strength of his potions would be restored or increased.
[4]SKINNER, Notes on the Plains Cree, p. 78.
[5]There was little intimacy, although no strict avoidance, between father and daughter. This may then signify that the berdache had not doctored his father because he had regarded himself in the role of his father's daughter and not as his father's son.
[6]A dance in which the Sacred Pipestem played the major role is described on p. 210.
[7]CADZOW, DONALD A., Peace-Pipe of the Prairie Cree (Indian Notes, Museum of the American Indian, Heye Foundation, vol. 4, New York, 1926), pp. 82-89.
[8]Ibid., p. 87.
[9]JEFFERSON, Fifty Years on the Saskatchewan, p. 76.
[10]SKINNER, Notes on the Plains Cree, p. 78.
[11]This is a common element in accounts of conjuring booth performances.
[12]CURTIS, EDWARD S., The North American Indian, vol. 18, Cambridge, 1928, p. 152.

Ceremonialism

VOWED CEREMONIES

The Sun Dance

The most difficult vow to fulfil and hence the one most likely to bring about the desired result, was the pledge to give a Sun dance. This occasion was the outstanding event of the ceremonial calendar. Large encampments, often of several bands, gathered in June or July to participate. It was the time for a great spurt of social activity; other dances were held; gambling and games went on continually; it was the ideal period for courtship.

The term for the Sun dance was *nıpakwe·cimuwin,* "Thirsting Dance," so called because the participants did not drink during its duration. Two Sun dance ceremonies were observed by the writer, one among the River People band in 1935, the other among the Calling River People band in 1934. The ceremony is still an active force in Plains Cree life.

In summary, the procedure was this: The dance was initiated in fulfilment of a vow. The pledger, always a man, either had his own Sun dance songs or else induced a man who did own such songs to conduct the ceremony, i.e., to lead in the singing. Any spirit power might grant the right to give the Sun dance, but usually it was Sun or Thunder.

The pledger chose four assistants who sang with him on the night of three new moons preceding the date set for the ceremony. The fourth and final preliminary singing took place in an enlarged tipi on the night before the dance. In the morning, a party of scouts set out to find a tree for the center pole. They acted as though they were seeking an enemy, and when they had found a suitable log, came back to camp and reported. A party went out, cut the tree, brought the center pole into camp. The lodge was built and an altar set up at the north side.

The dancing continued for several days and nights. Many

cloth and smoke offerings were given during this period, self-torture inflicted, innumerable prayers uttered. A general gift-giving occurred near the end of the dance. The ceremony was concluded by a procession in which everybody filed out of the lodge after touching the center pole.

To expand on this summary, we begin with the pledger inviting the several old men who were to assist him and, if necessary, would teach him the proper method of conducting the ritual. They met and sang during the nights of three new moons preceding the date set for the dance. The fourth pre-

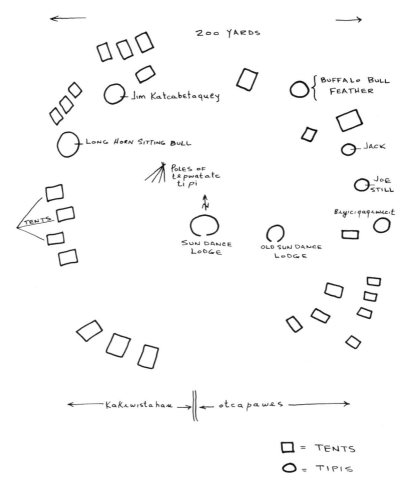

Fig. 16. Sun Dance Encampment. June 23, 1934. Crooked Lake Reserves. Because there was then a government prohibition on visiting a reserve other than one's own to attend a Sun dance, this ceremony was situated on the boundary between the kakiwistahan and the otcapawes bands of the Crooked Lake agency.

liminary singing occurred, as we have noted, on the night before the ceremony.

At this time a *wewahtahokan,* an enlarged tipi, was set up adjoining the site on which the Sun dance lodge was to be built the following day. The pledger went out in the evening to find a buffalo skull. He had usually cached one beforehand, and located it. He wrapped it in a cloth offering and carried it back to the lodge. He entered the tipi wailing and held his burden over a sweetgrass smudge. The skull was carried around the tipi and gently deposited on a bed of sweetgrass braids.

The pledger had previously chosen some man to be crier for the ceremony. This official, the Shouter, now stepped out the tipi door, which faced south, and called, *"He . . .* come and have a smoke.'' He thus invited the spirit powers to attend. After repeating this cry in four directions, the crier summoned old men and women into the lodge. Inside, six or eight male singers sat around in a circle. Three sweetgrass smudges were made around the tipi and one in the middle of the singers' circle. Two men held a folded rawhide over the three smudges successively and, after three feints at throwing, tossed it into the midst of the singers. The singers yelled and beat the hide. Some kept time by beating the hide with willow sticks; four of the singers beat drums; the man who led the singing shook a rattle.

Fig. 17. Preparing Drums for Sun Dance by Allen Sapp.

The two who had thrown the hide were chosen to cut tobacco and care for the pipes during the whole ceremony. They did not drink during the dance and were required to keep their eyes on the ground or on their work, so that they might not look at women. The two were called *okaskikot-cı·kanikewak,* Tobacco Cutters.

The four old men who assisted the pledger and taught him the ritual made pipe offerings. Each one was given a pipestem. The four stems were pointed in unison. Then the pledger took a rattle, addressed the supernaturals, and led the singers in his own power songs. After he had exhausted his repertoire, or his voice, his four assistants, each in turn, took the rattle, prayed, and led in the singing. The burden of all the prayers was that a ceremony very dear to the powers was about to be given, that the powers help the participants complete the Sun dance, so that mankind might be blessed. During the singing, those of the assistants who were not singing prepared ceremonial paraphernalia for the following day. They cut whistles out of bird bones; they braided loose sweetgrass; they attached cloth offerings to the sticks by which the cloths were hung.

After the singing was over, the company dispersed. The pledger and the crier, however, remained awake in the tipi all night. Just before the sun rose, the pledger walked to the south of the camp circle and made his way around the tipis, wailing and asking the people to help him in his purpose. Then the crier called those who were to search for the center pole. They were men who had acted as scouts for a war party.

The group of six to ten men entered the lodge and sat down. The pledger went up to the leader of the scouts, whose name had been called first, gave him a filled pipe, placed his hand on the leader's head and wailed, saying, "Help me complete this (vow that I have made)." The pledger repeated this with every scout; meanwhile, the pipe was lit and passed around. After the pipe had been smoked and its ashes emptied on a sweetgrass smudge, the Tobacco Cutters filled it again and gave it to the leader of the scouts, together with a cloth offering and a sweetgrass braid.

The scouts returned to their tipis, took their war paraphernalia, and met again in the woods. From the meeting place they scattered in all directions, proceeding as though they were scouting for the enemy. When one found a suitable tree for the center pole, he barked. The other scouts assembled at the tree and tied a withe around it.

186

Then they built a small fire near the tree, washed and painted their faces, put on their war gear. Four sweetgrass smudges were made at the base of the tree, one in each cardinal direction. A pile of boughs was deposited nearby. The leader made a pipe offering, then gave one bough to each scout. One of the group was delegated to count coup, telling of an expedition on which no one was killed. The reciter concluded with, "So let it be with this pole. When we stand it up, let nothing evil happen." Then he placed his bough in the withe which was tied around the tree. Each scout repeated this performance and then the party went back to camp.

They announced their approach with high pitched yells and entered the encampment as though they were spying on the enemy. They ran and ducked and crawled and dodged. Then the leader dashed up to the door of the preliminary lodge and sat down. The other scouts sat down behind him. The pledger came out and sang a power song. When he finished, the scout leader rose and kicked through a pile of branches. Thereupon all the spectators grabbed one of the branches, saying as they did so, "I'll kill a Blackfoot," or "I'll take a horse," as did the members of a war party when the scouts returned (c.f. p. 244).

Then the pledger asked the scout leader to report. "Tell your story, but take it easy (i.e., do not exaggerate)." There were two ways in which the leader might answer. If the pledger's father had been killed in battle, he would say, "I saw your father. He told me that he is well off and that he wanted his son to come for him soon." The other reply was, "I spied the enemy in his camp. He told me that he is well off and that he wanted his friend to come for him soon." The pledger thanked the scouts by repeating the ceremonial thanks, "hai."

While the scouts were coming into camp, the young men were decorating themselves and their horses. Two men who had taken women captives went from tipi to tipi leading out the girls and young women. All gathered at the lodge. A colorful procession started for the tree. In the van were the pledger and the leader of the scouts. The young women, on foot, followed them, each carrying a rope or a length of hide thong. The young men rode behind.

At the tree, sweetgrass smudges and pipe offerings were made. Four men armed with axes stood around the tree. The pledger sang three songs during which the ax men pretended to chop at the trunk. During the fourth song they cut it down so that it lay to the south. As the tree crashed to the ground the men fired their guns, and rushed in to break off a branch and to utter a wish, "I take a gun," or a similar expression.

The tree was quickly cleared of branches, a fork being left at the top. The women lined up in pairs on each side of the pole and fastened their lines to it. With the aid of the horsemen they dragged the log away. Just as they entered the encampment, men who had killed an enemy with a gun discharged their firearms into the tree.

The pole was set up to the north of the hole which had been dug to receive it, the butt a few inches from the edge of the hole, the forked top raised on a tripod. Those who brought the pole partook of berries which were passed around. When all had eaten, two men who had captured enemy women told the young men to mount their horses. They led each horseman to a young woman, who mounted and rode double with him. The riders aligned their horses in a row and rode around the camp circle singing. Then they broke ranks and went into the bluffs to bring back the Sun dance lodge timbers which were being cut.

They hauled the logs into the encampment with whoops and yells. The walls of the Sun dance lodge were made by setting up forked poles, about seven feet high, in a circle perhaps forty feet in diameter. Beams were lashed across the forks with rawhide thongs. Meanwhile the "nest" was attached to the center pole by one of the pledger's assistants. Bundles of brush were fastened in the fork of the pole and long cloth offerings attached to them. Other offerings were also suspended from the "nest." Guns, clothing, and sometimes stuffed images of spirit powers were hung on it. Representations of spirit powers were carved or painted on the center pole. At the bottom of the hole dug for the pole, cloths and sweetgrass were placed.

Lines were attached to the center pole and at a signal from the pledger it was raised into position, being steadied as it rose by two pairs of coupled tipi poles. Rafters were laid across the top of the lodge, resting on the wall beams and in the fork of the center pole. Leafy boughs and tipi covers enclosed the side walls and were occasionally placed over the roof. The preliminary lodge was stripped of its two tipi covers which were placed on the walls of the Sun dance structure. A fence or partition of intertwined boughs extended around the lodge, except in front of the entrance and the altar, some three feet in from the wall. It was made by driving stakes into the ground to a height of about four feet and

Fig. 18. Sun Dance. Raising the Center Pole. Little Pine Reserve, 1935.

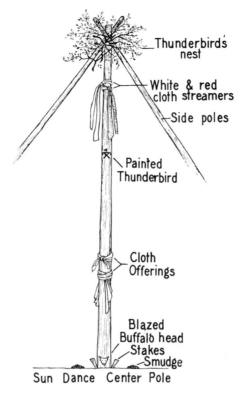

Fig. 19. Center Pole at Crooked Lake Sun Dance, June 23, 1934.

twining leafy branches between them. The dancers sat behind this fence and grasped it while dancing.

A great deal of prescribed ritualism accompanied the building of the lodge. For example, the first wall pole to be set up was the one which was on the west of the entrance. The first four rafters had to be placed in the cardinal directions; prayers were offered as they were set in position, and cloths tied to them. If the dance was the first given by the pledger, eight rafters were used in the lodge roof. When a man gave his second Sun dance, twelve rafters were laid on the roof. The number was increased by fours until a maximum of twenty-four rafters was reached. It is to be noted that *Maskwa* did not follow this custom in the 1935 dance, placing twenty-five rafters on a lodge which should have carried only twenty. One of the old men hinted that this was not the proper procedure, whereupon old *Maskwa* angrily retorted, ''If you don't like how I do things, do them yourself.''

While the structure was being erected, one of the pledger's assistants made the altar. This was placed at the north side of the lodge near the wall. It consisted of an excavation about sixteen inches square and four inches deep. A short peeled peg was planted in each corner of the excavation and in the center. The four pegs symbolized the four Thunders, one in each cardinal direction, the center peg represented Great *Manito*. Behind the excavation was set the buffalo skull upon which were laid cloth offerings and sweetgrass. Beside the skull two crook-shaped sticks were set up.

When the lodge was completed, the altar paraphernalia, skull, cloths, sweetgrass braids, tobacco, dance regalia, all were brought from the preliminary tipi into the dance lodge. The pledger and his assistants each took some article and, wailing, proceeded in single file to deposit their burdens at the altar. The number four and the use of sweetgrass smoke entered into this part of the ritual as they did in practically every phase of the Sun dance. Each man in the file held his burden over four sweetgrass smudges en route from the preliminary tipi to the dance lodge.

When the altar was completed, it was screened from the view of the spectators. The pledger and three assistants sat at each corner of the excavation. In unison, two of them lit pipes, blew puffs of smoke about them, and spoke to the spirit powers. Then the pipes were slowly passed along the edges of the excavation, each man taking a few puffs and passing the pipe clockwise to his neighbor. One pipe was held with the mouthpiece nearest the lip of the excavation and the other was passed with the bowl nearest and foremost. When each pipe had made a complete circuit four times, the chief assistant pulled off the pipe bowls from the stems and flung them to the ground.

The altar was then unscreened and the singers, eight or ten in number, took their places to the northeast of the center pole. They sat in a circle as they had in the preliminary tipi on the previous night and again the rawhide upon which they were to beat with willow wands was thrown into their midst. The spectators entered and sat against the bough partitions behind which the dancers reclined. Women sat in the southeast quadrant of the enclosure. Men sat around the western arc of the fence. Women dancers were placed on the eastern side, the men dancers on the western. The pledger always danced beside the altar.

At the start of the dance, however, the pledger sat among the singers, leading them in his own power songs. After a

Fig. 20. Inside the Sun dance lodge. Women dancers. Singers in the foreground.

Fig. 21. Inside the Sun dance lodge. Men dancers.

while, he was relieved by some other man who possessed songs, and so on, through the dancing, one song leader succeeded another. Each leader shook a rattle and was flanked by two drummers on each side. The other singers beat on the hide. Before a leader began his songs, he uttered a short prayer, mentioning how and where he had acquired the songs he was about to sing. One or two introductory songs were sung before the Sun dance songs proper were given.

As the music began, the dancers rose and danced in place, blowing on an eagle bone whistle which they held in their mouths. The dancers rested their hands on the top of the fence and rhythmically bent their knees, bobbing up and down. Each dancer kept his eyes steadfastly on the center pole, so that he might have only the supernaturals in mind while dancing.

The dance formerly lasted through four days. Recently the time has been cut. In the 1935 dance at Little Pine Reserve the dancing started in the late afternoon of one day, continued through the next two days and nights and ended on the afternoon of the third day. Few of the dancers participated throughout this period. Some had vowed to dance one or two days only; others had relatives substitute for them at intervals while they slept. The singing went on all throughout the dance period. When a song leader was changed, there might be a rest period of fifteen or twenty minutes. The singers left the lodge at their pleasure. If there were any lack of men to aid in the singing the Shouter impressed some into service. The singing was done by the men in the singer's circle, and by some of the women spectators.

Men who had vowed to do so were tethered to the center pole. Skewers were passed through the flesh of their breasts and lines attached the skewers to the pole. The men danced around the lodge enclosure, tugging at the lines in an effort to tear the skewers loose from their flesh. They were released after one song. Guns or buffalo skulls might be hung from skewers set into the flesh of the back, or horses tied to the skewers and led about.

These tortures were offerings to the spirit powers and were only done in carrying out a vow. Bits of skin might be cut out as offerings, and a finger, usually the little finger, chopped off for the same purpose. Throughout the dance, cloth offerings were brought up to the pledger who consecrated them. He held them up to his spirit helpers and asked them for the blessing desired by the donor. The offerings were then hung on the lodge.

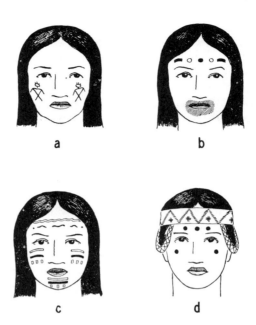

Fig. 22. Face Paintings of Four Women Participants in Sun Dance at Crooked Lake Reserve, June 23, 1934. Designs are imparted in a vision to the dancer or to the one who paints the design. a, Thunderbird in black on each cheek; b, Area around mouth, dark green, bars in red, circles blue; c, Solid lines and areas, red, others are blue; d, Beaded headband with beaded side pendants, marks in black.

No special costume was worn by the dancers. Most dancers fitted themselves out in their finest clothes and painted their faces in accordance with vision revelation (Fig. 22), or lacking this, in decorative fashion. Men who possessed or who could borrow articles from sacred bundles, put them on while dancing. Objects which were in any degree imbued with supernatural power were worn or carried through the ceremony. Sacred stones were placed beside the dancers; one participant in 1935 wore a mask used in the *wɪ·htiko* dance.

The dancers were allowed to smoke, but could not eat or drink. If rain fell during the ceremony, however, they were permitted to drink the rain water since it was believed that the rain was sent by spirit powers who pitied the thirsting dancers. Therefore, prayers for rain were a salient feature of every Sun dance. The pledger continually exhorted his supernaturals to bring on a storm and used every magical device in his power to secure that result. If, in spite of his prayers, the days were clear and cloudless, other men might bring their sacred stones or shields to him in the hope that prayers to the spirits resident in those articles might be of some avail.

Sometimes water was produced through shamanistic tricks. The pledger or one of his assistants might blow water through his whistle or tap the center pole for water. The liquids thus produced could be drunk by the dancers.

The dance period was one in which the presence of the supernaturals was very close and their imminence keenly felt. Hence, guards were posted at night to make sure that nothing untoward went on. They prevented the young men who were always "foolish" and to whom the sacred nature of the occasion meant little from holding trysts with girls or otherwise engaging in actions displeasing to the powers. Sexual abstinence was compulsory for the dancers and for those assisting in the ceremony throughout the duration of the dance. The pledger did not have sexual intercourse from the time he made his vow until the Sun dance was concluded.

Early in the dance period a fire was built in the lodge, to the northwest of the center pole, and kept smouldering to provide coals for the pipes and for the sweetgrass smudges. The firewood was supplied by a man who, as a novice, had tended the fires for a war party. He collected wood from the tipis and brought it into the lodge. On his entrance, the singers broke into a war song. The firewood collector entered the lodge carrying a load of wood, followed by a file of boys also carrying wood. They danced with a lively step for a few minutes. Then the collector recounted how he had looked after the fires on a war trip and so had earned the privilege of taking wood from the tipis. The wood was piled near the fire and the Sun dance songs were resumed.

Ranged against the partition near the fire sat the pledger's assistants, the Tobacco Cutters, and the Servers. Two Servers were appointed to perform the necessary menial tasks. The Shouter did not have any special place, but walked about acting as general overseer and manager of the ceremony. At frequent intervals during the dance period, boys and young men rode around the camp in a row abreast. They sang war songs, laughed, and joked among themselves. When they tired of this they dismounted and went off to play games or amuse themselves in some other manner. But soon two or three young men would begin to ride around the camp circle again and before long they would be joined by many others.

At one point in the dance period, the foremost fighters gathered and slowly advanced in a group to the dance lodge. The man with the highest deeds walked at their head. When the Servers saw them coming, they prepared a pipe and hand-

Fig. 23. Thunderbird Nest of Sun dance Lodge. Crooked Lake, 1934.

ed it to the leader of the party who puffed at it and passed it around the group. Then they entered the dance lodge singing, "Just below the sky (referring to Thunder?) that is my companion *(nikwɛmɛ).*" The fighting men formed a circle near the singers and danced. They went around in a clockwise direction. But, if any one of them had turned back to meet the enemy when all his comrades had fled, he was privileged to dance in a counter-clockwise direction outside the ring formed by the others. When one song had been sung, the leader stationed himself near the center pole, counted coup, danced alone for a short while after he had told his story, then rejoined the group. Each one in turn repeated this performance until all had recited their deeds.

Each of the men who counted coup contributed some clothes or horses which were given away. The clothes and the twigs which represented the gifts of horses were piled to the south of the center pole. When all the coups had been counted, the Shouter distributed these articles to the onlookers. He was at liberty to give the gifts to anyone he might choose. Usually the old and infirm received precedence, then presents were given to visitors from other bands or tribes. Men who themselves were known to be liberal would also receive some of the gifts. As each person received a present, he offered a prayer or a short paean of praise for the donor. When all the gifts had been distributed, the dance continued.

Frequently the Shouter would ask the singers to stop for a while and call out to the spectators that they be quiet. Then some man of prestige stood near the center pole and, facing the men, delivered a speech. Some twenty such speeches occurred during the ceremony witnessed in 1935. They lasted from three to fifteen minutes and though they touched upon many themes, each delivered essentially the same message. The speaker declared that the Sun dance was a ceremony blessed by the supernaturals and he exhorted the dancers not to falter but to complete their promises and vows. This sermonizing may have been introduced after contact with missionaries. One of the pledgers (there were two) of the 1935 Sun dance erected two five-foot poles, one on the east side of the lodge, one on the west. Attached to the top of each pole was a single eagle feather. No one had ever seen this done before and the pledger announced that he had received vision instructions to set up the poles. Several old men grumbled a bit at this unwonted innovation, but since it was purported to stem from supernatural suggestion, they had to accept it.

Once each day, during the forenoon, food was brought into the dance lodge and all the spectators and ceremonial assistants ate. The women who had prepared and donated the food were rewarded by having their names publicly announced by the Shouter. Fine-day and *Maskwa* asserted that in former days, no food was served inside the dance lodge and that the custom had been innovated some thirty years ago.

On the last day of the dance, a general gift giving took

place. The gifts given by a man were placed near the center pole; the giver and his family came forth and danced beside their gifts. Then the Shouter distributed the presents to visitors or to tribesmen. The gifts undoubtedly added prestige to the donor's name, but officially they were regarded as offerings to the supernaturals. The people who received the presents prayed for the welfare of the donors and by means of such prayers divine favor might be procured.

At the conclusion of the ceremony, everyone stood up, spectators included, and danced with their arms outstretched before them. Then all went out of the lodge in a file, rounding the center pole in a clockwise direction and touching it as they went by. The finale of the dance witnessed among the Calling River People on the Crooked Lake reserves was different. There the dancers came to the center of the lodge, stood in a circle around the pole, and danced. Several men leaned their heads on the pole and wailed. When the song was over, the dancers went out in random fashion, followed by the onlookers.

The Sun dance lodge was left standing, but could not be used again. Soon after the dance was over, the pledger gathered up all the cloth offerings that had been hung on the lodge and carried them deep into the bush where they would not be stolen or disturbed. There he left them.

Fig. 24. Structure of Old Sun dance Lodge. Crooked Lake, 1934.

198

If it happened that two men in the band had pledged to give a Sun dance, they could join forces and give one together. However, it often occurred that several people in a large encampment would have made such vows. In that case a number of Sun dances were given, one after the other.

While a woman might receive vision sanction to make a Sun dance and could vow to give one, she herself could not conduct the ceremony. She would have to induce her husband, or her son, to make the vow and act as pledger.[1]

The Smoking Tipi

Ranking next in importance to the Sun dance among the sacred ceremonies, was the Smoking Tipi *(pɪhtwowikamik)*. As with all vowed ceremonies, it was given in fulfilment of a pledge made to the supernaturals; in order to give it a man had to acquire the right either in a vision, or by purchase, or through inheritance.[2]

This ceremony consisted of a night-long singing session during which many prayers were said, offerings given, and pipes ritualistically manipulated. It was usually held in the spring in an enlarged tipi. This structure differed from the ordinary enlarged tipi in that it was built on a four-pole foundation. The four poles were laid on the ground, one pointing to each of the cardinal directions, their tops laid one over the other. An old woman was called to lash the top of the poles together. Before she tied the knot she said, "I am going to tie you, poles. May the one who promised to give this ceremony be well and may the next one who makes this ceremony be well also." (The informants could give no explanation as to why an old woman had to lash the poles, or why this particular formula had to be spoken. It may be noted that formulaic expressions were rare in Plains Cree ceremonialism.) The tipi was then set up by the men.

In the center of the lodge a round altar was made by excavating the sod to a depth of about three inches and a diameter of four or five feet. The depth of the excavation was increased each successive time that the host gave the ceremony. Four pegs were planted in the altar flush with the surface at opposing points on the circumference. A fire was built in the center of the altar. At the north side of the lodge, near the wall, four cloth offerings were draped over short upright stakes.

The pledger had four assistants. He also chose two young men who had to sit close to the fire, not moving throughout the ceremony. The ritual began after food had been served and eaten by all those in the lodge except the host, who neither ate nor drank during the rite. Two of the assistants came up and sat beside the two young men, each assistant near one of the pegs in the altar. The two smoked in unison, prayed to the spirit powers, and then passed their pipes along the perimeter of the altar just as was done along the rectangular Sun dance altars. Two men sat at the other two pegs, received the pipes, smoked them, and passed them on along the edge of the excavation. The pegs symbolized the thunders, one in each cardinal direction.

When this part of the ritual had been completed, two pipes were passed around the assembled company. Then four rattles were held over sweetgrass smoke and one handed to each of the pledger's assistants. The head assistant received the "chief" rattle. He sang his power songs aided by a chorus of the other assistants and of the women who were present. The other men in the lodge did not sing until they had received rattles. After the head assistant had sung through his power songs, he passed the chief rattle to the assistant sitting next to him, who then led the singers in his songs. Thus the chief rattle was passed around until every man who possessed songs of his own had an opportunity to sing them. The other three rattles were also passed around. Soon after the start of the ceremony, boys daubed with white clay entered the lodge, wailing. They carried offering cloths which they presented to the host.

The singing continued through the night. At dawn, the chief rattle was given to a man who sat near the door. This was the *"manito* person," so called because he was well versed in all the songs and procedure for the ceremony. The pledger had also confided to him the circumstances under which the vow was made. He sang a special set of songs connected with the office. As he sang, the servers shook the four cloths which were draped over poles at the back of the lodge, as though to wake them. The ceremony ended after the four assistants took places beside the pegs on the altar and passed the pipes as before.

The ceremony is replete with ritualized manipulations of pipes and rattles. The accompanying diagram, Fig. 25, represents the groundplan of the Smoking Tipi and the position of the participants at the start of the ceremony. Circles 1 and 2 represent the two young men who sit near the fire. They are called *kotinama·ketcikocpwa·kana,* "They who take the Pipe." Circles numbered 3 to 6 are the host's assistants, the

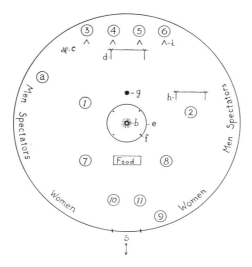

Fig. 25. Diagram of Lodge at Beginning of Smoking Tipi Ceremony. See text for key to numbered circles. a, Host; b, Central fire; c, Rattles; d, Pipe rack; e, Rim of altar excavation; f, Peg; g, Sweetgrass smudge; h, Pipe rack; i, Cloth draped over stake.

four old men who lead the ceremony, called *nıkanopıha · kanak,* "They who sit in front." 7 and 8 are two young men who take a small part in the ritual; 9 is the *"manito* person." 10 and 11 are servers, ceremonial aides.

The following account of the Smoking Tipi ritual gives it in fuller detail than the preceding description. It is keyed to the diagram (Fig. 25) for the sake of simplicity.

The host takes four pipes and, holding them together, passes them through the smoke of smudge *g*. First, he holds the mouthpieces in the smoke, then rotates the pipes clockwise to present the bowls over the smudge. He does this four times and then leans the pipes against rack *d*. A small peg is placed at the bowl of each pipe to keep it from tipping over.

1 takes a pipe from rack *d,* slowly hands it to 2 who places it against rack *h*. A server, 10, comes up and then 2 hands pipe to him. Server rotates pipe clockwise and hands it to 3. 1 takes another pipe, hands it to 2. Server, 11, comes up, takes pipe from rack *h* and gives it to 4.

Host and 3 rise and go over to sit near 1, beside one of the pegs of the altar. 4 goes to sit next to 2. 7 and 8 move up and sit at the altar, one at each of the two south pegs. Server takes coal from fire with cleft stick and holds it to the bowl of 3's pipe. 3 takes four puffs. Server does the same with 4.

3 holds up his pipe and prays. Then he points it in the cardinal directions, east, south, west, north. 4 watches 3 and duplicates all his motions. Both puff at their pipes in unison. When the pipes are well lit, 3 points the mouthpiece of his pipe to-

ward the peg near which he is sitting, holding the stem close to the ground. He slowly passes the pipe to 4, holding it close to the lip of the excavation all the time. 4 is meanwhile passing his pipe to 8 in the same way. When 8 takes 4's pipe, 4 turns to take the pipe 3 is passing to him.

8 passes the pipe to 7, who then gives it to 3. As each man gets a pipe he takes a few puffs before passing it on. When 3 has both pipes he gives them to the host who cleans them and replaces them on the rack. Host, 3, and 4 go back to their former places as do 7 and 8.

3 takes the four rattles which have been lying at c and gives them to the server who holds them over smudge g and shakes them four times. The server then goes up to 3, feints at giving him the rattles three times and hands them over with the fourth movement. 3 passes a rattle to each of the other assistants, 4, 5, and 6.

3 takes a pipe from the rack and hands it to 4. 4 lights it, holds it up as a smoke offering and replaces the pipe on the rack. This is done with another pipe also. The server then gives one of the pipes to 5 and one to 6. They hold them up as smoke offerings, then pass them on to be smoked around the company.

As soon as the pipes are passed, 3 shakes his rattle and sings. 4, 5, and 6, who also have rattles, sing with him. When the pipes have gone around the company, the singing stops for a while and the servers pass out food. They begin with 3 and proceed in a clockwise direction. After all have eaten, the younger men and women go home, taking with them the food they were not able to eat. Sometimes two or three boys, daubed with white clay, come into the lodge and stand near the altar, between 7 and 8. They carry cloth offerings and wail. The women in the lodge wail with them. One of the boys goes up to the host who asks him, "To whom are you giving this offering?" The boy answers, "It is something for Thunder (or for some other power)." The host takes the cloth and gives the boy some pemmican. The other boys do the same and then the host holds the cloths up to the spirits, prays, then hangs the cloths on the lodge wall.

Those who remain sing through the night. Shortly before dawn, the chief rattle is given to the host for the first time. He sings just one song and lays the rattle down. The server takes this rattle and the other three and holds them over sweetgrass smoke. With a sudden movement the server throws the rattles to 9, who is called *manitoayisı·yinıw, manito* person. 9 asks some of the younger men in the lodge to sit around him. He gives three of the rattles to them and leads them in singing special songs. He also sings his own power songs. While 9 sings, the server shakes the cloths which are draped over stakes at the back of the lodge, as though to wake them.

When 9 has finished, 3 goes to sit with 1, 4 with 2, 5 with 7, 6 with 8. They sit beside the pegs in the altar. The server passes one pipe to each of the pledger's assistants. They smoke in unison, following 3's movements, and pass the pipe along the circumference of the altar as was done at the beginning of the

202

ceremony. Then 3 holds the four pipes over the smudge and addresses the supernaturals. He talks for a long time and asks for many blessings. When he puts the pipes back on the rack, the server goes out and shouts, "Come and get the food that is left." The women in camp come up and carry off all the food. The server gives some food and water to the host. Then all go to their homes.

This ceremony is still given by the River People band on the Battleford reserves but was not witnessed by the writer. Skinner[3] did participate in the ritual during his 1913 visit to the Crooked Lake reserves. His account differs in some essentials from that given above. He noted that outside the lodge

a poplar pole crowned with leaves was erected, bearing a British flag, a square of red broadcloth, and a human figure of leaves, about three feet high, with a leafy crescent in each hand.[4]

F.E. Peeso also observed that beside the Smoking Tipi lodge "they set up an image and hung clothing upon it."[5]

Skinner goes on to tell of a stuffed image of a buffalo inside the lodge. Although there was a round excavation, there was none of the ritual smoking at the altar. This version of the ceremony seems to be a simplified one, as perhaps is also the contemporary practice of the River People.

D.A. Cadzow, in 1926, collected the ceremonial paraphernalia used in a Smoking Tipi ceremony given by an Indian of the Peepeekisis Reserve of the File Hills Agency. His account[6] is quite different from both Skinner's and mine. It describes the dedication of the four foundation poles in the forest and tells of a buffalo skull shrine. There is an elaborate symbolism of colors and ceremonial objects which is foreign to the writer's experience with the Plains Cree. The ceremonial objects illustrated by Cadzow (now in the Museum of the American Indian, Heye Foundation) were not mentioned by the writer's informants nor seen by Skinner. They do occur, however, in other ceremonial contexts. For example, the painted feathered crooks shown on p. 276 of Cadzow's article are identical with those used in the Sun dance. It should be noted that Cadzow's informant came of a band which was closely connected with the Assiniboin, just as Skinner's informants were close to the Plains Ojibwa.

Robert Jefferson also describes this ceremony.[7] It does not seriously differ from the account given by the writer save that in this source, too, there is no hint of the smoking at the altar. Jefferson's data were collected from the House People band.

Masked Dance

The *wihtikokancimuwin*, *"wihtiko-*like dance," was a masked performance often given during the Sun dance period. The *wihtiko* was a cannibalistic character in the folklore of the Wood Cree. Tales concerning this spirit power were sometimes told among the Plains Cree, but the spirit was never seen in the prairie country and imbued only the forest inhabitants with man-eating desires. Except for the name, this character does not figure in the dance.

The pledger carried a staff with deer hooves attached. He went from tipi to tipi and shook his staff over the heads of those men whom he wished to join him in the dance. As he did this he spoke in inverted fashion, saying, "I do not want you." The men so chosen followed the pledger into his tipi. There he offered up a pipe, rotating it in a counter-clockwise direction instead of clockwise as was done in every other ritual. He phrased his prayers conversely to the desired meaning. The dancers were furnished with an old tipi cover from which they cut the masks they were to wear. These were made of two rectangular pieces of hide sewn face to face along three sides and fringed around the edges. Round holes were made for the eyes and mouth, and a long tubular nose was attached. The men dressed in odd bits of old clothing, wore their own clothes inside out, and put on non-matching leggings. In addition to his mask and ragged clothing, one of them wore a calf robe on his back. Under it was placed a bundle of cloth which bulged out like a hump. He was called *sapotcikan* and always stood apart from the others.

Dressed in this way, they went out and danced at several places inside the camp circle. They clustered around the leader who sang and kept time by thumping his staff. All of them executed improvised and comic dance steps. The humped dancer stayed a few yards behind the group, doing his own comic routine, continuing after the song had stopped, looking up in apparent confusion upon discovering that he alone was dancing.

Then the group went from tipi to tipi where the owners had placed food upon the tripods that stood over every campfire. The dancers stalked the food as though it were an animal, suddenly shot arrows into it, and ran off, yelling, when they hit their mark. All through this performance they talked "backwards." When they missed their target, they ran to pick up the arrow, saying, "This is a fine lucky arrow. It never misses. I shall keep it forever," and broke it. A rider on horseback followed them and collected the food they hit. A crowd of onlookers trailed them, enjoying the fun and teasing the dancers.

Having made the round of the camp, they returned to the pledger's tipi. He stood in the center of the lodge and drew a circle on the ground with his staff. He held the staff in the center of the circle with his left hand while he distributed food to the dancers with his right. He threw the pieces of meat and fat at each one of the group, first feinting at throwing it three times. The pledger kept singing his power songs throughout the food distribution and the feast that followed.

The group slept in the lodge, and in the morning they danced around the camp again. Then they went out on a buffalo hunt, taking their masks with them. When they succeeded in killing an animal, it was spread out on its belly. The dancers put on their masks and stood around it, while the pledger danced at each leg of the carcass. A piece of hide was cut from the shoulder and haunch and offered to *"Manito* person,"* perhaps meaning whatever spirit power for whom this ceremony was conducted.

The meat was divided into parcels and carried back to camp by the dancers. They attached the intestines to their hair as braids, placed the stomach fat on their own abdomens as though they had a paunch, and used the carcass in other comic ways. When they approached the camp, women and children came out to meet and harry them, trying to pilfer their meat. Finally, they reached the pledger's lodge. He feinted at throwing his staff three times and on the fourth attempt tossed it through the smoke hole of the tipi. He did the same with the buffalo tongue which he carried. Each dancer in turn threw his parcel of meat through the smoke hole, and as he did so, dived through the tipi door.

The meat was prepared and eaten. The procedure of the preceding feast was repeated and again the dancers slept in the lodge. The next morning they danced again and then left camp and went off to some remote place. The humped dancer did not go with them but his mask was taken along. Deep in the bush they performed a final dance together, placed their masks and other regalia on the ground, and dispersed.

This ceremony was witnessed in 1934 on the Crooked Lake reserves. The dancing and ritual tallied with the above description except that the buffalo hunt was naturally omitted, not being replaced by substitutive activity.

The account of this ceremony given by Skinner[8] is substantially the same as that above.

Give A way Dance

The Plains Cree word for this ceremony has been translated literally as "a passing of something to each other."[9] It was usually given in the fall or early winter and was dedicated to a certain spirit power known as *pa·kahkus,* the "Bony Specter" of Bloomfield's texts.[10] An enlarged tipi was built, inside of which a post, crudely carved at the top with the representation of a face, was erected. This image of Bony Specter was set up in back of the central fire.

The ceremony opened with a feast. After all had eaten, the chief assistant to the pledger, and three other assistants, took places around the fire. The head man faced one of the assistants and the remaining two faced each other. The chief assistant carried a buffalo bladder full of hardened bone grease. A song was struck up and the head man danced toward the assistant as though to give him the bladder. The assistant danced forward also, but just before they met, the two danced backward, away from each other. The two assistants on the other side of the fire similarly danced to and fro. At the end of the song, the head man took a bite of the hardened grease and spit it on the fire. He then handed the bladder to his partner who turned and danced toward one of the other assistants. This continued until each of the four had danced with the bladder. The bladder was then passed to every man present; as he received it each one said, "I catch long life" or "I take many furs," or a similar expression. Finally, the server cut up the fat and gave everyone in the tipi a bit of it to eat.

The host rose, carrying an armful of clothes, and danced toward one of the men present, just as the head man had done with the bladder. When the song was ended, he gave the man one of the garments. He repeated this with various men in turn until he had given away all the clothes. After he had finished, and through four nights thereafter, a continuous round of gift giving went on. No dancing occurred during the day. Both in the ceremonial lodge and in the camp outside, couples danced facing each other, giving and receiving gifts. Men might dance with women; even the children participated.

A great deal of wealth changed hands and a man might emerge much more affluent than he had been previously. It was believed that one who was intentionally parsimonious would have bad luck with any accretion in wealth he might amass. Conversely, liberality brought prestige and supernatural blessings. Fine-day put it this way.

> If someone gives only poor little things for good gifts, he will generally not enjoy them. I was cheated like that once. But I didn't mind, even though afterward I didn't even have a horse with which to hunt buffalo. The one who cheated me got a fast horse, but couldn't make use of it because he [the man] grew blind soon after. The old people said, "He got blind because he cheated you. *Pa·kahkus* has strong power."

Children danced before the image, giving cloth offerings to Bony Specter. The cloths were tied to the pole. On the last night, four men danced in front of the image. They carried sticks to which were attached horsehairs plucked from every horse given away during the ceremony. These were fastened to the pole as an offering to the spirit power and the ceremony was thus concluded. The image and the cloth offerings were later taken by the pledger to some place where they would not be molested.

Another version of this dance was noted by Robert Jefferson who lived among the House People band.[11] Jefferson tells of a preliminary singing in the lodge in which a rattle was passed around, each man singing his own songs as he took it. The host sang first. During his song, guns were shot at four posts placed in the cardinal directions outside the tipi. This was not done by the River People band.

The ceremony is still given annually on the Little Pine reserve.

Prairie-Chicken Dance

This ceremony, as witnessed among the River People band in 1935, took place in a long lodge. In the center of the lodge a sapling was set up, its leafy top rising above the ridgepole. A cloth offering was attached to it, and a stone placed at the foot of the pole. The stone represented the spirit powers underground. As in every long lodge, there were two fires, one under each end of the ridgepole. The entrance was to the south.

Behind the rear fire was placed a stake on which several feather fans were hung. In front of the stake was a cushion of leaves and twigs on which were laid short sticks ornamented with prairie-chicken feathers. The fans and the sticks were taken by the dancers when a song was begun and replaced after each dance. The singers sat in a circle on the east side of the rear fire. They beat time on four drums. The host and his two assistants sat behind the fire and the guests sat around the lodge.

A preliminary pipe was offered and then the pledger took his place among the singers. He shook a rattle and led them in singing his own songs. The dancers made a circuit around the two fires. The step consisted in advancing one foot and drawing up the other. A few men imitated the dance of the prairie-chickens.

This continued through the night until every man who had songs took the rattle and led the singers. Two or three times during the night, food was served, consecrated, and eaten.

In this ceremony, too, gift giving played an important part. Those who were participating in a Prairie-Chicken dance for the first time were obliged to hand some gift to the Shouter who gave it to some one of those present. Once a man had given a suitable gift, he had the privilege of participating in the Prairie-Chicken dance whenever it was given. This system of obtaining the right to dance is similar to that employed in secular dances, the Pow-wow and the Sioux dance. It did not appear, to my knowledge, in any other of the vowed ceremonies.

The man who vowed the ceremony seen in 1935 received the right to conduct it from the spirit power, Bony Specter.

The dance of the Prairie-Chicken Warrior society may have been the forerunner of this ceremony.

Horse Dance

Two spirit powers, Weasel and Horse, were especially connected with this ceremony and it was made for them. *Pones,* "Little Paul," said of this dance:—

> It is not very hard to give the *misatimucimuwin,* the Horse dance, but only a few men are able to do it. On this reserve (Little Pine) only two can make it. Night-traveler was taught how to do it by his father. William Sap was given the power in a dream. I myself couldn't give the dance. But if I had vowed it, I would give the necessary things to Night-traveler and ask him to make a Horse dance. I would send him two offering cloths, sweetgrass, and berries. He wouldn't take anything for himself, but he would always be willing to do it. The food is provided by the women. Those who come to the dance bring as much food as they can spare.

The preliminary ritual was conducted in a long lodge. Pipes were offered, berries eaten, and songs sung. In front of the pledger was placed a stake to which bells were attached. He shook this in time with the song.

A young man who was chosen by the pledger to be leader of the ceremony danced carrying a weasel hide. He finally danced out of the lodge and tied the hide around the neck of his horse. The other young men filed out of the lodge and proceeded to paint and decorate their best horses. When the riders were assembled, the pledger and the singers came out of the lodge and stood near an upright pole on which cloth offerings had been hung. The horsemen rode around the group when the songs were sung, rearing and prancing their horses. At intervals they dismounted and, holding their mounts, danced in place. This continued for a day.

Elk Dance

The Elk dance, *wawaskecıwcimuwin,* was one of the few ceremonies in which women took an active part and, indeed, seems to have been pledged by women only. It has not been given on the modern reserves for many years.

A long lodge was set up, in which preliminary offerings were made. Two saplings were erected outside the lodge, about ten yards apart. The dancers, young boys and girls, lined up in pairs, every girl on her male partner's left. The woman who had pledged the dance came out and sang her songs to the accompaniment of a rattle. The couples danced around the two poles. As the boys passed the saplings, they rubbed against them, imitating the elk. The dancing continued until a feast was given in the evening.

Fine-day recalled a dance in which he had taken part.

> The woman (who had vowed to give the dance) asked to borrow some young people for the dance. Eight of us went. In the long lodge some old people were singing; she must have taught them her songs. The dancers were all young boys and girls dressed very nicely. She painted the boys with a white mark over the right eye, the girls with a yellow mark over the left eye. She herself had a white mark over the right eye, just like the boys.
>
> We went out and sat in a double file in front of the lodge. Boys and girls of the same age were paired. She (the pledger) told us what to do. Then she went up to one of the saplings (she was naked to the waist and smeared with mud), and held her hands up. "Father (i.e., Great *Manito*), this is your will. It must have been your doing that your child, the spirit power,

taught me this. I pray that all the young dancers may grow up and live to an old age.'' Then we danced. Her song was:—

> "Come thundering earth.
> White Elk, I will make you dance.''

"Thundering earth" meant that the dancers' steps resembled the noise made by a herd of elk.

After the first song, we sat down. The singers smoked and the pledger prayed again. "White Moose, I saw you thundering toward me. I am making this dance so that young people may grow old." Then we danced again, but singly, not in pairs. The young men made horns of willow wood and strapped them to their heads.

It was a very long dance. I would no sooner stop to rest than the singing would begin again. We danced all day.

Bear Dance

In the *maskwacimuwin,* Bear dance, a preliminary feast was given in an enlarged tipi and the customary pipe offerings made. Then the dancers went out of the lodge ranging themselves in a semicircle around the pledger and the singers. The men dancers were stripped to the breechclout; the women arranged their robes and painted their faces to give themselves a bear-like appearance.

The pledger spoke to the supernaturals reiterating the reasons why he had vowed to give the ceremony and mentioning the source of his prerogative. During his prayer, the dancers kneeled in a doubled-over posture. When the first song was intoned they looked up, peered about, moved clumsily — all in mimicry of bear behavior. One of their number shot his gun and all scattered as though they were fleeing from a hunter. A second song was begun and the participants gathered and danced in place, facing the singers.

Since this ceremony has long been neglected, the details of its performance are now vague. Many-birds averred that only those who had dreamed of the Bear power could participate, but Fine-day's testimony is probably nearer the actual circumstance.

> Only those who belonged to the dance ate (the preliminary feast) in the lodge. But anyone could join in the dancing. A person belonged to the dance after they had promised to give one or to give something away at a (Bear) dance for the recovery of a sick relative or for success on the warpath.

Pipestem Bundle Dance

In this ceremony, called *oskitciwcimuwin,* the bundle

210

was unwrapped in a long lodge set up especially for the dance. The stem was placed against a rack behind the rear fire. The Pipestem Bearer sat near it. The pledger might be the Bearer himself or any man who was empowered, through a vision or through former ownership of the bundle, to sing *oskitcı·* songs.

After the initial pipe offering was made a song was begun. The pledger, or some man chosen by him, had been sitting between the two fires during the offering and now danced around alone, making the circuit of the lodge four times. As he passed the Sacred Stem, he stroked his hand along it.

During the second set of songs, the dancer carried the Pipestem around and pointed it in the cardinal directions as he danced. Then food was passed, consecrated, eaten, and the dancer continued his performance again. The ceremony lasted until all the food had been consumed. Skinner[12] mentions this dance, saying that a pipe bowl was attached to the Sacred Stem which was then passed around and smoked. This ceremony is no longer given.

Round Dance

The name of this ceremony, *wasakamecimuwin,* literally means "dancing around." It was also called "night singing tipi" *(nanapawnikamowikamik).* The bundles in which braids of deceased relatives were kept figured in the dance. The night before the dance was to be given, preliminary songs were sung. The pledger and his assistants offered pipes and food and sang the dance songs. They notified the powers and the souls of the dead that a dance was to be given for them on the following night.

A long lodge was built and a sapling set up in the center, projecting above the ridgepole. On it were hung cloth offerings; at its base a stone was placed, as for the Prairie-Chicken dance. At the rear of the lodge was a rack on which the bundles were to be placed.

After preliminary pipe offerings and prayers, the bundles were brought in by their owners. The server took them and hung them on the rack. Four drums were passed over sweet-grass smoke, and were given to the pledger and to three assistants. One of the drums was designated as the chief drum. The man who held it led the others in singing his own songs. When the host had finished singing his songs, he passed the chief drum to the man next to him. Thus, every man owning songs appropriate to the ceremony sang them when he received the chief drum. The other three drums were similarly passed along.

At the first song, each bundle owner took his bundle from the rack and danced in a circuit around the two fires, holding it in his arms. At this time the souls of the dead were supposed to manifest their presence by whistling. After the first song, the bundles were returned to the rack where they remained during the rest of the ceremony. The dancing continued throughout the night. Food was served several times. Once in a while a young man would hood his face in his blanket and join in the dance. He capered about announcing that he was a ghost and so furnished comic relief.

Jefferson's notes on this ceremony state that a woman conducts the ceremony.[13] This was certainly not the case among the River People band where women never acted as hosts or pledger except in the Elk dance.

In a performance of this ceremony witnessed by the writer, ten bundles were brought in. The dance lasted until 2:00 A.M.

The Mite · Wiwin

The *mite · wiwin* differed from the other vowed ceremonies in that it was given and conducted by a group organized for the purpose. Membership in the group was obtained by persons who had vowed to join the ceremony in order to secure supernatural aid against sickness.

The ceremony was last given about 1875. It was always regarded with some suspicion by the Plains Cree because it dealt with the use of medicines, which might possibly be employed in sorcery. According to native testimony, it was introduced to them by the *otcipwewak,* the Ojibwa. The last leader of the ceremony among the River People was a man of that tribe. Moreover, Fine-day asserted that the songs used in the ceremony all had Saulteaux, and not Cree, words. In 1935 I could find only one survivor of the *mite · wiwin* members, Many-birds. She had joined as a substitute for her mother who had died before her vow to participate could be fulfilled.

The novices who were to be initiated were each told to bring a dog to the long lodge where the ceremony was held. The *mite · wiwin* leader came out to meet them. His body was painted red and he wore two otterskin armlets. He carried a sacred club, carved or inscribed with animal figures. At the entrance to the lodge, the novices lined up, holding their dogs leashed on rawhide thongs. Four songs were sung by the members and then the leader struck and stunned each dog with his club. Before delivering the blow he feinted at striking three times. The server grasped each dog by the head and by the tail, and, holding it before him, brought it into the lodge. The dogs were stretched out one behind the other. Songs were sung again and then the server took the dogs out to give them to the women who were to cook the meat.

After this an old man went around the camp with a rattle, singing. He summoned all the members who followed him into the lodge. Before he entered he stood at the doorway and prayed. The novices entered and, following the old man, made several circuits of the lodge. Each novice carried a bundle of hay in his arms, together with gifts of clothing for the members. The server took the hay from each novice, placed it on the ground, and spread a robe over it. The novice knelt on this cushion. The gifts were hung on the walls of the lodge.

At the place of honor, in the rear of the lodge, a bear hide was spread. It represented the Bear Spirit and was treated with great respect. Moss was placed at the head of the hide, an amulet on each paw, and a bowl of berries at the snout to feed the Bear.

Behind each novice stood a member of the society who instructed and directed the actions of the candidate. A song was begun and the members danced about holding the whole hides of animals in which medicines were stored. When the leader suddenly pointed his hide at a novice, he fell as though stunned by a blow. Upon being revived by the old man who was his mentor, the novice took a gift to one of the members and asked to be given medicine. The member tapped him on the back and extracted from his mouth that which had been shot into him and which had stunned him. It usually was a cowrie shell. Medicine was administered and the novice returned to his place.

The cooked dog meat was brought in and served. The leader offered his portion to the spirit powers and prayed. When he had finished the prayer, the assemblage repeated a word of thanks used only in this ceremony and in one other. It was *kana·kɛhkana,* defined by Lacombe[14] as "mot usité pour rendre grâce dans les festins de superstition." The common word for thanks in other ceremonies was *haı.*

All of the food which had been prepared had to be eaten

in the lodge. The bones were collected by the servers and deposited in an animal's burrow. Many-birds recalled that

> Sometimes, after eating, a person would feel nauseated, not being used to dog meat or to eating so much. Near the fire there was a stone on which moss and castoreum were placed. They would burn this; he would smell it and vomit.

The head, breast, and paws of the dog were eaten by four men who were the dance leaders. After the feast, one of these men stood up, prayed, and then danced around the lodge. He carried a cylindrical water drum and beat time on it as he danced. Behind him danced the four servers, each carrying a rattle. At the end of every dance song, the dancers stood around the bear hide and sang a special song. This was repeated by each of the dance leaders.

Many shamanistic tricks were performed during the ceremony. For instance, the server might rub medicine on his arm, plunge it into a boiling kettle, and pull out a piece of meat. It is noteworthy that the feats exhibited in the *mite·* lodge were accomplished by the aid of purchased medicines and not through direct vision revelation as in other ceremonies. Many-birds mentioned two other traits which differentiated this ritual from all others. Sweetgrass was not used in any part of the ceremony; men and women sat together and were not segregated into two groups.

The novices were taught the use and manufacture of medicines in return for their gifts. The medicines were wrapped in small packets and stored in the whole hide of a small animal. This hide was called *kaskɩpitakanak,* tied tightly, and was the badge of *mite·* membership.

SECULAR DANCES

Pow-wow Dance

The dance locally known as the Pow-wow is in Cree called *pɩtcitcɩwin,* Moving Slowly dance. It is one version of the widespread Omaha or Grass dance. Before it was introduced by the Assiniboin, there were few social dances; only those in the Warriors' lodge and the Scalp dance were of a secular character.

At the present time the Pow-wow is frequently held, has supplanted much of the religious ceremonialism, and provides the most common social activity of reservation life. The origin of the dance was related by Fine-day.

The Moving Slowly dance came from the south. A woman of the Mud House People (one of the village tribes of the Missouri, probably the Mandan) had four adopted children. She made feather bonnets for them and showed them how to dance. She said, "This dance will be all over and everybody will dance in it." So it is.

They would make a special feather bonnet which was worn by the woman leader of the dance. A different woman would wear the bonnet for each song. That is what I heard when I visited the Rocky Boy Reserve in Montana. The Moving Slowly dance as we do it now (without a bonneted leader) was first danced by the Stoney. This was at the time of the rebellion (1885). They danced four times around and then would capture one of our men. That is how we got it.

In the Pow-wow the dancers stand shoulder to shoulder in a circle and shuffle sideways in a clockwise direction. The singers stand in the center of the circle, beating a large double headed drum which is provided with four loops by which it is held by the singers or suspended from four sticks planted in the ground.

Connected with the dance is an hierarchical set of officers. Each reserve has its own dance hall, a rough shack in which the dances are held during the winter, and its own group of dance officials. At their head is the "dance chief" who supervises everything relating to the dance. Other officials are the crier, servers, "whip owners," "drum leg owners," and tobacco handler. Each office incurs an obligation of liberality and when a dance is held the officials must supply a large share of food and tobacco.

When an official decides to relinquish his position, he asks the singers to sing the song belonging to his rank. He dances alone and seizes the man to whom he wishes to transfer his status, ceremonially capturing him. The recipient of office gives his captor gifts of horses or clothing, varying in value according to the rank of the office.

The participants in the dance adorn themselves in their finest clothing. Feather bustles are seldom used. Roached head-dresses of porcupine and deer hair are worn in the dance and on all festive occasions. The food sticks and whistles used by other tribes in the Grass dance[15] are not common to the Plains Cree dance. An ornamental whip is used by one official to induce "wall flowers" to participate in the dance.

At the present time food is served during the dance without any ritualistic accompaniment. Cameron gives a spirited account of a Grass dance[16] in which the dance leader

215

carried a sword bound to a staff. Women brought in a kettle containing a dog which had been strangled for the occasion. The leader stalked the kettle as though it were an enemy and then speared the dog's head.

In the modern practice of the dance, the right of an individual to participate and the social prestige which accrues to him by participation is based on the amount of wealth given away in his behalf by his parents and relatives. When a child takes his place in the dance, as children freely do, his parents may give various articles to the crier. He announces the nature of the gift, for whom and by whom it is given. The crier (whose Cree title literally means "shouter") then distributes the gifts, usually to visitors and old people. A similar wealth distribution was formerly practised in the Warriors' lodge.

Another means of gift giving is employed during the dance. It is called *ekaskiputcikεht,* which literally means "cutting in." A man will step into the circle of dancers to the right of a woman whom he has chosen. When the song is over and the dancers go back to sit down, he presents her with a gift for the privilege of dancing with her. Women may "cut in" next to a man in the same way and later present him with a gift. Receiving a gift entails an obligation to return a more valuable present, and a rivalry of gift exchange occurs between the partners.

Solomon Blue-horn described the mechanics of the Pow-wow in this way.

> If you consider yourself to be a worthy man (i.e., one of some status) you can choose a woman and dance next to her. You give her something valuable. Then her husband tells her to invite you (to dance) and to give you something in return. A woman may pick a man worth more (of higher social status) than her husband. He will be glad, for she is showing that she considers him a big man.
>
> There are some women with whom everyone is afraid to dance. Their husbands are well off and both husband and wife are brave. If you touch her with gifts she'll give back much more than she gets. When a woman thinks that a man can't keep up with her in gift giving, she won't dance with him any more.
>
> To cut in, you follow the woman around the circle for a few steps. The person dancing to the right of her will hesitate a bit and you step right in. But, if the person to the right is the woman's mother, or her father's sister, or her sister, a man cannot cut in. And a man cannot cut in to dance with any of his woman relatives except his *nitcimus* (female cross-cousin) or *nitim* (sister-in-law). After the dance the man gives the Shouter the gift. The Shouter stands in the middle and announces who gave what to whom. Then he hands the present to the woman.

216

At the next dance, the woman cuts in on you and gives you a present.

You do not dance with a woman all the time, only very seldom. Sometimes the women fill the whole circle and the men all sit. Usually, half of the circle is composed of men, half of women. All this cutting in was brought back by the Cree who ran away to the States after the rebellion. They saw it done there. Before that, the only way to give presents was to put them in the center and tell the Shouter to give them to anyone he chose. That is still done when you give gifts for one of your relatives.

Suppose my brother's daughter just got married and this is the first time she is dancing after her marriage. I will put something in the center to be given away for her. Last year I gave clothing for my little girl who had joined in the dance. She was seven years old. I wanted to be kind to her and hope that she will have good luck. So I gave the presents. The old people who got them begged the spirit powers that the little girl have a long life. Once that is done for a child they cannot push her out of the dance. Yes, they let a child dance even if nothing has been given but they don't care for him. He isn't worth anything in that dance. A grown person who has never had anything given for him can give clothes or even a horse for himself. His wife will have to prepare food every time a dance is made. After a while he will be equal with the others.

Now, supposing a man lost his child. For four nights we can't bother him or invite him anywhere. On the fourth night we are sorry for him. The Dance Chief, the Shouter and a few others join and choose one man to invite the mourner. The invitation can't be refused.

That night we assemble and prepare a big feast. The news gets around pretty quickly. The men bring gifts for the mourner and the women bring gifts for his wife. All the presents are piled in the center of the hall. The Shouter announces, "We invited this person because we are sorry for his loss and because we want him to be with us. We are helping him so that he won't be ashamed to come to the dance." Then the mourner tells the Shouter to tell the people that he is thankful and that he will be in the dance just as he was before.

In 1925 a new Pow-wow custom was introduced on the Little Pine Reserve. A Cree visiting the Assiniboin on the Red Pheasant Reserve was "captured" by a dance society which had a special song. At the next Little Pine Pow-wow this Cree distributed gifts, announced that whenever the song he had learned from the Assiniboin was sung, his *kaupois* (cow boys) society would dance. His relatives formed the nucleus of the society, others joined by giving away a gift. The only function of the society is that only its members dance when the *kaupois* song is sung. The Pound-maker Reserve followed suit, recently organizing a similar society called *matcanesak* "worthless."

Dakota Dance

At intervals during the Pow-wow the singers strike up a song of livelier tempo, one belonging to the *pwatcimuwin,* "Dakota dance." The dancers' privilege to participate in the Dakota dance must also be secured through gift distribution. They dance individually in a circuit around the singers. During this dance, the singers are seated around the drum; during the Pow-wow they stand. The step is one unique to the Dakota dance; the toe is lightly tapped on the ground once before the full forward step is taken. The trunk is slightly inclined and the left hand usually held on the hip. Some dancers go through the pantomime battle as they dance, scouting, aiming, shooting, scalping.

The dance was introduced by the Dakota who fled to Canada after the battle on the Little Big Horn. The songs used in the Dakota dance and Pow-wow are sung to burden syllables since the Cree did not understand the Dakota words.[17]

Tail Wagging Dance

The "Tail Wagging dance" is a social dance that shows European influence. Men choose women as partners. A man whispers his choice to the Shouter who goes over to where the women are sitting and tells the girl that she has been chosen. She joins the circle of dancers (similar to the Pow-wow circle) and the man steps in beside her. At a change in the music, the dancers separate into couples and dance away holding hands. The man dances backward, the girl forward. Some men hold one arm around their partner's waist and grasp her hand with the other. At another change in the music the couples "line up and dance sideways" (?). Finally, they dance in a circle again. After the dance each man tells the Shouter what gift he has for his partner; usually, it is fifteen or twenty-five cents. The Shouter publicly calls the girl to come to her partner and receive the present. She comes up, shakes hands with the man, takes her money, and goes back to the women's side. After several hours of dancing the Shouter announces that it is time for the women to choose. The women pick partners, give them gifts after each dance.

This dance was introduced to the River People when those Cree who had fled to the United States returned. This is the "Cree Dance" of the Lemhi and Fort Hall Shoshone.[18]

Tea Dance

A social dance that is no longer given, but which was popular thirty years ago, was known as the Tea dance, called in Cree, *kıckwepehtawin,* "playing drunk." A large kettle of very strong tea was brewed. Berries and sometimes plug tobacco were added. This was drunk during the dance and was supposed to have an intoxicating effect. The dance is thus described by Jefferson.[19]

> The Indians sit around in a circle — either inside (a house) or out, according to circumstances, the men on one side and women on the other, each bearing a cup of some sort into which the "tea" is dished out periodically by a master of the ceremonies. Songs are started to the accompaniment of a drum, in which all join. Soon, the "tea" begins to work and they one after another get up and dance . . . (The dance) consists of sudden bendings of the knees, to give the body an up-and-down motion taking, at the same time, short steps of a few inches to the side. This sideward movement will carry each person round the circle to the original position all to the two-thirds measure of the drum.

BEAR CEREMONIALISM

The bear was highly respected and was considered to be a very powerful spirit helper. In addition to the proper term for bear, *maskwa,* several other titles of respect and euphemisms were used. They were:—

ukimawokusisa·n, chief's son
neokatewayisıyin, four-legged person
wa·kayos, round back
kakıspicit, rough feet
aya·pisiskısikos, little eyes

When a bear was located, the hunter addressed the animal and promised to give it a feast if the bear would allow itself to be taken. If the hunter were successful he later provided food for a modest ceremony wherein smoke offerings and berries were consecrated to Bear spirit power. Skinner was present at such a ceremony in which a prayer was addressed to Bear

> telling it that it had been slain to furnish food and begging its good will and future abundance of bears.[20]

There is some indication that a lapse of bear observances had occurred, perhaps due to the Plains influence on Cree culture. One of Skinner's informants indicated as much[21] and Fine-day made this statement:—

> I remember that, long ago, I saw an old man kill a bear in his den. He spread the bear out with its head toward the sun (to the south). He smoked a pipe, talked to the powers, offered the pipe to the bear. But in my day this was not done. We had no special way of hunting bears. I myself caught many with steel traps. But I have heard that they used to sing and make medicine before they went out to hunt for bears.

Coming-day said that when a bear was being butchered, a person who was suffering from an ailment would cut out a piece of the flesh. A man who had a pain in his shoulder would cut a piece from the shoulder of the carcass, saying, "I have a pain in my shoulder and now I cut it out." Another bear custom was described by Coming-day:—

> I have not seen this, but I have heard of it many times. When a bear was killed, a bit of the breast fat, some meat from the ribs, and the large intestine were boiled together. Then the people were called in. One man took the intestine, held it to his ear saying, "What is it? I don't understand you. He tells me that I shall have good luck on the warpath." He bit off a piece of the intestine and passed it on. He didn't really hear anything, it was only a wish. They passed the intestine all around, even to the women. They wished for all kinds of things until it was all eaten. Then they served the rest of the food.

While Bear was one of the most venerated and feared of the spirit powers — perhaps because he was so venerated — tales were told of men who had foiled him. The following story, related by Fine-day, illustrates the type of narrative in which the most sacred characters or objects are flouted by the *dramatis personnae*. The stories concerning *wı·sahket-ca·hk,* the mythological trickster, were considered as fabulous and imaginary tales by my informants. But incidents such as the following, in which the principal character was placed in a kinship relation to the narrator or to someone known to the narrator, were given somewhat greater credence.

> I knew one man who beat out a spirit power. It was my grandfather's *osima,* his parallel cousin, whose name was *pı·hpa·hkwat,* Pot-belly. When he was young he was afraid of nothing and he used to laugh at everything. He had many dreams, but nobody knew it for he would never tell anyone.
> When the frost was on in the fall, an old man got into a conjuring booth. A lot of people were there to listen and Pot-belly was also there. One spirit power came and the rattle on

the tipi shook to announce his presence. "You know who I am. I am *ukimaw okusisa·n*, Chief's-son." That is a name for Bear.

Then Pot-belly called out, "The one that's afraid of you calls you Chief's-son. But I call you *Kispa·tıkitcisk,* Shaggy-rump."

The spirit power answered, "I know you very well. You are Pot-belly. When the berries are ripe, I will watch for you and change you." The spirit got mad and stopped shaking the booth. It went on saying, "You are too young to know of all the people whom I have twisted and whose looks I have changed." Pot-belly answered, "Yes, but I am not a bit afraid of you. I will change your appearance."

When Pot-belly got home his father scolded him, but he was laughing all the same; it was so funny. Pot-belly bought a good gun, cut the barrel down, and cut the stock just long enough to hold. He bought a knife of the kind called flat knife, which was sharpened on both sides.

Now when the young men went out hunting they saw the berries ripening one at a time. It was close to the time when they should meet each other. Pot-belly oiled his little gun. The criers went around telling the people to move to where there were more berries. Pot-belly loaded his gun and sharpened his knife. His time was getting close. He went where there weren't many people. He started picking berries and before he had a handful the bear was out. It came out of a bush.

Pot-belly had his gun ready. As the bear jumped he aimed and fired, but the gun didn't go off, the cap missed fire. The bear struck the gun out of his hand. Pot-belly grabbed his knife and at the same time stuck his hand down the bear's throat and held it fast there. The bear kicked the knife out of his hand but he couldn't bite. They wrestled. Pot-belly tried to drag the bear over to where the knife was lying, saying, "Come on, we are going to fix each other." The bear gasped, "Let me go." Pot-belly said, "I am going to cut the hide from around your eyes and your ears." The bear was scared and tried to settle with him. "If you let me go, I will be there when you want to save a person from dying." Pot-belly answered, "No, you'll fool me. If I let you go you'll forget everything. I am going to drag you to where my knife is." "If you let me go, Pot-belly, I will give you power in battle. As many hairs as I have on me, so many shots will miss you." "No, we've got to fix each other." "Pot-belly, you have me. I'll give you my claws so that you can even cure those who have consumption." "No, I'll fix you when we get to my knife." "You've beaten me, Pot-belly, I promise to listen to you all the time. Wherever you are, I will be there also, under the ground. I will give you power to cure all the people that send for you to save them because I'll always be with you." "You promise a lot. People believe in you and then you fix them up and change their appearance." "You have beaten me and I promise you that I will give you all I say. There are two things you must not do. Never point at me with a gun or knife and never taste of me. But I will even give you something to save yourself with if you do eat of me." "If you promise me that truly I will let you go." "I do." He let him go. The bear went back into the bush, his mouth full of blood.

He told Pot-belly that there was a young fellow who had been hurt in the back. "They will try to get you to cure him. I will help you do it and that is how you will be sure that I am keeping my promise." The bear gave his middle claw to Pot-belly with which to remove the sickness. Pretty soon a man leading a good horse and carrying a gun, came up to Pot-belly. Sure enough, he wanted him to cure the boy. Pot-belly sang a bear song, put his finger on the boy's back, and drew the matter out. Before he started doctoring he told his story. "If Bear is here, listening under the ground, he will cure this boy." He did.

My grandfather went along to help Pot-belly sing. He told me this story many times. *Pɪ·hpa·hkwat* used the bearclaw many times. But he would always suck the last of the matter out with his mouth. He was one who had won out over a spirit power.

EAGLE CEREMONIALISM

Eagle feathers adorned most objects in ritualistic use and lent them additional potency. Eagle wings were carried as badges of prestige by important men in ceremonies. They were used as fans in hot weather and also utilized as fire fans. A man who needed eagle feathers for any purpose would make a pipe offering to Eagle spirit power. He would ask Eagle to allow itself to be taken. If he did manage to secure an eagle, a feast would be given in which pipe offerings were made and berries consecrated and eaten. The feathers were plucked out and the eagle carcass was abandoned in a secluded place. When the feathers were to be used on a war bonnet or on other martial regalia, the eagle was eaten.

The use of the pit ambush method of trapping eagles was not known. Eagles were shot or obtained by strewing bait about and allowing the birds to gorge themselves until they were unable to fly.

FIRST EVENT CEREMONIALISM

The first berries of the season were not eaten until a feast had been given. The feast was not a communal affair; each family group conducted its own ritual. The berries were cooked and an old man invited to consecrate them. After the usual pipe offering, he held up a bowl of berries. First Great *Manito* was invoked and thanked for allowing men to eat berries again. Then the bowl was held toward the sun. Sun was asked to do his work faithfully — to ripen the berries — since he had been put there for that purpose. The bowl was

222

next held to Thunder and this power was asked for rain. Finally, the bowl was lowered to the earth and Earth was asked to bring forth her fruits so that the children might grow to be old.

If the bowl of berries were too heavy for the old man to hold up, he might dip a braid of sweetgrass in the juice and hold it up instead. Then all the family partook of the berries.

Women were not permitted to pick or eat the first berries during their menstrual periods.

A concept expressed by Fine-day in describing this ritual probably reflects Christian influence. He stated that

> Earth Man (the first human in Cree mythology) was told that the first berries to be picked had to be boiled. The juice represents Great *Manito's* blood and is a feast for all the spirit powers.

A similar feast was sometimes given when a man killed the first wild fowl of the year. The offerings at the feast were especially directed to the souls of the dead, and the pipe was pointed as it was during the funeral feast.

A man might vow that he would give a ceremony when the first thunder would be heard in the spring. Unlike other vows this promise was not actuated by a desire for supernatural aid in a specific situation, but was made simply for the sake of conducting the ceremony.

As soon as the pledger heard the first peals of thunder, he built a large sweatlodge, using as many as one hundred willow sticks in its construction. In the center of the lodge a rectangular excavation was made to receive the hot stones. The pledger entered the sweatlodge alone and the server passed in the hot stones which were placed in the excavation. Four were placed in the cardinal directions and one was set in the center. Other stones were piled around these.

The men who were to bathe came in. A pipe was offered and smoked around. Cloths and berries were consecrated. The door of the lodge was closed. The pledger dipped a braid of sweetgrass into water and splashed the hot stones. Each of the five stones, which represented the Thunders, was sprinkled. The pledger, beating time with a stick, sang his songs and the other men sang with him.

After four songs had been sung, the pledger prayed and then asked the men to pray. They did so and then all of them wailed. The door was opened; they came out and lay on the ground to cool off. Berries were eaten and the ceremony concluded.

The first game killed by a boy, no matter if it were only a chipmunk, was carefully preserved. When the child's parents had collected enough food, they gave a feast in honor of the event. The boy's kill was placed in a deep vessel as though it were a large animal. Pipes and cloths were offered to the spirit powers. Many prayers were made asking that the boy be successful as a hunter. Gifts were distributed by the parents.

DOG FEAST

A ceremony in which the ceremonial eating of dog meat was the principal rite was given for the spirit powers of medicines. While it was often given in fulfilment of a vow, it might also be made to restore failing medicines to their full power, or to signalize their acquisition by a new owner.

An enlarged tipi was built for the ceremony. In the center a circular sod altar was made, raised several inches from the ground, and a fire built on it. The server brought in food which the leader of the ceremony offered to the supernaturals. Then the meat was passed around by the server. The head, legs, breast, and tail of the dog were placed in a separate vessel before the leader. When the server came to one of the men who were entitled to these portions, the leader handed out the appropriate part. On the right and left of the tipi door (as one entered), sat men who were given the right and left hind legs, respectively. Just inside the entrance was a man who got the tail and backbone. The right and left fore legs were given to men at the rear of the tipi.

Before the food was eaten, a pipe was offered, then passed around. As each man took the pipe, he said *kana·-kɛhkana·,* the word for thanks which was also used in the *mite·wiwin.* After the meal, the leader again offered a pipe and spoke to the supernaturals.

A peculiar feature of this ceremony was the manner of inviting guests. The server went to the tipis of the men who were invited and handed them a feather, dyed red or blue. When the guests came into the ceremonial tipi they returned the feather to the server. If a man forgot to bring his feather along, he was given an extra large portion of food. Just before the feast was begun, the leader sang a song during which this man had to stand, holding his bowl of food before him.

TIPI PAINTING

The paintings on a tipi cover usually represented the

owner's spirit helpers and those of the man who had named him. Since the woman of the household owned the tipi cover, her approval of the design had to be secured before it could be painted. Thongs were passed around the tipi at various heights to mark off guide lines for the drawing. Then the cover was laid flat and the men applied the varicolored paints. When they had finished, the cover was set up.

A fire was built in the tipi and food, tobacco, and sweetgrass brought in. If the man who had named the giver of the feast were alive he was called to lead the ceremony. Else some other old man was invited to make the offerings and consecrate the tipi cover.

The host passed a pipe over sweetgrass smoke and gave it to the leader saying, "Teach me how to sing songs." The leader took the pipe and offered it to his spirit helpers. The host meanwhile sent someone to invite all the old men who had power songs. Women were also invited to partake of the feast and to help with the singing.

Food was passed around to the people assembled in the tipi. The leader offered a pipe again, held some of the food to the powers, and prayed that the giver of the feast be blessed. Then all ate. When they had finished, the servers passed out four rattles. As in many other rituals, they feinted three times at passing the rattle before actually handing it to a man. The leader took the "chief" rattle and led the company in his own songs. After he was through, the chief rattle was passed to the next man and he sang his songs. So it went around until every shaman had led the singers.

The ceremony was concluded when all the food had been eaten. The leader presented his own rattle to the host as he went out.

When a cover which had been painted with vision designs was worn out, it was taken into the bush and spread. The owner beat it with a stick and then abandoned it.

A tipi cover design illustrated by Cadzow[22] involves a pictographic representation of Cree theologic concepts. The paintings seen by the writer were generally much simpler, merely representing one or more spirit powers. The painted designs on a tipi seen at the Crooked Lake Reserve are shown in Fig. 26.

Drawings of battle scenes on tipi covers were just coming into fashion when the buffalo life was ended. Few men had them. No ritual was connected with painting war exploits. Fine-day stated that a man who possessed such a tipi cover

225

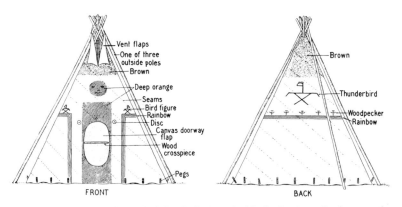

Fig. 26. Tipi of Long-horned-sitting-bull, Crooked Lake Reserve. Design seen by owner in a vision. Brown area at apex represents the sky. The rainbow lines on each side of the doorway are colored yellow, blue, brown, and green. The figure above the door represents the sun. The tipi had sixteen side poles.

was obliged to give a feast whenever he pitched it among a band not his own. *Maskwa* denied this.

It may be that both informants are partially right. Tipi covers painted with battle scenes were new and a body of customary practice had not yet grown up around their use. A man who pitched such a tipi among strangers might be considered guilty of an act of supererogation. He could establish his status, demonstrate his hospitality, and evince his basic adherence to traditional mores by giving a feast.

OFFERING POLE

The right to set up an offering pole could only be acquired in a vision. A certain spirit power, *manito·hkan, Manito*-like, granted the privilege and the pole was known by the same name. Gift offerings were tied to the pole or placed at its base. A log about five feet long was smoothed; eyes and a mouth were carved at one end. Two poles were lashed to the log, one on each side, to form arms. Sweetgrass, tobacco, and a cloth were laid in the bottom of the hole dug to receive the pole.

Pones described how he had dedicated his offering pole.

I told him (the spirit power of the pole) that whenever any persons, young or old, would give him something, to give a gift (i.e., a blessing) right back to them. I said that I would be living close by and that he should look after my children and be kind to all.

The best thing to give *manito·hkan* is blood soup. You

226

don't have to stand at the pole to give it. You must hold up the bowl of soup in your house and say *"manito·hkan,* we are giving you soup and we are eating it for you."

Offerings most commonly placed on the pole were tobacco, bows, arrows, feathers stripped to the quill except at the tip. At the present time the gifts to *manito·hkan* consist largely of worn out clothing, broken guns, old crockery. Dogs were not hung on the offering poles.

THE ELEMENTS OF RITUALISM

Certain phases of ritualistic procedure were present in all Plains Cree ceremonialism and may be abstracted and presented apart from any specific context. Although occurring in various juxtapositions, each element was to be found in practically every ceremonial activity.

Use of the Pipe

Foremost among these, in the sense that it inaugurated all ritualistic behavior, was the use of the pipe. Whenever there was occasion to call upon supernatural forces, a pipe was lighted and the spirit powers were summoned to have a smoke. The filled pipe was held over sweetgrass incense and handed to the man who was to do the praying. He drew a few deep puffs to set it going well and then held the stem upright before him at head level. He spoke in a solemn, almost chanted, cadence, always dedicating the first words to *kice· manito·,* Great *Manito.* The Creator was called upon to witness that his commands were being followed in the giving of smoke offerings.

Then the mouthpiece was swung around clockwise to the point of the compass where dwelt the spirit power who was to be addressed. This was a fixed locality for some powers, but more often was the place where the spirit had revealed itself to the supplicant. As the pipestem was held toward it, the power was invoked. The circumstances of the vision were repeated and the desired blessing requested. If the speaker had purchased or inherited the right to call upon the spirit power, he mentioned the name of the original visioner. After the petition was concluded, the pipestem was again turned clockwise and pointed toward a different spirit power, or perhaps to another place where the same spirit had appeared. Again a lengthy prayer was delivered and then the stem was shifted to yet another direction.

The number of places to which the stem was pointed varied with the worshiper and the particular situation. A shaman, while curing, might give smoke offerings to as many as five or six spirit helpers whose aid he requested. Ordinarily, a supplicant called only upon his own spirit helpers. At a funerary feast, however, the spirit powers which cared for the soul were given smoke offerings, although it was not often that they appeared in a vision. When the petitioner finished his prayers, he puffed at the pipe. If the tobacco were still burning it was a sure omen that the powers had smoked. If the pipe had gone out, it was re-lighted. Then it was passed around in a clockwise direction. Each man took a few whiffs and passed it on.

The pipe had secular as well as ceremonial usages. In social situations, such as in the Sioux dance or the Pow-wow, pipes were circulated without being offered up in prayer. Whenever men casually assembled, they passed a pipe among themselves. Smoking connoted a friendly and equitable relationship among the participants and was universal to all social intercourse. If a man had a request to make or a favor to ask of another, he shared a pipe before stating his desire. Tobacco was sent with every invitation or important message. Smoking the tobacco signified acceptance of the invitation or assent to the proposition stated in the message.

The concept underlying pipe offerings to supernaturals was that the spirit powers thus smoked in company with men. Having done this, they were bound to listen to the requests and, if at all possible, to accede to them.

Offerings

Material offerings were made whenever spirit powers were asked to exert their influence toward some particular end. Commonly, these offerings were pieces of trade cloth, bolt width and a yard or two long. One edge of the cloth was fastened to a small stick by which it was hung to a bush or a tree. By means of these offerings the grace of the spirit powers was procured. Cloth offerings were given under a variety of circumstances. The Sun dance lodge was always bedecked with multicolored offerings. A man setting out on the warpath would hang up a number of cloths, or vow to do so on his return. When a shaman was asked to cure, the gift taken to him was usually accompanied by several lengths of cloth for his spirit helpers. All offerings were eventually placed in the bush where no man or animal would molest them. Every ceremony entailed at least one cloth offering and often scores of them. Before the advent of traders, tanned hides were offered.

An old form of offering consisted of a large number of small rods. Willow sticks were peeled, pointed at each end, and painted. They were strung together on a sinew cord and hung up, or laid on the ground in a loose pile. One hundred such rods was the usual offering. Stick offerings of another type were the willow hooks placed on the Sun dance altar and also used in other ceremonies.[23] They were peeled wands, bent over like a shepherd's crook and held in shape by a sinew line. Two feathers were usually attached to the line and two to the bend of the stick. William Sap said that they represented an obsolete form of weapon.

Guns and clothing were also offered to spirit powers. They were similarly hung up in remote places. A very potent offering was made by cutting bits of skin from the arms and thighs, more rarely by hacking off a finger joint. These were enclosed in a buffalo bladder with tobacco, sweetgrass, a bit of charcoal, and then hung away. Torture by swinging from the center pole in the Sun dance lodge, or from a pole erected especially for the purpose, was considered to be an offering to the powers.

All offerings were consecrated before being given. A preliminary pipe was smoked and held toward the power to whom the offering was made. The purpose of the offering — to secure health or success in war, or to make good a pledge previously given — was repeated aloud.

Songs

An indispensable element of every ceremonial activity was the singing of revealed songs. While ritual smoking beckoned the spirit powers and offerings gratified them, songs placed a stamp of authenticity upon ceremonial procedure as emanating from genuine vision experience. To be accepted as a true vision innovation, a song had only to vary in minor details from one already known, such as the substitution of one word for another. Every grant of power from the supernaturals was accompanied by the imparting of a new song which was to be sung when the power was being exercised. These songs were owned by the visioner and could not be sung by others unless the right had been transferred. Certain secular songs, those used in gambling, in secular dances, in distributing gifts, could be sung by anyone.

229

Song texts consist of a few phrases, introduced and followed by burden syllables.

Round Dance Songs (Fine-day)

kɪcik	ninaskomikan	askɪ	ninaskomikan
the sky	blesses me	the earth	blesses me

naye·wutcikɪcikohk	ninimɪhaw	ahtcahk
up in the skies	I cause to dance	the spirits

naye·wutaskamakohk	ɪ·yinɪw
on the earth	the people

ninimɪhaw
I caused to dance

Masked Dance Songs (Fine-day)

nɪya	nitcewehtitan	nisaskahan	nɪya
I	I make it sound out	my staff	I

nitcewehtitan	nitastotin
I make it sound out	my hat

Warpath Song (Bare-ground)

osam	osawaskahk	ninipawin	manitowan·
because	on yellow grass	I stand	supernatural

nitɪapwin
is my eyesight

Smoking Tipi Songs (owner unknown)

nɪya	nohtawɪ	nɪwɪkimaw	kɪcemanito·
I	my father	I live with	Great *Manito*

nɪwɪkimaw	nɪya nohtawɪ	nɪwɪtapwemaw
I live with	I [with] my father	I am sitting

kɪcemanito·	nɪwɪtapwemaw
[with] Great *Manito*	I am sitting

A Woman Shaman's Song

iskutɛhk	nikanokucin	ɪyinaw	kitawanickaw
in the fire	I'll be seen	the person	will get up

The following types of songs were not individually owned:—

Gambling

nama kɪkwaɪ	kɪkayan	kama ye
nothing	you will have	for nothing

yimayɛn
you compete with me

Sung when Gifts Are Distributed

wesa	mɪwasinɪyiw	ukimaw	ototamowin
so	it is very good	the chief	his deeds

230

Sung by Camp Leader

nikan	nihaw	kahkakiw	nikan	nihaw	kihiw
ahead	he flies	the raven	ahead	he flies	the eagle

Sung by Men on War Party

ehpimuhtcan	nitcimus	niwapamaw
while walking	my sweetheart	I saw

atawiyah	miyocew	ma·ka
truly	good looking [she is]	but

niponeyimaw	ahwiah	niteyihtɛn
we will forget her	it pains	I think

amenitcimus	kicakihitihk	niwicipwehta·n
my sweetheart	I loved you	I am going away

itap anɛ	mina	kikawapamitin	pape maticiahkoh
sometime	again	I will see you	if we are alive

Sun Dance Songs

When the scouts returned to the camp

mahihkanak	piapahtatcik
the wolves [i.e., scouts]	when they come

ata·yohkan	omiawate
spirit power	makes merry

When a center pole is raised

mistik	kitawaniskaw	ata·yohkan
pole	wake up	spirit power

kitamiawatim		
will make merry		

Pledger's song at beginning of dance

mistik	nipowiw	manito·	kanawapimew
the pole	is standing	Manito	looks at him

Sun dance song (Fine-day)

pi·cim	niwitcihik	kitanipowean pi·cim
the sun	helps me	to stand	the sun

niwitcihik	kita pimohtean
helps me	to walk

Prayer

A major portion of every ceremony was devoted to speaking to the supernaturals. Prayers were lengthy, repetitious, detailed, and exhortatory. Supplicants addressed the spirit powers very much as they would address men. They called their attention to certain circumstances and said or implied that the powers were obliged to fulfil their contractual obligations.

The supernaturals were particularly apt to come to the aid of one whose plight was so bad that the spirits were moved to compassion. The one theme that runs through most prayers and invocations may be summed up in the phrase "pity me." Boys were visited by spirit helpers during vision quests because the powers felt sorry for the lad suffering from hunger and thirst. Girls, during puberty, were likely to secure visions, because they were terrified by the flow of blood, and the powers sought to allay their weeping. A man who prayed before a raid asked his spirit helper to grant him success because of his piteous condition. In leading the Sun dance prayers, *Maskwa* portrayed the sad state of reservation life and the "pity us" rang out clearly again and again. So it was with all speeches directed to the supernatural powers.

When *kıce·manito·* was addressed he was not urged to take any direct action. Prayers to Him simply asked that He look at, or regard, or witness, what was being done. The implication was that the ceremonial rites were done according to His will.

The matter-of-fact tone of prayers may be judged from the following examples:—

Pones, one of the two pledgers of the Sun dance witnessed in 1935, began the dancing with this invocation:—

> Our father, master of us all, of course I have to name you first. Look at this dancing. All Spirit Powers, I beg a good life for the people that are coming here to fast. Last fall when my children were having bad luck I promised you this lodge. Now I am glad and happy that it is being completed for me. I am satisfied and I think *manito·* is satisfied. Now give us good health for all the people. I cannot say more for I shall take up too much time.

Fine-day told how he had once vowed to swing from the center pole at the Sun dance, but decided instead to cut off bits of his skin and give them as an offering to his spirit helper. The reason he gave for the substitution was that there might have been menstruating women at the ceremony who might have spoiled his offering. When he hung away the bits of skin, he said:—

> Thunder, I promised you that I would swing from the pole. You know how it happened that I didn't do it. I am now going to fulfil my promise. I think it will be just as well for you to accept this skin as an offering. So I'll hang it up for you.

232

The Vow

The place of the vow in the religious complex has been mentioned in several connections. It was the accepted manner of contracting divine assistance in a crisis. A father whose son was critically ill not only called in a shaman, but also raised his hands to the heavens and spoke to a spirit power. He might promise to give the spirit a Sun dance or some other sacred ceremony. The life of the child was requested in return for the vow. A man did not often make a vow in order to secure health for himself. It was usually a sick person's parents, grandparents, or spouse who pledged themselves to undergo torture or hardships for him, for it was no easy matter to give a sacred ceremony. The pledger was often obliged to fast for a considerable time. Moreover, the giving of a ceremony entailed a considerable outlay of food, offerings, and gifts.

A man usually vowed to give a ceremony that he had a right to conduct. If he did not have the prerogative, someone who did, conducted the ritual for him. Should the favor asked of the powers be a minor matter, the vower would make a minor pledge such as a cloth offering or the promise to build a sweatlodge for the spirit.

The obligation to fulfil a vow was not canceled by the death of the one for whose welfare the pledge had been made. Similarly, even if a war trip ended disastrously, the vows that had been made upon setting out had to be fulfilled.

Food

Food was served at ceremonial occasions; curing rituals were an exception. The crier, in inviting people to a ceremony, usually called ". . . and bring your eating utensils along." Berries were always eaten at ceremonies. When platters of meat and berries and buckets of soup were brought into a ceremonial lodge, they were held over sweetgrass smoke before being set down. A bit of every kind of food that had been prepared was set before the leader of the ceremony. After pipes had been offered, the food was held up toward the spirit powers and they were asked to partake of it. Only after this was done could the food be eaten.

Just as taking the pipe posited a state of social equanimity among the smokers, so did eating together establish an amicable and propitious relationship among the participants.

Thus, when the spirit powers partook of the food offering, they could hardly turn a deaf ear to the petitions addressed to them by the host. Much of the ceremonialism may be interpreted as a projection of the rules of social intercourse to the sphere of the supernaturals. For example, every gift received imposed a reciprocal obligation on the recipient. A man who was given a new robe during some public distribution of wealth, often gave clothing away at the same ceremony or at one soon after. An old man who received a gift paid off his obligation by publicly praising and praying for the giver. In the same way cloth offerings were considered to be gifts to the spirit powers, in return for which they were duty bound by the rules of the social game to return favors in proportion and kind.

Servers

The manual tasks involved in carrying on the ceremonies were entrusted to the *oskapewisak,* "servers." Two men were chosen for the position at every ceremony. They passed out food, seated the guests in order of their rank, made the smudges, filled the pipes, and tended the fires. Only in the Sun dance were the two latter functions performed by special officers. In the Warriors' lodge these servers were permanent officers, but in ceremonies they were chosen by the host for the occasion. It was a position of honor for a young man. The servers had to observe certain ritualistic requirements in the manner of serving, and their bearing and appearance reflected credit or discredit on the ceremony. Therefore appointment to the position implied that the host had confidence in the abilities of the men he chose.

In minor ceremonies, the servers called the guests, made announcements, and distributed gifts. In the more elaborate ceremonies, as the Round dance and Prairie-Chicken dance, a Crier was appointed to perform these duties.

Smudge

The sweetgrass smudge was a universal component of all ceremonial practices, except the *mite·wiwin.* The grass *(Savastana odorata)* was gathered when long and plaited into braids. Before and at frequent intervals during every ritual, a bit of dried grass was broken off onto live coals. The resultant aromatic smoke was regarded as a purifying agent, as a means of dispelling mundane atmosphere and substituting an odor pleasing to the supernaturals.

Pipes which were to be offered were held over the smoke. All ceremonial accessories had to be passed through the incense. If a sacred bundle were to be handled, those who were to touch it washed their hands in the smoke and drew it over their bodies.

Pine needles and the stalks of a variety of grass called "raven stick" were also burned for this purpose. Special altars for the smudge were not made.

Miscellaneous Ritualistic Elements

Other common denominators of ceremonialism may be briefly mentioned.

All movements were in a clockwise direction. The pipe was passed, food served, and dancers moved, clockwise. Only during the Masked dance, when everything was reversed, were ceremonial motions made in a counter-clockwise direction.

Important guests were invited by name. Even though a man were already in the ceremonial lodge at the beginning of a ceremony, the Shouter called out so that all the camp might hear, "Flying-eagle, you are invited to come."

When the servers gave a rattle or any object, they often made three gestures as though they were giving it to the recipient and with the fourth actually handed it over.

Dancing was a part of many ceremonies. There were two principal dance steps. One, as in the Sun dance, consisted of standing in place and rhythmically bending the knees. The other, used in the Round dance, involved advancing one foot a few inches and drawing the other foot up to it.

Face painting was done in accordance with patterns and designs revealed in visions. Many, but not all, visions included instructions in the kind of painting to be done before the vision prerogative was exerted.

Men and women sat apart. The women sat to the right as one entered a lodge, the men to the left and at the rear.

The ceremonial number, four, was repeatedly used. Thus four smudges were built, four songs sung, four offerings made, four preliminary rituals held, four puffs taken upon lighting a pipe, and so on through each part of every ritual. When four objects or activities could be spatially oriented, they were laid in the four cardinal directions.

Thunder spirit power was more frequently called on than any other, and it was conceived as being multiple, residing in the four directions. Each thunder was associated with a particular color and cloth of that color was offered to the respective thunders. When food or whiskey was offered to the thunderers, the bowl was first held up to the Chief of the Thunders above, to the east for Red Thunder, to the south for White, to the west for Blue, and to the north for Black Thunder.

Sweatbath

The sweatbath was not common to all ceremonies, but was very often utilized. Sweatbaths could be taken for pleasure, as an offering to a spirit power, or as ritualistic cleansing preliminary to any ceremony. The sweatlodge was built, stones heated and passed inside. Sweetgrass was burned inside the sweatlodge and a pipe offered. Then the lodge was closed and water sprinkled on the hot stones. A set of four songs was sung and then the cover was lifted a little and the bathers rested. They sang two or three sets of songs in all and then came out of the lodge. They lay on the ground to cool off.

Bundles

Doctor Wissler has abstracted certain general features from Blackfoot ceremonialism.[24] Although the phrasing of the Plains Cree rituals was often quite different from those of the Blackfoot, the general characteristics were much alike. The basic Blackfoot conception of a ritual is

> something that brings about a relation, or rapport, between the supernatural source and a single individual.[25]

This was also true of the ritualism of Plains Cree bundles. Among the Cree, however, the bundles were not as elaborate nor did they play as important a part in the religious life. Of the various ceremonial features enumerated by Wissler, only a few were totally foreign to Plains Cree practice. These were the grouping of songs into sets of seven, the "receiving sign," the "wing movement," and the altar for smudges.

[1]Other accounts of the Plains Cree Sun dance which differ in some minor respects from that given here, may be found in the following sources: BROWNING, T.B., (A Note on the) Sun Dance (Proceedings, Canadian Institute, Toronto, third series, 1887-1888, vol. 6, Toronto, 1889), p. 40; CURTIS, The North American Indian, pp. 80-85 (Wood Cree); LANE, CAMPBELL, The Sun Dance of the Cree Indians (The Canadian Record of Science, vol. 2, Montreal, 1886), pp. 22-26; GODDARD, PLINY EARLE, Notes on the Sun Dance of the Cree in Alberta (Anthropological Papers, American Museum of Natural History, vol. 16, part 4, New York, 1919); PAGET, The People of the Plains, pp. 28-41; SKINNER, ALANSON, The Sun Dance of the Plains-Cree (Anthropological Papers, American Museum of Natural History, vol. 16, part 4, New York, 1919); JEFFERSON, Fifty Years on the Saskatchewan, pp. 40-49 (Stoney traits are included in this account of the Cree Sun dance).

[2]Since songs were tokens of supernatural visitation and hence of the right to give any ceremony, it was really the songs, rather than the ceremonies proper, that were revealed, purchased, or inherited.

[3]SKINNER, Political Organization, pp. 538-540.

[4]*Ibid.,* p. 538.

[5]PEESO, The Cree Indians, p. 53.

[6]CADZOW, DONALD A., Smoking Tipi of Buffalo-Bull the Cree (Indian Notes, Museum of the American Indian, Heye Foundation, vol. 4, New York, 1927), pp. 271-280.

[7]JEFFERSON, Fifty Years on the Saskatchewan, pp. 85-87.

[8]SKINNER, Political Organization, pp. 528-529.

[9]*Ibid., p. 533.*

[10]BLOOMFIELD, LEONARD, Plains Cree Texts (Publications, American Ethnological Society, vol. 16, New York, 1934), pp. 204ff.

[11]Quoted in SKINNER, Political Organization, pp. 533-534.

[12]*Ibid.,* p. 537.

[13]Quoted *ibid.,* p. 536.

[14]LACOMBE, Dictionnaire et Grammaire, p. 367.

[15]WISSLER, Shamanistic Societies, p. 862.

[16]CAMERON, The War Trail of Big Bear, pp. 134-138.

[17]An interesting case of differential diffusion occurred. After telling how the Dakota had sold certain dances to the Cree and how the Stoney had "captured" Cree to dance in the Pow-wow, Fine-day said, "But there was one dance the Dakota would not give to the Cree. Two men at a time would dance in it. It was danced to call the buffalo. They were afraid that we might get too many buffalo if we danced that dance."

[18]LOWIE, ROBERT H., The Northern Shoshone (Anthropological Papers, American Museum of Natural History, vol. 2, part 2, New York, 1909), p. 221.

[19]JEFFERSON, Fifty Years on the Saskatchewan, p. 73.

[20]SKINNER, Political Organization, p. 542.

[21]*Ibid.,* p. 541.

[22]CADZOW, The Prairie Cree Tipi, pp. 25-27.

[23]Illustrated in CADZOW, Smoking Tipi of Buffalo-Bull, p. 276.

[24]WISSLER, CLARK, Ceremonial Bundles of the Blackfoot Indians (Anthropological Papers, American Museum of Natural History, vol. 7, part 2, New York, 1912), pp. 246-278.

[25]*Ibid.,* p. 272.

Warfare

MOTIVES

Success in warfare was the high road to prestige. War exploits were the chief concern of the young men and constituted the stock topic of conversation among their elders. Women desired sons who would become famous warriors; girls despised the men who had never been on a war party. Raids netted the victorious warrior acclaim for his prowess and were the means for obtaining the wealth in horses which implemented his rise to high status.

The great enemies of the Plains Cree were the tribes of the Blackfoot Confederacy. Most war parties were directed against the Blood, Blackfoot, and Piegan; the heaviest losses suffered by the tribe were inflicted by these people. The Sarsi and Crow were often met in battle. Tribes less frequently encountered, but none the less bitterly hostile, were the Gros Ventre, Cheyenne, several of the Dakota divisions, Nez Percé, and Flathead. These enemy tribes were only to the south and southwest of the Plains Cree country, for the Assiniboin, Plains Ojibwa, and Wood Cree were friendly and close allies.

PROCEDURE OF THE RAID

Most military operations took the form of nocturnal raids on an enemy encampment. The objective was to get away with as many horses as possible, shunning any engagement with the pursuing forces unless it was absolutely unavoidable. If a group of hostile tribesmen were met in the course of workaday activities, the Cree attacked only if they heavily outnumbered their opponents. Otherwise, the men retired to their tipis and awaited a possible assault. Young bloods, however, often cast prudence aside and came to grips with a superior party, hoping thereby to gain greater glory. When the alarm was raised that a raiding party had made off

239

with horses, all the men in camp joined in hot pursuit. But unless the thieves were overhauled within a distance comfortably close to home, the chase was abandoned.

A raiding party could be organized and led only by a man who had vision sanctions to perform these functions. Previous experience in battle was another requirement for leadership. When a man who had these qualifications decided to undertake an expedition, he told his intention to several of his companions and relatives. They were usually eager to go along and they tried to keep their plans secret for a time, so that others might not prepare to join them. Recruits were not welcome because a large party was not as efficient as a small one. They agreed upon a date for the departure and thenceforth collected weapons and ammunition. Extra pairs of moccasins for the journey were prepared by their mothers and sisters.

For several nights prior to leaving, the members of the party sang war songs and danced in front of the tipis of men of rank. They received a small gift of tobacco, food, or ammunition from each tipi owner. On the night of their departure, they danced one final time and then scattered. Each went to his own tipi, gathered his belongings, and met the others at a preappointed place. They set out at first in a direction different from that they really intended to follow. This precaution was taken so that the party might not grow too large. There was always a superfluity of youngsters eager to join and though their presence handicapped the expedition, they could not be turned back, once they had found the group. Thus the first care of a war party was to dodge these youthful enthusiasts.

Parents were not always eager to see their beloved sons go off on the warpath and sometimes tried to dissuade them. In a tale recorded by Bloomfield, a chief's son is mocked by a woman because he has never fought the enemy. The boy is ashamed and his father consoles him with these words,

> Here, my son, dress yourself; do not be shamed; do nothing foolish to yourself. This is no way to be. I never bid you go to the scenes I need not name; I love you too much. Poor men are they who go on the warpath, [note well!] for they hope to steal horses; but you, your horse is handsome; he is fleet of foot. And you yourself are handsome; you are not poor, . . .[1]

But the father's words are to no avail and the boy goes out to meet the enemy.

This scene was frequently enacted in actuality, and the

social pressure on a young man was usually too great to be ignored. Men who had not participated in warfare were derided and ridiculed. Their names might be given feminine endings and young warriors might summarily tell them to join "their fellow-women." Thus, a war party usually had a full quota of boys anxious to establish themselves as real men via the proving ground of battle.

The party went on foot and usually traveled at night and slept during the day. Young men who participated in a war expedition for the first time were subject to special restrictions. They performed the menial tasks and might not eat raw meat, bone marrow, nor rib meat. For the amusement of the others, a novice would be blindfolded and given a club. He was told to hit a bone that had been placed on the ground. If he succeeded, he was permitted to suck out the marrow in the bone. Novices could not scratch their heads with their fingers, but used a stick for the purpose. They were not allowed to listen to the songs of the leader and were supposed to remain out of sight of the others when scouts returned to the party with a report of the enemy.

Every night that the party was in hostile territory, the leader sang his power songs and offered a pipe to his spirit helpers. He asked for supernatural aid and sometimes, while singing, said that he foresaw the position of the enemy camp. It was the leader's ability to prognosticate the course of events by the aid of his spirit helper that made vision sanctions so necessary for leadership of a war party.

The man with the best war record (who was not necessarily the leader) called the other members of the party, *nicimitik,* "my little brothers." On the warpath also, a man would address one who outranked him in deeds as "elder brother," irrespective of age or kinship affiliation.

The men amused themselves in many ways. They passed a pipe around and told stories. One man might have a girl in camp whom he wanted to win. He would take the pipe, point it to where she was and say, "To her *ahtcak,* soul, I point this pipe. I would like to see her in a dream tonight." Then he would take a piece of the large intestine of a buffalo, scrape it and bite off a piece. "Thus as I bite off this piece will I take a pinto mare for her." The group would laugh and tease him about his desires.

Another way of making merry would be to roast and cut the large intestine of a buffalo. The gut was doubled back on itself to make two layers. Both ends were tied and it was laid on the coals. When it was well done, the top layer was stripped off and the inside portion passed around. Each man cut off a piece representing his estimate of the length of his penis. A great deal of banter and joking went on.

Some men were known to have naturally short foreskins which did not completely cover the glans penis. Such men were made the butt of jokes. They were known as *peya·k*. The term was also extended to anyone whose actions were ridiculous or funny. If there were a *peya·k* with the party, one of the men, during a dull evening, would lift the *peya·k's* breechclout and say, "Come, you are invited." They would seat him on a piece of fat and tie a thong around his penis. He would be given the part of the buffalo intestine which adjoins the paunch to eat, for this was supposed to be the favorite food of the *peya·k*. A blanket would be hooded over his face and jokes made about how he was "peering through," just as did his male member. When he smoked a pipe, he held the bowl upside down and did other things which served as sources of jesting. The *peya·k* who resented the teasing brought redoubled ridicule and teasing on himself.

A warrior skilled in taking horses would often be squired by one or two less accomplished men. They cooked for him, mended his moccasins, and carried his load. In return he gave them some of the horses he took. These squires were either inexperienced boys who attached themselves to a noted fighter or older men who did not have the agility and skill necessary to a successful horse thief.

The leader made all the decisions and detailed the men to various duties. Dissensions were few, because of his recognized authority, and for another reason stated by an informant in this way:—

> If you were wise, on one of these raids you took care to be on good terms with the others of the party so that if they took horses and somehow you didn't get any, they would give you several. If a man were boastful, his partners might take a dislike to him. When the horses were taken and the enemy aroused, they might say to the boaster, "Go back and get horses for yourself as we did." The man who took horses disposed of them as he liked.

When the war party entered enemy territory, two scouts were sent ahead to survey the country. They were chosen by the leader for their ability and resourcefulness.[2] On their backs they wore wolf hides. The rest of the party remained in hiding during their absence.

When the scouts returned, they barked like coyotes or

howled like wolves to give notice of their approach. On hearing this signal the members of the party piled up a heap of branches or buffalo chips. The scouts dashed into the camping place and kicked through the pile. Each member of the party grabbed a bough or a chip, saying as he did so, "I have taken a black horse," or "I have captured a pinto mare," or some similar utterance.

After the scouts reported their discoveries, the party advanced to the enemy camp. Those who possessed shields, war bonnets, or other protective devices, unwrapped them, sang the related songs, and put them on. Some painted their faces. Each man prepared his weapons for instant action and carefully coiled a length of hide thong around his shoulder. The thongs were used to lead away the horses.

Under cover of night, the party deployed and entered the enemy encampment in pairs. They stealthily cut the horses loose and led them away. Gathering at an appointed spot, they rode hard until the pursuit had been shaken off. Should the pursuers catch up with them, the raiders dug a pit or trench atop an elevation, where they remained besieged until the enemy withdrew, as often happened, or until they could steal through the enemy cordon. Sometimes, however, they were so greatly outnumbered that the party was wiped out. Most of the valorous deeds that were later recounted took place during these combats. Men who were besieged sang their power songs to invoke the aid of supernaturals. While singing, they would beat time on their guns with a special stick which they carried.[3]

When the members of a Cree war party saw one of the enemy shot down, they would give the war whoop, yelling in a high pitch and clapping their hands over their mouths at the same time. Another kind of whoop called the "Blackfoot yell" was used when attacking the enemy or when a pursuer caught sight of the fleeing war party. This was also a high pitched yell, *he . . . yı*.

The "no flight" obligations found among some Plains tribes were not known to the Plains Cree. Two instances of "Crazy Dogs" were recalled by informants, but it seems that this was a novel and rare practice. "Crazy Dogs" were men who had received vision instruction to be unusually brave. During an engagement they danced continually, shaking a feathered rattle. When confronted by the enemy, they danced out into the open, advancing toward the hostile lines until they were shot down. The other members of the party used force to restrain the Crazy Dogs from exposing themselves.

THE RETURN

When the war party reached home, they signaled their coming by flashing mirrors in the sun. The leader gave advance notice of the casualties by flapping his robe once for every one of his fellows who had been killed. The whole camp came out to escort the returning raiders back to their tipis. The men who had taken scalps blackened their faces with charcoal they had saved from their campfires. When the women came up, the warriors smeared charcoal over their faces also.

In the exuberance of the welcome, the warriors were often stripped of their clothes and even their weapons taken and kept by their rejoicing tribesmen. Coming-day explained this practice as follows:—

> The reason why they give all their things away is because they might be killed the next time. Then who is going to have their belongings? (i.e., they won't have them anyway). They don't know when they are going to die and so they give away all their goods.

The warriors had, as it were, renounced rights to their personal possessions when they had staked both their lives and their belongings on the uncertainties of warfare. When they returned with glory and spoils they would not be petty enough to hoard their personal property. Jefferson even says that:—

> The custom was to rifle the tents of the near relatives of those who brought home scalps—probably with the idea that they were so transported with joy as not to notice the depredation. This was the next step, and all hastened to take what they could lay hands on; [so that a returned warrior was often obliged] to seek shelter and food in someone else's lodge. It paid a man better to devote his talents and audacity to horse-stealing rather than the acquisition of scalps, and yet this latter was infinitely more desired.[4]

Yet, even the taking of horses yielded few immediate material benefits to the successful raider. The captured horses were given to relatives and friends, so that out of a string of ten or twelve stolen animals, a man would keep only one or two for himself. Of course, the horses given away were not outright gifts. If a man gave several horses to his brother, the brother would come to his aid later when he needed horses, say, to purchase a sacred bundle or when he needed large amounts of food to give a ceremony.

A corollary to the concept that a man renounced his

rights to material possessions when he took to the warpath was the lack of mourning for a brave fighter who had been killed in combat. When a novice or some undistinguished young man fell in battle, his parents mourned for him just as they would have had he died at home. But when a Chief or a Worthy Young Man was killed, there was no wailing for him. When the news was imparted, the women sang a song in which they named the dead hero saying, "Yellow-horse (if that was his name) is a man," i.e., he died as a man should die. An experienced fighter knew the risks he was taking and was prepared to give up his life. A warrior might even instruct his companions not to bury him if he should be killed. By doing this he demonstrated the light-heartedness with which he regarded death.

As soon as the returning party entered the encampment, the Happy dance *(kamatcıwcimuwin)*[5] took place. The warriors stood in the center of the camp; the one who had accomplished the bravest deeds advanced a little ahead of his companions. Young women put on the feather bonnets and the other war paraphernalia used by the men in battle and carried the scalps taken by the men on sticks. They lined up in a row facing the group of warriors. Men with drums (Jefferson states that no drums were used) began a victory song and the women danced toward the fighters and then away from them. The returned veterans left the celebration as soon as they could and modestly remained in their tipis during the night dance which followed. In this dance both men and women participated, dancing shoulder to shoulder in a circle around the singers.

The first dance is described by Jefferson[6] in these words.

> It is a day dance and only women take part in it. Their faces and hands are blackened, like those of the men. No drum is used, and the songs are peculiar to the dance. All join in the tune and someone is inspired to set words that suit the occasion. In this recitative the name of the hero and his great deeds are extravagantly sung, with the chorus coming in at the end of each sentence. The whole performance is sweet to the men, who stand mute objects of admiration. The scalp wands are snatched from each other by the dancers, who progress round and round in time with the tune. At intervals, one virago or another pours forth fiendish sentiment in staccato song. Eventually, both sentiments and fury are exhausted and the party separates to meet again at night.[7]

SCALPING

Scalps were laced to willow hoops and the flesh side

painted red or yellow. Several scalps might be taken from a single corpse, since only a narrow strip was cut off by each scalper. After being carried in the Happy dance the scalps were sewn to clothing or attached to the Pipestem bundle. After the homecoming celebration, the scalp itself was little valued. It was the honor of being named and praised by the women, that motivated the young men in their fanatic quest for scalps. *Maskwa* once sadly remarked that "Many, many of the best young men were killed for the sake of being named in the Happy dance."

Sometimes the arms and legs or even the heads of enemy bodies would be brought back to camp. The women carried these trophies in the dance and later the children would kick them around. If there were an opportunity to take captives, enemy women and children were carried off. Men were always killed. The captives were guarded for a while and later, when they had grown accustomed to the Cree life, accepted as full members of the tribe.

WAR EXPLOITS

While the purpose of most war expeditions was to get horses, the mere taking of horses did not constitute a particularly meritorious deed. The criterion employed in rating war exploits was the degree of danger to which the man was exposed while accomplishing the feat. Thus a man who shot an enemy while he himself was under fire, outranked one who had killed an enemy from ambush. Similarly, one who had killed his man with a club had more to his credit than one who had picked off his opponent with a rifle. A man's rank depended to a large degree on the courage he displayed in battle. The old men accorded a warrior the precedence to which he was entitled by his proven valor. Rarely was there any complaint or argument against their judgment.

This concept was carried out logically in that the highest deed of all was to make peace with a hostile tribe. It required great courage to approach the enemy unarmed, for hostile peoples usually shot the Cree at sight. But considerable trade advantages could be derived from a peaceful parley and a few of the sturdiest men undertook such missions. Even after the Indians had been settled on reserves, occasional parties of Cree visitors were slaughtered by their Blackfoot hosts — at least so run the Cree accounts.

Another feat which brought great praise was the killing of an old man. Old men usually remained in their tipis and were surrounded by their friends. To get a scalp with gray hair a man usually had to fight off many of the old man's protectors.

Although the number and nature of the war deeds accomplished by a man counted for a great deal in many phases of Cree culture, there were but two occasions for the formal counting of coups. A man publicly recited his war feats only during the Sun dance and the Pow-wow. All the detail that could be remembered was mentioned. During a raid the men sometimes went out of their way to do something which they could later relate. *Maskwa* was once stealing out of a Dakota camp with three horses when he came across one of his companions slashing some hides that were staked out. There was momentary danger of arousing the enemy and the destruction of the hides in no way furthered the Cree purpose. When *Maskwa* later asked the man why he had wasted precious time in cutting up the hides, the reply was, "Just so that I would have something more to tell when I got back."

VENGEANCE PARTY

While the greater number of war activities were carried on by small detachments raiding for horses, larger parties were occasionally organized for vengeance. They were initiated by parents whose sons had been slain by a hostile tribe. The bereaved father and mother borrowed a Pipestem bundle and carried it among the various bands of Plains Cree, wailing and begging that the men help avenge the death of their son.

They often succeeded in recruiting a large party which set out against the offending tribe. Only on such occasions did women accompany a fighting expedition. They were taken along to cook for the men. The Warrior society policed the march, kept order and rounded up the stragglers. This was also the only time when the Warrior society, as a group, had anything to do with warfare. When the enemy was found, the attack was planned so as to annihilate the camp.

Fine-day stated that vengeance parties were no longer undertaken when he was a boy (1860 and after) because the increasing use of firearms had terminated this custom. A few guns, effectively used by the defenders, could inflict great damage on a large number of assailants.

INSIGNIA

The high esteem accorded to valor made for an elaborate

symbolism for the representation of battle accomplishments. The meanings and forms of the designations were not constant among the several bands and varied from time to time even within a single band. A feather tied in the hair signified that the wearer had taken a scalp. If the quill were stripped, except for a tuft at the top, it meant that the wearer had wrestled with and overcome an enemy. A stick with shavings curled at one end, also placed in the hair, denoted a wound. Two such sticks meant a wound in which the bullet had pierced the part of the body hit. Another way of representing a wound was to paint a mark on the part of the clothing which covered the scar. Red paint dripping from the mark symbolized blood flowing from the wound. A man who had held off the enemy singlehandedly slit the skirt of his coat into strips. Noted warriors wore fringes from the heels of their moccasins. A long horizontal stripe on a robe signified a long war trip. A cross marked on a robe proclaimed that the owner had engaged in a peace parley. A mark like an inverted U, sometimes with rectangular corners, was placed on various articles of clothing; each mark symbolized one captured horse. A heart-shaped mark also symbolized stolen horses. Members of a war party who had entrenched themselves to fight off the enemy were privileged to carry a hooped staff with feathers on it or a feathered hoop. The feathers symbolized the enemy.

METAPHOR OF BATTLE

One of the mechanisms whereby the war accomplishments of an individual were brought to bear on the social and religious system may be called "the metaphor of battle." A man established his right to perform a ceremonial act by referring to a somehow similar deed he had executed in warfare. For example, the man who cut the braid of hair from the head of a deceased person, told of a time when he had taken a scalp. Grasping the braid he said, "and this is how I cut that scalp," and snipped it off. The man who carried the corpse out of the tipi announced before doing so. "I killed an enemy in his tipi and dragged him out of it. Now I am going to take this body out." Only men who could metaphorically relate their ceremonial acts to their battle deeds were privileged to perform these functions.

When a tipi cover was appropriated for the Sun dance lodge built in 1935, *Sapostahɪka·n*, "Shooting-through," stepped up to a tipi and told how he had once slashed an

248

enemy's tipi. When he finished recounting the deed, he lightly struck the cover with a stick to symbolize his action and it was then taken down and put on the sides of the Sun dance lodge.

One of the riders in a Horse dance dropped an otterskin ornament. It could be picked up only by a man who had taken an otter fur, from the enemy. No one at the dance had done this except Basil Favel. He came up, told how he had shot a Blackfoot and taken a mirror, edged with otter fur, from the body. Then he picked up the skin which had been dropped, jocularly saying, "Yes, it was just like this fur. I think it must be from the very same hide."

The case history of a man's battle deeds was similarly imprinted upon the social and religious life. A war record brought a man to public notice time and time again throughout his life and so raised his prestige status.

A WAR RECORD

Fine-day was the most noted Plains Cree warrior still alive in 1935. In the closing years of the nomadic life he was generally recognized as one of the bravest men and best fighters in the tribe. During the 1885 rebellion he led the Plains Cree against the Canadian army forces. He has not included this exploit in the account of his war record which follows.

> The first time I went out was when I was very young. I heard that my brother was going away. I did not mean to do anything but follow my brother, and went along with the war party. When we got close to the Blackfoot we could hear them and see them hunting. The ground was level all around so that we could not hide. We stayed there, waiting for the night to come. The name of the leader was *otcι·pwam,* Pointed-thigh.
>
> Soon we couldn't see anything, it was getting late. The leader started to sing about his dreams. We were all listening; I sat amongst the others. All at once, a coyote yelled and scared me badly. When he stopped singing *tcatcwatcιw* gave a pipe to Pointed-thigh. As he handed the pipe over, he asked the leader what the coyote had said. Pointed-thigh answered, "You will have a very hard time. You had better go home."
>
> One of the men, *opinawewin,* told my brother to take the boy, Fine-day, home. He replied, "No, I will not go back because I came to look for those people before us." All the other men said that they were willing to go on. Again *opinawewin* told my brother to go home with me, but he said that he was going to stay. Then they told me to go home. Finally, I said, "No, when my brother goes back, I'll go with him." They started to plan how to hide. They could not hide along the river for the Blackfoot might see them there.

249

Then *tcatcwacıw* said to his brother, Pointed-thigh, "Let us go home. This isn't the only raid that we will ever go on. This scabby-necked boy will be in our way." He said, "All right." They all went back. On the way home, I had a very hard time keeping up with the men. They walked night and day. I got very sleepy; often I was just about asleep when I'd wake with a start. We got home at last. I had set out on that trip for nothing.[8]

From then on there were many fights. I would have gone but I was only a small boy and had nothing to shoot with. When I was a little older I started on another trip. *Apistatim,* Small-horse, was the leader. We arrived at the enemy camp. I was very young and inexperienced, but the leader chose me and two others (to go into the camp) to steal horses. They were *ka·kıcikawahtcapew,* Day-bow, and *kitowe·paı,* He-who-gasps.

The three of us went. It was a dark, cloudy night. There was no wind. When we were close to the tipis, the dogs started to chase us and bark at us. I dropped to the ground and saw the others running away. Three dogs came up, sniffed at me and ran on to follow my partners. I thought, "The dogs woke them, but I'll try anyway." I followed the dogs back to the tipi and reached there with them. I was very scared.[9] I saw a horse tied to the door. It had a white face, but it was too dark to see its color. It was a very good horse, the kind people keep tied right next to the tipi. I went up and put a rawhide thong around its neck. It was tied to the door by its foot and I cut that leash with a knife. I watched the door all the time and hid behind the horse. I was a short distance from camp and yet I didn't run, lest the dogs bark.

The men I had gone out with were back with the party when I returned. I took the horse there and told them that the camp was fast asleep. I waited there and the two started off again. Before very long they each brought back two horses. Two other men went off. Each went in their turn, until there were only two men who didn't have a horse to ride.

It was in spring and the morning was pretty close. We started running away. In the morning I saw that my horse, a sorrel, was the very nicest of the lot. The others said that they had taken the first horses they came to and had not gone right to the center of the camp as I did. My horse was in the poorest condition, because he had been used to chase buffalo. My horse played out and they left me behind about noon. It had been raining; they were sure that the enemy would follow the tracks in the mud. I didn't want to leave the horse so I dismounted and drove him along. I felt a choking in my throat. None of the party were my relatives so they did not wait for me.[10] But I had a good rifle and many cartridges. When I reached one ridge, I would see the Cree on the next one, far ahead.

Then my horse started to smell the tracks of the others and began to trot. He started to run. He went faster and faster and I caught the neck thong to stop him. I had to snub the thong around his nose, he wanted to go so fast. I jumped on and he was all right again. He had gotten over his tiredness.

The last time I had seen the others on a ridge, far away. Then I saw them again, I was already closer. They saw me and waited on a little hill. They said that they had waited for me on purpose, but I knew that they were lying. They had seen me riding up. When I got home I gave that horse to my mother.

We'll start another one. I went with *Musta·htak,* Bare-earth, who was of the West People. This was in winter, in the Eagle Moon (February). I ran a lot, because I went on ahead, scouting. We went two together, his name is Day-bow. We found the Sioux, camping on the Piegan River. Smoke came from a big bluff; we knew they were there. Nearby were buffalo herds.

We went back to the party and started for the enemy camps at night. It was day when we came up. It was very warm. We waited for night.

Our leader said, "We'll go along the creek where it is thawing out and get closer to the camps." We did so. All at once, we saw a rider, and then a bunch of them. We threw ourselves to the ground. Many Sioux were chasing buffalo. They killed buffalo close to where we were lying and came near our track.

We saw one coming from the camp on foot. We said, "We are all killed anyway (i.e., we are bound to be discovered and killed), we may as well shoot this one." We couldn't dig any pits because the ground was frozen. There were two Worthy Young Men with us. The Sioux missed us; he didn't see us. We chased him. He went over a hill. We headed him off. When we had been lying down, we had put on our battle clothes ready to fight.

I outran the others, there were two a little behind me. I stopped on a little hill and called, "Where are you going, my friend." He made a noise and pulled up his gun. I shot him. He turned and sat down facing us. I ran up to him. He got up. He turned to me. I threw my gun away and drew my knife. It had belonged to a dead man and it was a very risky weapon to use, especially for the first time. As soon as I grabbed this knife, I was afraid. My heart was beating, tum-tum. That's why I threw the gun away (?).

All my partners fell back, but I ran at him and didn't stop. I knew he was waiting to shoot me in the face, when I got close. I came up to him. He aimed right at me. I ducked and he missed. He was loading his gun again and I caught him by the hair. He was wounded in the hip and couldn't get up. I took his hair with an eagle feather stuck in it. He was not dead yet.

The other men came up and took what they could. When they were finished stripping him, he was hardly dead yet. We started off, there was no place to hide and we kept on. They didn't chase us right away. When they started after us we reached a place where there was shelter. One of our men was killed. There were no wounded. We got away from them.

When we got home with the scalps, the girls were dressed up and ready to dance. A row of girls faced a row of old men who drummed and sang. I was placed in the center and the girls danced around me, always looking at me. That showed that I had done something worth doing.

251

That was when I became a Worthy Young Man, for I had used a dead man's knife. The two Worthy Young Men who had been on the trip had seen me do all these things and that's why I became one of them. I was very young then, about fifteen or sixteen.

The third time I went out was with a Saulteaux, *Piwa·pis-kawa·sis,* Iron-child. We went to the Piegan who were in the United States, close to the mountains. We went out with a big bunch of men. A large encampment of Piegan was near a hill and on the other side of the hill was a smaller camp; I think it was another chief's band.

The leader sent me and his brother to see if the horses were tied up. Before we left, they told us where they would wait for us. We found a big corral full of horses right in the center of the tipis. We went back to the appointed place, but nobody was there. They had missed the place. My younger brother, who is still living, was in that party. I said to my partner, "Morning is coming, let us hide. They may steal some (horses) and we will get horses (from them)." We went back in the hill to hide.

In the morning, we watched one of the camps and didn't see a single horse. A rider went from that camp to the other to report the loss of all the horses. We dodged around that hill all day to keep out of sight. We waited all day. The Piegan caught up to our party of Cree and there was a fight. Many horses were killed. Iron-child was shot through the thigh and penis, but was not killed. The Piegan only got a few horses back and the Cree got away with all the rest, one hundred and fifty head. After Iron-child was wounded he rode for two days. Then they found some poles and built a travois to carry him in.

The next night we went down to where they had taken the horses. There were some in the corral again. The Piegan who thought that they had killed Iron-child were dancing. The dogs chased us and the Piegan shouted into the night, "Our brothers will shoot you down. They are watching closely." The Saulteaux I was with asked me if I could understand. I said "yes," and told him. They hadn't seen us, but just yelled.

I told my partner that it was going to be pretty hard to get a horse, but if we tried to walk home we would starve to death (before we reached home). He said, "That's right." There was a big cloud coming, it was very windy and there was a heavy rain. They quit dancing and went into their tipis.

We went into the camp. I passed one tipi and noticed a little opening. I thought it was for a gun. I was afraid, but went on. In the corral there were only twelve head and one little sucking colt. A gray horse was very nice looking. There were also two pintos and a buckskin. My partner was waiting outside the camp circle. He saw me at the horses so he came along. They were tied up inside the corral. I cut several loose. He asked me for two. I gave him a pinto and a blue. I opened the corral. As soon as I led the two out, the rest broke out and ran off down the wind. I hung on to those I had chosen. My partner was behind me. I waited for him. We had signals arranged, two whistles — a call and an answer. I wouldn't have found him if my horses hadn't whinnied to the others. I saw someone coming. I whistled. He stopped, but didn't answer. I whistled again. He gave the answer. We went off. The rest of the party were home two days ahead of us. The Piegan chief there was *Atcimusis,* Young-dog.

I gave the two horses to my sister. When we came home from a raid our relatives came out to greet us and kiss us. As each came up we would give him a horse.

I went on another trip with *Apistatim,* Little-dog. We went to the *Kakahkıwatcaınak,* the Crow. We went along the Rockies and got to them after a long trip. I was very thin then because I ran a lot. I was always scouting. The others cooked for me and sewed my moccasins. I was chosen to scout because I could do it well.

I found them just where their reserve now is. It was on the Good River where the two branches come together to form the Big Muddy River (Missouri). The Mud House People (Mandan?) lived there (also). I started back right away. We found our party and yelled that we had found some camps. The distance was three full nights. On the fourth night we came up to the camps. We found a good hiding place in the mountains and we decided to meet there. Some of the party waited there.

One man who died last year, Fighting-bear, went scouting for horses with me. We were the first of the party to go off. It was a moonlit night. They didn't have the horses tied, but men guarded them closely. On one side a lone tipi stood near a creek. We went there. Seven head of horses were there. At first we didn't take them because there weren't enough. But, in the main camp, there were many fires and men watching. We came back and took the seven horses. I took three and he took four. I took a good sorrel horse. He took a good black. There was one moose-colored gelding. The rest were poor horses.

We ran off. We couldn't find the place where we were supposed to meet the others and we went on. It was hardest to steal horses from the Crow. They would give chase for four days and four nights to recapture the horses.

Because it was a moonlit night the others couldn't get any horses. But just about daylight, the (Crow) young men fell asleep and the Cree took the very best horses in the bunch. There weren't many, but they were the very best. In the morning they were not yet out of sight of the Crow.

Many of the Cree were on foot, only a few had horses. Those on foot scattered into the bush. Those who had horses tied them up and hid in the grass. They remained there all day. One of the Cree pushed on with three of the horses. He went to the place where we had agreed to meet. We had arranged to wait there for two days before going on. One by one, they came there and found each other.

The Crow had killed three Cree. One of the novices and two very brave young men were killed. One of these was killed immediately. One was shot through the arm and kept on fighting. His rifle jammed. It took them a long time to kill him. He chased them off with a knife but was killed from behind with a club. The Crow told us about it many years later.

253

Three others were missing and unaccounted for. To this day we do not know what happened to them. Some whites, Americans, were hunting buffalo nearby and they might have killed them. Only three horses had been taken from the Crow by the others and with our seven it made ten in all. Years later, we became acquainted with the man from whom we had stolen the seven horses. He told us that he had heard us doing it, but he was all alone with his wife then and so he couldn't do anything. If he had been brave he could have killed the two of us. Had he shot one, the other would have run away. He was a coward and that is why we got away with the horses. Thirty-one Cree had started out from home. Only twenty-five came back.

The next time I went out the leader was *osa·katcıwew,* Coming-over-a-hill. He was of the East People. Just three of us who were on that trip are alive. There were twenty-eight on that trip. We didn't go out for a fight, only to get horses, but we knew that if the enemy caught us there would surely be a fight. We went out to get horses from the Sioux or from the *kane-hıawestcik,* "Cree Talkers" (Cheyenne).

The leader was known to be a great liar. On the fourth night out he offered a pipe and asked for luck. He started to sing. Then he knew what was going to happen from day to day, until we got to the enemy camps. He would find out all that. When that great liar said that he had found out something from his dream, it came true (?).

I went out scouting again and came very close to where the Mud House People were. It was a bright moonlit night. Our leader had foretold that the first bunch of horses that we came upon would not be enough. If we went on a little farther east we would have more than enough. He said that we would do something at the first encampment which would bring bad luck.

I came up to the first camp. We were close to the place where the leader had told us that we would have more than enough horses. But we had come a long way and were tired. I told my partner, "I am going to get some horses here. I am tired of walking." There were many horses there.

At night we crawled up. One of our party followed the two of us wherever we went and he came along. We saw three horses tied and made for them. When we were out of the bush, a little dog barked at us. I just went right up to a horse that was tied to a tipi door; it was a roan. My partner came up to get a black. The little dog quit barking and went into the tipi. The fellow who followed us got a little pinto that was tied up to a tipi. Among the tipis of the "Cree Talkers," were some canvas tents. We got out of sight with the three horses. I gave a very fat mare to my brother. Another fellow got a fat moose-colored horse. There were many horses, but our men couldn't find them because they were hidden somewhere. At last they came upon two mules and a horse that were hobbled. That was all they brought home, seven head.

I went out against the Piegan with another leader, *mahe·-hkan·icis,* Little-wolf. We reached the place where we had been with Iron-child and went a little west to the Cut Rock River. We found them camped on a flat in the bend of a river. The moon was darkened. I went up to a tipi with another fellow and took two pintos and one gray from the door. There were many horses tied to tipis, most of them pintos. Our partners came up from another side of the bend.

We ran off and ran all night. The next day the enemy caught up to us. I shot one down, but I was riding so fast that I couldn't stop immediately. My partner took everything, the scalp, the belt. He had taken three horses from the camps but they were not very good. The fellow I shot was riding a good horse. We took a scalp from each side of his head. I think the Piegan were afraid of us.

After we had this little fight, we ran on. We came up a hill and saw some horses with saddles. We thought they belonged to some Blackfoot and took them. But some men yelled at us and it turned out that they belonged to our party and had gone ahead of us. We brought home the scalps and the horses. The others had taken the horses that were outside the line of the camps and they were not much good. We got the best horses.

I went with another war party. Day-thunder was the leader. He had just married my sister. The berries were already ripe then. We were looking for the Piegan. There were five of us. We found a Piegan camp. Day-thunder had been scouting through his dreams (i.e., had foretold the future) and he was afraid of this bunch. He was told not to tackle them. We went around these and on to another camp.

This is where I was most scared in all my life. I and my brother went ahead to find the place where Day-thunder had seen the enemy camp in his dream. We looked from hill to hill, but there was none there. It was getting late and we went back. We tracked our party to a valley, but couldn't find them before night. In the morning we started out and looked for their tracks again. But we couldn't find the three others. The two of us carried water in a buffalo paunch and we emptied it. We didn't know what to do.

We went up the creek bed that day and the next night and found water. The other three had gone down the creek, while we were going up the creek. They found water. Close to where the creek joined a river was a bush where they slept. Their heads were toward a buffalo trail.

Now before we had set out, another party of Cree had gone out before us. They struck this same camp of Piegan. There were three of them, one was a little deaf. Two of them went around one side of the camp and the deaf man went around the other side, alone. The two heard some Piegan talking and fled. The deaf man couldn't hear them and walked right up to where they were talking. They chased him, but he was a very fast runner and got away.

Meanwhile we were coming down the creek, still looking for our three partners. The Piegan who were chasing the deaf man saw us and ran after us. We ran until we came to a big hole that had been used by a bear or a timber wolf. We had only one

255

gun. I put my brother in the hole and I sat outside to fight off the Piegan. The hole was so big that he could sit upright in it. I fought them off all day. As they came up, one by one, I shot them. Finally, they gave up and went back. I asked my brother if he had been frightened. He replied "No," but in a very low voice. During the fighting I had taken off all my clothes and left only my breechclout.

Then I said to my brother, "Do you know what you are wearing around your loins?" He said nothing. I said, "I know what this breechclout is for. I am a man. Our father is dead and so we will go back for more fighting."[11] Only once before had it happened that a man went back to the enemy camp after fighting them off all day.

While I had been fighting the Piegan, our three partners were sleeping back near their camp. An old man happened to see them and raised the alarm. Only old men were left in the Piegan camps since all the others were out after me. They thought they would have an easy time with only three Cree. But one of the Cree had a rifle and he picked off several of the old men at a distance. They got scared and retreated.

When we got back to the enemy camp, I heard a stallion neigh from the direction of the tipis. I thought that it must be in the shadow of the tipis and I crept up. A man came out of a house to urinate. I stooped down and pretended to be defecating. He went back in the house without saying anything. I ran back to my brother and said that we would go back to find some place to sleep. I planned to get the horses during the day.

While looking for a hiding place we found twelve fat horses hobbled in a little valley. We unhobbled them. We ran for two days and nights. On the third day, we killed a buffalo, but we just cut out a few strips of meat and tied them to the saddle. We didn't want to lose any time.

The first enemy camp that we had come to on our way out, the one Day-thunder had circled, was moving as we came past. We thought that we had avoided them but instead we had gone right to where they had moved. They chased us. We were going around the shore of a little lake. Instead of keeping right at the shore, we made a sudden turn into the hills and so lost them. I brought twelve horses home.

When I got back, I told the whole story. The chiefs said that only one other man had gone back after an all-day fight. They took me as the highest in the Rattlers' Tipi. Among the chiefs I would be called in to eat before some of the greatest chiefs. And a chief couldn't go between me and the fire, but would have to go around me. Since that time I was the head one in the Rattlers' Tipi, until the whites came and put an end to it all. The big chiefs had done much that was worth a great deal, but none of them had done what I had done.

The next story I am going to tell is not mine but my grandmother's. She often told it to me.

Southwest of Saskatoon is a place called Sand Hill. My grandmother's eldest and her youngest son were hunting there once and were killed by the Gros Ventre. The leaves were just beginning to turn color. She was very sad and told her husband to cry for help everywhere. The old man said, "I'll go." He gathered the chiefs in a tipi and told them about it.

One of the chiefs lent a sacred pipestem to the old man. These were about a yard long and nicely decorated. They were carried about as the priests carry Bibles. As soon as he got it, he began to cry aloud. That was at a place called Stony Hill, just this side of Carlton. The chiefs told him to go to the east and to the west. He went west first. Three of them went together. The old woman had to go along and they took another man to do the praying for them. She carried the stem across her back and whenever they came to a camp, they went all around crying the news, and finally, would go into the chief's tipi. She would go right up to the chief, put her hands on his head, and tell her story. If the chief had decided to go, if he meant to take the pipe, he would abuse my grandmother, saying, "What do you mean, coming around like this to take all our best young men and get them killed? You are only a lousy old woman and not worth having our men shot." They would say this as they were cutting tobacco on a board. Then she would know that they were going and would hang the pipestem on the chief's back-rest.

She went east as far as Indian Head. All the chiefs took the pipe. In the east she got the man who was the most powerful of all in his dreams to lead the party. His name was *kɪ·nikas,* Pointed. When she came back with the East People, the West People were already waiting. There were a bunch of them.

The old lady had an adopted daughter that she had raised — a good, hard-working girl. She gave the girl to *kɪ·nikas.* The girl led the expedition. Offering cloths were tied on her back. She walked ahead and *kɪ·nikas* told her where to go. When they camped, she slept alone ahead of the camp. On the fourth night out, *kɪ·nikas* sang. He said that they would have very good luck if the people would not be rash and raise the enemy alarm.

The Warriors led the party and kept them together. On the eighth night, *kɪ·nikas* sang again. Then the scouts came back and reported that the Gros Ventre were just ahead. *Kɪ·nikas* sang again and said that the Cree would ambush the enemy as they were pursuing our scouts.

So it was. But the Warriors had to slap the horses' faces so that they would not dash forward and reveal the ambush. It was the most successful battle the Cree had ever had. Some were wounded but none was killed.

Before the party had left, the old lady had asked her full brother, who was a chief, to go. He refused and moved away with ten tipis. But his men stayed with the war party. The other chiefs told her to unwrap the stem and to lay it before her brother. She did, but he only went around it. This chief couldn't feed all the women so he had to come back to the camp. When the victorious war party returned, they all laughed at and mocked this chief, who was so ashamed that he kept within his tipi. The other chiefs told my grandmother to sing her song, and she sang before him:—

When I asked you to go you refused me,
When I told you that I was poor.
But I tried to go.
I got to the Sweet Grass Hills when it was good.
When I told you this you were sitting here at home.
You are still sitting here.
At last I got to the Sweet Grass Hills.
And you are still sitting here at home.

Afterwards that song was sung by the women on the return of a successful war party.

I myself never saw a big battle like that. I know of only four times that happened. The old lady was my father's mother.

In this same fight, my grandmother's nephew was trying to get a horse and was lying on his belly. A Gros Ventre jumped up, ran up to him, and tried to shoot him with a bow. But he couldn't manage to string his arrow and so he hit the boy across the back with the bow. The boy spit blood and the Gros Ventre jumped into a trench. From then he was called, Strike-him-on-the-back. He had two other names, Rotted-scalp, and *misahe·gipwe·me-ta·s,* Loose-leggings-on-thigh. He evidently had no dream name.

Some men would have no dream name because there would be no old man around when they were born. This happened when a group of young people went into the forest for furs.

I got my name, Fine-day, from Strike-him-on-the-back. My other name was *O·miki·s,* Has-little-sores.

FOOTNOTES

[1]BLOOMFIELD, Plains Cree Texts, p. 63f.
[2]According to Skinner, scouts had to have propitious dreams for this function. My information is at variance with Skinner's in several other respects. I could find no evidence of "no-flight" obligations signalized by planting a knife in the ground, nor of the leader running the gauntlet or fire-walking, nor that a war leader had to be a member of the Warrior society; SKINNER, Political Organization, pp. 521-522.
[3]Cf. WISSLER, Ceremonial Bundles, pp. 266-267.
[4]JEFFERSON, Fifty Years on the Saskatchewan, p. 89.
[5]LACOMBE, Dictionnaire et Grammaire, p. 366, translated this word as "chante de la victoire avec danse." Jefferson calls it the "Scalp Dance" (SKINNER, Political Organization, p. 535).
[6]JEFFERSON, Fifty Years on the Saskatchewan, pp. 88-89.
[7]*Ibid.,* p. 89.
[8]This instance of the disbanding of a war party because of the presence of a boy and the occurrence of a bad omen was not unusual. Any omen interpreted as evil by the leader might lead to the abandonment of a raid. If one of the members of the party were killed, the others rushed home.
[9]In the recounting of personal war exploits, the narrator frequently states that he was frightened and terror-stricken.
[10]The ties of kinship were the strongest of societal forces. A relative would not have left Fine-day alone.
[11]By this reference to their dead father, Fine-day reminded his brother that they themselves had to establish their social status without the aid a father could give.

PART TWO

A COMPARATIVE STUDY OF
THE PLAINS CREE CULTURE

I: The Problem

The Plains Cree are a people who migrated from forests to plains within relatively recent times. The motives for this movement and the history of the migration have been treated in previous pages, together with an account of Plains Cree life as of 1860-1870. It is the purpose of this part of the study to describe and analyze the changes in the tribal culture which followed the change in environment. The acculturation to Plains life took place on an aboriginal level and there are no eyewitness accounts of the process. In order to understand what happened, therefore, we must compare the traits of the Cree before the migration with their customs after they had settled on the prairies. The relation between the "before" and the "after" stages of Plains Cree history helps in defining the relationship between Plains and Woodlands culture areas in North America. Therefore this study entails a comparative survey of the two areas as seen from the Saskatchewan region, home of the Plains Cree.

The historical evidence of the documentary sources reveals the westward advance of the Cree. In the period of first contact with whites (1690-1740) they are depicted as a powerful tribe, possessing a culture very much like that of some of their modern descendants, the present day Eastern Cree. Soon after trading posts were established in their territory they became dependent upon the traders for European manufactures and firmly wedded to the fur trade.

Two factors propelled them to the west. They became middlemen for the fur trade, carrying trade goods to the tribes of the hinterland in return for pelts offered by the more distant peoples. More important, as their own lands were trapped bare, they were forced to expand their bound-

---

Parts 2 and 3 of this volume are, with minor revisions, from the comparative sections of Dr. Mandelbaum's doctoral dissertation and are published here for the first time.

aries ever farther in order to secure an adequate supply of furs.

Even before the days of white influence, the Cree seem to have been an aggressive, warlike people. Upon being provided with firearms by the English, they easily overrode opponents who as yet had only aboriginal weapons. For a time the only limit to the extent of Cree conquests was that of sheer distance separating the regions of their farthest forays from the base of European supplies. This continued expansion brought them eventually into the prairies. They moved steadily farther into the open country, driving before them Gros Ventre and Blackfoot.

An additional factor which contributed to their military success was their alliance with the Assiniboin, whose warriors usually augmented the forces of the Plains Cree. Because of their several allies, the tribe could concentrate attacks on one part of its territory while their adversaries had to contend with assaults on numerous flanks.

For a time (from about 1740 to 1820), they shuttled in and out of the plains, trapping in the forests for part of the year, and during other seasons hunting buffalo. Finally some of the Cree broke with the Woodlands entirely and remained on the plains the year around, where they occupied territory formerly held by their Assiniboin allies. These Plains Cree continued their commerce with the Hudson's Bay Company, exchanging buffalo hides and pemmican for the required trade articles.

Thus it was that the Cree burst into the plains and stayed there. We cannot be certain, it is true, that buffalo hunting was not occasionally practised by some Cree before the advent of Europeans. Be that as it may, all documentary indications point to the fur trade as the immediate and paramount force in drawing Cree into the prairie country. Moreover, it is a strong tradition among the Plains Cree of today that their forefathers, at a not too remote date, wrested their present territory from the Blackfoot and other enemy peoples.

Here we have as well documented a case of migration into the Plains area as we may expect to find. An analysis of the changes which took place within this one culture should serve to shed light on the cultural background of other Plains tribes whose extra-Plains origin is suspected, but whose movements are not as clearly known or definitely marked. Plains Cree history is not to be taken as duplicating that of the Cheyenne, Gros Ventre, or Dakota. Each of these tribes must have had its peculiar historical context if, as appears to be the case, they did come into the plains from the east. But an understanding of the changes in Cree culture as between Woodlands and Plains makes clearer the relationship of the two areas and illuminates the potential cultural changes involved in any woodland to plains transfer.

Fig. 27. Consecrating the Sun dance Pole by Henry Beaudry.

Fig. 28. Pow-wow at the Battlefords by Allen Sapp.

Fig. 29. Kee-a-kee-ka-sa-coo-way (The man that gives the War Whoop), by Paul Kane.

II: The Eastern Affiliations of Plains Cree Culture

Professor Duncan Strong has characterized the horse culture of the central plains as a thin and uniform veneer, exhibiting many traits "more typical of the forest-hunting regions to the north than they were of the prehistoric plains themselves."[1] If this is true of the middle plains area, it should be all the more valid for the northern edge of the prairie country.

The comparative statements of this section chiefly encompass the Eastern Cree, the various Ojibwa groups, the bands of the Labrador peninsula, the Menomini and other Central Woodlands tribes. The primary emphasis is upon the relationship between the two Cree groups.

Material Culture and Economic Life

HOUSING

The Plains tipi finds its counterpart in the conical lodges of the east. Among the Eastern Cree, as with their Western congeners, the lodge poles are laid over a three pole foundation. The lodge cover, according to Skinner, consists of birch bark or of skins laid on individually. Two older sources, however, indicate that the cover was made of hides sewn together, as on the plains. Henry Ellis, writing in 1746, says that the tent covers of the natives residing at Fort Nelson, undoubtedly Cree, were made of moose or deer skins sewn together. The "Southern Indians," also Cree, who accompanied Samuel Hearne in 1769, erected a conical framework on which they raised a tent cloth made of dressed moose skins sewn together and cut in the shape of a fan.[1a]

Speck characterizes the dwellings of the Labrador tribes as a conical many-poled structure covered with birch bark in the southern part of the area, and with caribou skins in the north. The Wabanaki peoples live in "conical, tipi-like wigwams" covered with birch bark.[2]

Jones states that the Ojibwa have a conical lodge as one of their house forms. The Northern Saulteaux build a similar lodge on a foundation of four crotched poles, very much like the Smoking Tipi structure of the Plains Cree.[3] Skinner writes that the Menomini have only recently acquired a conical dwelling. A tipi house form is listed, but not described, for the Winnebago. The Prairie Potawatomi use tipis only occasionally.[4]

Among these Woodlands folk, only the Cree and Labrador peoples use the conical lodge as the principal dwelling. The poles of the Montagnais-Naskapi lodge are not taken down when camp is moved, and according to Skinner, the present day Eastern Cree do not sew the hides of the cover. However, the fire in the center and the smoke hole at the apex, even the fan-shaped tipi cover among the Cree of an

Fig. 30. Old Woman Getting Water in Early Spring by Michael Lonechild.

earlier day, bespeak a close resemblance to the familiar tipi of the plains. In this trait, as in many others, the Forest and Plains Cree customs are not dissimilar.

The domed lodge, mat or bark covered, forms the principal dwelling for the Central Algonkins. It is used by the tribes of southern New England, in the Labrador region, and also by the Eastern Cree and Northern Saulteaux.[5] The most common method of constructing the domed lodge is exemplified by the Menomini practice. Saplings are set upright, bent over, and lashed at the top to saplings set opposite them and similarly bent over.[6] This technique is used by the Plains Cree in constructing sweat lodges.

Another method of building a domed lodge involves arching an erect pole over until it touches the ground where it is made fast. Eastern Cree domed lodges are made in this fashion.[7] This technique is also known to the Plains tribe in the construction of temporary shelters.

A house form unknown to both the Eastern and Plains Cree is the rectangular, gabled summer house found among the Ojibwa, Menomini and Prairie Potawatomi. The Labrador manner of spreading a hide across poles to serve as a windbreak is reminiscent of the Plains Cree practice of stretching a hide between two erect poles set up for the same purpose.[8]

As far as dwelling form is concerned, the Plains Cree are at one with the Eastern Cree and with the Northeastern Algonkins. While not identical the essential structure of the conical tipi is common to both Cree groups. In this respect, the Labrador bands are close to the Cree, while the peoples of the Central Woodlands are farther removed. With the exception of the rectangular house form, the methods of constructing dwellings other than the tipi by the Central Algonkin are not foreign to the Plains Cree.[9]

CEREMONIAL STRUCTURES

The long lodge, triangular in cross section, which is erected for many Plains Cree ceremonies, is paralleled by the "two-fire wigwam" of the Eastern Cree. The eastern form is apparently used as a dwelling, as is a similar Northern Saulteaux structure.[10] The Mistassini of Labrador hold a feast in a large double tent. The name given for this ceremonial lodge is *cabatowa·n,* cognate with the Plains Cree term for the long lodge, *sapohtowa·n.*[11] Again, the conical dwelling of the Northern Saulteaux is set up on a foundation similar to that of the Plains Cree Smoking Tipi lodge.

The use of a long house for ceremonial purposes is common among the Central Algonkin tribes. The construction is quite different from the Plains Cree long lodge, however, since it involves an arched roof. Nevertheless, the idea of a two fire structure for ceremonial purposes extends even to the Lenapé.[12]

Again we find that the Hudson Bay Cree and certain Northeastern Algonkins share a distinctive trait, the long lodge, with the Plains Cree. The Central Woodlands practice is divergent, yet even there the long lodge is a ceremonial structure. While the long lodge seems to be a dwelling among the Eastern Cree, it may be a ceremonial structure as well.

The distribution of the hemispherical sudatory is more uniform. The sweat lodge used by the Eastern Cree, Northern Saulteaux, and Naskapi is the same as that of the Plains Cree. The Menomini type is also similar. Zaisberger describes a Lenapé sudatory nearly large enough to permit a man to stand upright in it, but otherwise it resembles the usual type.[13]

HOUSEHOLD FURNISHINGS AND UTENSILS

There are few data on the sleeping arrangements in the eastern conical lodges. Chippewa bedding consists of blankets or hides tanned with the hair on. Pillows are filled with duck feathers and a thin feather bed is used.[14]

Central Woodlands houses generally have elevated couches built around the walls. These serve the purpose of the willow rod back-rest familiar from the Plains.[15]

Horn spoons are not common in the east; a Naskapi spoon made of reindeer antler is illustrated by Turner, and Hodge, in the *Handbook of American Indians,* mentions specimens of mountain sheep and goat spoons from the "Northern Algonquian tribes."[16] The wooden ladles and spoons roughly carved by the Plains Cree are made in many highly finished and ornamental forms by the Central Woodlands tribes. The Naskapi forms are much more like the crude Plains Cree types. Mussel shells are used by the Menomini, especially for administering medicines.[17]

Legskin bags are much used by the Eastern Cree, but are laced at the opening instead of being covered with a flap as in the Plains Cree specimens. Speck lists the use of legskin bags as one of the boreal traits common to the Labrador and Eskimo cultures. They are not generally found in the Central Woodlands.[18]

The numerous woven bags of the Central Algonkins are foreign to the Plains. The Eastern Cree make netted carrying bags, but otherwise their bags are largely of the legskin type. The foetus skin bags described for the Plains tribe are not Eastern, as far as I know.

The truncated pyramid type of birchbark container is widespread. Illustrations of specimens from Mistassini, Menomini, and Eastern Cree show a similar type of construction involving seams on two sides and a one-piece pattern.[19]

Wooden bowls and dishes are used throughout the eastern forests but are generally hollowed out of knots rather than carved from sections of split logs as with the Plains Cree.[20]

Household utensils then, are much alike for Plains Cree, Eastern Cree, and Labrador; divergent for the Central peoples. The Plains back-rest is absent in the east; woven bags are not found on the plains. Bedding is probably similar among all the tribes. Horn spoons are Northeastern and Plains, not Central. Wooden spoons and bowls are found in all these areas. Legskin bags are also Northeastern and Plains Cree, not being known to the Central Woodlands. Birchbark containers, of the Great Lakes "mocock" type, are used in the three regions under consideration.

DRESS

The Plains Cree costume represents a type which has a far flung distribution. Women's dress in the region of Hudson Bay was noted by Ellis in 1746 as being a "petticoat" of deer, otter, or beaver skin prepared with the hair on. The sleeves are frequently separate from the body, being tied only with strings at the shoulders, and taken on and off at pleasure. According to Wissler, this use of sleeves as a separate and distinct garment extends throughout the Eastern Woodlands and into the Plains.[21] The woman's short leggings, usually gartered below the knee, are found among the Eastern Cree, Huron, Ojibwa and Menomini. Naskapi women, however, wear high leggings.[22] The woman's head covering of the Plains Cree has an analogue among the Eastern Cree which is described as a strip of cloth sewn at the ends to fit the head. This is probably Northern Saulteaux also.[23]

The breechclout drawn over a belt and hanging down in a flap or apron before and behind is worn by men among the Ojibwa, Winnebago, Menomini and the Indians of New England. Skinner does not specify how the breechclout is worn among the Eastern Cree and Northern Saulteaux, but since the latter form, at least, has quillwork ornamentation, it is likely that it is pulled over the belt and hangs down in a flap.[24]

There is some indication that the poncho shirt of the Plains was not aboriginally worn in the forests. Thus Henry Ellis in describing the Cree costume makes no mention of a shirt. Miss Densmore notes only a chest protector of muskrat skin for the Chippewa. Skinner tells of a deerskin shirt worn by Menomini men but does not describe it. The loose, sleeved shirt of the Ojibwa mentioned by Jones may be a post-European development.[25]

The tailored garments characteristic of the Eastern Cree, Northern Saulteaux, and Labrador peoples are not common to the Plains Cree, although the plains tribe occasionally made tailored coats having a hood attached.[26]

The single piece moccasin, with a seam around the outside of the foot, is not Eastern. The other Plains Cree type, with a seam extending from the toe to the tongue piece, is

271

worn by the Montagnais, Naskapi, Ojibwa and Menomini.[27]

The use of robes as an outer covering is a fundamental Eastern Algonkin trait. Willoughby quotes several early sources which describe the cloak-like robes worn by the natives of New England. A 1718 account of a Potawatomi village near Detroit states that buffalo robes, richly painted, are worn in winter. Naskapi robes are made of two deerskins sewn together. The care given to the drape and mode of wearing the annuity blanket among the Chippewa suggests that the robe was formerly an important article of dress. The use of the robe among the Menomini is set out in a mythical tale of a magic robe.[28]

Skinner's report on the Eastern Cree mentions cloaks of skin worn by both sexes. Each was fastened at the throat with a bone pin. The furs most highly valued by the French traders were those which had been sewn together and worn as robes by the natives. In the wearing, the fur became downy and the hide well greased and yellow in color. This kind of fur made the best felt and was called *castor gras*. A letter of 1686 indicated that the best of these came from the Cree country. In 1737 the Cree asked La Vérendrye to establish a fort at the north end of Lake Winnipeg, stating that the trade in *castor gras* would be very good there.[29] It is probable, then, that the Eastern Cree wore robes made of beaver skins sewn together.

Men's long leggings, attached to a belt around the waist, are worn throughout the Eastern and Central Woodlands. Naskapi leggings are aberrant in that they come up only to the middle of the thigh.[30]

The fur fillets of the Menomini bear a resemblance to certain types of Plains Cree headgear. The Northern Saulteaux and Naskapi[31] used caps but these are not adequately described. Birket-Smith's list of trait distributions shows that mittens are worn by the Naskapi, Beothuk, Algonkin and Ojibwa, as well as by the Eastern Cree.[32]

The Plains Cree type of woman's dress has a wide eastern distribution. The early Cree invaders of the plains probably carried this trait with them. Women's short leggings also are common to the Eastern and Central Woodlands with the exception of the Naskapi case. The Naskapi do not seem to have the double flap breechclout, but this may be due to lacunae in the accounts, a situation which may apply to the Eastern Cree. The use of the men's shirt among the Eastern tribes in pre-Columbian times is an open question, but a definite break occurs between the Plains tribe and the Eastern Cree in the matter of tailored clothing. The Plains Cree are not entirely ignorant of tailored garments, but make little use of them.

The traditionally older moccasin type common among the Plains Cree does not appear in the east, while the other Plains type is found both in Labrador and in the Central Woodlands. Long leggings are Eastern Cree and Central Woodlands, the Naskapi type again being somewhat different. Mittens are worn in all the Algonkin regions under consideration. Robes also are probably universal.

Plains Cree clothing, then, differs from Eastern Cree dress only in one significant stylistic respect, the use of tailored clothing. Evidence on the shirt, breechclout, and headgear is unsatisfactory, necessitating suspended judgment on these points. Central Woodlands dress is much like Eastern Cree, though differing also in the matter of tailoring. Labrador dress resembles the Eastern Cree costume to a large extent.

PERSONAL ADORNMENT

Alexander Henry noted that the Cree about Lake Winnipeg had their ears pierced and the holes filled with the bones of fish and land animals. Earrings are worn by Eastern Cree, Northern Saulteaux, Chippewa and Menomini. The pendant earring made of a shell disc is not mentioned for these eastern tribes.[33] While shell gorgets are not described in the ethnological literature, their eastern presence is proven by archeological specimens excavated from sites in the middle eastern states.[34]

Accounts of Eastern Cree hairdress differ. The elder Henry, in the passage cited above, states that men have their heads bare of hair except for a round place at the crown where it grows long. This tuft is rolled and covered with a piece of skin. The women arrange their hair into a roll over each ear. The men's hairdress described by Henry is characteristic of the Menomini and other Central Algonkins; the women's hairdress is common to the Labrador bands. Neither style was worn by the Cree of a later date. Skinner states that the Eastern Cree women wear two braids, at the ends of which ornamental bands are wound. Men formerly wore their hair loose or in two braids.[35]

Eastern Cree men are tattooed principally on the chest and arms, while women bear lip-chin tattoo lines. Both practices correspond to the Plains Cree practice. This style of women's tattoo is found throughout the Labrador and Eskimo areas. While the Menomini use tattoo for curative purposes only, the technique employed, pricking through a charcoal smear, is the same as the Plains Cree method. Birket-Smith lists both the pricking and needle-and-thread tattooing techniques for the Cree, but believes that the latter method made its way to the Ojibwa, Chipewyan and Cree in late times, coming from the west where it was aboriginally practised. The pricking technique is listed for the New England tribes and for certain Wabanaki peoples also.[36]

Arthur Dobbs in 1746 noted that the peoples of the Hudson Bay region painted their bodies with various realistic figures. The Eastern Cree, according to Skinner, paint their faces with either realistic or geometric designs. Face painting occurs throughout the Central Woodlands and Wabanaki territory.

None of the items of personal adornment enumerated for the Plains Cree are restricted to the plains and, with the exception of the shell gorget, all find close correspondence among the Eastern Cree. The earlier evidence on hairdress links the Eastern Cree with the Labrador peoples for one sex and with the Central Woodlands for the other; the later descriptions, however, tally with the Plains Cree form. The Cree groups are closer to the Labrador bands in the matter of tattooing, but are nearer the Central peoples in face painting.

THE FOOD QUEST

The pound technique in hunting is not often found in the east. William Jones does note the use of enclosures for securing buffalo, but this may be a result of Plains influence. Pounds for deer are mentioned but not described for the Beothuk. This is the only eastern reference to this hunting technique in the literature known to the writer.[37]

Spearing or shooting swimming animals is quite as productive a method of hunting in Eastern Cree territory as are the pounds on the plains. The Woodland Cree slaughter deer, caribou, and moose in great numbers when the animals are migrating. Hunters in canoes overtake the herds when they cross a body of water. Then the animals may easily be killed, sometimes even by punching in the side of the deer or caribou with a paddle. The Naskapi pursue the same method, making a prodigious slaughter.[38]

While the pound is not Eastern Cree, a fence similar to the chute attached to the pound is recorded for the tribe.

Poles with rags tied to them are set up in lines as the two arms of a triangle or in hourglass fashion. The animals follow them to the apex where hunters are stationed. According to Skinner this chute is set up only on ice. The Menomini, however, make a chute in the same fashion on land, felling trees to make the fence. Hunting fences are widely known, being found among the Naskapi, Beothuk, Huron, Neutral, New England aborigines, Ojibwa, Menomini, Winnebego, Miami and Illinois.[39]

The concerted hunt is not practised in the eastern forests because of the nature of the terrain, nor in the northeast because of the scattered population. Naskapi men on snowshoes drive deer into snowbanks where they are speared. This is also a Plains Cree practice. Menomini hunters attract does by bleating, just as the Plains Cree hunter attracts buffalo cows.[40] Snares and deadfall traps are used throughout the eastern areas.[41]

Fish are an important foodstuff to the Eastern Cree. John West, writing about 1820, states that the Swampy Cree subsist mainly on fish. As early as 1669, the Jesuits note that the Cree come down to the Sault from time to time to enjoy the abundance of fish there. Harmon and David Thompson comment on the abundant catch obtained by certain Eastern Cree bands.[42]

Birket-Smith cites his own field notes as the authority for the presence of a fish weir among the Eastern Cree, giving no description of it. He also lists this trait for the Montagnais, Winnebago and Iroquois, and as being found in New England, "Eastern Woodlands," New York, Ontario and Manitoba. Skinner asserts that the Northern Saulteaux do not build weirs, although they do set fish traps. This trap apparently operates on the same principle as the trough set at the apex of the Plains Cree weir.[43]

Other types of fish weirs differ from the Plains Cree form. The Winnebago set a weir at the base of an artificially constructed waterfall. The Prairie Potawatomi place a net at the apex of a V-shaped stone dam. William Jones states that the Ojibwa catch fish by means of a weir, but the type described by Densmore for the Chippewa is merely a close fence built across a stream. Men sit on it and fish with hooks and lines.[44]

The crude forked stick employed by the Plains Cree in spearing fish is roughly analogous to the two-pronged spear of the Eastern Cree. Fish spearing is widespread, although spear types vary from the single-headed Winnebago spear to the three-pointed leister used by the Ojibwa, Menomini, and the peoples of the Labrador and Wabanaki bands. The association of fish spearing with the use of fire to attract fish has been recorded from the Northern Saulteaux, Menomini and Ojibwa.[45]

The use of nets for fishing is common to the Eastern Cree and to many other eastern tribes. A suggestion that this may not be aboriginal is found in the testimony of a Northern Saulteaux informant, who claimed that nets were a European innovation.[46] Be that as it may, fishing with hooks, lines, gorges and seines has a varied and wide eastern distribution and does not extend to the Plains Cree.

Ellis names eleven varieties of wild fowl eaten in the Hudson Bay region that constitute an important part of the diet. The present day Eastern Cree shoot ducks and geese, or snare them. The Ojibwa use the same method as do the Plains Cree in clubbing wild fowl. They are able to do so, Jones adds, when the birds are fat and unable to rise.[47]

Skinner asserts that vegetal foods are almost unknown to the Eastern Cree, but goes on to mention that certain berries, roots, and plants are eaten. The Ojibwa collect a rich stock of berries and roots which include some varieties gathered by the Plains Cree. The Northern Saulteaux build a rack for drying berries, as is done among the Plains tribe, but unlike the Plains custom, a fire is built under the scaffold to hasten the process.[48]

There is abundant evidence from the *Jesuit Relations* and other early documents that some of the Cree gathered wild rice. The absence of this plant from the northern part of the Cree terrain may help explain Ellis' statement that the tribes of the Hudson Bay area have no dependence upon the fruits of the earth for their subsistence.[49]

Maple sugar is collected by the Central Woodlands people and prepared in a manner similar to that used by the Plains Cree tribe.[50]

When Skinner visited the Eastern Cree, the staple food in the winter was the rabbit. That this was not always the case is attested by a note in the *Jesuit Relations* for 1659-1660. The passage states that the abundance of deer in the Cree country is so great during certain seasons that the natives provision themselves for a year by smoking or freezing the meat. Ellis writes that the Indians kill very many deer every year from an unaccountable notion that the more they destroy, the greater plenty will succeed. Sometimes they leave as many as three or four hundred carcasses to rot, taking out only the tongues. These and other statements indicate that the Eastern Cree were primarily dependent upon large animals, deer, moose and caribou. Although starvation was known, the food supply seems to have been more ample than at present. It is interesting to note that when the buffalo failed in the Plains Cree territory, the taking of muskrat and of rabbit helped to keep the people from starving.[51]

The food supply of such Woodland people as the Menomini and Winnebago was more stable than that of the Eastern Cree because of the greater availability of vegetal foods and the practice of agriculture. Even among these peoples, however, hunting and fishing supplied the major portion of the tribal diet.[52]

When the food quests of the two Cree divisions are contrasted, we find certain basic similarities. Both divisions were largely dependent upon animals which congregated in herds. Both reaped the greatest harvests when the animals gathered in large numbers. The eastern method of overtaking the herds in water could not be followed on the plains. Although the pound method could be practised in a forested area, it seems better adapted to a more open, parkland terrain. The chute well may be a development of the deer fences used by the eastern peoples. Snares, deadfalls and decoys are common to both areas.

In the use of fish and the building of fish weirs, the plains tribe followed the customs of their eastern affiliates. The fish spear and fire fishing of the Plains Cree also link with eastern traits. Other methods of fishing were probably less feasible in the relatively waterless prairie country. The proportion of the various foodstuffs used by the Eastern Cree does not seem radically different from the Plains ratio in that large animals constitute the bulk of the supply, while fish, birds, small animals and plant foods are used secondarily. The greatest difference would lie in the apparently more limited use of vegetal foods by the Eastern Cree.

The Eastern Cree, in turn, are similar to the Labrador bands in food habits. The Central Woodlands differ radically only in having some small-scale agriculture, while in the utilization of plants they resemble the Plains Cree.

In brief, despite the absence of the buffalo and buffalo pound from the Eastern area, the fundamental food habits of the Eastern Cree are close to those of the Plains group. The plains environment was not suitable for the water pursuit of game and some fishing devices. It was favorable for the use of plant foods and the impounding technique.

FOOD PREPARATION

In the forest just as on the plains, meat is cut into strips and preserved by smoking over a slow fire or by drying in the sun. The *Jesuit Relations* of 1659-1660 states that the usual method of preserving meat is by smoking it. The Eastern Cree use a rectangular platform grill; the Chippewa build a frame over the camp fire; the tripod scaffold of the Northern Saulteaux is identical with a type used by the Plains Cree and, indeed, the other two forms are also known to the prairie tribe.[53]

The Eastern Cree, Ojibwa and Naskapi make pemmican. The word itself, of Cree origin, indicates that the early traders probably first learned of pemmican from the Cree.[54]

As on the plains, the Eastern Cree consider the tongue the choice part of the animal. The nose and heart are also delicacies.[55] The Plains custom of boiling split bones for the grease is also Eastern Cree, Chippewa and Naskapi.[56] While stone boiling is widely known, the usage of a container made of hide lining a hole in the ground does not extend eastward. Paunches are used as water containers among the Eastern Cree and Menomini.[57]

Methods of food preparation among the Eastern Cree differ in no essential from those outlined for the Plains division. Pit baking occurs among the Menomini, but takes the form of a large trench for baking corn.[58] Platform caches are set up by the Eastern Cree. The Menomini excavate pits to store wild rice.[59] The use of pits in the tipi floor for baking and the specific technique of stone boiling appear to be peculiar to the Plains. Otherwise both groups of the Cree, the Central and Northeastern peoples are quite uniform in this phase of their cultures.

TRANSPORT

A great dichotomy between Plains and Forest Cree exists in the means of transport. What the canoe is to the Woodland dwellers, the horse is to the inhabitants of the prairies. While the techniques involved in these two complexes differ widely, certain similarities may be observed in their effects on the life of the people. Both impart a range and mobility impossible without them. Both step up the returns of the hunt, the horse by its ability to outrun the buffalo, the canoe by making possible the pursuit of swimming animals. Both allow widely scattered groups to gather on occasions, as for the Plains Sun dance and for the annual rendezvous of the Eastern Cree. Both are immobilized during the winter, the horse being greatly handicapped by snow, the canoe by ice.

The horse complex was congenial to a people like the Eastern Cree in the sense that they already were a widely roving populace, accustomed to being scattered in small groups for a good part of the year, gathering in the spring and early summer. The shift from water to overland travel did involve a great re-adjustment. But the shift was not as violent as it would have been for a sedentary, village dwelling, agricultural people.

The two Cree divisions show similarities in winter travel. The two types of snowshoe used by the Plains Cree are made also by the Eastern Cree. The Ojibwa also have both types, the elongated style made in two pieces with one end upturned, the other having a rounded form. The long type, which has been called the Western Cree type, does not appear in Labrador or among the Menomini.[60]

The introduction of Eastern Cree dog sleds is attributed to Eskimo influence. It is probable, then, that the introduction of this trait to the Plains Cree via the Hudson's Bay Company ultimately stems from the same source. The sled tradition is not old in Labrador although the man-drawn toboggan is. The Eastern Cree also use toboggans, and in this they differ from the Plains tribe.[61]

Carrying straps are passed across the chest or forehead among the Ojibwa and Menomini. The Eastern Cree tumpline crosses the forehead.[62]

The dog is used as a draught animal in connection with the sled and toboggan in the eastern forests, but there is no indication of its employment as a pack animal. In hunting, the dog is used by the Eastern Cree, Menomini, and Wabanaki tribes.[63]

To recapitulate the comparative data on transport, the abandonment of the canoe and the acquisition of the horse by Cree peoples was not as great a dislocation as it might have been. In a measure, the Forest Cree were attuned to the nomadic life of the prairies. Winter travel is about the same in the eastern areas as on the Plains. Cree and Ojibwa have the same kind of snowshoes, as do the Plains Cree, differing from the other Central and Eastern Algonkins. The dog as a pack bearer and the use of the travois is Plains only, while the toboggan is Woodlands and not Plains Cree.

WEAPONS

The Western Woodland Cree who live in the forests north of the Saskatchewan River, use a bow which is sinew-backed and made of willow or birch. The simple bow is used by the Northern Saulteaux, Ojibwa, Huron, Labrador bands, Menomini, Winnebago and Prairie Potawatomi. Generally, use of the reinforced bow does not extend eastwards of the plains. Birket-Smith believes that the sinew-backed bows of the Menomini and Penobscot are of recent origin since the old records do not mention them.[64]

The arrows of the Eastern Cree are finished with two or three feathers. The Labrador bands have evidently adopted the Eskimo mode of using two feathers but the Naskapi, Menomini and Huron attach these vanes tangentially as do the Plains Cree. The Northern Saulteaux arrow is unfeathered.[65]

The distribution of the Mediterranean arrow release used by the Plains Cree is restricted to the Eastern Cree and Naskapi in the regions under consideration. The Eskimo and Chipewyan use the same release, suggesting a northern provenience for this trait. The Menomini use the tertiary release, and the Ojibwa apply the primary and secondary.[66]

The Ojibwa made use of wrist guards made of buckskin.[67] A toy cross-bow ("bow gun") was observed by Skinner among the Eastern Cree and by Speck among the Montagnais.[68] Presumably of European origin, it may have been brought in at a very early date and spread on an aboriginal level.

Bone-pointed spears were used by Eastern Cree and Ojibwa for both war and hunting. The Labrador people employ a bone-headed spear for caribou and bear.[69]

The war club of the Eastern Cree has a ball head with a stone set in it. This knobbed type and the flat "rabbit leg" shape are employed by the Ojibwa and Menomini. The club with flexible neck is not eastern.[70]

Shields were not used by the Eastern Cree or the Northern Saulteaux. Iroquois shields of bark or netted willows are evidently of a Southeastern type, like those seen by De Soto in 1539 among the Carolina tribes. Menomini informants stated that buffalo hide shields were once carried but were later abandoned.[71] Umfreville notes that some Cree on the prairies wore armor in addition to carrying shields.[72] A kind of pneumatic armor is described by Skinner for the Eastern Cree but the Plains Cree usually wore no armor.

Plains Cree weapons differ in several respects from those of the Eastern Cree and Central Woodlands tribes. The sinew-backed bow, the shield and the Plains club do not occur in the east. The Plains Cree share with Central and Northeastern peoples the simple bow and spear. The data on arrow feathers are inadequate but the Plains Cree type appears among several eastern groups. In arrow release usage the Central tribes differ from the others.

MANUFACTURES

The skin dressing technique of the Eastern Cree differs only in a few details from that of the Plains Cree. The initial fleshing is done with a bone implement which is obviously the prototype of the metal tool used by Plains tribes. This implement is also used by the Northern Saulteaux and Naskapi. Instead of the hoe scraper of the plains, a beaming tool is used. The hide is thrown over a log during the scraping process whereas on the plains it is usually pegged to the ground. It is to be noted, however, that the log and beaming tool are occasionally employed by the Plains Cree. The Eastern Cree work the hide with the hands instead of over a sinew rope. All other details are generally similar for the two groups.[73]

The use of a hoe scraper among eastern tribes is reported only for the Ojibwa.[74] The Naskapi use the beaming tool for dehairing. A scraper of the gun barrel type is used to remove the subcutaneous tissue. The hide is thrown over a log during these processes. The tanning mixture of brains, liver, and fat is applied, but is evidently not washed off as among the other tribes. The hide is worked directly after the mixture dries. Hides are sewn into bag shape and suspended over a fire to be smoked.[75]

The Menomini technique differs from that of the Plains Cree. The hair is removed with a knife. The hide is subjected to an additional soaking after being wrung, and is then rubbed with a wooden spatula.[76]

The painting of hides is common practice with the Eastern Cree, Naskapi and Menomini.[77] Quillwork is employed for decoration of skins from "Maine to Virginia and West to the Rocky Mountains, north of the Arkansas River."[78]

It is to be noted that the moose hair embroidery of the Huron and Penobscot is not made with the same technique as the Plains Cree horsehair decorations on moccasins.[79]

Beaded bands are made by the Chippewa with a technique similar to that of the Plains Cree, save that a square loom or a birch bark warp holder is used in place of the bow loom. This trait may not be aboriginal.[80]

The elaborate floral designs used by the Eastern Cree in decorative art are recent, according to the Cree themselves. The old art was realistic and geometric.[81] This is true also for the Plains Cree, where a study of old specimens bears out such assertions.

The Menomini cut leather thongs by a process similar to that used by the Plains Cree. Skinner lists a Menomini word for braided buffalo hair twine. The basswood bark twine, which serves many uses among the Chippewa and Central peoples, is not like the bark rope of the Plains Cree.[82]

Woodworking is somewhat more developed among the Eastern Cree than among their Plains affiliates. There is nothing like the profusion of woodworking, among any Cree-speaking group, however, as that found in the Central Woodlands.

Grooved stone axes were hafted in a split stick by the Eastern Cree. An illustration of an old Ojibwa axe shows the withe that forms the handle wound around the groove as with the Plains Cree types. The hafting of the Menomini grooved axe is not specified. The Northern Saulteaux and the bands of the Labrador Peninsula are said to have used unhafted axes.[83]

The prevailing style of pipe among the Eastern Cree is the "Micmac" type. This pipe form has a Central and Northeastern Woodland distribution, extending as far west as the Missouri River. The style is sometimes seen among the Plains Cree, but the prevailing Plains type, the "monitor" pipe, is not eastern. It is interesting to note that the two pipe styles illustrated by Skinner for the Northern Saulteaux correspond quite closely to specimens from the Blackfoot illustrated in Wissler's account.[84]

The ornamental stems used by the contemporary Plains Cree are similar to Menomini pipe styles.[85]

The use of *kinnikinnik* is long-standing among the Woodlands tribes. Red willow bark is smoked by the Ojibwa and Abenaki and also by the inhabitants of Western Pennsylvania, Virginia and the Green Bay region of Wisconsin. It is also used by several Plains tribes including the Omaha, Cheyenne, Comanche, Arapaho, Kiowa and Sioux. Bearberry leaves are used for the smoking mixture by the Ojibwa, Assiniboin and Blackfoot. Carver saw natives smoking these leaves in 1796 along Lake Michigan.[86] The Eastern Cree use both willow bark and the leaves of a plant that may be the bearberry. Both are also utilized by the Plains Cree.[87]

The tobacco pouches of the Central Woodlands people, as exemplified by Menomini specimens, are short, soft bags with a plain fringe, unlike the long tobacco bags of the Plains. The Plains Cree use both types, although the long style is the more common.

The practice of fire-making with the bow drill is common to Eastern Cree, Menomini and Northern Saulteaux. It is not known to the Plains Cree.[88]

Although the Eastern Cree and Plains Cree have no pottery, a tradition of pottery-making exists among the Northern Saulteaux, Menomini and Winnebago.[89]

The weaving of rabbitskin blankets is done with a similar technique among the Eastern Cree, the Northern Saulteaux and the Plains Cree. However, the strips of rabbitskin, rolled on the bare thigh, are wound on a stick, unlike the Plains Cree manner of preparing the strip. The Chippewa weave their blankets on a twine warp or use the same technique as in snowshoe netting.[90]

Of the several processes and artifacts discussed under this heading, there are very few that are not shared by the Plains Cree and some Eastern tribes in one form or another. The bow drill for fire-making and the use, or rather the recollection, of pottery-making are not found among the Plains tribe. The hair embroidery technique described for the Plains Cree is apparently not eastern.

Certain of the eastern forms are known to the Plains Cree but are used as an alternate to another, non-eastern trait. This is true of the pipe, the tobacco pouch, the use of willow bark in smoking. Traits recorded for the Woodlands groups as well as the Plains Cree include woven beaded bands, leather thongs, hair rope. The ornamentation of leather by quillwork and painting is universal to the groups of the areas here considered.

The Central Woodlands tribes are far better craftsmen than the Cree groups and the Labrador bands. This is especially true of work in wood. The Plains Cree elaborated the use of leather, but very few Eastern Cree techniques were forgotten on the Plains.

MUSICAL INSTRUMENTS

Skinner describes a double-headed drum from the

Eastern Cree, and mentions that a single-headed type is known to the Albany Cree. The tambourine drum, held by the thongs which stretch over the open face, is found in Labrador, among the Wabanaki bands and in the Central Woodlands.[91] Double-headed types are reported from the Ojibwa, Menomini and Penobscot. Speck states that in Labrador the double-headed drum is used by the people west of the St. Marguerite River (Mistassini, Lake St. John bands). East of that river the single-headed drum is used.[92]

The water drum associated with the Plains Cree *mite·wi-win* is Ojibwa and Menomini. In 1661 Radisson saw Cree using drums made of earthen pots filled with water and covered with "stagg's" skin.[93]

The disc rattle, used by one Eastern Cree band, and by groups in Labrador, corresponds to a rattle used by one of the Plains Cree societies. The hide rattles of the Plains Cree are shaped like the gourd rattles of the Menomini.[94]

Both single- and double-headed drums are found in all the areas under consideration. The hide rattle and straight drumstick of the Plains Cree are not eastern. The Eastern Cree and Naskapi use a bent drumstick. The water drum appears to be a trait that had been forgotten by the Plains Cree until reintroduced by the Ojibwa. A dried deerskin is beaten in the annual ceremony of the Lenapé.[95]

FOOTNOTES

[1] STRONG, WILLIAM DUNCAN, An introduction to Nebraska Archeology (Smithsonian Miscellaneous Collections, vol. 93, no. 10, Washington, 1935), p. 298.

[1a] SKINNER, ALANSON, Notes on the Eastern Cree and Northern Saulteaux (Anthropological Papers, American Museum of Natural History, vol. 9, part 1, New York, 1911), p. 12; ELLIS, HENRY, A Voyage to Hudson's Bay, London, 1848, p. 181; HEARNE, SAMUEL, A Journey from Prince of Wales Fort in Hudson's Bay to the Northern Ocean, J.B. Tyrrell, ed., Toronto, 1911, p. 74.

[2] SPECK, FRANK G., Culture Problems in Northeastern North America (Proceedings, American Philosophical Society, vol. 65, Philadelphia, 1926), pp. 279, 285.

[3] JONES, WILLIAM, Central Algonkin (Annual Archaeological Report, 1905, Toronto, 1906), p. 139; SKINNER, Notes on the Eastern Cree, p. 119.

[4] SKINNER, ALANSON, Material Culture of the Menomini (Indian Notes and Monographs, Museum of the American Indian, Heye Foundation, New York, 1921), p. 99; RADIN, PAUL, The Winnebago Tribe (Thirty-Seventh Annual Report, Bureau of American Ethnology, 1915-16, Washington, 1923), p. 104; STRONG, WILLIAM DUNCAN, The Indian Tribes of the Chicago Region (Field Museum of Natural History, Anthropology Leaflet 24, Chicago, 1926), p. 23.

[5] SKINNER, Material Culture of the Menomini, p. 99.

[6] *Ibid.*, p. 89.

[7] SKINNER, Notes on the Eastern Cree, p. 13.

[8]JONES, Central Algonkin, p. 138; SKINNER, Material Culture of the Menomini, p. 86; SKINNER, ALANSON, The Mascoutin or Prairie Potawatomi Indians; Part I, Social Life and Ceremonies (Bulletin, Museum of the City of Milwaukee, vol. 6, no. 1, 1924), p. 268; SPECK, Culture Problems, p. 279.

[9]"Eastern Cree" includes all Cree speaking people from James Bay to Lake Winnipeg. Synonyms for this term used here are, Forest Cree, Woodland Cree, Cree. It is to be noted that the Western Woodland Cree are yet another group who live to the north of the Saskatchewan River and west of Lake Winnipeg. The cultural and geographic boundaries of this division have yet to be defined. "Northern Algonkin" refers chiefly to Eastern Cree and Northern Saulteaux. "Northeast Algonkin" includes the Montagnais and Naskapi. "Central Algonkin" refers mainly to Menomini, Potawatomi, Sauk and Fox; these and the Winnebago are encompassed by "Central Woodlands." The Ojibwa (Chippewa) are mostly North Algonkin, although some southern bands of Chippewa have a Central Woodlands cast of culture.

[10]SKINNER, Notes on the Eastern Cree, pp. 14, 120.

[11]SPECK, FRANK G., Naskapi, The Savage Hunters of the Labrador Peninsula, University of Oklahoma Press, Norman, 1935, p. 202.

[12]SKINNER, Material Culture of the Menomini, p. 87; HARRINGTON, M.R., Religion and Ceremonies of the Lenapé (Indian Notes and Monographs, Museum of the American Indian, Heye Foundation, New York, 1921), p. 82.

[13]SKINNER, Notes on the Eastern Cree, pp. 14, 162; SPECK, Naskapi, p. 98; TURNER, LUCIEN M., Ethnology of the Ungava District (Eleventh Annual Report, Bureau of Ethnology, 1889-90, Washington, 1894), p. 300; HOFFMAN, WALTER JAMES, The Menomini Indians (Fourteenth Annual Report, Bureau of Ethnology, 1892-1893, part 1, Washington, 1896), p. 117; HARRINGTON, Religion and Ceremonies of the Lenapé, p. 125.

[14]DENSMORE, FRANCES, Chippewa Customs (Bureau of American Ethnology, Bulletin 86, Washington, 1929), p. 29.

[15]SKINNER, Material Culture of the Menomini, p. 91.

[16]HODGE, Handbook of American Indians, part 2, p. 625; TURNER, Ethnology of the Ungava District, p. 302.

[17]SKINNER, Material Culture of the Menomini, pp. 289-293; TURNER, Ethnology of the Ungava District, pp. 302, 306.

[18]SKINNER, Notes on the Eastern Cree, p. 50; SPECK, Culture Problems, p. 293; TURNER, Ethnology of the Ungava District, p. 301.

[19]SPECK, FRANK G., Mistassini Notes (Indian Notes and Monographs, Museum of American Indians, Heye Foundation, 1930), p. 438; SKINNER, Material Culture of the Menomini, p. 294; SKINNER, Notes on the Eastern Cree, p. 47.

[20]SPECK, Culture Problems, p. 281; SPECK, Mistassini Notes, p. 443; SKINNER, Notes on the Eastern Cree, p. 134; SKINNER, Material Culture of the Menomini, p. 287; DENSMORE, Chippewa Customs, p. 170.

[21]ELLIS, A Voyage to Hudson's Bay, p. 186; WISSLER, Costumes of the Plains Indians, p. 81.

[22]SKINNER, Notes on the Eastern Cree, p. 19; SPECK, FRANK G., Notes on the Material Culture of the Huron (American Anthropologist, n.s., vol. 13, no. 2, 1911), p. 211; JONES, Central Algonkin, p. 141; SKINNER, Material Culture of the Menomini, p. 125; TURNER, Ethnology of the Ungava District, p. 291.

[23]BALLANTYNE, R.M., Hudson's Bay, Edinburgh, 1848, p. 42; SKINNER, Notes on the Eastern Cree, p. 121.

[24]SKINNER, Notes on the Eastern Cree, pp. 35, 121; JONES, Central Algonkin, p. 141; RADIN, The Winnebago Tribe, p. 106; SKINNER, Material Culture of the Menomini, p. 116; WILLOUGHBY, CHARLES C., Dress and Ornaments of the New England Indians (American Anthropologist, n.s., vol. 7, no. 3, 1905), p. 501.

[25]ELLIS, A Voyage to Hudson's Bay, p. 186; JONES, Central Algonkin, p. 141; DENSMORE, Chippewa Customs, p. 31; SKINNER, Material Culture of the Menomini, p. 113.

[26]SKINNER, Notes on the Eastern Cree, pp. 17, 122; SPECK, Culture Problems, p. 279.

[27]WISSLER, Material Culture of the Blackfoot Indians, p. 151; SKINNER, Material Culture of the Menomini, p. 117.

[28]WILLOUGHBY, Dress . . . of the New England Indians, pp. 502-503; STRONG, The Indian Tribes of the Chicago Region, p. 18; TURNER, Ethnology of the Ungava District, p. 284; DENSMORE, Chippewa Customs, p. 33; SKINNER, ALANSON, The Menomini Indians: Social Life and Ceremonial

Bundles of the Menomini Indians; Associations and Ceremonies of the Menomini Indians; Folklore of the Menomini Indians (Anthropological Papers, American Museum of Natural History, vol. 13, parts 1-3, 1913, 1915, 1915), p. 263.

[29]INNIS, The Fur Trade in Canada, pp. 46, 96.

[30]TURNER, Ethnology of the Ungava District, p. 284; *see also* WILLOUGHBY, Dress . . . of the New England Indians, p. 502; SPECK, Material Culture of the Huron, p. 211: DENSMORE, Chippewa Customs, p. 31; SKINNER, Material Culture of the Menomini, p. 109.

[31]SKINNER, Material Culture of the Menomini, p. 109; SKINNER, Notes on the Eastern Cree, p. 121; TURNER, Ethnology of the Ungava District, p. 286.

[32]BIRKET-SMITH, KAJ, The Caribou Eskimos: Their Cultural Position (Report of the Fifth Thule Expedition, vol. 5, part 2, Copenhagen, 1929), part 2, p. 342.

[33]HENRY, Travels and Adventures in Canada p. 239; DENSMORE, Chippewa Customs, p. 36; SKINNER, Material Culture of the Menomini, p. 128; SKINNER, Notes on the Eastern Cree, pp. 24, 125.

[34]HODGE, Handbook of American Indians, part 1, p. 496.

[35]HENRY, Travels and Adventures in Canada, p. 239; SKINNER, Material Culture of the Menomini, p. 130; SPECK, Culture Problems, p. 293; SKINNER, Notes on the Eastern Cree, p. 24.

[36]SKINNER, Notes on the Eastern Cree, p. 23; SPECK, Culture Problems, p. 293; SKINNER, Material Culture of the Menomini, p. 134; BIRKET-SMITH, The Caribou Eskimos, part 2, pp. 186, 345.

[37]JONES, Central Algonkin, p. 140; CHAMBERLAIN, ALEXANDER F., The Beothuks of Newfoundland (Annual Archaeological Report, 1905, Toronto, 1906), p. 120.

[38]JEREMIE, NICHOLAS, Twenty Years at York Factory, 1694-1714; (his) Account of Hudson Strait and Bay. Translated from the French ed. of 1720. With Notes and Introduction by R. Douglas and J.N. Wallace, Ottawa, 1926, p. 38; *Perrot in* BLAIR, E.H., ed., The Indian Tribes of the Upper Mississippi Valley, Cleveland, 1911, pp. 107ff; WEST, JOHN, The Substance of a Journal During a Residence at the Red River Colony, London, 1824, p. 19; TURNER, Ethnology of the Ungava District, p. 277.

[39]SKINNER, Notes on the Eastern Cree, p. 25; SKINNER, Material Culture of the Menomini, p. 182; BIRKET-SMITH, The Caribou Eskimos, part 2, p. 330.

[40]TURNER, Ethnology of the Ungava District, p. 279; SKINNER, Material Culture of the Menomini, p. 185.

[41]BIRKET-SMITH, The Caribou Eskimos, part 2, pp. 158-159.

[42]WEST, Journal . . . at the Red River Colony, p. 55; THWAITES, The Jesuit Relations, vol. 54, p. 173; TYRRELL, David Thompson's Narrative, pp. 84, 111.

[43]BIRKET-SMITH, The Caribou Eskimos, part 2, p. 332; SKINNER, Notes on the Eastern Cree, p. 137.

[44]RADIN, The Winnebago Tribe, p. 114; SKINNER, The Mascoutin or Prairie Potawatomi Indians, p. 281; JONES, Central Algonkin, p. 140; DENSMORE, Chippewa Customs, p. 126.

[45]SKINNER, Notes on the Eastern Cree, pp. 271, 137; RADIN, The Winnebago Tribe, p. 114; BIRKET-SMITH, The Caribou Eskimos, p. 322; SKINNER, Material Culture of the Menomini, p. 201; KOHL, J.G., Kitchi Gami: Wanderings Round Lake Superior, London, 1860, p. 311.

[46]SKINNER, Notes on the Eastern Cree, p. 137.

[47]ELLIS, A Voyage to Hudson's Bay, p. 185; SKINNER, Notes on the Eastern Cree, p. 27; JONES, Central Algonkin, p. 140.

[48]SKINNER, Notes on the Eastern Cree, pp. 30, 138; KOHL, Kitchi Gami, pp. 318-323.

[49]THWAITES, Jesuit Relations, vol. 66, pp. 107ff; DOBBS, An Account of Countries Adjoining to Hudson's Bay, p. 36; HENRY, Travels and Adventures in Canada, p. 243; TYRRELL, Documents . . . of Hudson Bay, p. 96.

[50]KOHL, Kitchi Gami, p. 318; DENSMORE, Chippewa Customs, p. 123; SKINNER, Material Culture of the Menomini, pp. 165-172.

[51]SKINNER, Notes on the Eastern Cree, p. 25; THWAITES, Jesuit Relations, vol. 45, p. 227; ELLIS, A Voyage to Hudson's Bay, p. 182; MULVANEY, North-West Rebellion, p. 55.

[52]SKINNER, Material Culture of the Menomini, p. 173.

[53]SKINNER, Notes on the Eastern Cree, pp. 29, 133; THWAITES, Jesuit Relations, vol. 45, p. 227; DENSMORE, Chippewa Customs, p. 43.

[54]SKINNER, Notes on the Eastern Cree, p. 28; JONES, Central Algonkin, p. 140; TURNER, Ethnology of the Ungava District, p. 322; HODGE, Handbook of American Indians, part 2, p. 223.

[55]ELLIS, A Voyage to Hudson's Bay, p. 182; SKINNER, Notes on the Eastern Cree, p. 29.

[56]SKINNER, Notes on the Eastern Cree, p. 29; DENSMORE, Chippewa Customs, p. 44; TURNER, Ethnology of the Ungava District, p. 278.

[57]SKINNER, Notes on the Eastern Cree, p. 30; JONES, Central Algonkin, p. 140; DENSMORE, Chippewa Customs, p. 41; SKINNER, Material Culture of the Menomini, p. 195.

[58]SKINNER, Material Culture of the Menomini, p. 160.

[59]SKINNER, Notes on the Eastern Cree, pp. 31-32; SKINNER, Material Culture of the Menomini, pp. 150, 152.

[60]SKINNER, Notes on the Eastern Cree, p. 44; KOHL, Kitchi Gami, p. 333; SPECK, Culture Problems, pp. 279, 283; SKINNER, Material Culture of the Menomini, p. 212; DRUMMOND, T., The Canadian Snowshoe (Transactions, Royal Society of Canada, vol. 10, section 2, 1906), p. 312.

[61]SKINNER, Notes on the Eastern Cree, p. 43; SPECK, Culture Problems, p. 278.

[62]SKINNER, Notes on the Eastern Cree, p. 43; JONES, Central Algonkin, p. 142; SKINNER, Material Culture of the Menomini, p. 213.

[63]Perrot in BLAIR, The Indian Tribes of the Upper Mississippi, p. 107; SKINNER, Material Culture of the Menomini, pp. 185, 191; SPECK, Culture Problems, p. 283.

[64]CURTIS, The North American Indian, vol. 18, p. 67; SKINNER, Notes on the Eastern Cree, p. 135; JONES, Central Algonkin, p. 143; SPECK, Culture Problems, p. 278; SPECK, Material Culture of the Huron, p. 225; SKINNER, Material Culture of the Menomini, p. 320; RADIN, The Winnebago Tribe, p. 110; SKINNER, The Mascoutin or Prairie Potawatomi Indians, p. 298; BIRKET-SMITH, The Caribou Eskimos, part 2, p. 148.

[65]SKINNER, Notes on the Eastern Cree, pp. 24, 135; SPECK, Culture Problems, p. 278; TURNER, Ethnology of the Ungava District, p. 312; SKINNER, Material Culture of the Menomini, p. 325; SPECK, Material Culture of the Huron, p. 225.

[66]BIRKET-SMITH, The Caribou Eskimos, part 2, p. 316; SPECK, Culture Problems, p. 278; SKINNER, Material Culture of the Menomini, p. 327.

[67]JONES, Central Algonkin, p. 143.

[68]SKINNER, Notes on the Eastern Cree, p. 37.

[69]Ibid., pp. 25, 78; JONES, PETER (REV.), History of the Ojebway Indians: With Special Reference to the Conversion to Christianity, London, 186-?, p. 131; SPECK, Culture Problems, p. 278.

[70]SKINNER, Notes on the Eastern Cree, p. 78; SKINNER, Material Culture of the Menomini, p. 314; JONES, History of the Ojebway Indians, p. 132.

[71]SKINNER, Notes on the Eastern Cree, pp. 78, 165; SKINNER, Material Culture of the Menomini, p. 319; HODGE, Handbook of American Indians, part 2, pp. 546-547.

[72]SKINNER, Notes on the Eastern Cree, p. 78; UMFREVILLE, EDWARD, The Present State of Hudson's Bay, p. 188.

[73]SKINNER, Notes on the Eastern Cree, pp. 33, 125; SPECK, Naskapi, p. 216.

[74]JONES, Central Algonkin, p. 142.

[75]TURNER, Ethnology of the Ungava District, pp. 293-296.

[76]SKINNER, Material Culture of the Menomini, pp. 226ff.

[77]SKINNER, Notes on the Eastern Cree, p. 73; CHAMBERLAIN, ALEXANDER F., Indians of the Eastern Provinces of Canada (Annual Archaeological Report, 1905, Toronto, 1906), p. 129; SKINNER, Material Culture of the Menomini, p. 340.

[78]A.C. Fletcher in HODGE, Handbook of American Indians, vol. 2, p. 342.

[79]SPECK, FRANK G., Huron Moose Hair Embroidery (American Anthropologist, n.s., vol. 13, no. 1, 1911), pp. 4-6.

[80]DENSMORE, Chippewa Customs, p. 192.

[81]SKINNER, Notes on the Eastern Cree, p. 56.

[82]SKINNER, Material Culture of the Menomini, p. 251; DENSMORE, Chippewa Customs, p. 152.

[83]SKINNER, Notes on the Eastern Cree, pp. 51, 132; JONES, History of the Ojebway Indians, facing p. 131; SKINNER, Material Culture of the Menomini, p. 318; SPECK, Culture Problems, p. 280.

[84]SKINNER, Notes on the Eastern Cree, p. 143; WEST, GEORGE A., Tobacco, Pipes and Smoking Customs of the American Indian (Bulletin, Museum of the City of Milwaukee, vol. 17, part 1, Milwaukee, 1934), p. 372; WISSLER, Material Culture of the Blackfoot Indians, pp. 82-83.

[85]SKINNER, Material Culture of the Menomini, p. 263.

[86]WEST, Tobacco, Pipes and Smoking Customs, pp. 105-116.

[87]SKINNER, Notes on the Eastern Cree, p. 40.
[88]SKINNER, Notes on the Eastern Cree, pp. 33, 138; SKINNER, Material Culture of the Menomini, p. 301.
[89]SKINNER, Notes on the Eastern Cree, p. 127; RADIN, The Winnebago Tribe, p. 119; SKINNER, Material Culture of the Menomini, p. 282.
[90]SKINNER, Notes on the Eastern Cree, pp. 35, 128; DENSMORE, Chippewa Customs, p. 161.
[91]SKINNER, Notes on the Eastern Cree, pp. 41-42; BIRKET-SMITH, The Caribou Eskimos, part 2, p. 363.
[92]SPECK, Naskapi, p. 170.
[93]JONES, History of the Ojebway Indians, p. 134; SKINNER, Material Culture of the Menomini, p. 345; SCULL, Voyages of Radisson, pp. 91-92.
[94]SPECK, Naskapi, p. 172; SKINNER, Material Culture of the Menomini, p. 352.
[95]HARRINGTON, Religion and Ceremonies of the Lenapé, p. 94.

Social Organization

The bands of the Eastern Cree are more in the nature of vague geographic divisions than corporate entities. The earliest reference to Cree bands occurs in the *Jesuit Relations* of 1656-1658 in which Father Dreuillettes names four divisions of the "Kilistinons," evidently distinguishing one from the other by the territory each occupies. Skinner also names four divisions, also labeled by the geographical sectors each occupies. He adds that the environment militates against large communities and the Eastern Cree are scattered in family groups over wide areas. In the spring these groups meet at an appointed place, now the trading post, for two or three weeks.[1]

The spring rendezvous is an old pattern in Cree culture. Father Dablon, in lamenting the nomadic nature of the Cree, says that they assemble "only rarely" for markets or festivals. The Jesuits often noted that the Cree are a wandering, hunting people, difficult to convert because of their footloose habits. Yet there are a number of passages wherein Cree "residences," "villages," and in 1660 a "general fair," are recorded.[2]

Loosely organized as are the Plains Cree bands, the divisions of Eastern Cree are equally inchoate—perhaps more so. William Jones depicts a similar arrangement for the Ojibwa groups. The bands of the Labrador Indians consist merely of the joint occupants of a district. The Wabanaki tribes have only a little more formal organization. The one factor that encourages organization is the common spring meeting place.[3]

The concept of individual hunting territories held by the Northeastern Algonkins extends westward to the Northern Saulteaux, but not to the Eastern Cree.[4]

Although the Ojibwa recognize sib lineage, it does not greatly affect the band organization. South of the Ojibwa, sib descent and moiety groupings do play a part in the band set-up.

CHIEFTAINSHIP

Chieftainship among the Forest Cree is much the same as with the Plains Cree. Umfreville seems to be referring to the Eastern Cree when he says that they have no manner of government or subordination. The father or head of a family has no superiors. He gives advice and expresses an opinion but at the same time has no authority to enforce obedience. The youth of the family follow the father's directions, but rather because of filial affection and reverence than because of any strict exactment. Similarly, when several families go to war or to the factories to trade, they choose a leader. But the obedience paid to the leader is purely voluntary since anyone may leave at his pleasure. Once the enterprise is over the leader may not presume to any authority. Merit alone gives title to the position. However, a person who is an experienced hunter, who knows the topography thoroughly, who can speak well, who is a conjuror, or simply one who has a large family, will usually have some followers.[5]

Ellis' discourse on the native chiefs of the Hudson Bay region is in the same vein. He says that the chiefs are "chosen from the most ancient of the people, but chiefly for their Skill in Hunting, and Experience in Trade, Domestic Affairs and Valour in War . . ." He adds that their advice is followed rather through deference than obligation.[6]

Eastern Cree chiefs, in Skinner's version, were formerly the best warriors and most trustworthy men and were chosen by tacit consent. This is true of the Northern Saulteaux. Speck states that the Wabanaki chiefs lack any special power, while in Labrador there seldom are chiefs.[7]

There is a tendency for Ojibwa chieftainship to be hereditary. South of that tribe, Central Woodlands chieftainship is, in general, hereditary along sib lines.[8]

Chieftainship and band organization among the Eastern Cree corresponds to Plains Cree patterns. In both groups, bands are loose, little-coordinated units, largely moulded by geographical considerations. In both groups also, chieftainship is dependent on merit and valor; the power of the chief varies with the personality wielding it.

The Ojibwa chiefs are much like the Cree. Labrador bands are so diffuse that the need for group leadership is attenuated. The kinship structure and village life of Central Woodlands people make for a wide divergence from the ways of their northern neighbors.

An official who corresponds to the chief's crier of the

Plains tribe is recorded for the Ojibwa. One of the duties of the Menomini war leader is to act as the spokesman for the chief in making public announcements and speeches.[9]

Ojibwa councils are composed of the principal men of the band. Each may have his say, as with the Plains Cree. There are few data on councils of the Eastern Cree, but we may presume that they are of the same informal nature.[10]

SOCIETIES

Of the Warrior Societies found in the Plains, no trace exists in the Northern Algonkin area. The forest environment furnishes sustenance only for small scattered groups and allows communal gatherings for very short periods. Therefore there is little chance for the development of social forms which require larger bodies of people living together for a longer period.

Certain traces of such organizations do exist in the Central Woodlands. Menomini war leaders and warriors police the camp to guard the crop of wild rice against premature harvesting. An hereditary officer acts as commander and wears a special badge of authority. Other duties of the warrior police, as Skinner calls them, are to take charge of ceremonies, to act as chief's criers, to intercede in quarrels. The name for them is cognate with the term used for the Warrior Society among the Plains Cree. According to Skinner, the word was taken by the Menomini from the Ojibwa, who in turn got it from the Sioux. Skinner states that other Central Algonkin tribes, notably the Sauk and Fox, made use of police, but not in the same manner.[11]

While these police are strongly reminiscent of the Plains Cree warriors, it seems likely that the two represent peripheral cases of distribution of the trait complex from a common center. Indeed Lowie concludes that the custom was borrowed by the Central Algonkin, probably from a Dakota source.[12] Since the Eastern Cree and other Forest Algonkin peoples do not have such an institution, it is probable that the Plains Cree societies were also taken from a Dakota-speaking group.

RANK AND PRESTIGE

The means of acquiring prestige among the Eastern Cree, as on the Plains, lies largely in success in warfare. This is not explicitly stated in the literature but there are many compelling suggestions. Thus Mackenzie gives two motives explaining why a Cree engages in warfare, the first of which is "to prove his courage." In various accounts, the requirements for chieftainship always include "Valour in War," as Ellis puts it.[13] So it is with the Ojibwa. Peter Jones relates that the civil chiefs, who do not have to be warriors, seldom neglect an opportunity of engaging in warfare and "the more scalps they take, the more they are revered by their people." Menomini boys look forward from earliest youth to the time when they can become warriors. Winnebago men go on the war path to achieve the distinction that comes with war exploits.[14]

The search for glory fades out to the northeast and the Labrador bands are a markedly docile people. In their emphasis on prowess in war, the Eastern Cree are perhaps most divergent from the Northeastern Algonkins. The Eastern Cree, as far back as we know them, set a high value on war distinctions. When they first came onto the plains, they were already attuned to this significant aspect of the Plains way of life.

THE INDIVIDUAL LIFE CYCLE

Birth

The available sources yield little information on the birth customs of the Eastern Cree. There is a passage in Harmon's journal, presumably referring to the tribe, to the effect that birth takes place in a little hut erected for the purpose. The woman remains apart for about thirty days.[15] Comparative data from other tribes are also scanty. A support used by Winnebago women in childbirth is identical with the type employed by Plains Cree women.[16]

The Eastern Cree infant is placed in a moss bag much like the bag used for Plains Cree children. The Eastern cradle board differs in that the bag is sewn to the board instead of being detachable. The Ojibwa board has a rim like the Plains type, but also has the bag, filled with rotted wood, attached to the board. Menomini cradle boards have an angular instead of a U-shaped rim, but otherwise are similar to the Plains Cree type. The Menomini use a band instead of the bag, and cattail down is used as an absorbent.[17]

Harmon mentions a feast, given by Eastern Cree shortly after the birth, at which the child is named. The Northern Saulteaux give a naming feast for children "as soon as they are born." The Ojibwa celebrate the occasion similarly and the name is given by an old man or woman who takes it from a vision experience. Kohl indicates that the father of an Ojibwa child gives the name if he has the requisite vision, otherwise he invites a friend to name the child from his vision.[18]

Menomini children are given personal names, often vision revealed, by their parents. Sometimes a shaman called in to cure a sick child will rename the child. The Ojibwa also give new names to children as a consequence of illness. This parallels the Plains Cree custom.[19]

While the evidence on birth customs is far from full, there is enough to indicate that the Plains Cree customs are known to the Eastern Cree and Central Algonkins. The baby carriers of the two Cree groups are alike in most respects. The naming feast and vision names are Eastern Cree and Ojibwa. While the naming practices of the Central Woodlands people are different from those of the Cree, a correspondence crops up in the changing of names in illness.

Puberty

The several accounts of Eastern Cree girls' puberty customs are not uniform. Joseph Robson writes that a woman once in her life separates herself and lives three weeks alone. During that time those who administer to her leave food in certain places and immediately depart. Since this source is none too reliable, greater credence may be given to other observers.[20]

Harmon says that a girl runs into the woods upon experiencing her first menstrual flow and remains there for several days. She then returns to her tent and proceeds to pile up a stack of wood as high as her head to show that she will become an industrious woman. Hearne also states that the girl goes off a little distance and returns in five or six days. After this she wears a kind of veil made of beads.[21]

Customs differ among other Indian bands. Menstrual seclusion in a small hut built for the purpose is practised by the Northern Saulteaux at puberty only. Ojibwa girls are confined to the menstrual tent for a month.[22] Certain bands of the Labrador Peninsula seclude pubescent girls for three days. After this time, they wear a veil to ward off harmful influences.[23] There is a ten day period of segregation for Menomini girls at puberty. Thereafter seclusion continues for the duration of each menstrual period.[24]

The Eastern Cree and Ojibwa are at one with the Plains

Cree in the segregation at initial menstruation and in not using special lodges for subsequent menstrual periods. The cutting of wood by the Eastern Cree girl follows the Plains Cree custom, although the ceremonial return to the lodge is not eastern. The Central peoples differ in that every menstrual period is an occasion for seclusion.

Throughout the areas under discussion, contact with a menstruating woman is defiling, especially for sacred objects. The phrasing given to this concept by a Winnebago informant holds true for most eastern tribes. "Everything that is holy would immediately lose its power if a menstruating woman came in contact with it."[25]

Marriage

Eastern Cree marriages are arranged by the parents. The bride is brought to the groom by her father and mother. According to Mackenzie there is matrilocal residence. The man is coldly treated by his parents-in-law until the birth of a child.[26]

A special marriage custom is recorded for the Northern Saulteaux. The man makes the marriage proposal to the girl's father. If he is accepted, he tosses pieces of wood at the girl. For every one she catches, the groom must give a gift to her father.[27]

Objiwa parents arrange the match and the couple go off on a hunting trip together.[28]

The Naskapi suitor offers gifts to the parents of his prospective bride. If they consent to the arrangement, the man takes the girl to live with him.[29]

The proposal of marriage among the Menomini is initiated by the man's mother or sister. If the match is agreed upon by the parents, the couple live together without any further ado. Later there is an exchange of gifts between the two families. Winnebago parents arrange the marriage and a gift exchange follows. Residence is matrilocal at first, later patrilocal. The Prairie Potawatomi marriage procedure is similar, but includes the undressing and redressing of both the bride and groom by members of the affinal families of each.[30]

Several constants may be observed in the marriage procedures of Plains and Eastern Cree, Central and Northeastern Algonkins. The match is arranged by the parents; no particular ceremony accompanies the actual marriage; gift exchanges are made between the affinal families; residence is often matrilocal at first, then patrilocal. While such divergent traits as the redressing of the Prairie Potawatomi and the chip-tossing of the Northern Saulteaux occur, the fundamental pattern is uniform.

A plurality of wives is permissible although none too frequent among the Eastern Cree. Skinner asserts that polygyny was once common and the number of wives varied from four to five. But Ballantyne and Harmon note that most men content themselves with one wife. Robson gives two as the usual number, that being as many as a man can well maintain by hunting.[31] In general the ability to feed additional spouses is the chief consideration in taking more than one wife.

The Eastern Cree practise the sororate, a man usually taking the younger sister of his wife as a second wife. He considers it his duty to marry his wife's sister upon the wife's death.[32] The obligation to hunt for one's father-in-law is attested by Franklin and Robson.[33] From an early date, sexual hospitality was noted for the Cree and is also recorded for the Northern Saulteaux.[34]

An unfaithful wife among the Plains Cree may be punished with the loss of her hair, the tip of her nose, or even of her life. Evidently the Ojibwa punish adulterous wives in a similar way, for Peter Jones relates that divorce occurs only upon the enactment of some heinous crime, such as adultery. Before the separation ensues, the husband bites off the wife's nose. Adulterous Menomini wives may be killed or have their noses bitten off by the irate husband.[35]

In the practice of polygyny and the obligation to hunt for the father-in-law, the Plains Cree are like the Eastern Cree.

The kinship behavior and joking relationships of the Central Woodlands are related to the sib systems and hence are unlike the Cree practices.

Death, Burial, Mourning

There are differing accounts in the literature about the mortuary customs of the Eastern Cree. Skinner relates that the body is laid out straight and wrapped in bark. The personal belongings of the deceased are left on the grave.[36] Mackenzie tells of a grave lined with branches over which a kind of canopy is erected. Grave posts with figures of animals carved on them are placed on the grave. This may be more like Ojibwa practice than Cree.[37] Robson writes that when an Indian of the Hudson Bay region dies, he is buried with all his possessions. The corpse is placed in the grave on its haunches. The grave is filled up and covered over with brush on which some tobacco is placed. Nearby a pole is set up and skins are tied to it.[38]

The Northern Saulteaux practise several kinds of burial. Bark lined graves are common, the weapons and utensils of the deceased being placed at the head of the corpse. A pole with a strip of cloth tied to it is erected at the head of the grave. The grave house is a recent development among the Northern Saulteaux. Another type of burial is the placing of the bark-wrapped corpse in a wooden box. In one instance this box was placed on the cross beams of a log cabin. Sometimes the body is placed on an elevated scaffold or in the fork of a tree. Skinner adds that insane people are burned alive, or more recently, killed and then cremated. This probably refers only to cases of possession by the *wihtiko* or Cannibal Monster. The only means of annihilating the evil spirit in the possessed is by burning them.[39]

The Ojibwa do not carry a dead body through the door but cut a hole in the side of the lodge for the purpose. Peter Jones tells us that the head is placed toward the west and the pipe, gun, and other personal belongings placed beside the corpse. Over the grave, brush is piled, on which mats or bark are laid. This is done to secure the grave against rain. This may well represent the prototype of the grave houses of the Central Algonkins. During the winter season, the same author continues, the ground is frozen too hard to be excavated and the corpse is wrapped up and hung in the fork of a tree until the ground has thawed.[40]

Labrador burials are in shallow graves. The corpse is placed on the side in a sleeping position or in a sitting position. The body, together with the weapons and tools of the deceased, is wrapped in a blanket. The head is to the west and a birch bark hut is erected over the grave. Some Montagnais observed in 1631, removed a corpse through an opening in the side of the dwelling, not through the door.[41]

The Menomini use birch bark to wrap the corpse and to line the grave. The instance of an old medicine man, whose dying request it was to be buried in a sitting position, brings to mind similar death-bed requests among the Plains Cree. Over the grave small houses are built and a board is erected, marked with the totem animal of the deceased.[42]

The funerary rites of the Eastern Cree are only briefly described by Mackenzie, who states that the property of the deceased is destroyed and a feast is given. This feast is repeated annually. Skinner states that it was customary for the oldest man in the band to watch over the grave for two or three days in order that the spirit of the dead might not return and take away one of the living. Sometimes a barrier of fish nets is erected to exclude the spirit.[43]

The Northern Saulteaux abandon a lodge after the death. As soon as the body is interred the neighbors enter the lodge and take possession of the belongings of the deceased.[44]

Kohl describes a custom followed after the death of a child. A lock of hair is cut from the deceased and wrapped with the clothes and amulets of the dead child. This bundle is carried and cherished as though it were the child itself. During ceremonies, gifts are given and sacrifices made to the bundle. At the end of a year, a feast is given, the bundle is unfastened, the clothes and other articles given away, and the lock of hair buried.[45]

Other Ojibwa mortuary customs are described by Peter Jones who tells of a feast eaten at the grave. Part of the food is given to the spirit of the dead as a burnt offering. An old man makes a prayer to the spirit, enumerating its virtues when alive and asking that it depart quietly. The widow of the deceased then jumps over the grave and dodges among the trees in an effort to shake off the spirit of her departed husband.

Miss Densmore describes a "spirit bundle" carried by the Chippewa. A lock of hair is taken from the head of the deceased and wrapped with clothing and other articles. It is constantly carried about until a feast is given, the articles distributed and the lock of hair burned.[46]

There is little fear of deceased relatives' ghosts among the Northeastern Algonkin nor are there any rites for the spirit.[47]

The Menomini carry the corpse to the grave on the third day after the death. A feast in which the spirit is supposed to partake, is eaten beside the grave. A pipe is smoked and the widow cuts a lock of hair from her dead husband's head. She wraps it in cloth and cherishes it through the mourning period. When the body is lowered into the grave, the relatives of the deceased jump over it. Then the grave is filled in, and warriors count their coups, making a nick in a stick for every deed recited. This coup stick is set up beside the grave. The Sauk and Winnebago have similar customs.[48]

Mourning is evidenced among the Eastern Cree by cutting the hair, piercing the thighs and arms, and blackening the face. The Ojibwa likewise blacken the face, gash the arms and chest, and pour ashes over the mourners' hair. A widow mourns for a year.[49]

A Menomini widow blackens her face and leaves her hair uncombed. Relatives of the deceased gash themselves. A man is considered unclean for a year after a death has occurred in his family.[50]

The most common mode of burial in the eastern regions is interment in a bush-lined grave. This in itself is not at variance with the Plains Cree custom, but the specific construction of the Plains Cree grave does not seem to be Eastern. The position of the corpse, and the use of the grave house and grave posts, are other matters wherein the Plains practice differs from that of the Eastern peoples.

Tree burial is widespread, evidently because of the difficulty of excavating graves in winter. The burial box of the Northern Saulteaux may be connected either with the modern coffin or with the log vault of the Plains Cree which is apparently aboriginal.

The family of the deceased in all these areas disposes of the effects of the dead person, including the lodge, either by giving them away, destroying them, or burying them with the body. Taking the corpse out through an opening in the lodge wall is widespread.

Counting coup at the grave as done by the Menomini has a different function from the Plains Cree custom in similar circumstances.

The Ojibwa and Menomini cut a lock of hair from the corpse and include it in a bundle. However, they keep the bundle for a year only, whereas the Plains Cree keep it indefinitely as a family possession, adding braids of hair to it as members of the family die.

The fear that newly departed spirits will take a relative with them is absent only from the northeast in the areas under examination.

A feast soon after the death is common, but the Plains Cree ritual does not have close parallels in the east. Mourning is generally expressed by cutting or loosening the hair, gashing the body and blackening the face. With the possible exception of the last, these are known to the Plains Cree.

In all, the mortuary customs of the Plains Cree differ a good deal in details from the Eastern practices. However the whole attitude toward the dead, the handling of the corpse, and mourning customs are generally alike both on the plains and in the east.

[1]THWAITES, The Jesuit Relations, vol. 44, p. 325; SKINNER, Notes on the Eastern Cree, pp. 9, 57.

[2]THWAITES, Jesuit Relations, vol. 45, p. 227; vol. 46, p. 69; vol. 54, p. 173.

[3]JONES, Central Algonkin, p. 137; SPECK, Naskapi, p. 16.

[4]SKINNER, Notes on the Eastern Cree, p. 150.

[5]UMFREVILLE, The Present State of Hudson's Bay, pp. 43-44.

[6]ELLIS, A Voyage to Hudson's Bay, pp. 181-182.

[7]SKINNER, Notes on the Eastern Cree, pp. 57, 150; SPECK, Culture Problems, pp. 280, 283.

[8]JONES, Central Algonkin, p. 137; SKINNER, Material Culture of the Menomini, p. 51; RADIN, The Winnebago Tribe, p. 209; STRONG, The Indian Tribes of the Chicago Region, p. 21.

[9]JONES, History of the Ojebway Indians, p. 108; SKINNER, The Menomini Indians, p. 22.

[10]JONES, History of the Ojebway Indians, p. 127.

[11]SKINNER, The Menomini Indians: Social Life and Ceremonial Bundles . . ., p. 26; see also WISSLER, CLARK, Societies and Ceremonial Associations in the Oglala Division of the Teton-Dakota (Anthropological Papers, American Museum of Natural History, vol. II, part I, 1912).

[12]LOWIE, Plains Indian Age Societies, p. 910.

[13]Mackenzie quoted in SKINNER, Notes on the Eastern Cree, p. 79; ELLIS, A Voyage to Hudson's Bay, p. 181.

[14]JONES, History of the Ojebway Indians, p. 130; SKINNER, The Menomini Indians, p. 97; RADIN, The Winnebago Tribe, p. 157.

[15]HARMON, A Journal of Voyages and Travels, pp. 272, 298.

[16]RADIN, The Winnebago Tribe, p. 126.

[17]SKINNER, Notes on the Eastern Cree, p. 45; SKINNER, Material Culture of the Menomini, p. 214.

[18]HARMON, A Journal of Voyages and Travels, pp. 272, 292; SKINNER, Notes on the Eastern Cree, p. 151; JONES, History of the Ojebway Indians, p. 161; JONES, Central Algonkin, p. 136; KOHL, Kitchi Gami, p. 273.

[19]SKINNER, The Menomini Indians, p. 40; JONES, History of the Ojebway Indians, p. 161; DENSMORE, Chippewa Customs, p. 57.

[20]ROBSON, JOSEPH, An Account of Six Years Residence in Hudson's Bay. London, p. 52.

[21]HARMON, A Journal of Voyages and Travels, p. 293; HEARNE, Journey to the Northern Ocean, p. 304.

[22]SKINNER, Notes on the Eastern Cree, p. 152; RADIN, PAUL, Ojibwa Ethnological Chit-Chat (American Anthropologist, n.s., vol. 26, no. 4, 1924), p. 660.

[23]SPECK, Naskapi, p. 231.

[24]SKINNER, The Menomini Indians, p. 52.

[25]RADIN, The Winnebago Tribe, p. 136.

[26]SKINNER, Notes on the Eastern Cree, p. 57.

[27]Ibid., p. 150.

[28]JONES, History of the Ojebway Indians, p. 78.

[29]TURNER, Ethnology of the Ungava District, p. 270.

[30]SKINNER, The Menomini Indians, p. 29; RADIN, The Winnebago Tribe, p. 138; SKINNER, The Mascoutin or Prairie Potawatomi Indians, pp. 35-36.

[31]SKINNER, Notes on the Eastern Cree, p. 57; BALLANTYNE, Hudson's Bay, p. 56; HARMON, A Journal of Voyages and Travels, p. 293; ROBSON, An Account of Six Years Residence in Hudson's Bay, p. 51.

[32]SKINNER, Notes on the Eastern Cree, p. 57.

[33]FRANKLIN, Narrative of a Journey, p. 136; ROBSON, An Account of Six Years Residence in Hudson's Bay, p. 51.

[34]CARVER, Travels Through the Interior, p. 131; SKINNER, Notes on the Eastern Cree, p. 150.

[35]MACKENZIE, Voyages from Montreal, p. cxlvi; JONES, History of the Ojebway Indians, p. 80; SKINNER, The Menomini Indians, p. 30.

[36]SKINNER, Notes on the Eastern Cree, p. 80.

[37]Ibid., p. 81; DENSMORE, Chippewa Customs, p. 738.

[38]ROBSON, An Account of Six Years Residence in Hudson's Bay, p. 49.

[39]SKINNER, Notes on the Eastern Cree, pp. 166-167; COOPER, JOHN M., The Cree Witiko Psychosis (Primitive Man, vol. 6, no. 1, 1933), p. 22.

[40]KOHL, Kitchi Gami, p. 107; JONES, History of the Ojebway Indians, pp. 98-99.
[41]SPECK, Naskapi, p. 52.
[42]SKINNER, The Menomini Indians, p. 65.
[43]SKINNER, Notes on the Eastern Cree, p. 80.
[44]*Ibid.*, p. 167.
[45]KOHL, Kitchi Gami, p. 107.
[46]DENSMORE, Chippewa Customs, pp. 77-78.
[47]SPECK, Naskapi, p. 51.
[48]SKINNER, The Menomini Indians, pp. 63-72.
[49]SKINNER, Notes on the Eastern Cree, p. 81; KOHL, Kitchi Gami, p. 109; JONES, History of the Ojebway Indians, p. 101.
[50]SKINNER, The Menomini Indians, pp. 68-69.

Religion and Ceremonialism

SUPERNATURALS

The religious concepts of the Forest Cree have been formulated by Dr. J.M. Cooper. His paper offers data from contemporary informants and exhaustively covers the literature.[1] It is clear from Cooper's evidence that the present day Cree have the concept of a single Supreme Being. He is somewhere above, and is master of all things, including mankind. The deity is not of the aloof, remote type but is actively and directly influential in his relations with men.

This might seem different from the Plains Cree idea of an all powerful but distant Creator. However, Cooper states that the powers of a shaman, though coming from the Supreme Being in the last analysis, are immediately given by the "powagans," i.e., the spirit helpers.[2] Moreover, some of the citations given in the monograph itself point unmistakably to the idea of a Supreme Being who is too great to be petitioned directly. Thus Father Charles l'Allemant in 1627 stated that the Indians near Quebec believe in One who has created all "mais pourtant ils ne luy rendent aucun honneur." The testimony of contemporary Forest Cree includes these statements: "manitu was never sung to," and "often the conjurers tried to get the real (Supreme) Manitu to come to them so he could be better known, but they could not succeed."[3]

It is true that other evidence, especially from recent sources, indicates that the deity intervenes in human affairs. There is enough contradictory information, however, to suspect late influences in the development of this idea, although Dr. Cooper believes otherwise. "A review of the evidence, fragmentary as this evidence is for many sections of the far-flung Algonquian peoples, makes it reasonably clear that a Supreme Being belief is part of Algonquian culture as far back as our information goes."[4]

One annotation may be appended to this quotation. The evidence reviewed does not cover all the Algonquian peoples but only the Ojibwa, Cree, Montagnais, and Naskapi. Harrington's inquiries concerning a Supreme Being among the Lenapé revealed the concept of an all powerful Creator who is not directly worshipped. The antiquity of this belief is established by observations of Lenapé religion made by William Penn and Zeisberger.[5]

The Menomini cosmogonic scheme depicts several hierarchical levels in the heavenly regions. All the powers above are under a Supreme Creator who resides in the topmost stratum. He is the nominal head of the universe, but rarely figures in worship. More attention is paid to the lesser spirits who come into direct contact with mankind.[6] One Plains Cree informant averred that there were four heavenly tiers, but other Plains Cree disclaimed any knowledge of such an arrangement.

Radin's wording of the Winnebago concept may be quoted, for it applies equally well to the Plains Cree belief:

> Earthmaker (the Creator) is not supposed to bestow any definite blessings on man. He is, in a general way, expected to give them life. There is but little real worship of him because he is far removed from men and is supposed to come into relation with them only through his intermediaries, the spirits.[7]

The correspondence in belief among these various tribes is so close that it makes more plausible a theory of the leveling influence of missionary indoctrination. Two considerations weigh the scales in favor of a pre-missionary existence of this tenet. One is that the earliest and usually trustworthy chroniclers report the concept. Secondly, the idea is deeply ingrained into the religious views and practices of the tribes.

The very term used by the Plains Cree for spirit powers was noted by the Jesuit, Le Jeune, in 1633 as relating to supernatural forces among the Montagnais. The word as written by Le Jeune is "Atahocan," clearly cognate with the Plains Cree *atayo·hkan*.[8]

David Thompson is probably referring to Forest Cree when he says that the natives believe that the Great Spirit has placed all living creatures under the care of supernatural beings. They are the guardians and guides of every genus of bird and beast. Each *manito* has a separate command and care—one the bison, another the deer—thus the whole animal kingdom is divided among them.[9]

302

Among the Naskapi, every object, no matter how simple, has its patron spirit. There are spirits of animals, birds, fishes, insects, and plants. Any of them may be propitiated in order that men may benefit from them.[10]

The Ojibwa believe there are supernatural forces in charge of deer, bear, beaver, and other animals. They see powers connected with the sun, moon, stars, and trees.[11]

The schematic representation of the heavenly forces conceived by the Menomini includes supernatural powers of animals, natural phenomena, and of folkloristic characters. The Winnebago powers are drawn from the same categories and are of a like nature.[12]

Both the term and concept for personal supernaturals is the same among the Eastern Cree as it is with the Plains Cree.[13]

The Naskapi believe that one's personal spirit helper lives within the body. It must be placated lest misfortune ensue. This concept differs from that of the Cree in the abode, and in the means of pleasing the spirit, but the sense of a personal guardian is the same.[14]

Hoffman speaks of "tutelary daimons" and "guardian spirits" among the Menomini.[15] The Ojibwa and Winnebago have like concepts.[16]

Prominent in the mortuary rites of the Plains Cree is an invocation to the spirit of the deceased to depart quickly and not to linger about the camp. Should the spirit look back in its journey, one of its relatives will die. The Eastern Cree also are fearful lest the departing spirit take a relative along. The Chippewa hold the same notion.

The Menomini tell of two souls. One lingers about the grave after death. The other, called *tcebaı* (cf. Plains Cree *tcıpaı*), travels to the land of the dead. The lingering spirit is feared. Skinner notes that he came upon this belief in two souls among the Plains Cree. My data would bear him out, save that the two are rather manifestations of the same soul. That is, the soul that remains on earth is called *tcıpaı*; when it ascends, it is *ahtca·k*.[17]

The Montagnais-Naskapi word for soul is related to this, being *atcakw*. Despite the similarity in terms, the Labrador soul is a spirit helper, rather than the disembodied life-force. But it too resides in the body which it enters at birth, and leaves at death.[18]

The information concerning the belief in an Evil Spirit, *matci·manito·*, is perplexing. From the weak and tenuous manner in which this belief is held among the Plains Cree it could easily be of recent origin. Cooper's informants declared that there was an old belief in an Evil Spirit, or else equated it with the Cannibal Monster. However, the term occurs in a 1697 manuscript. Other early writers, Drage, Ellis, Wales, Umfreville, connect the Evil Being with the Cannibal Monster also. If the 1697 account of La Potherie can be explained away on the grounds of Christian influence even at that date, it appears that the belief in an Evil Spirit is not pre-European.[19]

It is not difficult to summarize the comparative evidence on religious ideology. The concept of a Supreme Being who delegates power to forces embodied in living organisms, natural phenomena and folkloristic characters, is universal in the areas with which we are concerned here. These forces are usually the direct supernatural aides of mankind, often in a personal relationship to individual men. The Central Algonkins aspire to blessings by many spirit powers while the Cree receive help from only a few. The underlying pattern is nevertheless similar. The Menomini cosmogony and the Naskapi soul-spirit are divergent. The life force, or soul, is generally something to be feared when it takes its leave of the body.

THE VISION QUEST

The Eastern Cree youth repairs to a secluded place in the forest and there fasts and prays until a spirit comes to him, usually an animal spirit power. It tells him what things he is to do, what tasks he must perform and what charms he must keep about him.[20] While fasting the boy remains on an elevated scaffold. If the vision comes during ordinary sleep, the dreamer retires to a tree overhanging a river and remains there for seven days. The vision quest among the Eastern Cree is associated with the *mite·wiwin*. Entrance into the ceremony must be made as a consequence of vision revelation. The Northern Saulteaux practice is similar.[21]

The Labrador peoples do not practise the fast-vigil but acquire visions in the course of ordinary sleep.[22]

Ojibwa boys fast on an elevated platform. The spirit helper appears in human guise, takes the dreamer to an assemblage of spirits where the blessings are conferred upon him. Evidently only boys may fast.[23]

Both boys and girls among the Menomini engage in a vision quest. They retire to a small lodge built in a secluded

304

place and there fast and pray until the vision appears. Specific boons are granted in addition to the general protection offered to the dreamer. Skinner points out that fasting by girls as well as by boys occurs elsewhere in the Central Algonkin region but specifies only the Woodland Potawatomi. He adds that Menomini children tell their dreams upon returning, unlike the Eastern and Plains Cree custom.[24]

Winnebago boys and girls go out to fast when they reach puberty. An account of a vision relates how a spirit comes in human form and takes the child to a lodge where many spirits are present. They grant him long life, war powers and medicines.[25]

The vision quest of the Eastern Cree closely parallels the Plains Cree type save for its connection with the *mite·wiwin*. Since there is some reason to believe, as we shall see later, that this ceremony is a comparatively recent introduction among the Cree, the connection may be a secondary one. That is, the vision quest of the Eastern Cree originally was quite similar to the Plains Cree form, later becoming associated with the *mite·wiwin*. The Ojibwa custom resembles that of the Cree. The fast and the formula of the vision in the Central Woodlands is not unlike the Cree case except for the participation of girls in the vigil. The Labrador customs differ in this matter.

SHAMANISM

The accounts of vision attainment cited above imply that many persons secured vision revelations. From this we may conclude that shamanism among the Northern and Central Algonkins was practised in varying degrees by a good part of each tribe.

The data on curative practices among the Eastern Cree is quite limited. Skinner states that doctors never suck wounds from bone tubes, but he does not say whether sucking without the tube is a Cree procedure. In general the emphasis seems to be on the use of medicinal plants more than on the aid of the shaman's spirit helpers.[26]

Naskapi curing, apart from the administering of certain medicinal potions, is afforded only by "the beating of the drum and the mumblings of the shaman, who claims to have control of the spirit which causes all disease and death."[27]

Speck cites Masson who says that the Montagnais-Naskapi shaman, in curing, administers no other medicine to bring about a cure than singing and blowing on the part affected, and sucking at it, "the intention of which is to counteract the machinations of their enemies."[28]

Shamanistic practices of the Central Woodlands tribes differ in that there is a specialization of shamanistic function. Thus there are four classes of Ojibwa shamans. There are those who cure by singing and accompanying themselves with a rattle. These are equipped with a set of small bones which they swallow and spit out as part of their procedure. They also administer medicines. The members of the second group perform magical feats, and usually are suspected of witchcraft. The third class of shamans is able to prophesy through the use of the conjuring booth. Lastly, there are the members of the *mite·wiwin* who acquire divinatory powers and are able to employ magical means of procuring game. They also are able to ensure a safe passage to the spirit world.[29]

It will be noted that all of these functions may be practised by a single Plains Cree shaman. Kohl describes an Ojibwa curing performance in which the doctor swallowed and brought up the bones, then blew and sucked through them. Finally he ejected from his mouth the illness he had sucked out of the sick person. Since Plains Cree doctors often perform sleight of hand tricks with the bone tubes they sometimes use to suck through, the Ojibwa method tallies with the Plains Cree curing technique.[30]

Menomini shamans are also grouped according to function. The *wabano* perform spectacular feats, the *je·sako* use the conjuring booth, the *mitäpwe* draw out intrusive objects sent by sorcerers. They blow and suck through a bone tube to bring out the cause of the illness.[31] Yet another class of shamans invoke aid from ghosts. All shamanistic powers are vision acquired.

The relationship of Northern Algonkin shamanism to that of the Central peoples has been considered by Speck. He shows that while the content is the same through both areas, the Northeastern groups lack the specialization of the Central Woodlands. Speck concludes that the non-specialized Northern form is older and that the specialized techniques represent a development from the older, simple form.[32]

This conclusion may be extended to embrace the Cree area also. The activities followed by shamans in curing are the same in Labrador, in the Central Woodlands and in the Plains and Forest Cree territory. Magical tricks, blowing, sucking, dosing with plant medicines are part of the curing technique in all these areas.

The employment of herbal medicaments among the Eastern Cree, and possibly the Ojibwa groups, seems to be of greater consequence than among other tribes.

The conjuring booth is often described in the early sources relating to the Forest Cree. Neither its construction nor the procedure involved in its use is notably different from that described for the Plains Cree. The same booth, built for similar purposes and utilized by the shaman in a like manner, is found in Labrador as well as in the Central Woodlands.[33]

A passage in Kelsey's Journal of 1690-1691 tells of magical protections in warfare. The description refers either to the Assiniboin or Cree, probably to both tribes. Kelsey enumerates the customs of the natives; his first and "Chiefest point" is a war bonnet made of birch bark adorned with feathers. It is fastened around the head with a piece of leather and falls down the back. The natives believe that it saves them from being killed. When used it is accompanied by songs sung by the maker of the bonnet who is usually the father or some kinsman of the wearer.[34]

Skinner describes a feathered war bonnet worn by the Eastern Cree but does not indicate whether the right to make it is a vision prerogative. Ornate garments worn in time of war and kept outside the lodge are also mentioned. These are probably very much like the war bundles of the Plains Cree.[35]

Ojibwa warriors carry their medicine bags with them on the war path. They are careful to place all their amulets and medicine in the bag so that the aid of their guardian spirits may be forthcoming. This is the same concept of protection as that which prevails among the Plains Cree, except that sacred hides are used instead of the shields, neckpieces, and other devices of the Plains tribe.

The war bundle of the Menomini contains all the necessary magical equipment for the whole party in a single parcel. Before an attack, the war leader distributes the contents of the bundle to the warriors. One may get a bird skin, another a feather, a third a pebble. Each receives some token which will guard him and lend him extraordinary prowess.[36]

Even among the Montagnais-Naskapi, a relatively peaceful people, protective devices are found. Instead of warding off the dangers of battle, however, Labrador charms guard against the vicissitudes of nature. There is a rich array of such charms, all vision granted. They correspond to the luck amulets of Plains Cree.[37]

In short then, the Plains Cree trait of donning special war paraphernalia made according to vision instructions, is not at variance with the Eastern Cree practice. The Central Woodlands warriors marshall all their devices in a single bundle which is also of vision origin. Even the inoffensive Labrador bands possess the underlying concept, albeit of such a general nature as to lose any sharp validity in a comparative analysis.

Since the ceremonialism of the Northern Algonkin is so scanty and that of the Central Algonkin so diverse from that of the Plains Cree, the necessity for vision prerogatives to give certain ceremonies can scarcely be traced eastward. Nonetheless, entrance into, and participation in, the Eastern Cree *mite·wiwin*, their principal ceremony, requires vision endorsement.[38]

Insofar as Menomini ceremonialism revolves around shamanistic performances, it is vision engendered. The Thunder and Buffalo cults are organized by those who have had a similar vision. The host in the Buffalo dance is quoted as saying "I am not doing this for idle pleasure, but because I was so commanded in my dreams."[39] The writer has heard a similar sentiment publicly expressed by the giver of a Plains Cree Sun dance. It is not clear from the account of other Menomini dances whether they must be granted in a vision.[40]

HUNTING OBSERVANCES

Cooper groups Eastern Cree religious phenomena into three divisions: the Supreme Being concept and cult; shamanistic practices; and a vast mass of hunting observances connected with the killing of game animals and birds, carried on by all the people.[41] It is in this last respect that the religious life of the Northern and Northeastern Algonkins differs most markedly from that of the Plains Cree. It is clear from Speck's analysis of Montagnais-Naskapi religion that most of the religious practice of these tribes, too, is directed toward a magical control of game in order to procure a stable supply of food.[42]

While hunting observances are known in the Plains tribe, they are but loosely observed and count for little. The great emphasis in Plains Cree religious activity is upon securing health and long life for the people. Bear ceremonialism of a limited kind is practised and some hunting medicines are known, but there is nothing like the almost frenzied attempt to secure magical control over game animals that occurs in Labrador. It may well be that the munificent and rarely failing supply of buffalo on the prairies made for a lessening of anxiety concerning the assurance of a food supply and hence for a partial loss of hunting magic.

ELEMENTS OF RITUALISM

The use of the pipe in Eastern Cree ceremonialism is attested to early and often in the historical sources. Both La Potherie and Dobbs characterize the Cree as Indians who use the "Peace Calumet." Kelsey's second "point" in the passage of the 1690 manuscript cited above describes an ornamented pipe stem which is passed around in councils. It is to be noted that here the pipe stem is the important ceremonial object, just as it is with the Plains Cree.[43]

Edward Umfreville is probably speaking of Wood Cree in a detailed account of the pipe ritual enacted when the Indians come into the post to trade. The pipe, made of stone, is filled with Brazil tobacco mixed with a native herb. The stem is three or four feet long and is decorated with bear claws, eagle talons, pieces of lace and variegated feathers. After the stem is affixed to the bowl and lighted, the agent takes it in both hands and points it to the east, to the zenith, to the west, and finally down to the nadir. He then smokes and passes the pipe to the Indian leader and so around to all, excepting the women. Plains Cree pipe procedure today is very much like that seen by Umfreville near Hudson Bay over two hundred and fifty years ago.[44]

Alexander Mackenzie recounts a smoking ceremony of the Cree at which many men were assembled. The officiating chief first turned to the east and blew a few whiffs in that direction. This was repeated for the other cardinal points and then the smoker made a speech (prayer?) to which the whole company responded with a "hooo!" Then the pipe was passed around. No one who bears a grudge against anyone else in the company may partake—nor may one who has had sexual intercourse within a day of the time of the ceremony. In a war council, those who take the pipe thus signify their willingness to take to the warpath.[45]

This report differs in some respects from the Plains practice. Blowing whiffs in the cardinal directions is still done on certain occasions among the Plains Cree. But the conditions under which the pipe must not be taken are not quite as restrictive, although it is felt that one who partakes in the pipe must be ceremonially clean and not repulsive to the spirit powers.

The Northern Saulteaux use the pipe ceremonially. Among the Montagnais-Naskapi smoking is the prime method of gratifying one's spirit helper.[46]

The Chippewa regard tobacco offerings as increasing the efficiency of a request to the supernaturals. The acceptance of tobacco when it accompanies a request signifies the promise to grant the entreaty. The offerings are those of the tobacco itself, rather than of the tobacco smoke.[47]

When Menomini bundles are opened, a gift of tobacco must be given to the bundle. Some of the old tobacco is taken out and smoked. The pipe is lighted and held up so that all the powers may smoke.[48]

In all, tobacco stands foremost as a means of attracting the grace of supernaturals. The Eastern Cree pipe ritual is very similar to that of the Plains Cree, while the smoke offerings of the Central and Northeastern peoples do not play as important a role in the rituals as among the Plains Cree.

Food offerings are given to the supernaturals among the Eastern Cree as they are among the Plains tribe. The Labrador bands throw part of the cooked meat they eat into the fire as a burnt offering. The Chippewa place food offerings beneath the ashes. In Winnebago feasts, the food prepared is first held up for the spirits.[49]

The Eastern Cree, like the Plains Cree, consider dog meat a delicacy. But the sacrificing of dogs, although known to the prairie people, is much more common in the forests. Father Allouez in 1666 reported that the Cree pay idolatrous worship to the sun by fastening a dog to the top of a pole and leaving it there until it rots. John McDonnell asserts that the only blood sacrifice offered by the Cree is a dog. Mackenzie observed that dog sacrifices are made at all feasts and that fat, white animals are preferred. Hind also says that dog sacrifices are very common.[50]

The *oskapewis*, the ceremonial server, is found among the Ojibwa and Menomini.[51]

The only reference I have from eastern tribes of a practice analogous to the Plains Cree use of sweetgrass, occurs in an account of a Menomini hunting bundle. A smudge is made with one of the medicines contained in the bundle and the men hold their weapons in the smoke.

Skinner appends a footnote saying that Sauk bundle customs are similar.[52]

But few references to cloth offerings appear in the literature dealing with eastern tribes. Kohl tells us that Ojibwa warriors hang up deer skins after a battle as an expiatory sacrifice. Offerings of clothing are mentioned for the Menomini.[53]

The use of sticks as sacrificial offerings was practised by the Menomini whom André visited in 1673. He saw a sheaf of small cedar sticks attached to a pole. Upon inquiring as to the purpose of the sticks, he was told that they were placed as a sacrifice or exhortation to the sun.[54]

Songs are individually owned and vision-granted among the Montagnais-Naskapi. The following quotation from Turner illustrates the prevalence of ritual singing and drumming:

> If a person is ill the drum is beaten. If a person is well the drum is beaten. If prosperous in the chase the drum is beaten; and if death has snatched a member from the community the drum is beaten to prevent his spirit from returning to torment the living.
>
> The drumbeat is often accompanied by singing which is the most discordant of all sounds supposed to be harmonious.[55]

Chippewa songs are also dream-inspired. They are used for war, curing, in any serious undertaking.[56]

Menomini medicines are valuable only when used in conjunction with the songs belonging to them. The most important factor in the use of Menomini bundles is the animating force of the songs. Possession of the songs belonging to a bundle is enough to permit the owner to use the power of the bundle.[57]

Although data on the use of songs by the Eastern Cree are few, it is likely that they too possess this characteristic. At least it is true that for the peoples all about them, Plains Cree, Labrador and Central Woodlands, singing is an indispensable element of ritual behavior. Songs are the means of proving past contact with the supernaturals and for effecting present liaison with them.

The sweat bath is taken for curative purposes among the Eastern Cree but its use as a ceremonial accessory is uncertain.[58] The Montagnais-Naskapi regard the sweat lodge as a means of strengthening the body and reinforcing the soul-spirit of the individual. Sweat baths are taken as a medium of control over bear and as a preparation for divining.[59]

The Chippewa enter a sweat lodge before the *mite·wiwin*

meeting. Menomini shamans sweat bathe before undertaking any serious or difficult task, and all men take sweat baths when they feel indisposed.[60]

The sweat bath is one of the traits linking all the tribes under consideration. Again the Eastern Cree facts are hazy, but quite probably they are in accord with those of the other peoples regarding the use of the domed sweat lodge in ceremonial situations.

Not all the elements of the Plains Cree ceremonialism occur to the east. While the pipe stem and smoking, the nature and prevalence of songs, the use of the sweat bath are important in eastern ritualism, food and cloth offerings, the ceremonial server, seem to have Central rather than Northern or Northeastern connections. The dog sacrifice is not widely distributed outside the Eastern Cree territory. The use of sweetgrass or other incense and the "pity me" refrain seem to be absent from the eastern regions, but gaps in the source material may account for this. Missing from the native theology of the northern, northeastern, and central forests is the place of the vow. The vow is the formal means for setting the ceremonial and ritual cycle in motion among the Plains Cree. It seems to be of little consequence in the religious set-up of the other tribes.

CEREMONIALISM

The absence of the vow is part of the divergence that exists between the ceremonialism of the Plains tribe and that of their Woodland affiliates. Apart from the *mite·wiwin*, none of the vowed ceremonies conducted by the Plains Cree are given by the Forest Cree. Since the northeastern Algonkins have little religious organization or group ceremonialism they share few Plains traits in these fields.[61] The Central Algonkins also have little in common ceremonially with the Plains Cree. Certain correspondences are present. Thus among the Menomini, the *je'saco* or conjuring booth shamans have their analogues to the west. The "Dreamers" dance is like the Pow-wow of the Plains Cree. The masks of the Dog dancers vaguely resemble the masked dancers described in a previous section.[62] But the motives for the ceremonies are not vows, nor are the resemblances more than faint except where patently attributable to a late development. In short, much of the ceremonial context of the Central Woodlands is different from that of the Plains Cree.

Six dances are enumerated for the Eastern Cree. Two are

concerned with warfare and will be discussed in the section dealing with that subject. The meagre details given for the others reveal no Plains Cree correspondences.

The one ritual whereby a basic ceremonial connection between the two Cree groups might be traced is the *mite·wiwin*. All the evidence, however, points to the diffusion of the ceremony in its complete form, and perhaps at a recent date, to all the Cree from the Ojibwa. In Eastern Cree territory, the *mite·wiwin* loses strength and importance in those parts distant from the Ojibwa boundaries. The Eastern Cree form of the ceremony is akin to the Ojibwa form.[63]

Among the Plains Cree, native tradition has it that the ceremony was imported from the Ojibwa proper, not from the Plains Ojibwa. The Plains Cree *mite·wiwin* leaders, as far as is known, were Ojibwa emigrants and the form of the Plains Cree ceremony was likewise Ojibwa. Furthermore the elements of the *mite·wiwin*, as the use of whole hides of small animals for medicine bags, are exclusively connected with that ceremony and are not deep rooted in Plains Cree magic-religious practices. In all there is ample reason to believe that the *mite·wiwin* among the Plains Cree is a fairly recent acquisition, received from an Ojibwa source, as it seems to be for the Eastern Cree also.

Plains Cree ceremonialism therefore has few correspondences among the peoples to the east of them. The reasons for this cultural hiatus are easily apparent. If the *mite·wiwin* is subtracted from Eastern Cree ceremonialism, little remains. The older Forest Cree situation may have been very much like the minimal ceremonialism in Labradorean cultures. If we assume with Speck that the Northeastern Algonkin represent the prototype of Algonkin cultures, then Plains Cree and Central Woodlands tribes represent two divergent developments from a common base.[64]

SECULAR DANCES, MINOR CEREMONIALISM, BELIEFS

The important secular dance of the present day Plains Cree is the Pow-wow, which is clearly one version of the Omaha or Grass dance. The Central Woodlands Dream dance is another version of the same dance. Both have been diffused from a Central Plains source at a comparatively recent date.[65]

The bear ceremonialism of the Plains Cree is not as

elaborate as the Northeastern or even the Central Woodland customs, but corresponds to the practice of both areas in the essentials. The Eastern Cree hunter speaks to the bear before killing it, explaining why it is necessary for him to do so. When the meat is cooked, part is offered to the spirit of the bear. This tallies with the usage of the Plains tribe.[66]

Montagnais-Naskapi bear ceremonialism is their major expression of institutionalized ritualism. Before slaying the bear, the hunter addresses it in polite terms, and also offers tobacco to the carcass after the kill. A feast is made when the hunters return to camp.[67] Menomini hunters of the Bear totem also speak to the animal before they kill it, apologizing for their action. A feast for the bear spirit is later given.[68] The bear observances of these tribes include the same gestures required of Plains Cree bear slayers.

A parallel to the method of catching eagles used by the Plains Cree occurs among the Prairie Potawatomi, who also allow the birds to gorge themselves until they cannot fly.[69]

First event ceremonialism of several types occurs in the Northeastern and Central areas. Cooper states that first-fruits sacrifices and first-fruits observances are strongly developed among the Cree of the James Bay region. Feasts are given when a boy brings down his first game or when the first annual bird of the season, such as a goose, is killed.[70]

A feast is given by the Eastern Cree when the first caribou of the season is shot. Certain parts of the animal are cooked, and the men of the band eat as much as they can. When a young man kills his first large animal he sits up all night singing and praying. A feast is given in his honor.[71]

The Ojibwa similarly give a feast when a youth kills his first big game animal. When a little boy shoots his first bird, his grandfather gives a "party" for him.[72] This is also done by the Menomini, both for the very first kill and for the first big game.[73] The Eastern Cree and Central Woodlands practice in this matter is the same as the Plains Cree custom.

The pole upon which sacrificial dogs are placed, which Allouez mentioned in his 1666 report, may possibly be related to the Plains Cree offering pole. E.R. Young tells of coming on a hill in the Cree country, upon which many trees had been cut down. The stumps had been carved into rude representations of the human form. Evidences of dog sacrifice were near by.[74]

The Cannibal Monster is known to the Eastern Cree, Ojibwa and Naskapi.[75]

Dwarfs bear the same name among the Ojibwa as among the Plains Cree. They are known to the Naskapi by a similar term.[76]

Visits to the land of the dead are related as occurring during an Eastern Cree *mite·wiwin* ceremony.[77]

Protective amulets are made in many varieties by the Montagnais-Naskapi, as has been previously noted. Most are granted in visions and are worn about the neck.[78] Cooper states that charms of various kinds are used by the Eastern Cree.[79] Chippewa charms are much like those worn by Plains Cree.[80] The Central Algonkins use charms and fetishes extensively.[81]

The use of sympathetic magic involving the making of an image is known among the Menomini. A doll of wood or grass is made, and touched with malevolent medicine on the part of the body where the victim is to be affected. The Ojibwa witch or sorcerer shoots the image with an arrow.[82]

The Eastern Cree tie up a bit of a child's navel cord and attach it to the cradle. This is also a Montagnais and Chippewa custom.[83] The navel cord pouch of the Plains Cree is regarded as a protective charm as is the bit of navel cord attached to Eastern cradles. All the beliefs and minor bits of ceremonialism described for the Plains Cree have widespread Eastern analogues. Bear and first event ceremonialism have an especially even distribution.

FOOTNOTES

[1]COOPER, JOHN M., The Northern Algonquian Supreme Being (The Catholic University of America, Anthropological Series, no. 2, Washington, 1934).
[2]*Ibid.*, p. 40.
[3]*Ibid.*, pp. 9, 16, 60.
[4]*Ibid.*, p. 66.
[5]HARRINGTON, Religion and Ceremonies of the Lenapé, pp. 18-24.
[6]SKINNER, The Menomini Indians, p. 73.
[7]RADIN, The Winnebago Tribe, p. 285.
[8]COOPER, The Northern Algonquian Supreme Being, p. 61.
[9]TYRRELL, David Thompson's Narrative, p. 82.
[10]TURNER, Ethnology of the Ungava District, pp. 272-273.
[11]JONES, History of the Ojebway Indians, pp. 83-84, 254.
[12]SKINNER, The Menomini Indians, pp. 73-81; RADIN, The Winnebago Tribe, p. 284.
[13]COOPER, The Northern Algonquian Supreme Being, pp. 39, 58; SKINNER, Notes on the Eastern Cree, p. 61.
[14]SPECK, Naskapi, pp. 41ff.
[15]HOFFMAN, The Menomini Indians, p. 64.
[16]RADIN, The Winnebago Tribe, p. 290; JONES, History of the Ojebway Indians, p. 88.
[17]SKINNER, The Menomini Indians, p. 85.
[18]SPECK, Naskapi, pp. 41-44.
[19]COOPER, The Northern Algonquian Supreme Being, pp. 39, 53-56.
[20]SKINNER, Notes on the Eastern Cree, p. 61.

[21]*Ibid.*, pp. 59-61, 154.
[22]SPECK, Naskapi, pp. 42-48.
[23]KOHL, Kitchi Gami, pp. 234-241; DENSMORE, Chippewa Customs, p. 70.
[24]SKINNER, The Menomini Indians, pp. 42-43.
[25]RADIN, The Winnebago Tribe, pp. 135, 304-307.
[26]SKINNER, Notes on the Eastern Cree, pp. 76-78.
[27]TURNER, Ethnology of the Ungava District, p. 270.
[28]SPECK, Naskapi, p. 225.
[29]JONES, Central Algonkin, pp. 145-146.
[30]KOHL, Kitchi Gami, p. 106.
[31]SKINNER, The Menomini Indians, pp. 197-199.
[32]SPECK, FRANK G., Penobscot Shamanism (Memoirs of the American Anthropological Association, vol. 6, 1919), pp. 273-278.
[33]ROBSON, An Account of Six Years Residence in Hudson's Bay, p. 49; CARVER, Travels Through the Interior, p. 123; TYRRELL, David Thompson's Narrative, p. 90; TURNER, Ethnology of the Ungava District, p. 273; JONES, Central Algonkin, p. 145; SKINNER, The Menomini Indians, p. 192.
[34]KELSEY, The Kelsey Papers, p. 19.
[35]SKINNER, Notes on the Eastern Cree, pp. 17, 78.
[36]SKINNER, The Menomini Indians, p. 114.
[37]SPECK, Naskapi, p. 226.
[38]SKINNER, Notes on the Eastern Cree, p. 61.
[39]SKINNER, The Menomini Indians, p. 202.
[40]*Ibid.*, pp. 206-213.
[41]COOPER, The Northern Algonquian Supreme Being, p. 42.
[42]*See especially* SPECK, Naskapi, p. 78.
[43]DOBBS, An Account of Countries Adjoining to Hudsons's Bay, p. 24; *La Protherie in* TYRRELL, Documents of Hudson Bay, p. 263; KELSEY, The Kelsey Papers.
[44]UMFREVILLE, The Present State of Hudson's Bay, p. 61.
[45]MACKENZIE, Voyages from Montreal, pp. clii ff., cxlix.
[46]SKINNER, Notes on the Eastern Cree, p. 144; SPECK, Naskapi, pp. 217-219.
[47]DENSMORE, Chippewa Customs, p. 145.
[48]SKINNER, The Menomini Indians, p. 96.
[49]COOPER, The Northern Algonquian Supreme Being, p. 28; SPECK, Naskapi, p. 81; DENSMORE, Chippewa Customs, p. 130; RADIN, The Winnebago Tribe, p. 310.
[50]SKINNER, Notes on the Eastern Cree, p. 65; *McDonnel in* MASSON, L.R., ed., Les Bourgeois de la Compagnie du Nord-Ouest. Récites du Voyages, Lettres et Rapports Inédits Relatifs au Nord-Ouest Canadien. Publié avec une Esquisse Historique et des Annotations, 2 vols., Quebec, 1889, 1890, p. 277; HIND, Superstitions and Customs, p. 260; MACKENZIE, Voyages from Montreal, p. cxlix.
[51]KOHL, Kitchi Gami, p. 85; SKINNER, The Menomini Indians, p. 177.
[52]SKINNER, The Menomini Indians, p. 138.
[53]KOHL, Kitchi Gami, p. 345; SKINNER, The Material Culture of the Menomini, p. 34.
[54]SKINNER, The Menomini Indians, p. 79.
[55]TURNER, Ethnology of the Ungava District, p. 325.
[56]DENSMORE, FRANCES, Chippewa Music II (Bureau of American Ethnology, Bulletin 53, Washington, 1913), p. 16.
[57]SKINNER, Material Culture of the Menomini, p. 66; SKINNER, The Menomini Indians, p. 94.
[58]SKINNER, Notes on the Eastern Cree, p. 14; ROBSON, An Account of Six Years Residence in Hudson's Bay, p. 50; ELLIS, A Voyage to Hudson's Bay, p. 188.
[59]SPECK, Naskapi, pp. 212-213, 150.
[60]DENSMORE, Chippewa Customs, p. 94; HOFFMAN, The Menomini Indians, p. 255.
[61]SPECK, Culture Problems, p. 280.
[62]SKINNER, The Menomini Indians, p. 171.
[63]SKINNER, Notes on the Eastern Cree, p. 65.
[64]SPECK, Culture Problems, p. 302.
[65]WISSLER, Shamanistic Societies, pp. 862-873.
[66]SKINNER, Notes on the Eastern Cree, p. 69.
[67]SPECK, Naskapi, pp. 95ff.
[68]SKINNER, The Menomini Indians, pp. 21, 213.

[69]SKINNER, The Mascoutin or Prairie Potawatomi Indians, p. 280.

[70]COOPER, The Northern Algonquian Supreme Being, p. 41.

[71]SKINNER, Notes on the Eastern Cree, pp. 73, 75.

[72]KOHL, Kitchi Gami, p. 86.

[73]SKINNER, Material Culture of the Menomini, p. 180; SKINNER, The Menomini Indians, p. 43.

[74]*Allouez in* KELLOGG, Early Narratives, p. 134; YOUNG, E.R., By Canoe and Dog Train Among the Cree and Saulteaux Indians, London, 1890, p. 84.

[75]KOHL, Kitchi Gami, p. 358; SPECK, Naskapi, p. 72.

[76]JONES, History of the Ojebway Indians, p. 156; SPECK, Naskapi, p. 72.

[77]SKINNER, Notes on the Eastern Cree, p. 65.

[78]SPECK, Naskapi, p. 225.

[79]COOPER, JOHN M., Field Notes on Northern Algonkian Magic (Proceedings 23rd International Congress of Americanists, 1928), p. 516.

[80]DENSMORE, Chippewa Customs, p. 107.

[81]SKINNER, The Menomini Indians, p. 92.

[82]*Ibid.*, p. 188; JONES, History of the Ojebway Indians, p. 146.

[83]DENSMORE, Chippewa Customs, p. 51; COOPER, Field Notes on Northern Algonkian Magic, p. 516.

317

WARFARE

The eager efforts of the early fur traders to divert the energies of the Eastern Cree from warfare to fur-gathering adduce proof in plenty for the martial nature of the tribe. The early documents leave no doubt but that the Cree waged war often and vigorously. Unfortunately the sources say little about the tribal procedure in preparing for warfare and engaging in combat.

The war customs of the Eastern Cree are briefly discussed by Skinner, who quotes Mackenzie for much of the data.[1] There are two motives for engaging in warfare. The first is to prove one's courage, which we may read as the desire for glory and prestige. The second is to avenge the slaying of a relative or tribesman.

When war plans are proposed, a council is held. If war is agreed upon, all those who intend to participate partake of the pipe that is passed around. Each one who smokes brings something with him as a token of his warlike intention or as an object of sacrifice. Mackenzie does not specify the nature of these offerings. They are hung on a pole nearby.

Before the departure of the war party, a dance is given in which the warriors enact the pursuit, battle, and final defeat of the enemy. Feasts are sometimes given at this occasion. In battle, war songs are sung. Scalps are taken by the victors.

The preliminary dance mentioned by Skinner differs from the war procedure of the Plains tribe. The formal war council may perhaps be the observer's formulation rather than the native practice. Among the Plains Cree also, a conclave of the men intending to go on the warpath is held, and the pipe passed around. Should any be present who cannot or will not accompany the party, they do not smoke with the others. This is not a specific war procedure, however, but is done in consonance with the general patterns of the culture which call for a meeting and pipe smoking when any significant matter is under consideration. Those who feel in any way at variance with the sentiment or purpose of the group do not smoke. This is not a hostile gesture nor one that is condemned by the others. It is merely the manner of signifying non-participation in any venture according to the regulations of Cree etiquette. Thus it is perhaps best to view the "war" council of the Eastern Cree as a general social usage rather than as a specific war custom. The Eastern Cree war songs and scalping practices also correspond to Plains conventions.

The great discrepancy between Eastern and Plains Cree warfare lies in the purpose of military activity. The Forest people go out to take the lives of the enemy; the Plains warriors are out to get horses and, if the opportunity presents itself, to secure scalps. Lack of information on war leaders and other usages prevents a closer comparison.

Northern Saulteaux war parties assemble at a secret place in the forest where the shaman performs certain magical acts. The objective of an attack is to annihilate the enemy, and return with their scalps. The victors rejoice with a feast and dance.[2]

The Ojibwa also plan to kill off the enemy. The leader of a war party must receive vision approval for the expedition. War trips are arranged in the winter. The war leader and his assistants sing power songs frequently, until the agreed date in the spring is reached. Before the departure, war dances are held in the lodges of the warriors and also at the "cemetery," according to Kohl.

On large expeditions a maiden is chosen to head the march. It may be parenthetically remarked here that an account of a Plains Cree vengeance party told of a young girl who was placed in the lead. Warriors may not scratch their heads except with a stick. Novices are not permitted to eat marrow. On approaching the enemy country, songs are again sung, pipes smoked, and the leader or some shaman prophesies what is to happen. During the engagement, scalps are taken and later affixed to hoops.[3]

The Ojibwa war dance as described by Peter Jones may be given at other times, but usually it is performed before departing on a war trip. The warriors dance around a pole, mimicking battle manoeuvres and engaging in sham fights. At intervals a warrior counts his coups, striking a pole as he does so.[4]

This dance is very much like one seen by Harmon among the Cree to the southwest of Lake Winnipeg. The dancers were about thirty in number, clothed in white antelope skins.

They had white earth sprinkled on their heads. In the center of the dance lodge there was a pole upon which a warrior armed with a hatchet counted coup.[5]

War bundles play an important part in Menomini warfare. The bundle owner gathers recruits and when the appointed time has arrived, leads them to a secluded place in the forest. There the bundle is ceremonially opened, sacrifices made, a war dance performed. Concerning this dance, Skinner tells us only that the participants "throw their bodies into dramatic postures." Then the party proceeds to the enemy country.

Before an attack is made, the bundle is opened and its contents distributed among the warriors. The objective is to take scalps which are later stretched on small hoops. A victory dance is given when the party returns. The warriors who have taken scalps carry them on sticks and dance about holding their trophies. After a while, the sister or some female relative of the warrior takes the scalp from him, giving him a gift in return. A man who has killed an enemy, the highest honor, is entitled to wear an eagle feather in his hair.[6]

The De Gannes manuscript of 1721 describes raids made by Illinois.[7] Small parties go out, the young men attend to the wants of the older warriors. Fetishes of reed mats enclosing feathers are carried along. When the enemy is encountered, the warriors vie to be the first to touch an enemy corpse or prisoner.

Winnebago war leaders must have special vision blessing. Revenge and glory are the motives for warfare. The party assembles outside the camp and partakes of a feast. War bundles are taken along.

Certain traits are common to the war practices of each tribe that has been considered. Proficiency in warfare is everywhere (Labrador excepted) the cardinal means of acquiring prestige. Scalps are taken and brought back as trophies. They are carried usually in the victory dance. The feast and dance in honor of the returned victors is a custom followed by all the warlike tribes mentioned above.

Although the Plains Cree warriors dance before the departure, there is no secret ritual performed as among the Eastern Cree and Central Woodlands groups. The mimetic war dance performed by the Eastern tribes seems to have been omitted by the Plains Cree and then freshly introduced as part of the Pow-wow, the Omaha dance.

The Ojibwa are closest to the Plains Cree in war

procedure. The vision requirement for war leaders, special restrictions for novices, invoking the supernaturals, prophesy before the attack, and the maiden in the van, are all known to both tribes. Since these traits are generally not Eastern Cree, the correspondence may be due to diffusion from a source common to both tribes.

The intent of war parties gives Eastern warfare a different emphasis from that of the Plains. Vengeance and glory are the priming motives in the east and warriors seek to dispatch their opponents as effectively as possible. Both motives are known to the Plains tribe, but are ancillary to the desire for horses. Hence the Plains Cree raider will relinquish an opportunity to kill the enemy, if there is any danger of losing the stolen horses in so doing.

FOOTNOTES

[1]SKINNER, Notes on the Eastern Cree, pp. 78-80.
[2]SKINNER, Notes on the Eastern Cree, pp. 165-166.
[3]KOHL, Kitchi Gami, pp. 340-345, 129.
[4]JONES, History of the Ojebway Indians, p. 133.
[5]HARMON, A Journal of Voyages and Travels, p. 44.
[6]SKINNER, The Menomini Indians, pp. 96-130.
[7]STRONG, The Indian Tribes of the Chicago Region, p. 11.

Summary

When the comparative data given in this section are recapitulated, we find that in only a few respects are the Plains Cree radically divergent from the Cree of the east. The Northeastern Algonkins lack some of the traits common to both Cree groups, but the patterns they do possess are held not only by the Plains and Eastern Cree, but to a large degree by the Central Woodlands tribes as well. It seems that the cultures of the Central area represent one kind of specialization away from the Northeastern Algonkin base, while the Plains Cree manifest another type of specialization from the common base.

Under the rubric of material culture we have seen that the Woodland Cree and Labrador bands are close to the Plains tribe in housing, ceremonial structures, household furnishings. The Central Woodlands are divergent in these respects, but their customs are not entirely alien to those of the other regions. In personal adornment and dress, the use of the tailored garment by the Northern and Northeastern Algonkin is the only difference of a major order among the tribes considered.

The use of the horse and of the buffalo differentiate the Plains tribe from the Eastern peoples, but it has been noted that these factors did not fundamentally alter the Eastern food and transport habits.

Food preparation varies in no essentials in any of these areas. The forms of certain weapons—the bow, the club, the shield—are restricted to the Plains tribe. But the Eastern types of the bow and club are also known to the Plains Cree and the shield may once have been used by certain Eastern peoples. The Plains Cree have developed work in skin to a higher level of attainment than their forest kindred. Otherwise the handicraft of the two Cree groups is similar. The Labrador manufactures are parallel to the Eastern Cree while the Central Woodlands people are better craftsmen than any of the other groups. The distribution of musical instruments is pan-Algonkin for most types.

In those phases of social organization which have been scrutinized, the general tenor of the Eastern Cree patterns carries over into the Plains Cree conventions. The nature of bands and of chieftainship is similar for the Cree of the forests and of the plains. The Northeastern peoples also share these aspects of social relationships, although in some of these tribes, chiefs and even band organization may scarcely be said to exist. The Central Woodlands are diverse in these respects.

The Warrior Society of the Plains tribe has no comparable institution in the east. The policing organizations of the Central Woodlands and the Plains Cree Warriors may have been taken over from a mutual, possibly Plains center. Rank is everywhere channeled by war prowess except in the peaceful northeast.

The Plains Cree birth customs are known to the Eastern and Central Algonkins. Naming differs in the Central area, but is close to the Plains Cree usage in the matter of name changing. Girls' puberty rites among the Eastern Cree and Ojibwa are generally like those of the Plains tribe. The observances of the Central Woodlands people are different but the same attitude toward menstruation is held in all the areas. A uniform pattern in marriage prevails throughout the regions under examination, although the Eastern Cree practice of the sororate is not found in the Plains tribe. Death customs differ in details among the tribes, but a correspondence in underlying patterns may be noted.

The religious ideology of all the groups is intrinsically alike. In the vision quest, only the Labrador peoples are markedly dissimilar. Shamanistic procedure is the same in the east and in the west, although there is a specialization of shamanistic function in the Central Woodlands.

The Plains Cree deviate from the Eastern Cree patterns in their neglect of hunting magic and development of group ceremonialism instituted by vows. The various elements of Plains Cree ritualism—the use of the pipe, songs and sweat lodge—are also paramount ritual considerations among the Eastern people. Smoke and cloth offerings appear to have only Central Woodland analogues. The use of sweetgrass, the characteristic Plains Cree manner of invoking supernatural sympathy, and the vow are not Eastern. Those customs we have classified as minor ceremonies are generally alike among the peoples here considered.

The war customs of Eastern Cree, Plains Cree and Central Woodland tribes have a good many traits in common. The presence of the horse brought about a new motivation for Plains warfare which was added to the war motives found among the forest peoples.

We are now in a position to visualize what happened to Eastern Cree groups when they settled on the plains. The abandonment of the canoe and acquisition of the horse did not disrupt the old ways too violently. The Cree of the plains relinquished tailored clothing, hunting magic, perhaps also pottery and the sororate. They gained many ceremonial forms and the society organizations. This profit-and-loss statement is not as simple when the details of various traits are taken into account. Plains Cree forms in bags, birth customs, and other considerations are not identical to Eastern Cree traits. But there is enough similarity to make the postulation of a basic correspondence, in most aspects of the Forest and Plains cultures, a justifiable affirmation.

III: The Plains Affiliations of Plains Cree Culture

Dr. Clark Wissler has enumerated twenty-one traits which are particularly characteristic of Plains culture.[1] The Plains Cree share seventeen of these traits. In three items of the list, limited use of roots and berries, special rawhide work, and special bead techniques, their practices closely approach those of most tribes of the plains. The remaining one of Wissler's criteria has to do with the general absence of fishing on the plains. But the Plains Cree are not the only prairie tribe which catches and eats fish.

The impression given by this checklist concerning the cultural position of the tribe within the Plains area is borne out by the comparative account which follows. The western affiliations of Plains Cree culture are presented in more condensed form than the eastern comparisons, and are largely confined to a consideration of the tribes of the northern plains country.

Material Culture and
Economic Life

HOUSING

The Plains Cree tipi closely resembles those of the other tribes of the northern plains. The chief point of difference among the various Plains tribes is in the number of poles used as a foundation. The three pole foundation of the Plains Cree structure is also used by Assiniboin, Gros Ventre, Cheyenne, Arapaho, Teton Dakota, Pawnee, Mandan, Arikara, Ponca, Oto and Witchita. The four pole foundation is characteristic of Blackfoot, Crow, Sarsi, Shoshone, Omaha, Comanche, Hidatsa, Kutenai, Flathead and Nez Percé. Outside of the Plains area, the Thompson and Shuswap have the four pole foundation; the Ojibwa and Winnebago have a three pole base.[2]

The four pole foundation has its distribution largely on the western side of the Plains, while that of the three pole foundation is to the east. In this trait the Plains Cree follow the custom both of their woodland relatives and of their northern plains neighbors, with the exception of the Blackfoot. The conical dwelling is known to all the Plains people, and is the sole house form for many of them. This likewise holds true for the inhabitants of the northern forests and of the Mackenzie Basin.

CEREMONIAL STRUCTURES

The long lodge of the Plains Cree seems not to extend farther into the bison area.

The enlarged tipi for ceremonial occasions is found among the Dakota and possibly the Blackfoot. The domed sweat lodge is widely used in the Plains area, usually constructed in a manner similar to the Plains Cree form.[3]

HOUSEHOLD FURNISHINGS

The tipi lining, or back wall, is known to the Blackfoot, Assiniboin, Gros Ventre, Sarsi, Crow and Dakota. Since a similar device appears in the wigwams of the Menomini and Ojibwa, it may be that this contrivance is more generally known in the Woodlands than is evident from the literature.[4]

The location of the fireplace, with the place of honor behind the fire and directly opposite the door, is common to the peoples of the northern plains. Back-rests of willow rods are widely distributed over the whole Plains area.[5]

While horn spoons are generally used in the Plains, wooden spoons are also known. Horn spoons are rarely found in the Woodlands.[6]

The failure of the Plains Cree to adopt the parfleche which they observed among neighboring tribes is noteworthy. Used by most of the Plains tribes, the parfleche is known in the Plateau area as well.[7]

The legskin bag is known to the Blackfoot and perhaps to other Plains tribes.[8]

Rawhide bags, made in a single piece, sewn along parallel sides and having a flap, are found among the Assiniboin, Gros Ventre, Blackfoot, Sarsi, Cheyenne, Arapaho, Dakota, Shoshone, Bannock, Ute, and Nez Percé. The Plains Cree specimens differ from the types common to these tribes in that they are generally unpainted and are sometimes sewn along two adjoining sides.[9]

Birchbark containers are not made by Plains tribes other than the Plains Cree and possibly the Plains Ojibwa. Wooden bowls are found throughout the Northern Plains.[10]

DRESS

The typical woman's dress of the Plains, made of two whole skins and having a cape-like shoulder piece sewn in as a yoke, is also worn by the Plains Cree. The more common woman's dress of this tribe, however, follows the Eastern pattern, being suspended over the shoulders with cords and having detachable sleeves. Wissler has pointed out the correspondences betwen the two dress patterns and suggests the ''technological descent'' of the Plains type from the Eastern Woodland type. The two styles are so similar that a Plains Cree woman could easily have worn either type without feeling that she was transgressing any canons of modish dress.[11]

Short leggings of the ankle to knee type are worn by

women among the Assiniboin, Northern Shoshone, Mandan, Hidatsa, Dakota, Blackfoot and Crow.[12]

The men's shirt worn by Plains Cree is similar to that of the Assiniboin, Gros Ventre, Blackfoot, Dakota, Crow and other Plains people. There is some indication that the shirt was formerly not as widespread in the area as it has been in historic times. Wissler mentions the use of the shirt by the Eastern Dené and Cree to indicate that the trait may be regarded as a Northern characteristic. Since we have seen above that the Eastern Cree men in early times probably did not wear shirts, the Mackenzie region may have been the source of the diffusion of this trait both to Plains and Woodlands. It seems probable, however, that when the Cree were making the transfer from forest to prairie, the shirt was being worn in both areas.[13]

The breech cloth was used throughout the buffalo area in historic times and was worn like that of the Cree.[14] The buffalo robe was a standard article of dress for men and women among all Plains tribes.

Mittens are known from the Blackfoot, Gros Ventre and Omaha, as well as from the Plains Cree.[15]

The single piece moccasin with a seam around the outside of the foot is traditionally the oldest type among the Blackfoot, as among the Plains Cree. The Cheyenne also say that this type is oldest although an outer sole is now sewn onto the Cheyenne moccasin. The simple form, without the attached sole, is made by the Assiniboin, Blackfoot, Gros Ventre, Sarsi and Shoshone. The two piece type, with a tongue inset and a seam from toe to tongue, is worn by Assiniboin and Teton Dakota among Plains tribes. In this case it would seem that the Plains Cree tradition is erroneous, for the two piece moccasin is Woodland and the one piece more generally Plains. A three piece type, consisting of tongue, upper, and sole, which is widespread in the bison area, is not known to the Plains Cree.[16]

A hat made of an oblong piece of rawhide, like that of the Plains Cree, is reported for the Arapaho and Piegan.[17] Women's headgear is little worn in the Plains. The feather bonnets worn on ceremonial and war occasions are known from the Dakota and many other Plains tribes.

PERSONAL ADORNMENT

Tattooing by the pricking method as used among the Plains Cree is practised by the Assiniboin, Blackfoot,

Dakota, Crow, Hidatsa and Mandan. In the southern part of the area, the Oto, Osage, Ponca, Omaha and Quapaw use the same method of tattooing.[18]

Women's hairdress throughout the area is like that of Plains Cree women. The hair is parted in the middle and plaited into a braid on each side. Although the styles of men's hairdress differ, the wearing of a braid on each side of the head is common.[19]

Shell gorgets are worn by many of the peoples of the area, and the use of shell earrings is very common. Face painting is equally widespread.

THE FOOD QUEST

The chute and pound method of securing buffalo was practised by the Assiniboin, Northern Blackfoot, Cheyenne and Plains Cree. The Cheyenne abandoned the use of the pound while they were still living a nomadic life.[20]

In the concerted buffalo hunt, in methods of stalking and ambushing large game and in the use of snares and deadfall traps, the other tribes of the Northern Plains are not radically different from the Plains Cree.

Fish weirs are described for the Blackfoot, Cheyenne and Nez Percé. The Cheyenne type is merely a fence across a stream, while the Blackfoot and Nez Percé types closely approximate the Plains Cree construction.[21] Other methods of securing fish are rarely found among the people of the plains who made little use of fish for food.

In the utilization of vegetal foods, the Plains Cree are very similar to the other tribes of the Missouri-Saskatchewan area.[22]

The digging stick survives in Blackfoot and Crow ceremonies. The forms used by Gros Ventre, Hidatsa, Mandan, and Dakota, as well as by the Crow and Blackfoot, are much like the Plains Cree type.[23]

FOOD PREPARATION

Pemmican is made throughout the Plains area.[24] Meat is cut into strips and dried in the sun or over a fire by all the Plains tribes.[25] The tongue is everywhere held to be the choice part of the buffalo and is often collected for ceremonial use.

Stone boiling in a hide pouch is known from the Blackfoot, Teton Dakota, Assiniboin and Gros Ventre.[26]

Both pit and elevated caches are made by the Blackfoot.[27]

TRANSPORT

Saddle frames of the styles used by the Plains Cree are made by the Assiniboin, Dakota, Cheyenne, Arapaho, Mandan and Comanche. The pad saddle has a wide distribution among the aboriginal horse riders.[28]

The travois is used through the whole Missouri-Saskatchewan area. Although the Crow appear to be an exception, it is known that they used the dog travois, and made a kind of horse travois to carry wounded or disabled tribesmen.[29]

The Assiniboin and Blackfoot used the netted oval carrier on the dog travois, as did the Plains Cree. The Dakota, however, employed this type on the horse travois. The rectangular frame type is Gros Ventre, Arapaho, Sarsi and Blackfoot. The Blackfoot practice is like that of the Plains Cree in that they employ the net carrier with dogs and the ladder (rectangular) carrier with horses.[30]

The only means of water transport among the Crow and Blackfoot is a raft over which tipi covers are laid, a form which may be analogous to the bull boat of the Assiniboin, Dakota, Mandan, Arikara and Hidatsa. The hide ferry of the Plains Cree is probably related to these types.[31]

The carrying strap is known to several Plains tribes, but as the horse and dog are used as burden carriers it is less frequent than in the Woodlands. Blackfoot women carry firewood with a line slung across the shoulders; the Dakota, Hidatsa and Omaha make similar use of a burden strap.[32]

Snowshoes are generally unknown on the plains, although the Omaha and Ponca are mentioned as using a type of snowshoe. Sleds and toboggans are known to few tribes in the area.[33]

Birket-Smith's table on the distribution of the use of dogs as pack animals cites only one source, relating to the southern plains, for the occurrence of this trait in the buffalo region. Wissler, however, indicates that the dog was used as a pack animal throughout the area.[34]

WEAPONS

The simple wooden bow is the prevailing type among Plains tribes generally, even where the sinew-backed bow was also used. The latter type was made by the Blackfoot, Cheyenne, Arapaho and Gros Ventre. Wissler states that all arrow types in the Missouri-Saskatchewan area are three-feathered; the feathering is probably laid on as among the Plains Cree. The Mediterranean arrow release is apparently not found elsewhere in the Plains.[35]

The combined bow and spear is known to the Assiniboin, Dakota, and, according to Wissler, to other tribes "in the Missouri Valley." Round buffalo hide shields are used by warriors of most, if not all, Plains tribes. The suggestion that armor made of several thicknesses of skin was once used and later abandoned, occurs in the traditions of the Blackfoot as it does in the historic literature of the Cree. War and hunting spears are widespread in the bison area.[36]

War clubs with stone heads, or with stones encased in hide, are known from most of the peoples of the region.[37]

MANUFACTURES

Methods of skin dressing do not vary a great deal throughout the area. The Assiniboin and Blackfoot techniques are very close to the Plains Cree process. Wissler suggests that the fur trade may have had a leveling influence on this trait complex, but states that

> . . . we get hints from many journals that indicate a general distribution of this [soft tan] process from Peace River to the Gulf of Mexico and from California to New England.[38]

The chisel-like flesher has a wide distribution through the Woodlands and Plains. The adze scraper, however, seems to be restricted to buffalo-hunting tribes. The use of the frame for stretching hides is frequently found in the Plains, as is rubbing the hide over a twisted sinew cord. The beaming tool of the split leg bone type is not Plains, but other forms of this utensil are found in the area. Wissler concludes that skin dressing methods among the buffalo hunting tribes are different from those employed by the inhabitants of other areas. This is true in that the adze scraper and the twisted sinew cord are largely restricted to the Plains. In most steps of the tanning process, however, the Plains methods correspond to those of the Woodlands.[39]

All the tribes of the northern plains decorate their clothing with quillwork, beadwork and painting. Plains Cree quillwork techniques are similar to those used by Blackfoot, Gros Ventre and Assiniboin.[40]

Hide thongs are the primary means of fastening employed by the buffalo hunting tribes. The Cheyenne and probably other peoples make a rope of twisted buffalo hair. The Blackfoot manufacture cord from the bark of a shrub, probably the same plant as is used for the purpose by the Plains Cree.[41]

Work in wood and stone in the Plains generally is much the same as it is among the Plains Cree. Stone mauls, arrowheads, and perhaps knives were made. The chief manufactures in wood were bowls and pipe stems.[42]

Long bags for tobacco and pipes are known to the Blackfoot, Assiniboin, Dakota, Cheyenne, and Crow. The Plains Cree style closely resembles that of the Blackfoot.[43] Pipes of the monitor and elbow shapes are known to most of the tribes of the Northern Plains. The use of *kinikinik*, either of red willow bark or bear berry leaves, is found among all the tribes of the area.

Fire-making with a simple drill is reported for the Crow, Arapaho, Hidatsa, Dakota, and possibly the Blackfoot. The bow-drill which Skinner mentioned for the Plains Cree may also have been used by the Dakota.[44]

The rabbit skin blanket is not made by other Plains tribes east of the Rocky Mountains. There are traditions of the use of pottery among Blackfoot, Cheyenne, Gros Ventre and Assiniboin. The Village tribes of Missouri are known to have had a pottery-making technique.[45]

MUSICAL INSTRUMENTS

The tambourine drum is used by the Assiniboin, Blackfoot, Gros Ventre, Hidatsa, Mandan, Arapaho, Crow, Iowa and Omaha. The rawhide rattle used by the Plains Cree is made by many of the buffalo hunting peoples. Whistles of bird bones probably have an equally widespread distribution.[46]

Summary

In review, Plains Cree material culture is very close to that of the other Plains tribes. Only two of the traits widely spread in the area are not found among the Cree. These are the use of the parfleche and of the hard-soled moccasin. Few elements of Plains Cree material culture differ from those encountered elsewhere in the Missouri-Saskatchewan area. The ceremonial long lodge, birchbark containers, snowshoes, the Mediterranean arrow release, and the rabbitskin blanket are the only material items which the neighboring Plains tribes do not share with them.

A conical lodge is the primary house form for the boreal peoples as well as for the plains dwellers. The hemispherical sweat lodge is similar in construction throughout the areas we are here examining. The general arrangement within the dwelling is also similar in east and west.

Household utensils differ considerably between Plains and Northern Woodlands. Horn spoons, willow rod back-rests, and the parfleche are Plains artifacts. Birchbark vessels are not made by the buffalo hunters and the legskin bag is known only on the northern fringe of the Plains country.

The costume of the Northern Algonkins is like that of the Algonkins and Siouans of the Plains in most details. The Eastern use of tailored garments is the major difference. Plains Cree moccasin types are also worn by other prairie peoples even though the type which prevails on the Plains has not been adopted by the tribe.

Methods of personal adornment are parallel for Woodlands and Northern Plains. Tattooing, face painting and the use of earrings, are known to most tribes of both regions. Women's hairdress is generally alike although the fashions of men's hairdress exhibit a greater variance between and within the areas.

Use of the buffalo pound is apparently restricted to four tribes of the Northern Plains and is most highly developed among the Assiniboin and Plains Cree. It seems likely that these two peoples developed this technique from the widely known use of hunting fences and game drives.

These basic similarities between the food quests of the two Cree divisions apply also to the wider consideration of the Forest and Plains areas. In both regions, large game animals which collect in herds furnish the bulk of the food supply. Vegetal foods are more intensively used in the Plains, while fish are utilized to a greater extent in the Woodlands. It is to be noted, however, that all Forest bands make some use of plant food, and a good many tribes of the Northern Plains eat fish at times. Methods of preparing food are basically alike in both regions.

Means of transport and travel are utterly divergent in most respects between the forests and northern plains. We may again stress the fact, however, that both the canoe and the horse people live a roving life, are scattered in small groups for long periods, and gather annually in large encampments.

Those weapons which differentiated Plain Cree armament from that of the Eastern Cree also distinguish the Northern Plains war and hunting equipment from that of the Northern Algonkin. The sinew-backed bow, the shield and the flexible-necked club are not generally found in the

Woodlands. It must be noted that the sinew-backed bow has only a limited distribution in the Plains and is everywhere an alternate to the simple bow. The possession of the Mediterranean arrow release by the Cree groups is apparently due to Northern influence.

The chief point of difference in skin dressing techniques between the Plains and Woodlands is the use of the adze scraper in the west. Methods of leather ornamentation are similar in both regions. Handicraft work with skins reaches a greater point of development in the Plains. Work in wood and stone is broadly alike for Northern Plains and Northern Woodlands. The rabbit skin blankets of the Woodlands are not generally made in the Missouri-Saskatchewan region; the pipe styles and long tobacco pouches are not usually found in the forest country.

The tambourine drum is used by most tribes of both areas. The bone whistle is widespread although rattle forms differ.

Since the material cultures of the Plains Cree and the Northern Algonkins are basically similar, and since Plains Cree material culture is very much like that of the tribes of the Northern Plains, it follows that there is a basic correspondence between the material cultures of Northern Plains and Northern Woodlands. Restricted in distribution to the Plains area are the adze scraper, back-rest, buffalo pound, horse gear, and certain styles of tobacco pouch and pipe. The Forest traits which do not extend into the Plains are the canoe, long lodge, birchbark vessels, snowshoes, rabbitskin blanket, Mediterranean release, the "Micmac" pipe and tailored clothing.

FOOTNOTES

[1]WISSLER, CLARK, The American Indian, New York, 1922, pp. 218-220.
[2]WISSLER, Material Culture of the Blackfoot Indians, pp. 110-111; BIRKET-SMITH, The Caribou Eskimos, pp. 297-301; DOUGLAS, FREDERIC, Indian Leaflet Series (Denver Art Museum, vol. 1, Denver, 1932), Leaflet no. 19.
[3]DENIG, Indian Tribes of the Upper Missouri, p. 578; WISSLER, Material Culture of the Blackfoot Indians, p. 106; HODGE, Handbook of American Indians North of Mexico, part 2, p. 662.
[4]WISSLER, Material Culture of the Blackfoot Indians, p. 110.
[5]Ibid., p. 110.
[6]Ibid., p. 46; BIRKET-SMITH, The Caribou Eskimos, pp. 308-312.
[7]SPIER, LESLIE, An Analysis of Plains Indian Parfleche Decoration (University of Washington Publications in Anthropology, vol. 1, no. 3, Seattle, 1925), p. 108.
[8]WISSLER, Material Culture of the Blackfoot Indians, p. 74; BIRKET-SMITH, The Caribou Eskimos, p. 139.
[9]WISSLER, Material Culture of the Blackfoot Indians, p. 76.

[10]BIRKET-SMITH, The Caribou Eskimos, pp. 306-307.
[11]WISSLER, Costumes of the Plains Indians, pp. 65, 82-83.
[12]WISSLER, Material Culture of the Blackfoot Indians, p. 139; LOWIE, ROBERT H., The Material Culture of the Crow Indians (Anthropological Papers, American Museum of Natural History, vol. 21, part 3, 1922), p. 226.
[13]WISSLER, Material Culture of the Blackfoot Indians, pp. 135-136; WISSLER, Costumes of the Plains Indians, p. 51.
[14]WISSLER, Material Culture of the Blackfoot Indians, p. 153.
[15]BIRKET-SMITH, The Caribou Eskimos, p. 343.
[16]GRINNELL, GEORGE BIRD, The Cheyenne Indians, 2 vols., New Haven, 1923, p. 58; WISSLER, Material Culture of the Blackfoot Indians, p. 151.
[17]KROEBER, ALFRED L., The Arapaho (Bulletin, American Museum of Natural History, vol. 18, part 1, New York, 1902), p. 52; WISSLER, Material Culture of the Blackfoot Indians, p. 124.
[18]BIRKET-SMITH, The Caribou Eskimos, pp. 345-346.
[19]WISSLER, Material Culture of the Blackfoot Indians, pp. 152-153.
[20]Ibid., p. 50; GRINNELL, The Cheyenne Indians, p. 258.
[21]WISSLER, Material Culture of the Blackfoot Indians, p. 39; GRINNELL, The Cheyenne Indians, p. 114; SPINDEN, HERBERT J., The Nez Percé Indians (Memoirs of the American Anthropological Association, vol. 2, 1908), p. 211.
[22]WISSLER, Material Culture of the Blackfoot Indians, p. 42.
[23]LOWIE, ROBERT H., The Tobacco Society of the Crow Indians (Anthropological Papers, American Museum of Natural History, vol. 21, part 2, 1919), p. 171; WISSLER, Material Culture of the Blackfoot Indians, p. 22; WISSLER, CLARK, North American Indians of the Plains (Handbook Ser. no. 1, 2nd ed., American Museum of Natural History, 1920), p. 80.
[24]WISSLER, Material Culture of the Blackfoot Indians, p. 44.
[25]See DENIG, Indian Tribes of the Upper Missouri, p. 581; WISSLER, Material Culture of the Blackfoot Indians, p. 24.
[26]WISSLER, Material Culture of the Blackfoot Indians, p. 45.
[27]Ibid., p. 97.
[28]WISSLER, CLARK, Riding Gear of the North American Indians (Anthropological Papers, American Museum of Natural History, vol. 17, part 1, 1915), pp. 31, 36.
[29]LOWIE, The Material Culture of the Crow Indians, p. 220.
[30]WISSLER, Material Culture of the Blackfoot Indians, pp. 90-92.
[31]Ibid., p. 87; LOWIE, The Material Culture of the Crow Indians, p. 219; LOWIE, ROBERT H., The Assiniboine (Anthropological Papers, American Museum of Natural History, vol. 4, part 1, 1909), p. 15; HODGE, Handbook of American Indians, part 1, p. 156.
[32]WISSLER, Material Culture of the Blackfoot Indians, p. 281; BIRKET-SMITH, The Caribou Eskimos, p. 338.
[33]DORSEY, J.O., Omaha Dwellings, Furniture, and Implements (Thirteenth Annual Report of the Bureau of Ethnology, Washington, 1896), p. 281; WISSLER, Material Culture of the Blackfoot Indians, p. 97.
[34]BIRKET-SMITH, The Caribou Eskimos, p. 338; WISSLER, The American Indian, p. 31.
[35]WISSLER, Material Culture of the Blackfoot Indians, pp. 159-161; BIRKET-SMITH, The Caribou Eskimos, p. 317.
[36]LOWIE, The Assiniboine, p. 28; WISSLER, Material Culture of the Blackfoot Indians, pp. 162-163.
[37]HODGE, Handbook of American Indians, part 1, p. 313. WISSLER, Material Culture of the Blackfoot Indians, p. 163.
[38]WISSLER, Material Culture of the Blackfoot Indians, p. 65; DENIG, Indian Tribes of the Upper Missouri, pp. 540-541.
[39]WISSLER, Material Culture of the Blackfoot Indians, pp. 67-70.
[40]Ibid., p. 62.
[41]GRINNELL, The Cheyenne Indians, p. 172; WISSLER, Material Culture of the Blackfoot Indians, p. 53.
[42]See WISSLER, Material Culture of the Blackfoot Indians, p. 31.
[43]Ibid., pp. 71-72.
[44]BIRKET-SMITH, The Caribou Eskimos, p. 352; WISSLER, Material Culture of the Blackfoot Indians, p. 32.
[45]WISSLER, North American Indians of the Plains, pp. 43, 74.
[46]BIRKET-SMITH, The Caribou Eskimos, p. 364; WISSLER, The American Indian, p. 154.

Social Organization

The band divisions of most North Plains tribes are quite like those of the Plains Cree. The band is a loose unit, occupying a certain sector of the tribal territory, having a recognized chief or head man. As Wissler puts it in depicting the group organization of North American hunting peoples, "The simple band is the fundamental unit and as such is little more than the voluntary association of individuals under an able leader."[1]

The bands of the Blackfoot, Gros Ventre, Assiniboin, Arapaho and Teton Dakota are of this nature. The names of Plains bands are more often of the sobriquet type than geographical references.

The annual rendezvous of the Northern Algonkins is paralleled in social function by the Sun dance encampment of the Plains peoples. In large measure, the band divisions of the Northern Plains tribes are similar to those of the Forest people.[2]

Blackfoot chiefs are chosen and hold office exactly as do those of the Plains Cree. The criteria of industry, liberality, and valor are requisite for the position in both tribes.[3] The means of attaining chieftainship and the duties involved in the office seem to be similar throughout the Missouri-Saskatchewan area. In all the tribes also, the council is composed of those men whose age, wealth, and military achievements give them a high prestige status.

Within the memory of living Plains Cree, men of prestige purchased the right to perform dances from the members of Dakota and Assiniboin societies. The non-graded nature of Plains Cree Warrior Societies, their functions of dancing and policing, link them with the Assiniboin and Dakota types. From the manner in which the society organizations were adopted within fairly recent times, it is my impression that the tribe took over the concept bodily from their Assiniboin allies.[4]

Social standing everywhere in the Plains is dependent upon war achievements. It is to be noted that the Plains Cree esteemed military prowess as much as any tribe in the area.

THE INDIVIDUAL LIFE CYCLE

Natal observances among the Assiniboin are much like those described for the Plains Cree. The custom of hanging the after-birth on a tree is followed by the Dakota.[5]

Among most Plains peoples names are given by an old person selected for the occasion. A feast generally accompanies the naming. Plains Cree names more often refer to vision experiences than to incidents of warfare. The reverse is the case for most of the Northern Plains tribes. Names are usually changed in consequence of war exploits rather than as a way of curing childhood illness. The Gros Ventre, however, are like the Plains Cree in the latter custom.[6]

Assiniboin cradles are exactly like those of the Plains Cree. Blackfoot and Crow cradles do not have an arch at the head.[7]

Girls' puberty rites among the Cheyenne resemble the Plains Cree custom in that the girl is secluded for a short period and on her return stands over incense smoke. Menstrual lodges are not common in the area. In all tribes, contact with a menstruating woman is dangerous, especially to sacred objects.[8]

For the majority of the Northern Plains tribes, marriage is the same simple procedure it is among the Plains Cree. The parents generally arrange the match, the couple occupy a new tipi with few or no ceremonial activities to inaugurate the mating, and gifts are exchanged between the affinal families. Mother-in-law avoidance is generally observed and usually the groom is obliged to hunt for or give gifts to his father-in-law. The levirate and sororate are reported for several tribes, but as with the Plains Cree, they are not strictly obligatory. Divorce occurs through simple separation, although sometimes the man publicly renounces his spouse. Adultery among the Blackfoot is punished by the loss of the woman's nose, elsewhere by other physical inflictions.[9]

Scaffold burial is the most common form of interment among the peoples of the Northern Plains. The other burial forms described for the Plains Cree, graves, "vaults," and placing the corpse in a tipi, are also found among some tribes. The methods of signifying mourning observed by the Plains Cree are followed by the other inhabitants of the area. Property distribution, personal mutilation and neglect of personal appearance, are the conventional modes of mourning. The cutting of a lock of hair from the corpse is an Assiniboin practice. Unlike the Plains Cree, but resembling the Eastern Woodlands custom, the braid is disposed of at the end of the year.[10]

In several aspects of life cycle practice and in social organization, then, the fundamental patterns of the Plains Cree are also those of other occupants of the Missouri-Saskatchewan area. It must be noted again that the correspondences are rarely absolute likenesses. Thus scaffolds were more common than graves as means of burial for most of these tribes. The reverse was true for the Plains Cree. Both forms of burial, however, were known in the area.

In the matter of so-called Warrior Societies, the Plains Cree organizations are not as highly elaborated as those of most other tribes of the region. Kinship relations and sib systems have not been dealt with in this discussion. These important topics should be included in more extensive comparisons among Plains peoples than can be made here.

In many respects the social life of the Algonkin-speakers of the north resembles that of the Plains Algonkin-speakers and their neighbors. A major difference lies in the development of Warrior Societies among the buffalo hunters.

FOOTNOTES

[1]WISSLER, The American Indian, p. 161.
[2]*See* WISSLER, CLARK, The Social Life of the Blackfoot Indians (Anthropological Papers, American Museum of Natural History, vol. 7, part 1, 1911), pp. 3-5; DENIG, Indian Tribes of the Upper Missouri, p. 431.
[3]WISSLER, The Social Life of the Blackfoot Indians, pp. 22-25.
[4]*See especially* LOWIE, Plains Indian Age Societies, pp. 902-912.
[5]DENIG, Indian Tribes of the Upper Missouri, pp. 516-517; WISSLER, The Social Life of the Blackfoot Indians, p. 28.
[6]WISSLER, North American Indians of the Plains, p. 92; WISSLER, The Social Life of the Blackfoot Indians, p. 16; LOWIE, ROBERT H., Social Life of the Crow Indians, (Anthropological Papers, American Museum of Natural History, vol. 9, part 2, 1912), p. 215; LOWIE, The Assiniboine, p. 38; KROEBER, ALFRED L., Ethnology of the Gros Ventre (Anthropologial Papers, American Museum of Natural History, vol. 1, part 4, New York, 1908), p. 182.
[7]DENIG, Indian Tribes of the Upper Missouri, p. 519; LOWIE, Material Culture of the Crow Indians, 1922, p. 220.
[8]LOWIE, Social Life of the Crow Indians, p. 220; DENIG, Indian Tribes of the

Upper Missouri, p. 524; WISSLER, Social Life of the Blackfoot Indians, p. 29; GRINNELL, The Cheyenne Indians, p. 129.

[9]*See* WISSLER, The Social Life of the Blackfoot Indians, pp. 9-14; WISSLER, North American Indians of the Plains, p. 91; KROEBER, Ethnology of the Gros Ventre, p. 180; GRINNELL, The Cheyenne Indians, pp. 137, 153; DENIG, Indian Tribes of the Upper Missouri, p. 510.

[10]WISSLER, North American Indians of the Plains, p. 92; WISSLER, The Social Life of the Blackfoot Indians, pp. 30-32; DENIG, Indian Tribes of the Upper Missouri, pp. 570ff; KROEBER, Ethnology of the Gros Ventre, p. 181; LOWIE, Social Life of the Crow Indians, pp. 226-228.

Religion and Ceremonialism

Father Schmidt has examined the religious beliefs of the Plains Algonkin and concludes that the creation of the world and man by the Great *Manito* is the central idea of all Algonkin religion. His evidence, although meticulously gathered, is hardly convincing.[1] Lacking among the tribes of the Northern Plains is the clear-cut Supreme Being concept that we find in the east. For several of these tribes, the Sun may be said to approach the nature of the Great *Manito* of the Woodlands, but the character of this deity is not constant in all phases of religious practice.

Although the supreme delegator of supernatural powers is not commonly present in the ideology of the Northern Plains peoples, the concept of delegated power is universal in the area. The many discussions concerning the nature of the Siouan *wakan* and like concepts among other Plains tribes reveal a strong similarity to the Plains Cree idea of supernatural power. Among the plains dwellers generally, the all-pervading forces emanate from some indefinite source; for the Plains Cree the ultimate source of power is not quite as indefinite, although remote and vague.[2]

Throughout the Plains there is belief in a great range of supernatural beings. Spirit powers manifest themselves as animals, birds, or other living organisms. Everywhere natural phenomena and folkloristic characters are visualized as spirit powers. There seems to be no aboriginal concept of an Evil Being in the area.

According to Dr. Ruth Benedict the forms of the guardian spirit concept and the vision quest vary greatly among Plains tribes. Nevertheless this author cites the Crow quest to illustrate certain traits widely diffused in the Plains. The vision is induced by isolation, fasting and self-torture. The tutelaries are usually animals, although they appear in human form. They confer a blessing, give a song, or describe some memento which is to serve as a token of the vision.

If the Crow practice is taken as typical of the region, the Plains Cree vision quest neatly fits into the Plains pattern. The quest by girls and the specific trait of chopping off a finger as a preparation for the fast, are not customary among the Plains Cree. Otherwise Lowie's accounts of Crow quests apply equally well to the Plains Cree.[3]

Most Plains men seek to acquire a guardian spirit through a vision and hence there is no special shamanistic class. Those whose spirit helpers prove to be especially powerful become renowned medicine men.[4] Curing by blowing, sucking, singing, and the performance of tricks, is universal to the shamanistic procedure of the Missouri-Saskatchewan region. Throughout the Northern Plains, as among the Plains Cree, shamanism is individualistic. Hence shamanistic associations are rare.[5] The administration of medicinal plants is often classed apart from shamanistic curing proper, but all forms of treatment are usually believed to be of vision origin.[6]

A comparison between Blackfoot and Plains Cree bundles reveals a great similarity in form and function. Both types are individually owned, transferable, vision-granted, and have unique songs and rituals. The Blackfoot bundles, however, are more complex in composition, ritual, and ceremonial attributes than are the Plains Cree bundles. While the latter are restricted in use largely to warfare, the former may figure in a vow made in order to cure a sick person, or may influence the success of a horse race. Moreover, the Beaver and Sun dance bundles of the Blackfoot are integral elements of group ceremonies, whereas only the Pipe Stem bundle of the Plains Cree figures significantly in ceremonial dances.

Bundles are known to all other tribes of the Northern Plains. Although they may differ in content and ritual, their source and function is similar to that of the Blackfoot and therefore, to a large extent, like the Plains Cree form.[7]

Wissler cites Paul Kane's remarkably full description of the Sacred Pipe bundle of the Plains Cree and concludes that, in the main, Kane's account holds true also for the Blackfoot. The Gros Ventre, Arapaho, Cheyenne, Teton Dakota, Assiniboin, Hidatsa, Omaha, Pawnee and Crow possess similar ritual traits.[8]

The prerogatives acquired through visions among the Plains Cree are much like those found among other tribes of the area. Everywhere there is a firm association of vision blessing and war achievement. While the conjuring booth is not known, Gros Ventre shamans are tightly bound in the same fashion as are Eastern conjuring booth shamans. Upon communicating with spirits, the Gros Ventre medicine man frees himself of his bonds.[9] Vision sanctions are usually prerequisites for giving ceremonies among the Northern Plains tribes. Among those people who build buffalo pounds a shaman must supervise their construction, as with the Plains Cree. Vision blessings may be transferred among all the tribes and among most these may become economic assets.[10]

The Plains Cree Sun dance seems to have been taken over in its full form from the Assiniboin. Following Spier's tabulation of traits, we find that the Plains Cree ceremony links most closely with the dance of the Blackfoot, Gros Ventre, Arapaho, Cheyenne and Assiniboin.[11]

In addition to the Sun dance and *mite·wiwin,* ten other vowed ceremonies are performed by the Plains Cree. None of these ten appear to be given by other Northern Plains tribes. Similarities do occur. Thus the Blackfoot Horse dance resembles the Plains Cree dance of the same name in some respects. The Assiniboin Horse dance is utterly different from the Plains Cree form, although it was supposedly derived from the Blackfoot. Few Assiniboin dances correspond to any of the ten ceremonies. The masked dancers of the Assiniboin are like those of the Plains Cree. The Prairie-Chicken dance also is common to both tribes, but Lowie says that the Assiniboin borrowed it from the Cree.[12]

The Plains Cree ceremonial system seems to have few correspondences with the ceremonies of any other group. The Plains Cree apparently took over certain bits of ceremonial procedure, isolated them from their former context, and elaborated them in consonance with the vowed ceremony pattern.

The present day secular dances are, as we have seen above, recent acquisitions. Although Wissler tentatively classed the Plains Cree "Pow-wow" with the Central Woodlands Dream dance, it seems to be much more akin to the Western or Plains form of the Grass dance.[13]

Specific bear rituals are reported only from the Assiniboin and Plains Ojibwa. Throughout the Plains, however, there is a high respect for the bear.[14]

Dog flesh is eaten on certain ceremonial occasions by the Blackfoot, Dakota, Crow and Sarsi, but among none of the tribes is there any ceremony similar to the dog feast ritual of the Plains Cree.[15]

Navel cord pouches among the Assiniboin contain tobacco and are hung around the neck of the child, as is commonly done among the Plains Cree. Amulets also are of common occurrence.[16]

The Crow, and probably other tribes, believe that evil magic may be done by making an image of the victim, as the Plains Cree believe. Tales concerning the *wihtiko*, Cannibal Monster, are not told in the Plains. Dwarfs play an important role in many myths. The offering pole does not seem to be known in the Plains beyond Plains Cree territory.

Most of the basic elements of Plains Cree ritualism are commonly used in the Missouri-Saskatchewan region. The use of the pipe, sweetgrass, the sweat bath, singing and feasting usually are part of ceremonial activity of any kind. Cloth offerings are given by the Arapaho, Assiniboin and Crow. However, these tribes do not make cloth offerings as lavishly and as often as do the Plains Cree.

The constant "pity me" refrain in Plains Cree prayer stands out as clearly in Blackfoot and Gros Ventre supplications. The vow is a motivating force in a great many Northern Plains ceremonies.[17]

In summary, the religious patterns of the Plains Cree are in large part shared by the other peoples of the Northern Plains; details of ceremonial practice are similar but there seems to be a remarkable absence, from the rest of the area, of the Plains Cree vowed ceremonies.

Apart from their special development of the concept of a Supreme Being, the general cosmogonic scheme of the Plains Cree corresponds to that held by their Plains neighbors. The nature of the vision quest is broadly the same throughout the region. Shamanism also is essentially uniform. Sacred bundle ritualism is more highly developed among most of the other North Plains tribes than with the Plains Cree, although all share a similar concept about sacred bundles.

The various vision prerogatives and ritual elements enumerated for the Plains Cree find their counterparts elsewhere in the region. The Sun dance of the tribe is much like that of several other Plains people. Only in the ten vowed ceremonies are the Plains Cree unique: these are the Smoking Tipi, *wihtiko* dance, Give Away dance, Prairie-Chicken dance, Horse dance, Elk dance, Bear dance, Bee dance, Pipe Stem Bundle dance and Round dance. Ceremonies bearing similar names are known to other tribes, but save for the name, they bear little resemblance to the

Plains Cree forms. Some of these ceremonies are known to the Plains Ojibwa, but it is probable that most of the non-Saulteaux elements in Plains Ojibwa culture have been taken directly from the Plains Cree. Hence these eastern associates of the Plains Cree have not been included in this discussion.

FOOTNOTES

[1]SCHMIDT, W., High Gods in North America, Oxford, 1933, p. 109.

[2]WISSLER, North American Indians of the Plains, p. 106; LOWIE, ROBERT H., The Religion of the Crow Indians (Anthropological Papers, American Museum of Natural History, vol. 25, part 2, 1922), p. 318; DENIG, Indian Tribes of the Upper Missouri, p. 486.

[3]BENEDICT, RUTH F., The Concept of the Guardian Spirit in North America (Memoirs of the American Anthropological Association, no. 29, 1923), pp. 15-16; LOWIE, The Religion of the Crow Indians, pp. 323-343; LOWIE, ROBERT H., The Crow Indians, New York, 1935, pp. 237ff.

[4]BENEDICT, The Concept of the Guardian Spirit, p. 67.

[5]WISSLER, Shamanistic Societies, pp. 858—859.

[6]LOWIE, The Religion of the Crow Indians, p. 373.

[7]WISSLER, Ceremonial Bundles, pp. 107ff; WISSLER, North American Indians of the Plains, pp. 109-110.

[8]WISSLER, Ceremonial Bundles of the Blackfoot Indians, pp. 165-168; LOWIE, The Assiniboine, p. 51; LOWIE, The Crow Indians, p. 269.

[9]KROEBER, Ethnology of the Gros Ventre, p. 223.

[10]WISSLER, Ceremonial Bundles of the Blackfoot Indians, pp. 272ff; BENEDICT, The Concept of the Guardian Spirit, pp. 77-78.

[11]SPIER, LESLIE, The Sun Dance of the Plains Indians (Anthropological Papers, American Museum of Natural History, vol. 16, part 7, 1921), pp. 478, 496.

[12]WISSLER, Societies and Dance Associations of the Blackfoot Indians, pp. 456-458; LOWIE, The Assiniboine, p. 56.

[13]WISSLER, Shamanistic Societies, p. 865.

[14]HALLOWELL, A. IRVING, Bear Ceremonialism in the Northern Hemisphere (American Anthropologist, vol. 28, no. 1, 1926), p. 73.

[15]WISSLER, Societies and Dance Associations of the Blackfoot Indians, p. 453; GODDARD, PLINY EARLE, Dancing Societies of the Sarsi Indians (Anthropological Papers, American Museum of Natural History, vol. 11, no. 5, New York, 1914), p. 473; WISSLER, Shamanistic Societies, p. 862; LOWIE, ROBERT H., Military Societies of the Crow Indians (Anthropological Papers, American Museum of Natural History, vol. 11, New York, 1913), p. 204.

[16]LOWIE, The Assiniboine, p. 38; KROEBER, Ethnology of the Gros Ventre, p. 275; WISSLER, North American Indians of the Plains, pp. 92, 110.

[17]WISSLER, North American Indians of the Plains, pp. 124-126; HODGE, Handbook of American Indians North of Mexico, part 1, p. 604; KROEBER, The Arapaho, p. 283; LOWIE, The Assiniboine, p. 59; LOWIE, The Religion of the Crow Indians, p. 426; KROEBER, Ethnology of the Gros Ventre, p. 222; WISSLER, Ceremonial Bundles of the Blackfoot Indians, p. 253.

Warfare

The war customs of the Gros Ventre and Assiniboin are especially close to those of the Plains Cree. In both tribes warfare is undertaken either by small raiding parties or by larger vengeance expeditions. Crow and Assiniboin war leaders must have vision sanctions giving them power to lead a war party. These leaders sing while on the warpath, summoning the aid of their supernatural helpers.

Blackfoot warriors dance before their departure; this trait is not generally practised by other tribes, however. War parties usually start out on foot throughout the Northern Plains. Novices perform the menial labor and are subject to practical jokes.

Scouts of Gros Ventre and Crow war parties duplicate the actions of Plains Cree scouts in howling like wolves and kicking through a pile of buffalo chips on their return.

Among all tribes scalps are mounted on hoops and carried by women in the dance given to honor the victors. The scalp dances of the Assiniboin, Cheyenne and Gros Ventre, are almost identical to the Happy dance of the Plains Cree. The symbolism of war deeds and what we have called the metaphor of battle are found everywhere in the plains country.[1] The organization of Oglala Dakota war parties seems to vary from the pattern followed by the Plains Cree,[2] but war customs among most of the prairie tribes are generally similar.

FOOTNOTES

[1]KROEBER, Ethnology of the Gros Ventre, pp. 191ff; WISSLER, Ceremonial Bundles, p. 267; DENIG, Indian Tribes of the Upper Missouri, pp. 544ff; LOWIE, The Assiniboine, pp. 28ff; LOWIE, The Material Culture of the Crow Indians, pp. 252ff; LOWIE, Social Life of the Crow Indians, pp. 230ff; GRINNELL, The Cheyenne Indians, p. 252; WISSLER, Shamanistic Societies, p. 873.
[2]WISSLER, Societies and Ceremonial Associations, pp. 54-61.

Summary

The Plains Cree faithfully mirror those usages common to the tribes of the Northern Plains. Only in a few matters is there a divergence. The material culture of the tribe is truly typical of the Plains area, lacking from the array of Plains traits only the parfleche and hard soled moccasin. The Plains Cree are by no means the only people of the region to make some use of fish and hence in this custom they do not stand alone.

Social organization is also consistent in those aspects which have been treated in this paper. The Warrior Societies of the Plains Cree are not elaborately ritualized, being simpler versions of the societies of the neighbors from whom they were taken.

Religious concepts, too, are fundamentally alike throughout the Northern Plains, save for the more definite concept of a Supreme Being among the Plains Cree. It is in ceremonialism that there is the greatest discrepancy between the Plains Cree and the other Plains tribes. In elements of ritualism and in the Sun dance the tribe is very close to its neighbors. The list of ten vowed ceremonies, however, finds no near parallel in the area, nor do these ceremonies appear in the Woodlands. As far as our investigation has gone, they stand as unique to this tribe. Plains Cree warfare is very much like that of nearby Plains peoples.

The status of the Plains Cree as an unequivocally Plains tribe can scarcely be denied. Yet the tribal culture also bears most of the traits characteristic of the Northern Algonkin. Plains Cree culture is like a palimpsest upon which the stamp of Plains life has been superimposed over an unfaded Woodland design.

PART THREE

CONCLUSIONS

Conclusions

Outstanding differences in the cultural resources of the two Cree divisions are immediately apparent. The canoe is exclusively Woodlands, the horse and horse gear exclusively Plains. The primary food animal is the buffalo in the plains, the caribou, deer, and moose in the forested region. The most productive hunting method is the pound in the plains, the spearing of swimming animals in the woodlands.

When the Cree came into their new environment, they gave up their old means of transportation, depended on a different food animal, and hunted it in a new manner. But these innovations did not unduly dislocate the Forest patterns, for the eastern life was already attuned to a widely roving existence and to seasonal slaughter of the principal food animals when they collected in herds.

The more abundant food supply which presumably lured the Cree into the plains in the first place, made possible certain developments in social and religious organization. The people could now gather in large encampments for a considerable period because of the ample supply of buffalo meat. Although the annual rendezvous is an old Woodland custom, it was limited both in duration and in the numbers taking part because of the restricted food supply. The buffalo herds, on the other hand, furnished enough meat to sustain large assemblages for a much longer period of time. As the societies and group ceremonies of the Plains were thus made possible, the Plains Cree readily took over these social phenomena from their new neighbors and apparently developed some new ones.

The munificent food supply in the plains also made for a reduction of hunting observances and magic. We may hazard the guess that the recurrent famines in the northeast sustained a general anxiety which manifested itself in the manifold hunting rites of the boreal forests. When the Cree found themselves in an environment wherein the food supply rarely failed, it seems likely that their anxieties were allayed

353

and the efforts to control game supernaturally were largely relinquished.

In most other phases of their culture, the immigrant Cree were already so close to the ways of the plains dwellers that there was little conflict of custom. The parallels between the two Cree groups also occur among peoples of a wider territory.

There is a basic similarity between the cultures of the Northern Algonkin, the Labrador peoples, and the Central Woodlands. Briefly expressed, it comes to this. The core trait complexes of the Northeastern area are generally held by the Northern Algonkin and, to a lesser degree, by the Central Woodlands People. In warfare and religion the Northern Algonkin have developed away from the Northeastern level. The inhabitants of the Central Woodlands have specialized still further away, both in these respects and in others. Central Woodlands handicraft, social organization, and ceremonialism are more elaborate than that of the Eastern Cree and far richer than that of the Labrador "starvelings." The more abundant economic resources of the Central peoples are undoubtedly prime factors in making possible these elaborations.

The basic substratum that underlies the cultures of these areas extends also to the Plains. The peoples of the Northern Plains share a long list of traits with the Eastern tribes. Most of these widely distributed traits appear among the Labrador groups.

All this was indicated by Edward Sapir in 1916.

> If for instance, it could be shown, as seems not unlikely, that all or most of the cultural differentia constituting the Plains culture area arose at times subsequent to the development of most of the features characterizing the Eskimo and Eastern Woodland culture areas, we should be compelled to conclude that, from an historical standpoint, the Plains area is a subgrouping of some kind when contrasted with the relatively primary groupings of the Eskimo and Eastern Woodlands areas.

Another passage from the same work stresses the importance of filling out the historical picture of Plains-Woodland relations with comparisons from other areas.

> Taking the Plains culture area, for example, we may either think of it as a specialized form of culture based on a more general Eastern Woodland culture; or we may prefer to see in it a culture blend in which participate tribes originally belonging

354

to the Eastern Woodland, the Southeastern, the Plateau, and possibly the Southwestern culture areas. The latter view seems more tenable to me, though particular emphasis should, I believe, be placed on the historical relation between the Plains and Eastern Woodland areas.[1]

Several cautions must be observed in dealing with these results. Although we have postulated a widely-shared base of common cultural participation, the various tribes by no means present a uniform appearance. As Spier has pointed out, each tribe displays its individuality in the final form and combination with which it stamps the common traits.[2] Moreover certain important cultural aspects such as mythology, games, and kinship organization have not been treated in this work. Although it is the writer's opinion that comparative analysis of these aspects will reflect the same situation as those phases which have been considered, that remains to be determined.

It is to be noted also that the trait comparisons have applied only to Woodlands and Northern Plains. The cultural affiliation between the Plains Cree and the Mackenzie Athabascans, for instance, would probably place the cultural status of the tribe in clearer perspective.

Our chief conclusions then, are:—

1. The Plains Cree are among the latest arrivals into the Plains area. The fur trade, together with the firearms which it introduced, was instrumental in motivating and facilitating the tribal migration.

2. The older Woodlands culture of the Cree quickly took on an overlay of Plains traits. This was not at all difficult because there was already considerable agreement between Forest and Plains cultures. The primary differences between the two lay in the development of group functions on the plains, made practicable by the superior food supply which the buffalo herds offered.

3. Underlying the patterns possessed by both the Cree of the Woodlands and those of the Plains, are certain cultural common denominators which extend throughout the Northern Plains and the Woodlands.

4. If we assume that the Northeastern Algonkin represent an archaic cultural adjustment as Speck believes, then Plains and Central Woodlands cultures may be considered as divergent developments away from this old base.

Our primary interest in this study has been to secure an insight into the historical career of one tribe, the Plains Cree.

The wider comparisons have been designed to illuminate the changes which took place within this aboriginal culture following on the shift in environment.

FOOTNOTES

[1]SAPIR, EDWARD, Time Perspective in Aboriginal American Culture: A Study in Method (Canada Department of Mines, Geological Survey Memoir 90, Anthropological Series no. 13, Ottawa, 1916), pp. 44, 45.
[2]SPIER, LESLIE, Problems Arising from the Cultural Position of the Havasupai (American Anthropologist, vol. 31, no. 2, 1929), p. 220.

APPENDIX

Appendix A
Month Names and Other
Terminologies

Thirteen months were recognized, reckoned from new moon to new moon. Their names were:—

1. *Kıce·pıcim*, Great Moon, or *Apıhtapıpunpıcim*, Midwinter Moon (approximately January). Another name for this month was, Loving Care Month, for every animal carefully looked after their young during this time to keep them from freezing.
2. *Mikicıwpıcim*, Eagle Moon.
3. *Miskıhpıcim*, Goose Moon.
4. *Ayikıpıcim*, Frog Moon.
5. *Sakıpakawpıcim*, Leaves Appear Moon.
6. *Pınawewıpıcim*, Eggs Laying Moon, or *Paskawehowıpıcim*, Eggs Hatching Moon.
7. *Pas·kowıpıcim*, Feather Moulting Moon.
8. *Ohpahowıpıcim*, Start to Fly Moon.
9. *No·tcıhıtopıcim*, Breeding Moon.
10. *Pinackopıcim*, Leaves Change Color Moon.
11. _____ , Falling Leaves Moon.
12. *Okaskatano·pıcim*, Frozen Over Moon.
13. *Pıwahtcakinacı·spıcim*, Scattering Moon (twigs fall from trees and are scattered over the sand).

The month names listed by other writers differ in a few respects, but are substantially in agreement with the above; Lacombe's list has ten terms in common with the list given here, Paget lists ten of the above terms, Skinner nine, and Umfreville nine.[1]

During the day, time was reckoned by the height of the sun above the horizon. Terms for time were descriptive of the sun's position. Noon and the time following was *atcıhtcikıcikan*; midnight and the night hours following were called *atcıhtcitipiskaw*.

Terms of measurement were:—

Peukotcihtc, One thumb's (width).

359

Peukwanohitinahk, One grasp. The width of four fingers.
Eskopihkipitonɛhk, Up to elbow. From tip of thumb to point of elbow.
Tawaskıkan, Mid breast. From center of sternum to tip of thumb on outstretched arm.
Peukonisk, the distance between the outstretched arms.

Stars which could be named by my informants were relatively few.

Eka·katchtetatcahkos, Star which doesn't move. North Star.
Otcekatahk, the three stars in the handle of the dipper or the whole dipper.
Okınanic, Pleiades.
Wapanatcahkos, Daylight Star. Venus.
Okıma·wakanictitcik, the three chiefs. Three bright stars, close together, in the southwest.
Atcahkoskocoit, Tailed Star. Evening star which appears in the southeast (in summer) which seems to have a tail (?).
Mahıhkanmeckano, Wolf Road. The milky way.
Matotisan, Sweatlodge. Half circle of little stars seen early at night in winter.
Okınanis, Little lumbar vertebrae.

The moon and sun were thought to be worlds with luminous earth. During eclipses of the sun, men would fire their guns at the darkened sun to bring it back to normal size.
Cloud names were:—

Pecaskwaw, long clouds, Cirrus.
Manɛnaskwaw, scattered clouds, Cumulus.
Emihkwestwahk, red sky. Portends change in weather.
Kaskewaskwahk, black clouds.

Place names were descriptive or commemorative. There were many of the latter type, such as, Where the Women Were Killed, Where Two Crow Were Scalped. Examples of the former type were, Little Sand Hills, Red Earth Place. A few place names referred to mythological incidents, as Sliding Hill, where the trickster slid down an incline and marked it with a deep groove. Such references were not common.
Some of the river names were:—

Kısaskatciwancı·pı, Swift Current River. Saskatchewan.
Onotinto·cı·pı, Fighting River. Battle River.
Kıhtcıcı·pı, Great River. North Saskatchewan.
Wawaskecıwcı·pı, Elk River. South Saskatchewan and Red Deer rivers.
Apistcıcıpıcis, Little Creek. Milk River.
Pıkano·cıpı, Piegan River. Missouri (?).

Directional terms were:—

Natakham, To the water places, North.
Nimitaw, No end, South.
Mamihk, Down stream, East.
Natimihk, Up stream, West.

In giving directions, the speaker orientated himself as though he were facing north. Hence the term for southwest was *natimihk otɛ*, this side of west.

These terms are peculiarly appropriate to the prairie habitat and would not apply, in their literal sense, in the Hudson Bay-Lake Superior terrain. Lacombe gives entirely different terms for the cardinal directions. In his orthography they are:

Kıwetınok, north (from term for north wind?).
Sâwan, south.
Wâpanok, toward rising sun, east.
Pakısamotâk, west (to setting sun?).[2]

Sign language was not much used by the River People band. *Maskwa* commented:

> We recognized the signs, but we didn't know how to make them. The Beaver Hills People band [westernmost of Plains Cree bands] know them very well.

Some of the signs for tribes were:

Cree, hand cutting across throat.
Blood, finger across mouth.
Blackfoot, grasp foot.
Plains Ojibwa, finger on nose.
Gros Ventre, motion of protruding abdomen.
Crow, flap hands.
Flathead, hands to side of head.
"Fish Men" (who lived west of Rockies), wriggle hands in imitation of fish movement through water.

Signaling was done by flashing mirrors in the sun. Most warriors carried a mirror, handsomely encased, around their necks. The meaning of the flashes was previously agreed upon by the men.

A column of smoke was sent up by a man who had become detached from his group and could not find them again. The members of the group sent up an answering smoke signal to guide him home.

Sentries arranged a series of whistles for communication. Sometimes it happened that the enemy would approach and, hearing the whistles, imitate them. Since they did not know the sequence of calls their presence would be revealed. Whistling was done by exhaling through pursed lips, never with the fingers. A sharp intake of breath through pursed lips was also classed as a whistle.

Trail marks were left to guide friends who might follow. A stake driven into the ground pointed the direction of the march. A buffalo shoulder blade might be placed near the stake and inscribed with a pictograph representing the chief of the group. If many buffalo were to be had in the direction of the march, buffalo chips were placed around the stake. If an attack had taken place, the pictograph represented a wounded man.

FOOTNOTES

[1]LACOMBE, Dictionnaire et Grammaire, under month names in French; PAGET, The People of the Plains, p. 29; SKINNER, Notes on the Plains Cree, p. 87; UMFREVILLE, The Present State of Hudson's Bay, pp. 54-55.
[2]LACOMBE, Dictionnaire et Grammaire, pp. 418, 526, 588, 634.

Appendix B
A Vision Experience and
Its Consequences

The following narrative is presented as recorded from the lips of the interpreter. The informant, Fine-day, tells of a dream in which the Sun spirit power, appearing as a beautiful young woman, granted him the power to make a Sun dance. The spirit also instructed him to give certain names to the sons he would have.

When the eldest son was born, Fine-day wanted to give the child the revealed name but his elders decided against it, and another man named the infant. When the boy grew up, he fell sick and his life was in danger. Fine-day believed that the illness was due to the fact that the proper name had not been given to the boy. He vowed to make a Sun dance, although it was forbidden by the whites. The boy recovered, and later the Police Commandant allowed the ceremony to be given.

> When I was a small boy somebody came to me in a dream and invited me to go along. I followed him. As I was walking along behind him, he stopped and I looked ahead. I saw a clearing in which a young woman was sitting on the west side. I entered on the north side but before I got to the center of the space the girl flew up. I was sorry, for I liked the girl—she was so beautiful. He who invited me was that little stone.[1]
>
> Pretty soon the same one came and invited me again. As soon as he did I remembered the girl. I wanted to see her again. I followed him. As soon as he reached the clearing he stopped. I went straight on. The girl was sitting in the same place. I got a little further into the circle than I had the last time before she turned her head and smiled at me and then flew up.
>
> The next night I got an invitation to the same place. I went in. I got a little further before she turned, smiled at me, and flew up. I thought that the next time I would get pretty close to her before she would fly away.
>
> The fourth night I came up to her. Just before she turned her head I grabbed her and she stood there. She sat down and

363

asked me what I thought to do by catching her. I told her that I liked her very much and I would like to take her for my wife. The girl said, "Yes, but only for a little while." Then she stood up.

The one that invited me generally stood behind my back. When the girl stood up the little man told me, "That's the sun." I stood close to her, almost touching her. "Look here," she said. She pulled a bow painted blue out of her side. She felt at her side again and this time pulled out a bow painted yellow. The one that stood behind my back told me that the blue bow was the Winter Hawk Bow (*pipunacinahtcapi*), and the yellow one was Raven Bow (*kɛhkɛhkaohtcapi*).[2] Every time he spoke to me he whispered so that the girl should not hear.

The girl asked me, "Do you know that Blue Bow?" I gave her its name. "Do you know the other?" I told her, "It is Raven Bow." She said, "Yes." She told me, "I will be with you only for a little while. Follow the one that stands behind you wherever he takes you and wherever he goes. He will show you the Sun dance and all the things that I direct. I am the real boss of all those things."

My guide said to me, "Now you must choose how many Sun dance lodges you are going to use. This one is the first one given to you." I told him I will use all those that were there—although some I could hardly see. "All right," he said. Then I went home. He followed me to my tipi and left me there telling me, "I'll be with you right along." As I grew I watched the Sun dance and thought—"That is what was given to me."

Every night I got an invitation from the same man when I was a boy. Once we went some place and all of a sudden he stopped. I could see posts around in a circle. I thought, "This is a Sun dance lodge." The man answered in his mind, "Yes." I understood his thoughts.[3]

The next night the man led me back and the posts were a little higher. The next two nights they were still higher. On the following night the posts stood way up and there were some poles laid across the top to the center pole. On the fifth night I saw that the lodge had already been used.

When I looked around I could see roads coming into the place from all directions. On the sixth night I saw a Sun dance lodge that had never been used. I went in there. The one who led me told me to sit down and said that I would dance there. I sat down. He himself stood by the center post. He told me to stand, and I did. I looked around and saw somebody (a man standing at the end of the woman's side),[4] his body plastered with white mud, his face painted with yellow, red on his eyes, and a streak of red across his mouth from ear to ear.

My leader asked me if I knew him. I said, "No." When I took a good look at the man I saw that he was wearing a raven skin cap on the left side of his head. Across the raven's eyes was a strip of red cloth with little pieces of tin, sewn on where the eyes are supposed to be.[5] He came up and stood beside my guide. "I am the *oskapewis*, the server, in this lodge." He said this to the one who led me, but I heard him also. "I am always on the right side of the door post. I am going to give him this cap." He handed the raven skin to my leader. "I give him this white clay with which he shall paint his body as I do. But I am not giving him (the right) to be an *oskapewis*."[6] I understood all he said. My leader put the skin on my head and repeated what had been told him.

"Now look here," the server said. He showed me the excavation and an old buffalo skull in it with horns on.[7] He said, "Ever since there has been a Sun dance lodge I have this job. At the first Sun dance a live buffalo stood there (at the altar). This skull stands for that buffalo. But all these things will be told to you in the future by old people.[8] I have worked in this place long and I want you to look at it." I saw a buffalo rising there. He wasn't very big but he was stocky. He shook his body. The next look I had, there was nothing there but an old buffalo skull. But I saw a buffalo hide over it with weasel skins sewed on. "That's the thing the buffalo skull gives you. You see how it is made. That will be your robe in the future."

Before I had this dream, ever since I was a little boy, I wanted to have a buffalo robe with horns attached to it. When I was told that it was to be my robe I took it and spread it out. It had the head skin and horns on.[9] Just below the horns a bell and an eagle feather were sewn on. From there, right down the back to the tail there were eight whole weasel skins. The whole hide of each weasel was tanned, even the claws were attached.

The server said, "That robe and the Sun dance lodge are given to you. Use this robe when you make a Sun dance. In the future some old men will tell you what this Sun dance is for. Now you and your partner can go." After I went out, I looked around. I saw a lot of Sun dance lodges which had never been used. They stretched in a row over a hill as far as I could see. Those I had seen unfinished before were still there.

One day when I was older I saw the Saulteaux girl that I told you of before (whom he married). I hung back at first because I was shy. But when I took a good look at her—it was the girl I saw in my dream.

I lived with her. Sometimes I went to the Blackfoot country to fight and left her for almost a year. I would leave ponies with her. When I came back they were gone. She had traded them all to buy food and clothing because I was not there to provide for her. But I always brought back more horses.

After we had been living together for four years,[10] I came back from a raid and found a little boy had been born to her. Now I remembered that I must name the child after the Blue Bow. I told my wife that I must name the child. It was a fine looking baby with gray eyes because my mother[11] and my wife's father had gray eyes. My wife told me, "You had better wait first. I will ask my father what he thinks about it, and you ask your grandfather what he thinks."

I went to my grandfather and told him about it. He sat for quite a while thinking. At last he took his big red pipe. He lit it and pointed it (as an offering to the spirits). He smoked and set it in front of him. "Now, my grandchild, you have not thrown away any print.[12] You had better wait until you have enough print to put away and then you can name your son."

My wife did the same. She asked her father what he thought about it, whether her husband should name the child. He said that I had not thrown any print away and that I should wait until I had done so before I named the child. "You had better get somebody else to name the child," he finally said.

Now I knew what preparations should be made for a child naming. I took my saddle horse and another horse. The camp was at Indian Head (in the Qu'Appelle River Valley) and I left to go to the Hudson's Bay post at Carlton. That is quite a distance. I sold the horse I was leading and bought prints in twelve colors, and some tobacco.

While I was away my father-in-law prepared food. I had three sisters-in-law and my mother-in-law; all were cooking. My second oldest sister-in-law had a fine-looking husband (*Ato·kien*), a Stoney. In Cree his name was *ukimawkɛhkɛhk*, Chief-of-the-ravens. He was a fine looking man and could doctor.

He was on my`mind as a good man to name my boy as I came home. When I got back my father-in-law came to me with tobacco, cut and ready to smoke. He asked me whom I would choose to name my boy. I told him, "Your son-in-law *(Ato·-kien)*." He was a Stoney, but he could speak Cree. My father-in-law called *Ato· kien*. When *Ato·kien* came in I filled a pipe, burned sweetgrass, and held the pipe over it. I gave the pipe to him, then I passed the cloths over the smoke. He was holding the stem waiting for me to tell him what it was for. "Now, *nitcewam*, my brother-in-law, the reason why I called you is to name my boy." He lit the pipe and laid it down. He took the cloths and held them up in the directions where his spirits were. He pointed each print separately. It took a long time, for there were twelve prints. In his prayers he always mentioned Great *Manito* first—who is father of all. With every print he asked that the boy grow up to be an old man. Then he sent his wife to get his father-in-law. "Tell your father that all the people may come in now."

All the food that had been cooked was brought into the tipi. I could hear my father-in-law shouting and naming all the old men in camp to bring a plate and cup.[13] The Stoney asked his wife to bring his rattle. The tipi wasn't very big so they opened part of it (by raising the tipi cover). There was not room enough for all so some women sat outside.

I had been burning sweetgrass right along. The Stoney took his rattle. After he prayed to Great *Manito* and all the spirit powers, asking that the boy grow up to be an old man, he sang four different songs. After he finished, he put the rattle on the ground and told me to go and bring my son. I took my baby in. He took the child in his arms. "Now Thunder that stays on top of the mountain, you are called *kapiwapickwac totinepiw*, He-who-sits-wearing-an-iron-cap. That's the name you had. So I give this child that name. You will take care of him and he will grow up to be an old man and a good man with everything that is useful to him while he is living." Then he passed the baby to the next old man who called him by his new name and said, "*Kapiwapickwac totinepiw*, I hope you will be a good hunter when you are old enough to chase buffalo." Then to the next one, "*Kapiwapickwac totinepiw*, I hope you'll have lots of horses." So, with all the old men, and then to my wife. She named the child and kissed him. Then outside to the old women. They did the same. I heard one old woman say, "*Kapiwapickwac totinepiw*, I hope you will be a great horse stealer." "*Kapiwapickwac totinepiw*, I hope you will kill lots of buffalo." I didn't hear them all.

I lived with my wife and so we had another boy. We had a girl, too. When my eldest son was nearly a young man and when the girl was ten years old, my wife died. I had just come to this very place where we are now. That was forty-eight years ago (1887). The girl in my dream told me she would be my wife only for a little while. But I made a mistake not to name the child as I was told in my dream.

After the rebellion quite a big bunch of us went south. I went with them. I had my second wife with me. When we were a long way from here, my eldest son sickened. We continued on, but went slowly. At last we couldn't go any further. The boy was dying. The others went on for we had no food. I sat near my boy and my mind was pretty heavy. I thought of what I had been told to do. The names I should have given were always on my mind.

I went out. I stretched my arms up. "Now, *Manito*, my father, you have given the Sun dance lodge for people to pray to you that all be well. I am afraid of losing my son. But I will put up a Sun dance lodge. Tell all the spirit powers to try and help me finish the Sun dance. Although the Sun dance has been stopped by the white man, you are the boss of everything. By your help I will be able to finish it. So help me, *Manito*, to finish this Sun dance that I am promising."

I went back into the tipi. I sat up, but I was pretty sleepy. At daylight I lay down beside my sick son. My wife got up. She lit the fire. We had a blanket over his head. He was breathing pretty fast. I told my wife, "I think he is sleeping now." I fell asleep; suddenly someone told me, "Partner, get up before the sun is up." I jumped up and went out to wash my face. I sat down near my boy and I thought, "What is this for?"

The sun began to rise. As soon as it is above the ground I heard him (the sun) singing. Nobody spoke. I listened and he sang four times. I knew the song. The words are, "Now is the Sun dance talked about." My wife and children did not hear him, only I did.

My boy began to get better. I was pretty sure that I would be able to make a Sun dance because I had heard the sun singing. Those who had gone ahead got to the big camp at Little River and told them of my trouble. My brother-in-law, brother of my present wife, started right out to bring food to me. When he came we started eating for we were pretty hungry. While we were eating my boy raised his head and looked at the food. He said he would like some too.

My brother-in-law had brought some bread from a store. I think it was the first bread we had seen. I asked my boy what he wanted. He pointed to the bread although he didn't know what it was. I took the crust off and gave him some of the soft inside.

When my other relatives heard that I was in a bad fix, they came with food. My younger brother and two more brothers-in-law came. They told me, "You have to move camp." I didn't like to go because my boy seemed to be getting better. But I had to. They hitched up a travois and put my boy in it. They tied thongs at the end of the travois so that they could lift the travois up when they came to a hole.

We stopped once. As soon as we did, the men cut trees to make a shade. The boy wanted to eat right away. We had lots of food then and we gave him whatever kind he wanted—but not much. Within ten days he was able to walk around and herd horses for me. I told my brother that I had made the promise. They told me, "You won't be able to do it."[14] I told them that I had to make it. They went to the store and bought two long print cloths for me. I got back here in the fall. This was after the buffalo were gone, but I used to go south on to the open prairie for foxes.

I had a bit of good luck in the beginning of that winter. I killed a silver fox, but the fur was not very good. When the storekeeper in Battleford heard that I had a silver fox they came here to get it, but the most I could get was $150. That was enough for the cloth offerings. I had just a little bag of berries. I bought more. But I kept the little bag I started with separate.

At the first new moon in the beginning of winter, I invited an old man, *Mitcewakan*, because he had made a few Sun dances before. When the Sun dance lodge was first given to me the server said, "The old men will teach you how to act in the Sun dance." After eating, I asked him to show me how to make the Sun dance. At first he didn't say anything. After he ate, "You must have four men who understand it. You can invite *Pietciw* from Red Pheasant Reserve, *Wapuyah* from Thunder-child has made one or two, *Pimuhteaciw* from Little Pine, and myself."

The next day I started off. While I was on the road I thought of what the old people would be satisifed with most, whiskey or food. As a rule the old men like whiskey best. So I went to Battleford. I didn't see anyone to get whiskey for me. Then I saw a half breed whom I knew well. I asked him. "How much do you want?" "Four bottles." In a short time my friend came with four bottles of whiskey. He put them in my rig. I hitched up and went home.

I brought the four men here. Toward evening, after we had our meal, I made everything ready—the cloths and the sweetgrass. I had a stone pipe myself and I borrowed three others. When there is a Sun dance four pipes are generally used. I filled the four pipes and passed each of them over the sweetgrass smoke. I took the bottles and unwrapped them. I gave each man a bottle. I had four cloths of different colors. I passed them over the sweetgrass smoke and gave each man a cloth.

They held their pipes up, but did not speak. I said to them, "You have all made a Sun dance before and I want you to show me how. You have heard that I am going to make one.

No doubt somebody (some spirit power) gave you the dances you have made."

After I told this they thanked me for it. They told me to open the bottles and to pour them all in a clean pan. Then *Wapuyah* spoke first. "You are doing the right thing. That is the way I was told to do. But still there is a long distance yet that you don't see." He began the story of *Aski·win*, the first man and the Sun dance. And they all told me this story. They said that they would teach me all winter, but it was very hard to make a Sun dance because it had been stopped by the white men. All the people around when they heard that I was going to make a Sun dance said that I couldn't do it. I wasn't afraid but thought that I could do it with the help of the sun and of Great *Manito*.

After I emptied the bottles in the pan they took the pipes and held them up. "Now, *kıce·manito·*, our father, see this stem. You have given us the Sun dance to make and I want you to help that it may be carried on." They all spoke pretty nearly the same. Then I lit the pipes for them. After they smoked, they started to sing Sun dance songs.

I had a rattle. They used that when they sang. Each man when he finished singing asked *kıce·manito·* and all the spirit powers to help them to make the Sun dance. I used to invite the four men every month and they taught me all about the Sun dance. During the time those old men instructed me, each night Thunder gave me songs. That is why I didn't get discouraged.

The rest of the account related how Fine-day managed, by persistence, to secure the permission of the Mounted Police Commandant to make the ceremony. When the Indian Agent discovered that his orders had been overruled, he did not get angry, but sent several wagon loads of food to be distributed to the assembled Indians. To Fine-day this was proof positive that the ceremony and the vision in which he had received the right to make it had been divinely inspired.

FOOTNOTES

[1]This refers to a small stone of peculiar shape which Fine-day picked up and treasured when he was quite young. The stone is unusual in that one side rises to a perfect hemisphere; the obverse is flat. Oddly shaped stones and pebbles were believed to be imbued with a Spirit Power. Since the stone was the one sacred object Fine-day then had, it is not surprising that it was the spirit of the stone which first appeared to the boy.

[2]Questioned later as to the meaning of the two bows and their names, Fine-day stated that he had never heard of the bow names before the vision, nor had he ever heard of anyone else dreaming of bows. The symbolic representation of sons by bows is, as far as I know, unique to this vision.

[3]This is common in accounts of visions. The participants need only think of a thing and their thoughts are known to the others.

[4]Where the servers, *oskapewisak*, are usually stationed.

[5]Fine-day later made a ceremonial headdress of a raven's hide modeled after the one he had seen in the vision. It is still in his possession. During Sun dances he paints his face according to the description above.

[6]The informant could not furnish any further explanation. The supernatural character had granted certain rights, but made it clear that he did not grant the privilege of acting as server. This is all the more puzzling since the servers were appointed and did not need supernatural sanctions to fill the office.

[7]The altar in the Sun dance.

[8]i.e., You will have to be instructed in the actual ritual of the Sun dance by old men who know it.

[9]An instance of wish fulfilment via the visions.

[10]Any span of time or enumeration of events is apt to have the ceremonial number four prefixed to it. Thus "four years" or "four scalps" may be read as "several years" or "several scalps."

[11]This informant showed no apparent evidences, either morphological or cultural, of any white ancestry.

[12]i.e., You have not made offerings of cloth to the spirit powers. It was necessary for a man to propitiate the spirits with many offerings before any act involving the supernaturals could be undertaken.

[13]This is the common procedure in feasts. The leading men are summoned by name. The purpose of the summons is indicated by the request that they bring their eating utensils.

[14]The Canadian Department of Indian Affairs had issued orders that the Sun dance was to be prohibited. After many Cree had been sent to jail every year for participating in the ceremony, the order was rescinded.

Appendix C

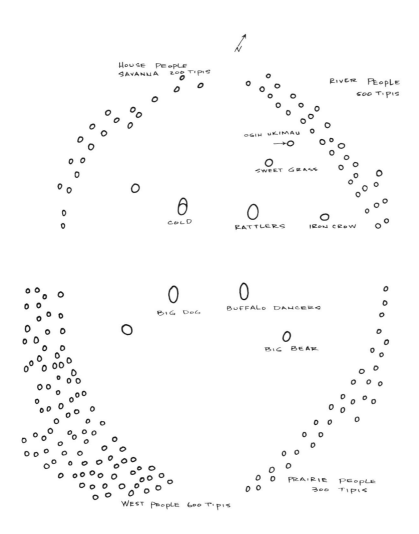

Fig. 31. Camp Circle. From a sketch drawn by Fine-day of a Spring encampment about 1870.

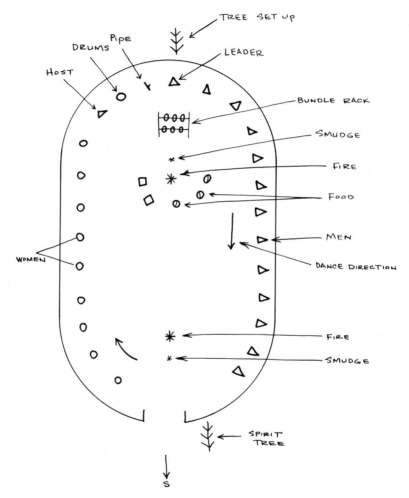

Fig. 32. Braid Bundle Dance. Also called Round Dance. In the performance witnessed, the two saplings, "Spirit trees" on which cloth offerings were hung, were set up outside the dance lodge.

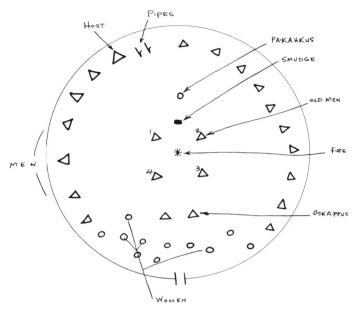

Fig. 33. Give away Dance.

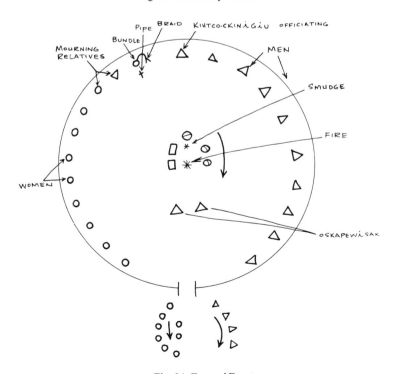

Fig. 34. Funeral Feast.

373

DRUM

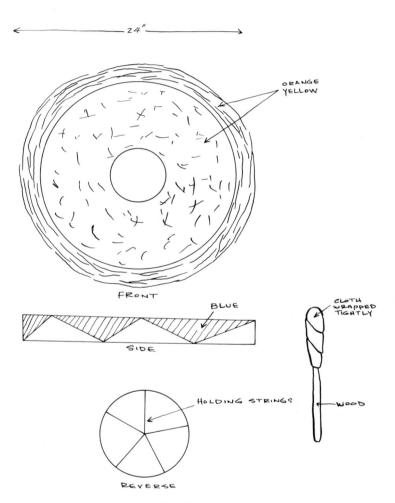

24"

ORANGE
YELLOW

FRONT

BLUE

SIDE

CLOTH
WRAPPED
TIGHTLY

HOLDING STRINGS

WOOD

REVERSE

Fig. 35. Drum.

BIBLIOGRAPHY

Bibliography

BALLANTYNE, R.M. Hudson's Bay. Edinburgh, 1848.

BELL, C.N. Journal of Henry Kelsey (Transactions, The Historical and Scientific Society of Manitoba, n.s., no. 4, Winnipeg, 1928).

BENEDICT, RUTH F. The Concept of the Guardian Spirit in North America (Memoirs of the American Anthropological Association, no. 29, 1923).

BIRKET-SMITH, KAJ. The Caribou Eskimos: Their Cultural Position (Report of the Fifth Thule Expedition, vol. 5, part 2, Copenhagen, 1929).

BLAIR, E.H., ed. The Indian Tribes of the Upper Mississippi Valley. Cleveland, 1911.

BLOOMFIELD, LEONARD. The Plains Cree Language (Atti del XXII Congresso Internazionale degli Americanisti, Roma, Settembre, 1929, pp. 427-431, Roma, 1928).

Sacred Stories of the Sweet Grass Cree (Bulletin 60, Anthropological Series, no. 11, National Museum of Canada, Ottawa, 1930).

Plains Cree Texts (Publications, American Ethnological Society, vol. 16, New York, 1934).

BROWNING, T.B. (A Note on the) Sun Dance (Proceedings, Canadian Institute, Toronto, third series, 1887-1888, vol. 6, p. 40, Toronto, 1889).

BURPEE, LAWRENCE J., ed. Journals and Letters of Pierre Gaultier de Varennes de la Vérendrye and his Sons. With Correspondence between the Governors of Canada and the French Court, touching the Search for the Western Sea. With Introduction and Notes by Lawrence J. Burpee (The Champlain Society, Toronto, 1927). *See COCKING, MATTHEW*.

CADZOW, DONALD A. The Prairie Cree Tipi (Indian Notes, Museum of the American Indian, Heye Foundation, vol. 3, pp. 19-27, New York, 1926).

Peace-Pipe of the Prairie Cree (Indian Notes, Museum of the American Indian, Heye Foundation, vol. 4, pp. 82-89, New York, 1926).

Smoking Tipi of Buffalo-Bull the Cree (Indian Notes, Museum of the American Indian, Heye Foundation, vol. 4, pp. 271-280, New York, 1927).

CAMERON, DUNCAN. The Nipigon Country, 1804. With Extracts from his Journal (In Les Bourgeois de la Compagnie du Nord-Ouest Récits de Voyages, Lettres et Rapports inédits Relatifs, au Nord-Ouest Canadien, Publié avec une Esquisse Historique et des Annotations, par L.R. Masson. Deuxième Série, pp. 229-300, Quebec, 1890).

CAMERON, WILLIAM BLEASDELL. The War Trail of Big Bear. Boston, 1927.

CAMPBELL, HENRY COLIN. Radisson's Journal: Its Value in History (Proceedings, State Historical Society of Wisconsin at its Forty-Third Annual Meeting, pp. 88-116, Madison, 1896).

CARVER, JOSEPH. Travels Through the Interior Parts of North America, in the Years 1766, 1767, and 1768. London, 1778.

CHAMBERLAIN, ALEXANDER F. The Beothuks of Newfoundland (Annual Archaeological Report, 1905, pp. 117-122, Toronto, 1906).

Indians of the Eastern Provinces of Canada (Annual Archaeological Report, 1905, pp. 122-136, Toronto, 1906).

CHARLEVOIX, PIERRE FRANCOIS XAVIER DE. Journal of a Voyage to North America. Translated from the French of Pierre Francois de Charlevoix. Edited, with Historical Introduction, Notes and Index, by Louise Phelps Kellogg, Ph.D., 2 vols. (The Caxton Club, Chicago, 1923).

CHITTENDEN, HIRAM MARTIN, and RICHARDSON, ALFRED TALBOT. Life, Letters, and Travels of Father Pierre-Jean De Smet, S.J., 1801-1873. 4 vols., New York, 1905.

COCKING, MATTHEW. An Adventurer from Hudson Bay. Journal of Matthew Cocking from York Factory to the Blackfeet Country, 1772-1773, etc. L.J. Burpee, ed. (Transactions, Royal Society of Canada, vol. 2, section 2, 1909).

COOPER, JOHN M. The Cree Witiko Psychosis (Primitive Man, vol. 6, no. 1, pp. 20-24, 1933).

Field Notes on Northern Algonkian Magic (Proceedings 23rd International Congress of Americanists, pp. 513-518, 1928).

The Northern Algonquian Supreme Being (The Catholic University of America, Anthropological Series, no. 2, Washington, 1934).

COUES, ELLIOTT, ed. New Light on the Early History of the Greatest Northwest. The Manuscript Journals of Alexander Henry and of David Thompson. 3 vols., New York, 1897.

CULIN, STEWART. Games of the North American Indians (Twenty-Fourth Annual Report, Bureau of American Ethnology, Washington, 1907).

CURTIS, EDWARD S. The North American Indian, vol. 18, Cambridge, 1928.

DAVIDSON, D.S. Knotless Netting in America and Oceania (American Anthropologist, n.s., vol. 37, pp. 117-134, Menasha, 1935).

DENIG, EDWIN THOMPSON. Indian Tribes of the Upper Missouri. Edited with Notes and Biographical Sketch by J.N.B. Hewitt (Forty-Sixth Annual Report, Bureau of American Ethnology, Washington, 1930).

DENSMORE, FRANCES. Chippewa Customs (Bureau of American Ethnology, Bulletin 86, Washington, 1929).

Chippewa Music II (Bureau of American Ethnology, Bulletin 53, Washington, 1913).

Menominee Music (Bureau of American Ethnology, Bulletin 102, Washington, 1932).

DE SMET, PIERRE-JEAN. Oregon Missions and Travels over the Rocky Mountains in 1845-1846. Reprint of the original edition, New York, 1847 (Early Western Travels, 1748-1846, Edited with Notes, Introduction, Index, etc., by Reuben Gold Thwaites, vol. 29,

Cleveland, 1906). *See CHITTENDEN, HIRAM MARTIN, and RICHARDSON, ALFRED TALBOT.*

DOBBS, ARTHUR. An Account of the Countries Adjoining to Hudson's Bay in the Northwest Part of America. London, 1744.

DORSEY, J.O. Omaha Dwellings, Furniture, and Implements (Thirteenth Annual Report of the Bureau of Ethnology, Washington, 1896).

DOUGLAS, FREDERIC. Indian Leaflet Series (Denver Art Museum, vol. 1, Denver, 1932).

DRUMMOND, T. The Canadian Snowshoe (Transactions, Royal Society of Canada, vol. 10, section 2, 1906).

ELLIS, HENRY. A Voyage to Hudson's Bay. London, 1848.

FINE DAY. Incidents of the Rebellion, as Related by Fine Day (Canadian North-West Historical Society, Publications, vol. 1, number 1, Battleford, Saskatchewan, 1926).

FRANKLIN, JOHN. Narrative of a Journey to the Shores of the Poplar Sea in the Years 1819, 20, 21, & 22. Philadelphia, 1824.

GODDARD, PLINY EARLE. Beaver Texts; Beaver Dialect (Anthropological Papers, American Museum of Natural History, vol. 10, parts 5 and 6, New York, 1917).

Dancing Societies of the Sarsi Indians (Anthropological Papers, American Museum of Natural History, vol. 11, no. 5, New York, 1914).

Notes on the Sun Dance of the Cree in Alberta (Anthropological Papers, American Museum of Natural History, vol. 16, part 4, New York, 1919).

GRINNELL, GEORGE BIRD. The Cheyenne Indians. 2 vols., New Haven, 1923.

HALLOWELL, A. IRVING. Bear Ceremonialism in the Northern Hemisphere (American Anthropologist, vol. 28, no. 1, 1926).

Kinship Terms and Cross-Cousin Marriage of the Montagnais-Naskapi and the Cree (American Anthropologist, n.s., vol. 34, pp. 171-199, Menasha, 1932).

Was Cross-Cousin Marriage Practised by the North-Central Algonkian? (Proceedings, Twenty-Third International Congress of Americanists, New York, 1928, pp. 519-544, New York, 1930).

HARMON, D.W. A Journal of Voyages and Travels in the Interior of North America, D. Haskell, ed. Toronto, 1911.

HARRINGTON, M.R. Religion and Ceremonies of the Lenape (Indian Notes and Monographs, Museum of the American Indian, Heye Foundation, New York, 1921).

HASKELL, D.W., ed. See HARMON, D.W.

HAYDEN, F.V. Contributions to the Ethnography and Philology of the Indian Tribes of the Missouri Valley (Transactions, American Philosophical Society held at Philadelphia, for promoting Useful Knowledge, n.s., vol. 12, article 3, Philadelphia, 1863).

HEARNE, SAMUEL. A Journey from Prince of Wales Fort in Hudson's Bay to the Northern Ocean, J.B. Tyrrell, ed. Toronto, 1911.

HENRY, ALEXANDER. Alexander Henry's Travels and Adventures in the Years 1760-1776, M.M. Quaife, ed. Chicago, 1921.

Travels and Adventures in Canada and the Indian Territories between the Years 1760 and 1776. 2 parts, New York, 1809.

HENRY, ALEXANDER and THOMPSON, DAVID
See COUES, ELLIOTT, ed.

HIND, HENRY YULE. Of Some of the Superstitions and Customs Common Among the Indians in the Valleys of the Assiniboine and Saskatchewan (The Canadian Journal, n.s., vol. 4, pp. 252-262, July, 1859).

Narrative of the Canadian Red River Exploring Expedition of 1857 and of the Assiniboine and Saskatchewan Exploring Expedition of 1858. 2 vols., London, 1860.

HODGE, FREDERICK WEBB, ed. Handbook of American Indians North of Mexico (Bulletin 30, Bureau of American Ethnology, part 1, Washington, 1907, part 2, Washington, 1910).

HOFFMAN, WALTER JAMES. The Menomini Indians (Fourteenth Annual Report, Bureau of Ethnology, 1892-1893, part 1, pp. 3-328, Washington, 1896).

HORNADAY, WILLIAM T. The Extermination of the American Bison (Report, United States National Museum, for 1886-1887, pp. 369-548, Washington, 1889).

INNIS, H.A. The Fur Trade in Canada. New Haven, 1930.

JEFFERSON, ROBERT. Fifty Years on the Saskatchewan (Canadian North-West Society Publications, vol. 1, no. 5, pp. 1-160, Battleford, Saskatchewan, 1929).

JÉRÉMIE, NICHOLAS. Twenty Years at York Factory, 1694-1714; (his) Account of Hudson Strait and Bay. Translated from the French ed. of 1720. With Notes and Introduction by R. Douglas and J.N. Wallace. Ottawa, 1926.

JONES, PETER (REV.). History of the Ojebway Indians: With Special Reference to the Conversion to Christianity. London, 186-?

JONES, WILLIAM. Central Algonkin (Annual Archaeological Reports, 1905, pp. 136-146, Toronto, 1906).

KANE, PAUL. Wanderings of an Artist among the Indians of North America from Canada to Vancouver's Island and Oregon through the Hudson's Bay Company's Territory and Back Again. London, 1859.

KELLOGG, LOUISE PHELPS, ed. Early Narratives of the Northwest. New York, 1917.

Journal of a Voyage to North America, Translated from the French of Pierre Francois Xavier de Charlevoix. With Historical Introduction, Notes and Index by Louise Phelps Kellogg, Ph.D., 2 vols. (The Caxton Club, Chicago, 1923).
See CHARLEVOIX, PIERRE FRANCOIS XAVIER DE.

KELSEY, HENRY. The Kelsey Papers. A Journal of a Voyage and Journey Undertaken by Henry Kelsey—in anno 1691. With an Introduction by Arthur G. Doughty and Chester Martin. Ottawa, 1929.

KOHL, J.G. Kitchi Gami: Wanderings Round Lake Superior. London, 1860.

KROEBER, ALFRED L. The Arapaho (Bulletin, American Museum of Natural History, vol. 18, part 1, New York, 1902).

Ethnology of the Gros Ventre (Anthropological Papers, American Museum of Natural History, vol. 1, part 4, New York, 1908).

LACOMBE, ALBERT. Dictionnaire et Grammaire de la Langue des Cris. Montreal, 1874.

LAHONTAN, BARON. New Voyages to America. 2 vols., London, 1703.

LANE, CAMPBELL. The Sun Dance of the Cree Indians (The Canadian Record of Science, vol. 2, pp. 22-26, Montreal, 1886).

LOWIE, ROBERT H. The Assiniboine (Anthropological Papers, American Museum of Natural History, vol. 4, part 1, 1909).

The Crow Indians. New York, 1935.

The Material Culture of the Crow Indians (Anthropological Papers, American Museum of Natural History, vol. 21, part 3, 1922).

Military Societies of the Crow Indians (Anthropological Papers, American Museum of Natural History, vol. 11, pp. 145-217, New York, 1913).

The Northern Shoshone (Anthropological Papers, American Museum of Natural History, vol. 2, part 2, New York, 1909).

Plains Indian Age Societies: Historical and Comparative Summary (Anthropological Papers, American Museum of Natural History, vol. 11, part 13, New York, 1916).

The Religion of the Crow Indians (Anthropological Papers, American Museum of Natural History, vol. 25, part 2, 1922).

Social Life of the Crow Indians (Anthropological Papers, American Museum of Natural History, vol. 9, part 2, 1912).

Societies of the Crow, Hidatsa and Mandan Indians (Anthropological Papers, American Museum of Natural History, vol. 11, part 3, 1913).

The Tobacco Society of the Crow Indians (Anthropological Papers, American Museum of Natural History, vol. 21, part 2, 1919).

MACKENZIE, ALEXANDER. Voyages from Montreal through the Continent of North America to the Frozen and Pacific Oceans in 1789 and 1793 with an Account of the Rise and State of the Fur Trade. 2 vols., New York, 1902.

MACKINTOSH, W.A. Prairie Settlement: The Geographic Setting. Toronto, 1934.

MANDELBAUM, DAVID G. Friendship in North America (Man, vol. 36, no. 272, pp. 205-206, London, 1936).

MARTIN, R.M. The Hudson's Bay Territories and Vancouver Island. London, 1849.

MASSON, L.R., ed. Les Bourgeois de la Compagnie du Nord-Ouest. Récits de Voyages, Lettres et Rapports Inédits Relatifs au Nord-Ouest Canadien. Publié avec une Esquisse Historique et des Annotations. 2 vols., Quebec, 1889, 1890.

McDONNELL, JOHN. Some Account of the Red River (About 1797), with Extracts from his Journal, 1793-1795 (In Les Bourgeois de la Compagnie du Nord-Ouest, Récits de Voyages, Lettres et Rapports Inédits Relatifs au Nord-Ouest Canadien. Publié avec une Esquisse Historique, Première Série, pp. 265-295, Quebec, 1889).

McDOUGALL, JOHN. Pathfinding on Plain and Prairie. Toronto, 1898.

MICHELSON, TRUMAN. The Identification of the Mascoutens (American Anthropologist, n.s., vol. 36, pp. 226-233, Menasha, 1934).

Oüenebigonchelinis confounded with Winnebago (American Anthropologist, n.s., vol. 36, p. 486, Menasha, 1934).

Preliminary Report on the Linguistic Classification of Algonquian Tribes (Twenty-Eighth Annual Report, Bureau of American Ethnology, Washington, 1912).

Some Algonquian Kinship Terms (American Anthropologist, n.s., vol. 34, pp. 357-359, Menasha, 1932).

MORRIS, ALEXANDER. The Treaties of Canada with the Indians of Manitoba and the North-West Territories. Toronto, 1880.

MULVANEY, C.P. The History of the North-West Rebellion of 1885. Toronto, 1885.

PAGET, AMELIA M. The People of the Plains. Toronto, 1909.

PALLISER, JOHN. Papers Relative to and Further Papers Relative to the Explorations by Captain Palliser of that Portion of British North America which lies between the North Branch of the River Saskatchewan and the Frontier of the United States; and between the Red River and Rocky Mountains. London, 1859.

PEESO, F.E. The Cree Indians (The Museum Journal, University of Pennsylvania, vol. 3, pp. 50-57, Philadelphia, 1912).

PERROT, NICOLAS. *Abstract from* Memoire sur les Moeurs, Coutumes et Relligion des Sauvages de l'Amerique Septentrionale: written about 1715-18 (Paris, 1864) in The French Regime in Wisconsin—I (Collections, State Historical Society of Wisconsin, vol. 16, Madison, 1902).
See THWAITES, REUBEN GOLD, ed.

PETITOT, EMILE. On the Athabasca District of the Canadian North-West Territory (Proceedings, Royal Geographical Society, and Monthly Record of Geography, vol. 5, pp. 633-655, London, 1883).

QUAIFE, M.M., ed.
See HENRY, ALEXANDER

RADIN, PAUL. Ojibwa Ethnological Chit-Chat (American Anthropologist, n.s., vol. 26, no. 4, pp. 491-530, 1924).

The Winnebago Tribe (Thirty-Seventh Annual Report, Bureau of American Ethnology, 1915-16, Washington, 1923).

ROBSON, JOSEPH. An Account of Six Years Residence in Hudson's Bay. London, 1752.

SAPIR, EDWARD. Time Perspective in Aboriginal American Culture: A Study in Method (Canada Department of Mines, Geological Survey Memoir 90, Anthropological Series no. 13, Ottawa, 1916).

SCHMIDT, W. High Gods in North America. Oxford, 1933.

SCULL, G.D. Voyages of Peter Esprit Radisson (Prince Society, Boston, 1885).

SHEA, JOHN GILMARY. Early Voyages Up and Down the Mississippi by Cavelier, St. Cosme, Le Sueur, Gravier, and Guignas. With an Introduction, Notes and an Index by John Gilmary Shea. Albany, 1861.

SHEA, JOHN GILMARY, ed. Early Voyages Up and Down the Mississippi. Albany, 1902.

SKINNER, ALANSON. The Mascoutin or Prairie Potawatomi Indians: Part I, Social Life and Ceremonies (Bulletin, Museum of the City of Milwaukee, vol. 6, no. 1, 1924).

Material Culture of the Menomini (Indian Notes and Monographs, Museum of the American Indian, Heye Foundation, New York, 1921).

The Menomini Indians: Social Life and Ceremonial Bundles of the Menomini Indians; Associations and Ceremonies of the Menomini Indians; Folklore of the Menomini Indians (Anthropological Papers, American Museum of Natural History, vol. 13, parts 1-3, 1913, 1915, 1915).

Notes on the Eastern Cree and Northern Saulteaux (Anthropological Papers, American Museum of Natural History, vol. 9, part 1, New York, 1911).

Notes on the Plains Cree (American Anthropologist, n.s., vol. 16, pp. 68-87, Lancaster, 1914).

Political Organization, Cults and Ceremonies of the Plains Cree (Anthropological Papers, American Museum of Natural History, vol. 11, part 6, New York, 1914).

The Sun Dance of the Plains-Cree (Anthropological Papers, American Museum of Natural History, vol. 16, part 4, New York, 1919).

SPECK, FRANK G. Culture Problems in Northeastern North America (Proceedings, American Philosophical Society, vol. 65, pp. 272-311, Philadelphia, 1926.)

Huron Moose Hair Embroidery (American Anthropologist, n.s., vol. 13, no. 1, pp. 1-14, 1911).

Mistassini Notes (Indian Notes and Monographs, Museum of American Indians, Heye Foundation, pp. 410-457, 1930).

Naskapi, The Savage Hunters of the Labrador Peninsula. University of Oklahoma Press, Norman, 1935.

Notes on the Material Culture of the Huron (American Anthropologist, n.s., vol. 13, no. 2, pp. 208-228, 1911).

Penobscot Shamanism (Memoirs of the American Anthropological Association, vol. 6, pp. 238-288, 1919).

SPIER, LESLIE. An Analysis of Plains Indian Parfleche Decoration (University of Washington Publications in Anthropology, vol. 1, no. 3, pp. 94-112, Seattle, 1925).

Problems Arising from the Cultural Position of the Havasupai (American Anthropologist, vol. 31, no. 2, pp. 213-222, 1929).

The Sun Dance of the Plains Indians (Anthropological Papers, American Museum of Natural History, vol. 16, part 7, 1921).

SPINDEN, HERBERT J. The Nez Percé Indians (Memoirs of the American Anthropological Association, vol. 2, 1908).

STRONG, WILLIAM DUNCAN. The Indian Tribes of the Chicago Region (Field Museum of Natural History, Anthropology Leaflet 24, Chicago, 1926).

An Introduction to Nebraska Archeology (Smithsonian Miscellaneous Collections, vol. 93, no. 10, Washington, 1935).

TACHÉ, ALEXANDRE. Esquisse sur le Nord-Ouest de l'Amerique. Montreal, 1869.

THOMPSON, DAVID. David Thompson's Narrative of his Explorations in Western America, 1784-1812. Edited by J.B. Tyrrell (The Champlain Society, XII, Toronto, 1916).

THWAITES, REUBEN GOLD, ed. Early Western Travels, 32 vols., Cleveland, 1904-1907.

The French Regime in Wisconsin-II, 1727-1748 (Collections, State Historical Society of Wisconsin, vol. 17, Madison, 1906).

The Jesuit Relations and Allied Documents. Travels and Explorations of the Jesuit Missionaries in New France, 1610-1791. The Original French, Latin and Italian Texts, with English Translations and Notes. Illustrated by Portraits, Maps, and Facsimiles. 58 vols., Cleveland, 1896-1901.

Radisson and Groseilliers in Wisconsin (Report and

Collections of the State Historical Society of Wisconsin, vol. 11, pp. 64-96, Madison, 1888).
See DE SMET, PIERRE-JEAN.

TURNER, LUCIEN M. Ethnology of the Ungava District (Eleventh Annual Report, Bureau of Ethnology, 1889-90, pp. 167-359, Washington, 1894).

TYRRELL, J.B., ed. David Thompson's Narrative of his Explorations in Western America, 1784-1812 (The Champlain Society, XII, Toronto, 1916).

Documents Relating to the Early History of Hudson Bay. Edited with Introduction and Notes by J.B. Tyrrell (The Publications of the Champlain Society, XVIII, Toronto, 1931).

UMFREVILLE, EDWARD. The Present State of Hudson's Bay, Containing a Full Description of that Settlement, and the Adjacent Country; and Likewise of the Fur Trade. London, 1790.

VERENDRYE, PIERRE GAULTIER DE VARENNES DE LA
See BURPEE, LAWRENCE J., ed.

VERWYST, CHRYSOSTOM. Missionary Labors of Fathers Marquette, Menard, and Allouez in the Lake Superior Region. Chicago, 1886.

WEST, GEORGE A. Tobacco, Pipes and Smoking Customs of the American Indian (Bulletin, Museum of the City of Milwaukee, vol. 17, part 1, Milwaukee, 1934).

WEST, JOHN. The Substance of a Journal During a Residence at the Red River Colony. London, 1824.

WILLOUGHBY, CHARLES C. Dress and Ornaments of the New England Indians (American Anthropologist, n.s., vol. 7, no. 3, pp. 499-508, 1905).

WILSON, GILBERT L. The Horse and Dog in Hidatsa Culture (Anthropological Papers, American Museum of Natural History, vol. 15, part 2, New York, 1924).

WISSLER, CLARK. The American Indian. New York, 1922.

Ceremonial Bundles of the Blackfoot Indians (Anthropological Papers, American Museum of Natural History, vol. 7, part 2, New York, 1912).

Costumes of the Plains Indians (Anthropological Papers, American Museum of Natural History, vol. 17, part 2, New York, 1915).

General Discussion of Shamanistic and Dancing Societies (Anthropological Papers, American Museum of Natural History, vol. 11, part 12, New York, 1916).

The Influence of the Horse in the Development of Plains Culture (American Anthropologist, n.s., vol. 16, pp. 1-25, Lancaster, 1914).

Material Culture of the Blackfoot Indians (Anthropological Papers, American Museum of Natural History, vol. 5, part 1, New York, 1910).

North American Indians of the Plains (Handbook Ser. no. 1, 2nd ed., American Museum of Natural History, 1920).

Population changes among the Northern Plains Indians (Yale University Publications in Anthropology, no. 1, pp. 1-20, New Haven, 1936).

Riding Gear of the North American Indians (Anthropological Papers, American Museum of Natural History, vol. 17, part 1, 1915).

The Social Life of the Blackfoot Indians (Anthropological Papers, American Museum of Natural History, vol. 7, part 1, 1911).

Societies and Ceremonial Associations in the Oglala Division of the Teton-Dakota (Anthropological Papers, American Museum of Natural History, vol. 11, part 1, 1912).

Societies and Dance Associations of the Blackfoot Indians (Anthropological Papers, American Museum of Natural History, vol. 11, part 4, New York, 1913).

Structural Basis to the Decoration of Costumes among the Plains Indians (Anthropological Papers, American Museum of Natural History, vol. 17, part 2, New York, 1916).

YOUNG, E.R. By Canoe and Dog Train Among the Cree and Saulteaux Indians. London, 1890.

INDEX*

Abenaki, 282
Adaptation, to plains life. *See* Environmental adaptation
Adoption, 127
Adultery, 148, 295, 338
Aged, 58, 62, 85, 127, 140, 143, 144, 197, 216; men, 81, 109, 110, 121, 175, 186, 213, 222, 225, 246; women, 83, 88, 145, 154, 199
Ages, 142
Agriculture, 24, 277
Albanel, Charles, 17
Alcohol, 24–25, 29, 30, 37, 108
Algonkin, 18, 24, 34, 98, 272, 305, 306, 308, 312, 340, 341; Central, 268–70 passim, 273, 291, 293, 294, 296, 304, 305, 315; Northeastern, 20, 269, 289, 294, 297, 313. *See also* Confederacy, Algonkin-speaking
Allemant, Charles l', 301
Alliances: with Assiniboin, 8, 19, 20, 21, 22, 31, 38, 39, 42, 262; with Ojibwa, 24; with Saulteaux, 8. *See also* Confederacy
Allouez, Claude Jean, 16, 310
Amulets. *See* Charms
Annual cycle, 77–78
Antelope, 57
Arapaho, 282, 327, 328, 329, 331, 333, 337, 342, 343, 344
Arikara, 327, 331
Armor, 280
Arrow release, 95, 280, 332
Arrowheads, 60, 94, 95
Arrows, 94–95, 280, 331; in games, 127–28, 129; in hunting, 55, 56. *See also* Arrowheads; Arrow release

Assiniboin (Stoney), 7, 8, 19–27 passim, 31–42 passim, 61, 62, 105, 112, 117, 214, 217, 239, 282, 327–33 passim, 337, 338, 342, 343, 344, 347
Astronomy, 360
Athapascans, 20, 24, 31, 34, 36, 39
Aulneau, Jean Pierre, 24, 25, 38

Back-rests, 91, 270, 328
Badger, 69. *See also* Divining, badger blood
Bags: bark fiber, 92; foetus skin, 92; legskin, 91, 270, 328; rawhide, 91, 328; tanned hide, 91; woven, 270
Ballantyne, R. M., 295
Band organization, 105–06, 289, 337. *See also* Bands, Plains Cree; Council, Band
Bands, Plains Cree: Beaver Hills People (Upstream People), 11, 361; Calling River People, 8, 9, 11, 57, 151, 183, 198; House People, 10, 11, 204, 207; Parklands People (Willow Indians), 10, 11; Prairie People (Cree–Assiniboin), 9–10, 11; Rabbit Skin People, 9, 11; River People, 10–11, 57, 117, 183, 203, 207, 212, 218; Touchwood Hills People, 10, 11
Bannock (tribe), 328
Beadwork, 81–85 passim, 92, 101, 102, 282, 332; loom, 101–02, 282. *See also* Ornamentation
Bear ceremonialism, 219–22, 313–14, 343
Bear dance, 210
Beauharnois, Charles, 25

*Compiled by Barbara ElDeiry

Beaver (tribe), 39
Beaver bundle, 342
Beds and bedding, 91, 94, 270, 333
Beothuk, 272, 274
Berries, 54, 75–77; in ceremonials, 172, 174, 188, 209, 213, 219, 222, 223, 233; first fruits, 222–23; gathering of, 75, 276
Big-bear, Chief, 107–08
Big Dog society, 117–18
Birds: eagles, 222, 314; eggs, 69; prairie chickens, 69; wild fowl, 69, 223, 276
Black-bear, Chief, 105
Blackfoot, 7, 8, 11, 31, 33, 34, 38–42 passim, 62, 63, 83, 89, 99, 120, 239, 262, 282, 327–33 passim, 337, 338, 342, 343, 344, 347
Blakiston, Lieutenant, 41
Blood (tribe), 8, 239
Blue-horn, Solomon, 4, 125, 216
Bows: construction, 94, 280; cross-bows, 95, 280; in games, 127, 128, 129; in hunting, 55, 56, 95, 96; with knife, 95, 332; simple, 94, 280, 331; sinew-backed, 280, 331; strings of, 60, 94; in warfare, 95. *See also* Arrows
Boys, 55, 58, 59, 87, 110, 134, 143, 144, 159–60, 195, 224, 232, 304. *See also* Children
Breechclout, 81, 271, 329
Buffalo: chase, 55–57, 330; chips, 60, 93; decline of, 42, 45, 51, 52; hunting of, 52–59, 77, 115, 205, 262, 274, 275, 330; migration of, 52; pound, 33, 38, 52–55, 177, 178, 330, 343; robe, 81, 82, 329; stalking, 57, 330
Buffalo Dancers' society, 111, 117
Buffalo spirit power. *See* Spirit powers, buffalo
Bundles. *See* Sacred bundles
Burial, 150–52, 295–97, 338; cave, 151; ceremony, 152; chamber, 150; cremation, 296; feast, 153, 296–97, 373; grave, 150, 295, 298, 338; grave cleaning, 154; grave houses, 150, 151, 296; mass, 151; mounds, 151, preparation for, 151, 295, 296; scaffold, 296, 338; tipi, 151; tree, 151, 296, 298. *See also* Dead; Death;

Mourning
Butchering, 55, 58, 220

Calendar, 359
Caller, chief's, 109–10, 290
Cameron, Duncan, 40
Cameron, William, 116, 215
Camp: circle, 113, 117, 121, 371; leader, 110; organization, 113, 121
Cannibal Monster (*Wihtiko*), 296, 304, 314, 344
Caribou, 274, 314
Carried on the back bundle, 154, 158, 174, 211–12. *See also* Dead, Hair of
Carver, Joseph, 32, 33, 282, 283
Ceremonial, 140–41, 152–54, 183–236, 308, 312–14, 343–44; clothing, 82, 83, 194, 204, 210, 212, 215; comedy in, 204, 212; face painting, 87, 194, 209, 210, 212; fire, 175–76, 195, 199, 207, 208, 211, 225; food, 141, 153, 172, 174, 197, 200, 204, 205, 206, 208–13 passim, 215, 219, 224, 225, 233–34 (*See also* Berries); music, 97, 98, 140, 175, 178, 183–84, 185, 186–87, 191, 208; officers, 185, 186, 191, 193, 195, 197, 199, 200, 201, 202, 204, 206, 208, 209, 211, 213, 214, 215, 224, 225, 234, 310; paraphernalia, 99, 186, 191; pipes, 96, 140, 153, 154, 172, 199, 200–02, 204, 309, 310, 344; right to participate, 183, 199, 208, 209, 211, 212, 218, 226; structures, 90–91, 183, 185, 186, 188, 198, 199, 206, 207, 209, 210–13 passim, 223, 224, 269, 327. *See also* Bear ceremonialism; Bear dance; Dakota dance; Dog feast; Eagle ceremonialism; Elk dance; First event ceremonialism; Give away dance; Horse dance; Masked dance; *Mite-wiwin*; Offering pole ceremony; Pipestem bundle dance; Pow-wow dance; Prairie-chicken dance; Round dance; Smoking tipi ceremony; Sun dance; Tail wagging dance; Tea dance; Tipi painting

392

Charlevoix, Pierre Francois Xavier de, 23
Charms, 164, 165, 213, 307, 315, 344
Cheyenne, 9, 234, 262, 282, 327–33 passim, 338, 342, 343, 347
Chiefs and chieftainship, 106–110, 117, 245, 290–91, 337; behavior of, 107–09; choice of, 106, 108, 290, 337; duties of, 106, 107, 109, 152, 337; hierarchy, 108; multiple, 108; recognition by Hudson Bay Co., 108. See also Warrior chiefs
Childbirth, 139, 292, 338
Children, 85, 140, 143–44, 150, 205, 206, 207, 209, 246. See also Boys; Girls; Infants
Chipewyan, 40, 274
Chippewa. See Ojibwa
Clothing, 81–84, 143, 271–73, 328–29
Cocking, Mathew, 33
Cold society, 116, 117
Comanche, 282, 327, 331
Coming-day, 4, 119, 126, 127, 147, 149, 150, 163, 176, 178, 179, 220, 244
Confederacy: Algonkin speaking, 19, 20; Blackfoot, 8, 239
Conjuring booth, 167, 168, 175–76, 178, 220, 306, 307, 312
Containers, 92, 270, 328. See also Bags
Contests. See Games and contests
Cooking. See Food preparation
Couches, 270
Council, Band, 109, 110, 172, 173, 290, 291, 337
Coup, counting, 112, 118, 152, 187, 197, 247, 297, 298, 320
Courtship, 146–47
Cow boys society, 217
Cradleboard, 140, 292, 338
"Crazy Dogs," 243
Cree: Albany, 284; Western Woodland, 8, 280; Woodland, 3, 8, 12, 15, 42, 43, 163, 164, 165, 204, 239, 261–84 passim, 289–98 passim, 301–15, 319, 320; for Cree, Forest and Cree, Eastern see Cree, Woodland
Cree language, 16, 22, 25, 34, 42, 43; dialects, 11, 12; pronunciation, 5; syllabics, 180
Crier, 55, 109, 290–91
Crime, 122–24; blood vengeance, 122, 319, 347; murder, 122 (See also Murder, justifiable); theft, 123. See also Law and order; Punishment
Crow, 9, 239, 327–31 passim, 338, 341–44 passim, 347

Dablon, Claude, 16, 17, 289
Dakota, 9, 15, 18, 19, 20, 31, 34, 111, 218, 239, 247, 262, 291, 328–33 passim, 337, 338, 343; Teton, 327, 329, 330, 337, 342; Oglala, 347
Dakota dance, 218
Dances and dancing, 111–112, 183–198, 204–19, 240–45, 312–13, 320, 321, 337, 347
Dead: children of, 110, 144; hair of, 152–54, 211, 297, 298, 339, (See also Carried on the back bundle); land of the, 153, 158, 180, 303, 315; names of, 142; property of, 152, 154, 155, 295–98, 339 (See also Inheritance); revisiting of earth by, 144, 153, 158; soul of, 158, 212, 223, 297, 303. See also Burial; Death; Mourning
Death, 120, 150–55, 245, 295–98, 338–39. See also Burial; Dead; Mourning
Decoration. See Ornamentation
Deer, 39, 68, 77, 274, 275
De Gannes manuscript, 321
de Smet, Pierre Jean. See Smet, Pierre Jean de
Dialect. See Cree language
Diseases and illness, 42–43, 141, 162–70, 233; frost bite, 170; insanity, 296; measles, 45; shaman-induced, 163, 164; smallpox, 40, 42, 44, 45, 46; starvation, 43, 51; tuberculosis, 44, 170; worms, 170; wounds, 170. See also Healing; Medicines
Divining, 175–76, 306, 311; badger blood, 176; scapulimancy, 177; in warfare, 175, 241; water scrying, 177. See also Conjuring booth

Dobbs, Arthur, 32, 274, 309
Doctoring. *See* Healing
Dog feast, 224
Dogs, 51, 61, 66–68, 115; care of, 66–67; in ceremonials, 66, 212, 213, 216, 224; as draught animals, 66, 67, 279, 331; as economic asset, 66; in hunting, 279; naming of, 67; sacrifice of, 66, 213, 310, 314. *See also* Dog feast; Meat, dog
Dream dance, 312, 313
Dress. *See* Clothing
Dresses, 83, 85, 271, 328
Dreuillettes, Father, 289
Duluth, Daniel Greysolon, 21
Dwarfs, 178–80, 315, 344

Earrings and ear decoration, 85, 273, 330
Eater-of-raw liver, 61
Elk, 39, 68, 77
Elk dance, 209–10
Ellis, Henry, 267, 271, 276, 290, 292, 304
Environmental adaptation, 3, 34–35, 38, 46, 261–63, 353–56
Eskimo, 19, 24, 270, 274, 279, 280
Evans, James, 180

Face painting. *See* Ornamentation, face
Feather (informant), 61
Fine-day, 4, 61, 62, 63, 67, 68, 73, 78, 84, 86, 99, 106, 110, 114, 118, 121, 122, 127, 132, 133, 144, 160, 161, 162, 164, 166, 168, 169, 177, 180, 197, 207, 209, 210, 212, 214–15, 220–23, 225–26, 230, 231, 232, 247, 249, 363–69
Fire: making, 92–93, 276, 283, 333; place, 89, 90, 267, 328; prairie, 57. *See also* Ceremonial, fire; Fuel
First event ceremonies, 222–24, 314; berries, 222, 314; game, 223, 224, 314; thunder, 223
Fish, 71–74, 275–76, 330
Fisher (informant), 61
Fishing methods, 71–74, 77, 275–76, 330; angling, 74, 275, 276; nets, 276; spearing, 73, 275, 276; traps, 275; weirs, 71, 72, 73, 77,

275, 330
Flathead, 9, 38, 130, 239, 327
Folklore and mythology, 157, 220–22, 272. *See also* Cannibal Monster; Dwarfs
Food, 55, 58, 68–76, 274–78, 330; in ceremonials (*See* Ceremonial, food); of children and infants, 142–43; sharing, 55, 73, 78, 107; storage, 58, 59, 276, 278, 330. *See also* Birds; Fish; Food preparation; Meat; Vegetal foods
Food preparation, 58–59, 278, 330; boiling, 59, 75, 76, 278, 330; drying, 58, 74, 75, 278, 330; pit baking, 59, 69, 74, 278; roasting, 59; smoking, 276, 278. *See also* Pemmican
Fox (tribe), 291
Franklin, Sir John, 37, 295
Fuel: buffalo chips, 60, 93; firewood, 66, 93, 100, 195; grease, 60, 93
Fur trade, 17–22, 25–31, 34, 35, 38, 39, 46, 261; and economic dependence, 16, 29, 30, 37, 39, 261–62; and social change, 20, 21, 22, 23, 28, 29, 30, 34, 37; and territorial change, 20, 30, 261–62
Furniture, 91, 270, 328

Gambling, 128–33, 183
Games and contests, 127–37, 183. *See also* Gambling
Ghost dance, 180
Ghost lodge, 117
Ghosts, 158
Gift giving (gift exchange), 62, 106, 107, 108, 112, 118, 119, 120, 122, 123, 127, 144–48 passim, 162, 173, 184, 197, 198, 206–08, 213–18 passim, 224, 240, 244, 294, 338. *See also* Give Away dance
Girls, 55, 136, 143, 145, 160, 187, 232, 304, 320, 342. Menstruation; Puberty
Give Away dance, 178, 206–07, 373
God. *See* Supreme Being
Gophers, 51, 69
Grass dance. *See* Pow-wow dance
Graves. *See* Burial
Green Grass World. *See* Dead,

land of

Gros Ventre, 7, 9, 31, 36, 39, 239, 262, 327–33 passim, 337, 338, 343–44 passim, 347

Guns, 23, 30, 35, 37, 41, 96; in hunting, 39, 56, 96; muzzle-loading, 96; rifles, 96; in warfare, 96, 262

Hair and hairdressing, 85, 273, 330

Happy dance, 245, 246

Harmon, Daniel, 39, 61, 275, 292, 293, 295, 320–21

Headgear, 84, 271, 272, 329

Healing, 98, 141, 162–70, 177, 178, 220, 222, 305–06, 342; blood letting, 169; blowing, 167, 306, 342; bone setting, 169; singing, 162, 306, 342; smoke inhalation, 169; sucking, 163, 167, 306, 342. See also Medicines

Hearne, Samuel, 267, 293

Henday, Anthony, 29

Henry, Alexander: the elder, 33, 273; the younger, 35, 38

Hidatsa, 327, 329, 330, 331, 333, 342

Hind, Henry Yule, 41–43, 45, 51, 56, 57, 62, 71, 75, 96, 310

Horse dance, 63, 208–09, 343

Horsehair; decoration, 102; rope, 65, 103

Horses, 32, 34, 38, 39, 41, 51, 60–66, 154–55; breeding of, 63; care of, 63, 64, 110; as economic asset, 63; as gifts, 62, 122, 146, 165, 244; in hunting, 55, 56, 62, 64; naming of, 65–66; in religion and ceremonial, 63, 195, 205, 209; riding gear, 65, 331; theft of, 41, 62, 63, 242–43, 247; wild, 64. See also Horse dance; Transportation

Housing, 87–90, 267–69, 327

Hudson's Bay Company, 9, 10, 17, 20, 21, 22, 25, 28, 29, 33, 37, 66, 67, 74, 85, 140, 262

Hunting, of bear, 219; of buffalo, 52–59, 274, 275; of caribou, 274; of deer, 39, 68, 77, 274, 275; of elk, 39, 68, 77; magic, 68, 308, 310; of moose, 39, 68, 274; observances, 308–09; territory, 289. See also Trapping

Huron, 271, 280

Hygiene, personal, 85, 121, 139, 140

Illegitimacy, 147

Illinois, 275, 321

Illness. See Diseases and Illness

Infants, 139, 140, 292

Informants, 4. See also Bluehorn, Solomon; Coming-day; Feather; Fine-day; Lives-in-a-bear-den; Many-birds; Maskwa; Night-traveler; Pones

Inheritance, 154–55, 178, 199. See also Dead, property of

Iowa, 333

Iroquois, 17, 28, 275, 280

Jesuits, 15–18, 22–25, 275, 276, 278, 289, 301, 302, 310

Joking, 242, 347; relationships, 124, 127, 295

Jones, Peter, 292, 295, 296, 297, 320

Jones, William, 267, 271, 274, 275, 289

Kane, Paul, 342

Kelsey, Henry, 21, 29, 30, 307, 309

Kinnikinnik, 97, 282, 333

Kinship, 105, 106, 107, 108, 124–27, 141, 295

Kiowa, 282

Kit-fox society, 117

Kutenai, 327

Labrador tribes, 266–71, 273, 274, 276, 277, 279, 280, 282, 283, 284, 289, 290, 292, 293, 296, 303–07 passim, 309, 310, 311

Lacombe, Albert, 42, 361

Lahontan, Baron, 19

Language. See Cree language

La Potherie, Claude Charles, 23, 304, 309

La Verendrye, Pierre Gaultier, 24–28, 31, 44, 60, 272

Law and order (maintenance of), 122–24; by chief, 107; by men of prestige, 115, 122; by warrior police, 291. See also Pipestem, Sacred; Punishment; Vengeance

Leggings, 81, 83, 271–72, 329
Le Jeune, Paul, 302
Lenapé, 269, 284, 302
Le Sueur, —, 23
Lewis and Clark expedition, 38, 39
Lives-in-a-bear-den, 4, 163
Lodges: conical, 267, 327; domed, 268; long, 269, 327; warrior, 113
Lynx, 69

McDonnell, John, 44, 310
McDougall, John, 42
MacKenzie, Alexander, 36–38, 81, 291, 292, 294, 295, 296, 309, 310, 319
Magic: concoctions, 95; in doctoring, 162, 306; sympathetic, 164, 315, 344; in warfare, 95, 307. *See also* Charms
Mandan, 38, 327, 329, 330, 331, 333
Manito, 140, 145, 153, 158–59, 302; evil M., 158, 303–04, 341. *See also* Supreme Being
Many-birds, 4, 77, 142, 210, 212–14
Marest, Gabriel, 22
Marquette, Jacques, 16
Marriage, 105, 106, 146–50, 294, 295, 338; age at, 148; ceremony, 146; choice of partner, 146–47, 148, 294; cross cousin, 124, 127; levirate, 338; polygyny, 148, 295; separation, 150, 295, 338; sororate, 295, 338; wife exchange, 149, 150. *See also* Adultery
Martin, R. M., 45
Mascoutin, 17
Masked dance, 98, 204, 205
Maskegon, 42
Maskwa, 4, 54, 69, 81, 99, 164, 165, 190, 197, 226, 232, 246, 247, 360
Measurement, 359–60
Meat: bear, 220, 314; buffalo, 55, 58, 205; butchering, 55, 58; deer, 276; dog, 66, 115, 213, 224, 310, 343; eagle, 222; gopher, 51; horse, 64; muskrat, 43, 51; rabbit, 276. *See also* Pemmican
Medicine, 212–14, 224, 305, 306, 311, 315; bags for, 165; herbal,

165, 170, 305, 307, 342; hunting, 170, 310; love, 164; purchase of, 66, 165, 177, 224. *See also* Healing; *Mite•wiwin*
Menomini, 266–84 passim, 291–98 passim, 302–07 passim, 310, 311, 312, 314, 315, 320
Menstruation, 145–46, 293–94; contamination by, 145, 294, 338; seclusion during, 145, 160, 293, 338; taboos, 145, 223. *See also* Puberty
Metaphor of battle, 248–49, 347
Metis, 43
Miami, 275
Missouri tribes, 9, 24
Mistassini, 269, 270
Mistawasis, Chief, 10
Mite•wiwin, 66, 97, 165, 304, 305, 306, 311, 312, 313, 315, 343
Mittens, 83–84, 272, 329
Moccasins, 60, 83, 102, 146, 240, 271–72, 329
Monsoni, 23, 25, 26, 27, 34
Montagnais, 267, 272, 275, 280, 296, 302, 303, 305, 307, 308, 310, 311, 314, 315
Moose, 39, 68, 274
Mosquitoes (society), 120–21
Mourning, 152–55, 297, 298, 339
Murder, justifiable, 122. *See also* Crime, murder
Music. *See* Songs, Musical instruments
Musical instruments, 97–99; buzzers, 99; drums, 97, 98, 185, 193, 208, 211, 212, 214, 215, 218, 219, 245, 283, 284, 311, 333, 374; flutes, 99; rattles, 98–99, 185–86, 193, 200, 202, 208, 209, 213, 214, 225, 243, 284, 306, 333; whistles, 54, 55, 99, 193, 333
Mythology. *See* Folklore and mythology

Naming, 140–42, 292–93, 338; ceremony, 140, 292, nicknames, 141; renaming, 141, 293, 338
Naskapi, 267, 269–72 passim, 274, 275, 278, 280, 281, 294, 303, 304, 305, 307, 308, 310, 311, 314, 315
Navel cord bag, 139, 143, 344
Necklaces, 60, 85, 273, 330

396

New England tribes, 268, 271, 272, 274, 275
Nez Percé, 9, 239, 327, 329, 330
Night-traveler, 4, 173–74, 208
Nipigon, 25
Nipissing, 28
North West Company, 34

Oblates, 41, 42, 361
Offering pole ceremony, 226–27
Offerings, 188, 199, 226, 228–29, 309–11, 344; body parts, 193, 229; cloth, 54, 140, 159, 162, 163, 171, 172, 173, 184, 185, 186, 193, 198, 199, 200, 207, 209, 211, 223, 224, 226, 227, 228, 311, 344; clothing, 227, 229; food, 151, 153, 211, 213, 223, 297, 310; hides, 229; pipe, 54, 140, 143, 151, 153–54, 159, 162, 171–74 passim, 184, 186, 187, 191, 200, 204, 208–11 passim, 219, 222–28 passim, 309, 310, 344; sticks, 229, 311; tortures, 193, 229
Ojibwa, 8, 34, 266, 267, 268, 270–84 passim, 289–98 passim, 303–07 passim, 310, 311, 313, 314, 315, 320, 327. See also Saulteaux (Plains Ojibwa)
Old people. See Aged
Omaha, 282, 327, 329, 330, 331, 333, 342
Omens, 180–81
Ornamentation: bags, 92; body, 85, 86, 87, 159, 212, 273, 274, 329, 330; centre pole, 188; clothes, 81, 82, 83, 85, 102, 246, 271, 332; face, 86, 87, 118, 274, 330; hides, 281; musical instruments, 97–98, 102; pipes, 96; pipestem, 172, 174, 246, 309; tipi, 89, 102, 224–26; tobacco pouches, 97; weapons, 95, 102. See also Beadwork; Horsehair decoration; Ribbon applique; Quillwork
Osage, 330
Oto, 327, 330
Ottawa (tribe), 20

Paipwat, Chief, 141
Palliser, Capt. John, 41, 42, 43, 45, 77

Pawnee, 327, 342
Peace negotiations, 18, 21, 25, 41, 43, 62, 173, 246
Pemmican, 58, 278, 330; fish p., 74
Penn, William, 302
Penobscot, 280, 284
Perrot, Nicolas, 18
Petitot, Emile, 23, 24
Piegan, 8, 31, 32, 44, 239, 329
Pipes, 96, 282, 333. See also Offerings, pipe; Pipestem, Sacred; Pipestem Bundle
Pipestem, Sacred, 122, 172–74, 210–11, 342
Pipestem bearer, 111, 172–74, 211
Pipestem bundle, 122, 172–74, 210–11, 246, 342
Pipestem bundle dance, 210–11
Place names, 360
Ponca, 327, 330, 331
Pones, 4, 208, 226, 232
Poor, 62, 107, 110, 115, 119–20
Pooyak, Baptiste, 176
Population, 7, 40–41, 52
Potawatomi: Prairie, 267, 268, 272, 275, 280, 294, 314; Woodland, 305
Pottery making tradition, 93, 283, 333
Poverty. See Poor
Pow-wow dance (Grass dance), 84, 98, 120, 214–17, 218, 228, 247, 343
Prairie-chicken dance, 207–08, 343
Prairie-chicken society (Hairy Legs society), 116, 117
Prayer, 140, 143, 145, 153, 158, 159, 162, 163, 174, 184, 186, 193, 194, 197, 198, 199, 204, 209–11, 213, 214, 222–28 passim, 231–32, 297, 304, 344
Pregnancy, 139. See also Childbirth
Prestige, 51, 62, 63, 105–11, 113, 119–20, 147, 170, 197, 198, 207, 216, 222, 239, 249, 290–92, 321, 337
Prophecy, See Divining
Puberty, 145–46, 159–61, 293–94, 304–05, 338
Punishment, 115, 116

Quapaw, 330

Quillwork, 81, 83, 84, 85, 92, 101, 281, 332. *See also* Ornamentation

Rabbit: meat, 276; skin blankets, 93, 94, 283, 333; snaring, 69
Races. *See* Games and contests
Radisson, Pierre Esprit, 17, 18, 28, 284
Range and territory, 3, 7–12, 15–46, 105, 261–63; seasonal changes in, 10, 16, 40, 43, 52, 77–78, 262
Rank. *See* Chiefs; Prestige; Warrior societies; Worthy Young Men
Rattlers dance, 112
Rattlers society, 112, 114, 116, 117, 118
Rebellion of 1885, 4, 7, 43, 107, 171
Religion, 157–82, 301–11, 341–45
Reserves, 7–12; Carlton, 10; Crooked Lake, 9, 151, 198, 203, 205, 225; Duck Lake, 10; Edmonton, 10; File Hills, 8, 9; Little Pine, 11, 173, 193, 203, 207, 217; Peepeekisis, 8, 203; Piapot, 10; Poundmaker, 217; Rocky Boy, Montana, 7; Saddle Lake, 10; Sweet Grass, 11, 107, 203; Touchwood, 10
Ribbon applique, 102
Richardson, Sir John, 37
Ridicule, 78, 124, 241
Riel, Louis, 43
Ritual. *See* Ceremonial
Robes, 81–82, 272, 329
Robson, Joseph, 293, 295
Ropes: bark, 102, 282; buffalo hair, 60, 102, 282, 332; horsehair, 65, 103. *See also* Thongs
Round dance, 174, 211–12, 372

Sacred bundles, 87, 121, 122, 154, 170–74, 194, 236, 297, 307, 342. *See also* Carried on the back bundle; Pipestem bundle; War bundles
Sacred objects: offences against, 123, 145, 181, 294, 338
Sarsi, 8, 38, 42, 239, 327, 328, 329, 331, 343
Sauk, 291, 311

Saulteaux (Plains Ojibwa), 8, 9, 20, 25, 42, 97, 105, 164, 165, 212, 239, 328, 343; Northern, 267, 269, 271, 272, 273, 276, 278, 280–83 passim, 289, 290, 292–98 passim, 304, 310, 320
Scalping, 245–46, 247, 319, 320, 321, 347
Sewing and sewing materials, 60, 88, 89
Sex: abstinence, 143, 195; deviation (*See* Transvestites); education, 144, 145. *See also* Adultery; Virginity
Shamans, 53, 54, 55, 68, 98, 140, 146, 162–70, 175, 176, 177, 180, 195, 214, 225, 293, 301, 305–08, 312, 320, 342, 343. *See also* Divining; Healing
Shelters, temporary, 89, 90
Shields, 95, 280, 332
Shirts, 81, 271, 329
Shoshone (Snake), 9, 31, 32, 44, 327, 328, 329
Shouter, 185, 186, 193, 195, 197, 198, 208, 216, 218, 234
Shuswap, 327
Signs and signals, 56, 244, 361, 362
Silvy, Antoine, 22
Sioux, 18, 20, 21, 23, 25, 27, 282, 341
Sitting Up Until Morning Ceremony, 118
Skinny Stoney, Chief, 112–13
Slave, 24, 36
Smet, Pierre Jean de, 40
Smoking, 96, 97, 228; in ceremonials, 96, 140, 153, 154, 172, 191, 194, 200, 201, 202, 227, 228, 309, 310, 344; to indicate assent, 228, 309, 319. *See also* Kinnikinnik; Pipes; Tobacco
Smoking tipi ceremony, 77, 90, 178, 199–204
Snake (tribe). *See* Shoshone
Snares. *See* Trapping
Social organization. *See* Band organization.
Societies. *See* Cow boys society; Mosquitoes; Prairie-chicken society; Rattlers society; Warriors society
Songs, 97, 160, 170, 171, 229–31,

311; ceremonial, 140, 175, 178, 183, 185–87, 191, 193, 195–98, 200, 202, 204–19 passim, 223, 224, 225, 229–31, 306, 344; in curing, 162; gambling, 131; in hunting, 54, 55; lullabies, 143; in warfare, 174, 240, 241, 243, 245, 320, 347

Soul, 158, 212, 223, 297, 303

Spears, 95, 280, 332

Spirit helpers, 54, 97, 102, 110, 140, 143, 145, 157–64 passim, 169, 170, 175, 178, 193, 194, 225, 228, 241, 243, 303, 307, 310, 342

Spirit powers, 52, 66, 153, 157, 158, 159, 161, 171, 173, 181, 183, 185, 186, 194, 204–07 passim, 210, 211; Bear, 63, 172, 210, 213, 219–22, 228; Bony Specter, 178, 206, 207, 208; Buffalo, 52, 63; Dog, 161; Eagle, 181, 222; Evil, 158; Ghost Stone, 153; Horse, 63, 161, 208; Manito-like, 226; Old Man, 153; Old Woman, 153; Sun, 63, 183, 222; Thunder, 63, 183, 191, 223, 232, 235, 236; Touching, 153; Weasel, 63, 208

Sports. See Games

Star-blanket, Chief, 10

Stoney. See Assiniboin

Summer house, 268

Sun dance, 66, 77, 98, 144, 183–99, 247, 343

Sun dance bundle, 342

Supreme Being (Kice•Manito•), 153, 157, 161, 172, 173, 191, 209, 222, 227, 232, 301, 302, 303, 304, 341. See also Manito•

Sutherland, George, 10

Sweatbath, 223, 236, 311, 312, 344

Sweatlodge, 81, 90, 223, 236, 269, 311, 312, 327

Sweetgrass, Chief, 89, 107

Sweetgrass, 145, 153, 154, 171, 172, 173, 185, 186, 187, 191, 195, 200, 211, 223, 225, 226, 233, 234, 235, 310, 311, 344

Swimmer, Chief, 127, 163

Syllabics. See Cree language, syllabics

Taboos, 81, 126, 142, 145, 161–62, 172, 223

Taché, Alexandre, 41

Tail wagging dance, 218

Tanning, 59, 60, 68, 281, 332

Tattooing, 86–87, 273–74, 329–30

Tcimaskos, Chief, 106

Tea dance, 219

Territory. See Range and territory

Thompson, David, 31, 35, 36, 44, 45, 60, 71, 275, 302

Thompson (tribe), 327

Thongs, 65, 69, 88, 102, 147, 175, 225, 243, 282, 332

Time (of day), 359

Tipi, 87–91, 327; construction of, 87, 88, 327; cover, 88–89, 225–26; decoration, 89, 224–26; lining, 89, 328; ownership, 89

Tipi painting ceremony, 224–26

Tobacco, 30, 96, 97, 143, 151, 154, 171, 172, 186, 191, 219, 225, 226, 228, 310, 344; pouches, 97, 283, 333. See also Smoking

Tools: axe, 282; bow drill, 93, 283, 333; digging stick, 69, 75, 136, 330; knife, 95; parfleche, 91, 328; scraper, 281, 332; for tanning, 59, 60, 281, 332

Toys: bull-roarers, 99; cross bows, 95, 280; deer calls, 99; slings, 134; sticks, 134; tops, 134

Trading: with Europeans, 16, 19–20, 22, 28–31, 33, 35; intertribal, 8, 19, 20, 24, 28, 31, 35, 38, 165. See also Fur trade

Transportation, 30, 99–100, 278–79, 331; boats, hide, 100, 331; canoes, 30, 33, 274, 275; rafts, 100, 331; snowshoes, 99, 279, 331; toboggans, 66, 67, 279, 331; travois, dog, 61, 67, 331; travois, horse, 65, 331. See also Horses; Tumpline

Transvestites, 166–68

Trapping, 30, 68, 77, 275, 330

Treaties, 43

Tribal comparisons (summaries), 323–25, 349, 353–56

Tumpline, 100, 279, 331

Umfreville, Edward, 34, 35, 44, 61, 280, 290, 304, 309

Ute, 328

Utensils, 91–94, 270–71, 328; cups,

horn, 76; dishes, bark, 92; dishes, wood, 92, 270, 328, 333; knives, 95, 333; mauls, 93; snow scoops, 92; spoons, horn, 60, 91, 270, 328; spoons, shell, 91, 270; spoons, wooden, 91, 270, 328. *See also* Bags; Containers; Tools

Vegetal foods, 74–76, 276, 330; flour, 74, 75; rice, wild, 276, 278, 291; sugar, maple, 76, 77, 276; turnips, Indian, 74, 77. *See also* Berries

Vengeance, 107, 108, 122, 247, 319, 347

Virginity, 147

Vision experience, 363–69. *See also* Vision quest

Vision prerogatives, 52, 86, 87, 89, 95, 97, 98, 118, 140, 157–64, 170, 171, 175–78, 194, 197, 199, 211, 226, 227, 229, 240, 241, 293, 308, 320, 321, 342, 343, 347. *See also* Vision quest

Vision quest, 145, 159–61, 232, 304–05, 341–42

Vows, 178, 183, 193, 197, 199, 208–12 passim, 223, 224, 233, 344

Wabanaki, 267, 274, 276, 279, 284, 289, 290

Wales, William, 304

War bundles, 170, 171, 307, 321

Warclubs, 95, 280, 332

Warfare, 17–21 passim, 23, 25, 32, 33, 34, 36, 37–43 passim, 239–58, 319–22, 347; clothing, 240, 307, 329; dance, 319, 320, 321, 347; insignia of, 247–48; leader, 240–42, 290, 291, 307, 320, 347; magic, 320; motives, 62, 239, 246, 247, 292, 319, 320, 338; nature of, 239–43, 249–58; paraphernalia, 243; prestige in, 110, 120, 246, 247, 290; prisoners, 246; protection in, 95, 170, 243, 307, 332; return from, 244, 321; sacred bundles in, 170, 171, 307, 321; sanction for, 240, 241; scouts, 242, 243, 347; warwhoop, 243. *See also* Metaphor of battle; Scalping; Weapons

Warrior chief, 113, 117

Warrior police, 291

Warrior societies, 98, 110–20, 247; dances, 111, 112, 115, 117, 118, 119; functions of, 113–16, 122, 152, 247; lodge, 113, 117; rivalry between, 117–19; servers in, 113–14

Weapons. *See* Arrows; Bows; Guns; Knives; Shields; Spears; Warclubs

Weather: thunderstorms, 98, 223; W. control, 170; W. forecasting, 180, 181

Weaving, 93, 94, 283

West, John, 275

Windbreaks, 89, 268–69

Winnebago, 270, 275, 280, 283, 292, 294, 302, 303, 305, 310, 321, 327

Witchita, 327

Women, in ceremonies, 118, 146, 172, 187, 188, 191, 193, 197, 199, 205, 209, 212, 213, 225, 235, 245; games of, 132–36; influence of, 146; as property owners, 58, 64, 66, 78, 89, 155, 225; work of, 58, 59, 60, 69, 74, 75, 76, 88, 89, 93, 100, 102, 113, 121, 151, 154. *See also* Childbirth; Menstruation

Woodlands tribes: Central, 226, 269, 270, 272, 274, 276, 277, 282, 284, 290, 291, 293, 294, 306, 307, 311, 312, 314, Northeastern, 282, 314

Woodwork, 92, 102, 270, 282, 333

Worthy young men, 110–11, 120, 122, 152, 245

Wrestling, 136